7/25/9.

D1236227

# Moltke, Schlieffen, and Prussian War Planning

# Moltke, Schlieffen, and Prussian War Planning

**Arden Bucholz**

BERG

New York/Oxford
Distributed exclusively in the U.S. and Canada by
St. Martin's Press, New York

Published in 1991 by
**Berg Publishers, Inc.**
Editorial offices:
165 Taber Avenue, Providence, RI 02906, U.S.A.
150 Cowley Road, Oxford OX4 1JJ, UK

Library of Congress Cataloging-in-Publication Data
applied for. No. 90-39333

British Library Cataloguing in Publication Data
applied for. No. 355.02130943

Printed and bound in Great Britain
by Billing & Sons Limited. Worcester

# Contents

# Acknowledgments

In many ways this is the other half of the story begun in my volume on *Hans Delbrück and the German Military Establishment: War Images in Conflict* (1985). This is so for several reasons. For one thing, history was a dominant field of knowledge in the nineteenth-century world. In both university and army, historical images and methodology played major roles. Second, many of the primary sources relating to Delbrück also refer to Prussian war planning. The reasons for this are tied to the fact that both Delbrück and the general staff were forced to deal with the possibilities of a future war during a long era of peace. As Schlieffen said on more than one occasion, we must study the past to gain the knowledge which the present refuses to give us. As Delbrück might have said, there is no way of judging the future, but the closest humans can come is by examining the past. Finally, many who helped with this book were colleagues, scholars, and librarians who also aided in the work on the Delbrück project.

Various portions of *Moltke, Schlieffen, and Prussian War Planning* were presented in rough form in a number of forums: in November 1986, for Mrs. Judy Tryka and her History Forum Seminar at SUNY Brockport; in spring 1987, as the chapters were first drafted during a SUNY sabbatical semester, for Jim Dingemann, Albert Nofi, and their colleagues in the New York Military Affairs Symposium; Sky Books International heard the developing structure twice, at the CUNY Graduate Center in March and at the School of International Affairs at Columbia in June of that year. During a year with the SUNY Program at Brunel University, London, 1987/88, a suggestion of my chairman, Professor Lynn Parsons, the basic framework was presented a half dozen times: to Professor Brian Bond's war studies class and his Institute of Historical Research Seminar at King's College, London; to Professor Anthony Glees's modern German politics class at Brunel; to the Seminar in Modern British and European History at the University of Edinburgh, thanks to Dr. Terry Cole and Dr. Richard Mackenny;

to the M.Phil. seminar at the Centre of International Studies at St. Johns College, Cambridge, courtesy of Professor Harry Hinsley and Dr. Richard Langhorne and, finally, to a workshop in the Militärgeschichtliches Forschungsamt, Freiburg, thanks to Dr. Wilhelm Deist's invitation and great personal kindness. Professor John C.G. Röhl looked over the general outline, talked through various possibilities, and offered encouragement during an afternoon in Kingston, Sussex. Professor Michael Howard received me cordially at Oriel College, Oxford, and listened to an outline of the project. My colleague in the SUNY Program at Brunel, Dr. John Halsey, listened cheerfully to the outline framework discussed during various bus trips to Uxbridge, Stonehenge, Wales, and elsewhere. Professor Dr. Wilhelm Scharfe of the Department of Cartography, Freie Universität, Berlin, was most helpful in supplying bibliography on Prussian-German mapmaking.

A number of colleagues read various drafts. Professor John Kutulowski read an early and a late version and responded with pages of comments, questions, and suggestions, always encouragingly. My *Doktorvater*, Professor W.H. McNeill of the University of Chicago, read an intermediate draft and made sound suggestions. Dr. Stig Förster of the German Historical Institute, Washington, D.C., read a late draft and gave me detailed pages of comments and suggestions. My colleagues, Professors Kempes Schnell, Steve Ireland, and John Kutolowski, wrestled helpfully through the chapters at our breakfasts during the summer of 1989. My friend and colleague Dr. Neil Johnson listened to several outlines of the project and carefully reviewed the penultimate draft from an anthropological perspective. Professor Dennis Showalter of Colorado College gave the manuscript an intelligent and useful reading for the publisher. Professor Ulrich Trumpener of the University of Alberta read the manuscript thoroughly and made helpful suggestions toward the end.

Various groups of librarians were instrumentally important in the completion of this work. The U.S. Army Military History Institute, Carlisle Barracks, Pennsylvania, appointed me an Advanced Research Associate in the summer of 1985, enabling me to work in their library, which is filled with excellent primary materials on the pre-1914 German army. Dr. Ed Drea was especially helpful during that visit. Mrs. Norma Lawrence and Mr. Robert Gilliam of Drake Library, SUNY Brockport, tracked down hundreds of interlibrary loan requests during the past half decade. Librarians at the

Bundesarchiv-Militärarchiv, Freiburg, especially Dr. Fleischer, were effective in laying out various bundles of documents so that my weeks there were efficiently spent. Dr. Gerhard Heyl, Director of the Bayerisches Hauptstaatsarchiv-Kriegsarchiv, Munich, received me cordially, arranged large numbers of archival documents, and facilitated photocopying. Dr. Mary Jo Orzech of the Brockport Academic Computing Center was helpful in the final laser printing process.

Our neighbors and friends, John and Ginny Pawlik, took care of our home while we were in England.

I am grateful to Sue, Merritt, and Mark Bucholz for supporting this venture amid the various ongoing activities of family life.

To all these I am most grateful. For the errors which remain, I alone am responsible.

Arden Bucholz
Waterport, New York
March 1990

# Abbreviations

BAMA  Bundesarchiv-Militärarchiv, Freiburg
BHSA  Bayerisches Hauptstaatsarchiv, Abteilung IV,
       Kriegsarchiv, München
DC     District Command
GGS   Großer Generalstab (Great General Staff)
GS     Generalstab (General Staff)
LC     Line Command
MGFA  Militärgeschichtliches Forschungsamt
MTP   Military Travel Plan
RRS   Railroad Section
TGS   Truppen-Generalstab (Troop General Staff)

# Introduction
# War Planning and the
# Prussian-German Experience

The present world situation in many ways resembles that of Europe toward the end of the last century. More and more we appear to be in a time period similar to the one preceding World War I. Specifically, both are eras of planning for future war: (1) in periods of rapid technological change; (2) with an arms race of increasingly complex, costly, and destructive weapons; (3) with the existence of several large, competing alliance systems; and (4) in a time of very great specialization of labor in the bureaucracies which deal with these matters. In spite of the current détente, the structures, institutions, weapons, and plans undergirding contemporary war are still in place.

The basic framework of war today, especially size, space, and time considerations, first confronted war planners in about 1890: armies much larger than a million men, campaign areas greater than forty thousand square miles, and time pressures of sufficient magnitude that planners feared that a delay of seventy-two hours might lose the war. The corresponding statistics for the contemporary world are combined NATO-Warsaw Pact European forces of over four million men, campaign areas spread across ten planetary zones, and time pressures from weapons effective against targets four to six thousand miles, but less than an hour, away. Nuclear weapons have fundamentally changed international relations because they have dramatically raised the stakes. Today a basic error can have far greater consequences than was true in 1914 or in 1939. Yet many of the problems security analysts must deal with today have their roots in the prenuclear era.[1]

One of these problems is the planning process. World War I was

---

1. A phrase used by Professor John Mearsheimer in describing his research on contemporary security issues, quoted in Brigitta Carlson, "Good Teachers: Honoring A Tradition," *University of Chicago Magazine* 78, no. 2 (Winter 1986): 15. A pioneering analysis of this problem within a global framework is found in William H.

the first war in world history which was preplanned in the sense that it was not only thought, written, and talked about in general, but was specifically laid out on paper in complex time tables, mobilization charts, and plans for men, weapons, and supplies. These plans were then "practiced" through war games, staff rides, and large-scale maneuvers before the war itself was declared. These forms of preplanning lasted not for days, weeks, or months, but for decades.

This book seeks to apply new theoretical perspectives to investigate the creation and development of modern war planning. It is not intended to be a definitive study. Quite the opposite. It is an attempt to suggest possibilities for further work, to open up the study of modern armies to new approaches. As readers will see, the fit between unconventional perspectives and traditional historical images is not always close. By looking at familiar material from a new point of view, this study will hopefully suggest fruitful lines of inquiry. One that immediately suggests itself is application of these perspectives to the larger and more complex problem of the opening round of World War I and the war planning processes of Austria-Hungary, Russia, France, Britain, and Germany, all seen in comparative perspective.

### Armies as Organizations

My approach has its roots in the study of the Prussian-German army and particularly its general staff. The standard image of that organization was formed after 1945 by such works as Walter Görlitz's *History of the German General Staff* and Gordon Craig's *Politics of the Prussian Army.*[2] Here the general staff is predominantly represented as noble, feudal, and reactionary – one of the conservative bastions of the industrial feudal state. Even Eckart Kehr's otherwise iconoclastic essays, Fritz Fischer's two foundational volumes, John Röhl's work on Second Reich notables, and Elizabeth Hull's *Entourage of Kaiser Wilhelm II* do not diverge very much from this standard interpretation.[3]

---

McNeill, *The Pursuit of Power: Technology, Armed Force, and Society since A.D. 1000* (Chicago, 1982), chaps. 6–8.

    2. Walter Görlitz, *History of the German General Staff* (New York, 1957); Gordon Craig, *The Politics of the Prussian Army* (New York, 1955).

    3. Fritz Fischer, *Germany's Aims in the First World War* (New York, 1967) and

Recent scholarship on the German army, however, stresses its growing professionalization and the corresponding development of a meritocracy. By 1895, 50% of the officer corps was middle class. Half of the War Academy classes were secondary school graduates. By 1913, 70% of the Great General Staff (GGS) was bourgeois, and of those in the most crucial positions in the Mobilization Section and Railroad Section (RRS), 84% were bourgeois. Erich Ludendorff, Herman Kuhl, Wilhelm Groener, Gerhard Tappen, Erich Zöllner – most of the key posts were held by members of the meritocracy.[4] The dominant ethos within this war planning cadre called for a continuous, reliable, and predictable level of performance, minimizing dependence on particular individuals.[5] Documents from Wilhelm Groener's papers demonstrate the Railroad and Mobilization Sections' repeated concern for the *Leistungsfähigkeit* or work capacity of each segment of the mobilization plan. The Military Travel Plan (MTP) described large-scale "transportation paths" for shipping the million-man army like so many units on a factory production line.[6] This is very different from the cavalry regiment, the Junker *noblesse de style*, and the militaristic ethos – brainless virility mixed with punctilious brutality – often said to dominate the Prussian army.[7]

---

idem, *War of Illusions: German Policies from 1911 to 1914* (New York, 1975); John C.G. Röhl, *Germany without Bismarck: The Crisis of Government in the Second Reich, 1890–1900* (Berkeley, 1967) and idem, ed., *Kaiser Wilhelm II: New Interpretations* (Cambridge, 1982); Eckart Kehr, *Economic Interest, Militarism, and Foreign Policy: Essays on German History*, trans. Grete Heinz, ed. Gordon Craig (Berkeley, 1977); Elizabeth Hull, *The Entourage of Kaiser Wilhelm II, 1888–1918* (Cambridge, 1982).

4. Cf. Ulrich Trumpener, "Junkers and Others: The Rise of Commoners in the Prussian Army, 1871–1914," *Canadian Journal of History* 4, no. 1 (April 1979): 29–47; Michael Geyer, "German Strategy in the Age of Machine Warfare, 1914–1945," in Peter Paret, ed., *Makers of Modern Strategy from Machiavelli to the Nuclear Age* (Princeton, 1986), pp. 527ff.; Detlef Bald, *Vom Kaiserheer zur Bundeswehr, Sozialstruktur des Militärs: Politik der Rekrutierung von Offizieren und Unteroffizieren* (Frankfurt, 1981), pp. 35ff. and idem, "Zum Kriegsbild der militärischen Führung im Kaiserreich," in Jost Düllfer and Karl Holl, eds., *Bereit zum Krieg: Kriegsmentalität im Wilhelminischen Deutschland, 1890–1914.* (Göttingen, 1986), pp. 154ff.; Theodor Fontane deals with these social changes, cf. Ernest K. Bramsted's *Aristocracy and the Middle Classes in Germany: Social Types in German Literature, 1830–1900* (Chicago, 1964), pp. 228–68.

5. *Militär-Adreßbuch (Taschen-Rankliste) aller Offiziere und oberen Militärbeamten der Standorte Groß-Berlin, Charlottenburg, Potsdam und Spandau sowie des Gardekorps* (Charlottenburg, 1913); Görlitz, *German General Staff*, p. 127.

6. Groener Papers, roll 18, no. 33.

7. Fritz Stern, "Prussia," in David Spring, ed., *European Landed Elites in the Nineteenth Century* (Baltimore, 1977), p. 61. Tim Travers argues that historians should shift their attention away from the faults and merits of individual com-

Armies are large public monopoly organizations, created and maintained primarily to compete against each other on future battlefields.[8] At the utmost bounds of this competition, one or both of the organizations will suffer some degree of death. Because armies serve as instruments of death, a point which cannot be overemphasized, and because of their size and the extent and manner in which they command the loyalties of their society, they are unique among the organizations of human social life.[9] General staffs, the "brains" of armies, an organizational innovation of nineteenth-century Prussia, are relatively small but complex units with potential for great impact on their societies by virtue of the fact that they plan, coordinate, and above all command when war breaks out. Because armies are essentially future oriented, that is, they exist primarily to deal with future contingencies, and because their activities threaten, entangle, and often submerge their citizenry in the ultimate stage of human life, their position as some of the first modern organizations in traditional societies has often been commented upon.[10]

---

manders, which has largely characterized First World War historiography up until now, and should pay more attention to the concept of the army and its activities as a system. Cf. *The Killing Ground: The British Army, the Western Front, and the Emergence of Modern Warfare, 1900–1918* (London, 1987), p. 27.

8. Graham Allison comments on organizational theory in *Essence of Decision: Explaining the Cuban Missile Crisis* (Boston, 1971), pp. 69–100. For Germany, Peter-Christian Witt comments on research on German bureaucracy prior to 1918 in his essay, "The Prussian Landrat as Tax Official, 1891–1918," in Georg Iggers, ed., *The Social History of Politics; Critical Perspectives in West German Historical Writing since 1945* (Leamington Spa, 1985), pp. 139ff. Not a great deal of attention has been paid by scholars to the Prussian-German bureaucracy. Two examples, neither of which deals with the military, are Herbert Jacob, *German Administration since Bismarck: Central Authority versus Local Autonomy* (New Haven, 1963) and John R. Gillis, *The Prussian Bureaucracy in Crisis, 1840–1860: Origins of an Administrative Ethos* (Stanford, 1971).

9. For a broad-ranging essay on armies as organizations of social change cf. Barton C. Hacker and Sally L. Hacker, "Military Institutions and the Labor Process: Noneconomic Sources of Technological Change, Women's Subordination, and the Organization of Work," *Technology and Culture* 28, no. 4 (October 1987): 743–75.

10. See especially Lucian W. Pye's seminal discussion, "Armies in the Process of Political Modernization," in John J. Johnson, ed., *The Role of the Military in Under-developed Countries* (Princeton, 1962), pp. 69–89; Edward Shils, "The Military in the Political Development of the New States," in David E. Novack and Robert Lakachman, eds., *Development and Society: The Dynamics of Economic Change* (New York, 1964), pp. 392–404; Morris Janowitz, *The Military in the Political Development of the New Nations* (Chicago, 1964); Samuel P. Huntington, *The Soldier and the State* (Cambridge, Mass., 1957); Amos Perlmutter, "The Military and Politics in Modern Times: A Decade Later," *Journal of Strategic Studies* 9, no. 1 (March 1986): 5–15; Michael Geyer, "The Militarization of Europe, 1914–1945" in John Gillis, ed., *The*

To illuminate the Prussian experience this work will employ organizational theory, a field of inquiry now a quarter century old which has been applied mainly to analyze business organizations such as railroad and automobile companies and governmental bureaucracies such as welfare and health care agencies. This book will employ three kinds of organizational perspectives. One is primarily developmental: it looks at organizations in the transition from traditional to modern. The second is environmental: it examines organizations at specific moments in time within their cultural contexts. The third is instrumental: it focuses on military organization as a policy instrument, with particular reference to knowledge, transportation, and communication as mechanisms of change.

Two useful perspectives of the developmental kind are those of Max Weber and Robert Michels. Their work is relevant for two

---

*Militarization of the Western World* (New Brunswick, 1989), pp. 65–102. Those who have dealt with Prussia have not concentrated on the military or the general staff. For example, Hans Rosenberg, *Bureaucracy, Aristocracy, and Autocracy: The Prussian Experience, 1660–1815* (Boston, 1966); John C.G. Röhl, "Higher Civil Servants in Germany, 1890–1900," in James J. Sheehan, ed., *Imperial Germany* (New York, 1976), pp. 129–54: Otto Hintze approaches the topic, but he does not concentrate primarily on the late nineteenth century, for example, in Felix Gilbert, ed., *The Historical Essays of Otto Hintze* (Princeton, 1975). Martin van Creveld skirts the fringes of war organization in both *Supplying War: Logistics from Wallenstein to Patton* (Cambridge, 1977) and *Command in War* (Cambridge, Mass., 1985); finally, there is Stanislav Andreski's *Military Organization and Society* (Berkeley, 1971), a book of which I have never been able to make sense despite the title. Peter F. Drucker, *The New Realities* (New York, 1989) deals with the relationships between organizations and knowledge, pp. 218–64. The most recent attempt to deal with offensive war and ideas in a comparative framework is Jack Synder, *The Ideology of the Offensive: Military Decision Making and the Disasters of 1914* (Ithaca, 1984). In dealing with the Prussian army as an organization, readers may note what may seem to them a terminological fuzziness in regard to the treatment of army size and bureaucratic titles and subdivisions. The reason for this is that the sources disagree. This is particularly true of the size of the army but it also applies to names of units within the bureaucracy. For example, those who have written on the general staff disagree on whether the divisions within it should be called departments, sections, or bureaus. This book focuses on the organizational activities and the work done, trying to lay out a new approach to understanding the Prussian military as an organization instead of tracking the minutiae of numbers, bureaucratic offices, and titles. The MGFA handbook (Militärgeschichtliches Forschungsamt, ed., *Handbuch zur deutschen Militärgeschichte, 1648–1945*, 5 vols. [Munich, 1979]) gets around this problem by adopting a standard framework. For example, for the period 1890–1914, it says that GGS internal organization basically did not change. I think it did change, and I argue specifically how it changed, but I leave to further researchers the job of going beyond the structure laid out here and specifying the minor details of bureaucratic life.

reasons. First of all, both lived in Prussian Germany during the period under consideration. Their writing has a primary source quality. Second, both were concerned with the pathology of organizations: they sought to understand organizational change. Weber delineated the transition from earlier traditional or patrimonial forms to more modern or rational ones. In his typology Weber described the supplanting of traditional administrative methods by rational bureaucratic forms. In doing so, he identified six areas for consideration: (1) division of labor; (2) hierarchy of offices; (3) performance regulations; (4) separation of personal from official; (5) selection by technical qualification; (6) employment as a career. Michels also dealt with the change from patrimonial to rational management. He provided an influential analysis of the shift of power from titular rulers to nominal subordinates, from generalists to technical specialists. Michels perceived oligarchic tendencies in this process. He believed that power tended to shift into the hands of an elite minority and that this shift was built into the very structure of organizational arrangements.[11]

In using perspectives of the second category, which describe organizations as cultural institutions, recent work on large-scale organizations emphasizes their historical context, often called the task environment.[12] Task environment is the specific domestic and foreign context in which war planning takes place.[13] This approach is the one customarily applied by historians.

A third perspective useful for understanding twentieth-century armies is derived from the work of those who focus on the organizational impact of knowledge and of transportation and communications methods. In this category, three writers in particular stand out. John Kenneth Galbraith defines technology as the systematic use of organized knowledge applied to practical skills.[14] The creation and use of technology results in the division and subdivision of

---

11. Hans H. Gerth and C. Wright Mills, eds., *From Max Weber: Essays in Sociology* (New York, 1946), pp. 196–204; A.H. Henderson and Talcott Parsons, eds., *Max Weber: The Theory of Social and Economic Organization*, (Glencoe, Ill., 1947), pp. 329–36; Robert Michels, *Political Parties*, trans. Eden and Cedar Paul (Glencoe, Ill., 1949). Cf. Wolfgang J. Mommsen's two books, *The Age of Bureaucracy: Perspectives on the Political Sociology of Max Weber* (New York, 1974) and *Max Weber and German Politics, 1890–1920*, trans. Michael S. Steinberg (Chicago, 1984).

12. W. Richard Scott, *Organizations: Rational, Natural, and Open Systems* (Englewood Cliffs, N.J., 1981), p. 13.

13. Ibid., pp. 13–18.

14. John K. Galbraith, *The New Industrial State*, 2d ed. (London, 1972), chap. 2.

labor into components so that tasks become coterminous with established areas of scientific and engineering knowledge. In other words, modern organizations break down their tasks, and therefore to some extent their basic structure, partially or substantially on the basis of knowledge. This process has many ramifications. The more thoroughgoing the application of technology, the longer the task cycle. As technology becomes discrete to one piece of work, the procedures to accomplish it become inflexible and harder to change. Manpower becomes more specialized since organized knowledge can only be applied by those who possess it. The organization employing technology itself becomes more complex in order to bring the work of a host of independent technicians to a coherent whole. As individuals specialize in discrete areas and as the task is further subdivided, more information is needed. Finally, Galbraith believes that power passes to those who have the knowledge necessary for important decisions. Technology is that commodity, the possession of which gave the RRS of the GGS its "knowledge advantage" over other departments. In sum, twentieth-century organizations depend on knowledge in very important ways, and that dependency shapes their structure, processes, and personnel. Two specific works illustrating the application of Galbraith's general approach are those of Chandler and Beniger. Each one deals with the impact of technology upon a single area of industrial organization.

Alfred D. Chandler, Jr., writes that nineteenth-century railroad and telegraph companies were the first modern business organizations.[15] They provided fast, regular, and dependable services essential for high-volume production and nationwide distribution. They were the first to require a large number of full-time managers to coordinate, control, and evaluate the activities of widely scattered operating units. New technology was required to carry high volume safely and efficiently. The task of size, space, and time coordination on such a vast scale required a new kind of organization. This organization had its origins in the transportation and communication business.

James Beniger describes a nineteenth-century "crisis of control" in which innovations in information processing and communications technology lagged behind innovations in energy application.[16] Rail-

---

15. Alfred D. Chandler, Jr., *The Visible Hand: The Managerial Revolution in American Business* (Cambridge, Mass., 1977).

road transportation evolved so quickly that its progress surpassed the development of the means to control and communicate with it. Following Max Weber, Beniger argues that foremost among solutions to this crisis was formal bureaucracy. Management instituted a wide range of innovations in organization, programming, information processing, and communication. Overall, increases in speed, size, and space accelerated the need for control. At times new technology outran the means to control it.

This work will examine Prussian war planning within an historical framework, emphasizing developmental, environmental, and instrumental perspectives. Specifically, the book will analyze the impact of the increasing demand for scientific and technical knowledge on the practical task of war planning. It will describe the impact upon the war planning process of its bonding with technology – the increasing need for bureaucracy, mechanical transportation, and electrical communication as essential components of twentieth-century war making.

## Prussia: Identity and Security

The first deep-future-oriented war planning system originated in the kingdom of Prussia in the nineteenth century. Following its validation in the wars of German unification, these bureaucratic processes were extended into the Second Reich after 1871 and were subsequently employed for both World Wars I and II. Prussian war planning evolved in an historical setting of great complexity. Prussia's own unique characteristics merged after 1871 with those of the rapidly industrializing new nation. Some would say that after 1871 the other German sovereignties underwent a process of "Prussianization." Either way, this new nation, the Second German Reich, was created amid the structures, culture, and ideas of a very ancient, traditional way of life. The uniqueness of Prussia had long been noted. Alexis de Tocqueville described Frederick the Great's state as a political and social hybrid, a curious combination of *tête moderne* and *corps gothique*.[17]

---

16. James Beniger, *The Control Revolution: Technological and Economic Origins of the Information Society* (Cambridge, Mass., 1986).

17. quoted in Rudolf von Thadden, *Prussia: The History of a Lost State* (Cambridge, 1987), p. 79.

This same contradiction dominated Prussia and Germany in the nineteenth century. During the forty-three years following 1871, traditional ways of life were confronted with a number of abrupt challenges. Ralf Dahrendorf called Imperial Germany an industrial-feudal society. Economic and social life were out of balance, and this imbalance was made worse by the speed of change. The Second Reich had insufficient time to absorb the quantitative and qualitative change confronting it prior to 1914. World War I represented such a fundamental watershed for all European states that, in the case of Germany, which was teetering precariously between traditional and modern, the lost war was altogether too much.

Although we cannot deal with all of these issues, some of the most interesting and suggestive may be approached by grouping them under two headings, identity and security. Each of these may be thought of as symbols standing for larger pools of issues, conflicts, and ideas, as paradigms suggesting some of the pathologies, fractures, and tensions inherent in the process of change from traditional to modern patterns.

The problem of identity may be stated as follows. Every nation-state is continually developing. Sometimes there are periods of rapid change when this development seems to get out of hand. During the late nineteenth century, Germany entered such a period. It was a time of essential schizophrenia: the state appeared at the same time monarchical and constitutional in its politics, agrarian and industrial in its economy, and feudal and egalitarian in its society. Was the Second Reich to be a modern constitutional state like England or France, or was it to remain a traditionally conservative monarchy like Russia or Austria-Hungary? Was its economy to become a modern industrial one like England's, or was it to remain a traditional agriculturally dominated system like Russia's? Was the Reich to attain a modern egalitarian class structure or retain its feudal and hierarchical character? The point was that it had some of each. Having both traditional and modern identities complicated everything. This identity crisis was reflected in Germany's love-hate relationship with England. Many Germans aspired to England's world power and its wealth, while deriding England as a nation of shopkeepers which had lost its cultural (read traditional) soul. England had had many of the same problems as Germany; however, the English had centuries, instead of a few decades, to deal with them.[18]

9

The problem of security is related to that of identity. Identity involves the self-image of the society. Security has to do with how the state is ordered and determines its boundaries, both physical and psychological. It is concerned with the nature of modern state formation and the problems involved in holding new nations together, especially those created in war and revolution. For Germany the question became, was the Second Reich to be a modern continental, or even colonial, world power like England or France, or was it to break apart, slipping back to traditional provincial separatism at the level of its constituent parts, like Prussia, Bavaria, and Württemberg? How were the new urban social classes to be incorporated into and enfranchised within the new nation?

As we know from post-1945 history, new nations are fragile constructions. They are fraught with political, ethnic, religious, and social conflict. So it was with the Second Reich. To the generation which brought it into being, Imperial Germany appeared to be perennially confronting enemies – domestic and foreign – who sought at least to impede its "natural" movement to a place in the sun of world politics, if not to break apart the new state cemented by the military conquest of German princelings and European great powers. Like George Washington in the farewell address to his new nation in 1796, Bismarck also feared the disintegration of the new state from within and without. Unlike the fledgling United States of America, which was a truly nonindustrial society, flanked by vast oceans and weak colonial provinces, the new Federal Reich of Germany, carved out of the center of Europe, was on the brink of explosive industrialization. To the southeast stood the Habsburgs, a world power since the fifteenth century. To the west was the Second French Republic, which harbored the traditions of Napoleonic imperialism. Both were recently defeated and therefore dangerous neighbors. Directly east were the Romanovs, whose armies in the previous century had sacked and burned Berlin. In this potentially lethal arena, fueled by hyperindustrialization, social Darwinism, and a high-technology arms race, security was always a paramount concern.

Identity and security may be defined in a number of ways. One of the most visible is in the development of nationalism. Again a basic

---

18. See Harold James, *A German Identity, 1770–1990* (London, 1989), especially chaps. 1–4.

imbalance existed, and this imbalance, defined in terms of a lag in development between two kinds of nationalism, cultural and political, began in the early nineteenth century. It is said that a German national identity was first defined in terms of its culture – language, literature, and folklore – and that this took place during the Napoleonic wars as a reaction against imposed French cultural forms. The Germanies became a cultural nation before they were a political nation. In contrast, political nationalism lagged behind: only after 1870 did the Germanies become a unified state.

Thus modern Germany has been described as an example of belated or delayed development, which was the result of a double lag: in politics cultural nationalism came before political nationalism, while in society industrialization preceded social modernization. This double lag affected both identity and security. The Germans could not decide if they were a modern constitutional state or a traditional monarchy; a modern industrial economy or a traditional agricultural system; a modern egalitarian society or a traditional feudal hierarchy. In fact they were both at once and were in rapid transition from one to the other in the forty-three years from 1871 to 1914. Having both a traditional and a modern identity complicated the security problem. Uncertain of their basic character and forced to define and defend this ambiguity in a world in which English and French national culture were well established, domestic and foreign enemies appeared legion in German minds. Under pressure from too much happening too fast, the schizophrenia of identity was united with the paranoia of security.

In each of these aspects, tradition and modernity, identity and security, Prussia shared in certain respects the problems and tensions of many new nations built upon old societies. In other ways Prussia was unique. As in all such collisions between past and present, certain continuities were preserved, others were lost, still others were transformed. One of the continuities both preserved and transformed was the relationship between Prussia and its military establishment.

As Otto Büsch wrote a quarter century ago of the unique integration of social life and the military in the eighteenth century, scholars have recognized the military as central to Prussian life and character throughout its existence.[19] The army was the main

19. Otto Büsch, *Militärsystem und Sozialleben im alten Preußen, 1713–1807* (Berlin, 1962).

instrument for its incessant expansion in the century and a half before 1914. This process occurred in four great bursts. There were two in the eighteenth century, from 1740 to 1763 and from 1772 to 1795, and two in the nineteenth century, in 1815 and from 1864 to 1871. As its land area quadrupled, Prussia transformed itself. From a seventeenth-century northern European electorate, it became an eighteenth-century great power kingdom, a nineteenth-century European empire, and a twentieth-century world power. The military, the major mechanism of this unexpected and unlikely transformation in the two centuries before 1914, was also the dominant vehicle of its demise thereafter.

Imperial Germany was the only state in modern Europe created and destroyed by war in less than a century. The dilemmas of the Second Reich therefore relate closely to its war planning system. To put it another way, the organization of war assumed a crucial role in both Prussia and the Reich. Means and ends always threatened to become confused, influencing, perhaps dominating, its history in ways unusual even for the European powers of its time. As a prototype for the study of modern war planning, therefore, Prussia represents a significant case history. Prior to 1914, Prussian war mechanisms assumed a leading role within the bureaucratic forms of the modernizing German state. In a sense, Prussia wrote the book on this particular aspect of modern life.

## War Planning as Process

Armies posed the largest and most significant management and control problem in the nineteenth-century world.[20] By the 1870s and more clearly in the 1890s Prussian war planners were confronted with an enormous problem – how to move, shoot, and communicate with several million men, almost a million horses, and their weapons, equipment, and supplies. Confronted with such a task in an environment dominated by fear and anxiety, they responded by creating the first deep-future-oriented war planning process. Deep-future orientation implies planning ahead one to five years and more. This process was put together gradually and haphazardly, not by men trained at the Harvard Business School, but by men brought up as professional soldiers. There was little con-

---

20. Beniger, *Control Revolution*, p. 279.

scious development, and it is probable that the creators never fully recognized the nature of their accomplishment. In retrospective, however, it seems that only an integrated, systematic modern organization could have achieved the results attained. Seen from this perspective, Prussian war planning has four interactive parts: organizational, representational, educational, and analytical. Each part depended on the systematic application of knowledge – engineering details for railroads, mathematical formulas in maps, historical images in education, and all of these used together in war games.

The organizational encompassed the general staff, an agency for thinking about, planning for, and ultimately directing future war. It conducted research on potential enemies and campaign areas. It prepared war plans before war was declared and tested out parts of that plan in war games, staff rides, and maneuvers. Members of "the brain of the army," as Spencer Wilkinson called it, were said to be the crème de la crème of the Prussian army. Selection meant accelerated promotion, better choice of assignments, and opportunities to work closely with the leading commanders. Above all, the general staff slowly became a modern organization, a working umbrella framework which spread out across the land, comprehensive and national. The Berlin GGS format and procedures were replicated at corps and division level. Specific mechanisms integrated the GGS into the rest of the army. One of these was the principle of theory and practice, carried out through staff and line rotations, the continual movement of officers between Berlin, the corps, and divisions. Other integrating mechanisms were organizational and procedural: the chief of staff system, the District Commands (DCs), and, above all, the railroad Line Commands (LCs). Even the Horse Purchase Commissions might be regarded as one of these integrating mechanisms because, like all the rest, it was connected to the war plan.

The war plan was the sine quo non which animated the organization. It was the hidden agenda, the boundary which both separated and joined peace and war. It gave the chief of the general staff his legitimacy and influence as primus inter pares among Prussian and Reich bureaucrats. Everyone knew that if war came, the GGS would be in charge. A relatively small, if highly prestigious organization in peacetime, its authority within the bureaucracy depended preeminently on its role within a theoretical future, one defined by the next war.

The second aspect of the war planning process was representational. This was embodied in the Land Survey Section. This agency provided a clear, precise, and useful image of the land. It laid down detailed procedures – trigonometric, topographic and cartographic – for creating and revising this image. Through summer field experience and winter drawing exercises, map creation was a widely known procedure among general staff officers and, indeed, throughout the army. Obtaining maps was the first step in war games, exercises, staff rides, and maneuvers. Not only was the image clear and precise, but the procedures used to obtain it and its integration into exercises trained the eye and mind in the intellectual relationships between armies and landforms. There was a good deal of visual literacy achieved in teaching those arcane and subtle relationships between size, space, and time so important for twentieth-century war.

The third aspect was educational. It included not only the well-known Berlin War Academy, but also the Pioneer and Artillery and Engineering Schools. Above all it meant a philosophy which saw education, particularly as it was embodied in history, as crucial for learning war during peacetime. Within it was encompassed the genesis of a comprehensive modern educational system, including regimental and divisional schools and libraries. It included the general staff technical publishing business carried out through the Military History Section and the Berlin publisher E.S. Mittler, which for over a century spewed out books, articles, and journals on military topics. Military history became a technical specialty. In late nineteenth-century Prussia, the Schlieffen school of history within the army complemented the Prussian school of history within the professoriate: both were idealist and national.[21] It included the orientation with which the RRS introduced itself to newly assigned officers which, by 1911, lasted nearly all day. Above all it encompassed a state of mind in which continuing education, particularly historical, was seen as an essential ingredient in war planning.

The fourth component was analytical. The war game was the keystone of Prussian war planning because it integrated the other three elements under simulated battle conditions. The organizational component provided the personnel, the setting, and the

---

21. Arden Bucholz, *Hans Delbrück and the German Military Establishment: War Images in Conflict* (Iowa City, 1985), pp. 1–44.

motivation; the representational the maps, charts, and visual literacy; and the educational the uniform body of training, procedures, and historical images. The war game exercised these elements in a profoundly theoretical yet eminently practical manner. Above all, it was a method of thinking about war in its essential two-sidedness. Armies, after all, are rival organizations: their ultimate function is to be tested one against another. War gaming structured this competition, allowing simulations, simple models of complex real situations. It tested officers, ideas, and plans against each other. Careers were made, lost, and sometimes redeemed in war games. Although not directly predictive, they were an exercise in understanding what future problems were most likely to arise. As an organization more or less immune from daily tests of efficiency but created for future contingencies, the army used the war game to examine hypothetical models of the future. By 1910 not only the GGS and the regiments, divisions, and corps, but the RRS, the LCs, and the War Ministry engaged in cumulative, serial war gaming, carried out under security codes and classifications. The games generated questions. The questions were submitted to field tests. The field tests yielded new data.

The binding tie between the planning process and the war plan was knowledge. By 1914, the MTP was the only phase in the seven-stage war plan which was expected to guarantee uniform, consistent, and regular performance – the delivery of huge masses of men, equipment, and supplies within a given time and space. The MTP was based upon the systematic application of knowledge, especially physics and engineering knowledge, to the practical skill of making war. Knowledge divided the task into components, increased the cycle time, created specialized personnel and complex organization, necessitated deep-future-oriented planning, and ultimately shifted power to the Mobilization Department and RRS, which alone possessed the specialized information necessary for the most important decisions.

This then was the Prussian war planning process in its organizational, representational, educational, and analytical aspects. Although each was interactive with the others in various ways, there is no presumption of uniform development. In fact the situation was quite the opposite. Although the War Academy was strong in the 1860s, by the 1890s it was much less so. The Land Survey Department, having reached a high level of technical proficiency in the 1890s that included photogrammetrics and stereophotography, afterward turned its hand mainly to map production. Personnel decisions made outside the general staff often changed its evolution. A poorly chosen department head sometimes meant that that department ossified, with its work transferred elsewhere. Only the RRS, under the pressures imposed on it by the war plan, appears to have developed uniformly, expanding in size, growing in complexity, procedures, and knowledge, extending power and influence from Berlin to the furthest boundaries and lowest echelons of the Second Reich.

The sources and development of that war planning process will be described in the following pages. Chapter 1 describes the origins and growth of the Prussian war planning process from its genesis in the 1790s to its sudden and extraordinary validation by Helmuth von Moltke, between 1864 and 1871. In his sixties, Moltke almost single-handedly reshaped the GGS during the years 1857 to 1871, creating the prototypical deep-future-oriented war planning bureaucracy. Building upon powerfully entrenched traditions, it was fused, tested, and changed by the brutal, practical experience of the last Napoleonic and first industrial mass wars. Chapter 2 deals with the decades 1871 to 1891, a period of reorganization and consolidation of Prussian military procedures during which the changes of the previous seven years were extended into the Reich. The newly independent GGS became a preeminent Prussian office. Modern bureaucratic methods began to take form, fitting and shaping procedures, routines, and standards. With the retirement of Bismarck and the replacement of the elderly first generation leadership by Wilhelm II and his entourage, an abrupt transition began. The domestic and foreign task environment darkened. Imperial Germany entered a period first of bureaucratic chaos and then of gradual alienation from Russia, France, and England. In this somber setting, the general staff was forced into drastic change. It evolved from an organization directing many hundred thousands in single-opponent, six-week wars of annihilation to one orchestrating millions in a multiple-opponent, two-hundred-twenty-four-week war of attrition.

Chapters 3 and 4 describe the transitional period (1891–1905) during which this took place. Chapter 3 describes Alfred Graf Schlieffen as the re-creator of Prussian war planning. He broadened and galvanized the separate threads of the basic structure created under Moltke and Waldersee, building the mature planning system that operated during Moltke the Younger's ten-

16

ure. His traditional background, combined with exposure to modern task-oriented planning techniques uniquely suited him to adapt the GGS to its twentieth-century role. Chapter 3 details the first "loading" of this system from 1891 to 1896, with the million-man army and years of substantial military buildup on the one hand and the search for a strategic plan for deploying these forces as the task environment turned increasingly black on the other. Chapter 4 describes the evolution of the strategic enigma of the two-front war and three-million-man army from 1897 to 1905, known to posterity as the Schlieffen Plan. Chapter 5 deals with the years 1906 to 1913, the era of Helmuth von Moltke the Younger as chief, a period in which army size was put on hold while the naval "risk" fleet was built and full-fledged technocratic war planning was established. Chapter 6 describes the period of frantic military buildup in the final year of peace, 1914, to show how this great peacetime military mechanism readied itself to plunge into the unexpectedly brutal experience of industrial mass war.

# Chapter 1
## Prussian War Planning
## Genesis and Validation, 1794–1871

### Background, 1794–1857

It has been argued that the French Revolution and its wars had fundamentally transformed warfare in the decades just before Helmuth von Moltke joined the Prussian army in 1819. Historiographically this change is attributed largely to factors outside of armies themselves, political and social factors which changed France and in turn transformed the French military, its strategy, and its tactics. This interpretation was established a century ago by historians such as Hans Delbrück.[1] A second interpretation, advanced by Jean Colin, French War Academy commandant before World War I, emphasized a more material or technical explanation. According to Colin, improvements in the latter half of the eighteenth century in artillery, army organization, road building, and cartography were responsible for the transformation.[2]

Briefly stated, artillery changes associated with Jean de Gribeauval and the brothers du Teil, improved the technical qualities of artillery, reduced its weight, and allowed Napoleon to employ massed guns for tactical breakthroughs. Innovations in organization led to creation of the division and the corps. Self-contained units of twenty to forty thousand men became Napoleon's main

---

1. Bucholz, *Hans Delbrück*, chaps. 1, 2, and 3.; cf. Hans Delbrück, *Das Leben des Feldmarschalls Grafen Neidhardt von Gneisenau*, 2 vols. (Berlin, 1880); idem, "Über die Verschiedenheit der Strategie Friedrichs und Napoleons," in *Historische und politische Aufsätze* (Berlin, 1886), pp. 324–25; idem, *Die Strategie des Perikles erläutert durch die Strategie Friedrichs des Großen* (Berlin, 1890); idem, *Geschichte der Kriegskunst im Rahmen der politischen Geschichte*, 4 vols. (Berlin, 1900–1920), 4: 255–522. The last-named work, Delbrück's pathbreaking masterpiece, is now available in paperback from the University of Nebraska Press as the *History of the Art of War in the Framework of Political History*, in Walter Renfroe's excellent translation.

2. R.R. Palmer, "Frederick the Great, Guibert, Bülow: From Dynastic to National War," in Peter Paret, ed., *Makers of Modern Strategy from Machiavelli to the Nuclear Age* (Princeton, 1986), p. 95; cf. Jean Colin, *The Transformations of War*, trans. L.H.R. Pope-Hennessy (London, 1912).

element in maneuver. Maps began their modern transformation in the eighteenth century, providing for the first time a correct two-dimensional representation of war theater based on mathematical triangulation. In 1809 Napoleon possessed one of the first examples of this new breed, a rare hand-drawn set of 1:100,000 maps of Europe west of Russia. In the late 1780s the first modern highways were begun in Prussia; these were some two hundred miles in length and linked the Ruhr with Bavaria. Napoleon was a road and bridge builder of the first rank, and after 1815 Prussia inherited the French road system of its new Rhenish and Westphalian provinces.[3] What did these innovations mean for military activities? Taken all together, their impact was to increase the possibilities for creating, sustaining, and managing larger and more destructive armies. The stage was set for the Prussian phase in the development of war.

Defeated by a new kind of army in the years 1806 and 1807, Prussia began to create its own. The royal government which Moltke joined in 1819 had begun to transform itself in much the same way that other developing states had in reponse to confrontations with the overwhelming power of more advanced states. The process, begun in 1806, lasted for the rest of the century. However, by 1822, four distinct features were already visible which set Prussia apart: these were the organizational, educational, representational, and analytical aspects of its war planning.

The general staff, a new creation in the annals of war management, originated in a series of memorandums written by Prussian Colonel Christian von Massenbach. As early as 1795 he wrote that a state with a large, well-disciplined, maneuverable standing army was like a powerful but blind lion, unless it protected this army with men who thought ahead during peace so that the first step in a war was made without danger, secretly, and did not destroy in a few months the fame of half a century. He proposed that the existing army staff be reorganized into three brigades, each charged with operational studies for a given geographic area, that the staff prepare war plans against all possible contingencies, that it hold

3. McNeill, *The Pursuit of Power*, pp. 166–75; Larry Addington, *The Patterns of War since the Eighteenth Century* (Bloomington, 1984), pp. 18–19; Creveld, *Command*, pp. 60, 290; Josef Konvitz, *Cartography in France, 1660–1848* (Chicago, 1987), pp. 56ff.; W.O. Henderson, *The State and the Industrial Revolution in Prussia, 1740–1870* (Liverpool, 1958), p. 37; J.H. Clapham, *The Economic Development of France and Germany*, 4th ed. (Cambridge, 1963), pp. 104–9.

regular exercises to familiarize its members with terrain problems, that it collect intelligence on foreign armies and conditions, and that its members alternate between service with the general staff and duty with troop units.[4]

The innovations contained in this memorandum are four. The first is the study and researching of potential enemies and future fields of action, a knowledge-based deep-future orientation unusual at the time but characteristic of all modern organizations. Second is the preparation of specific war plans for contingencies during peacetime, that is, before the war had been declared, before it was likely, before danger was imminent. Third is a set of staff exercises to work out in mock format what might happen in particular terrain situations against specific foes, applying theoretical forma- tions to sets of contexts whose parameters were in various ways numerical. These exercises emphasized the study of history defined as battles fought in a concrete geographical context. Fourth is the marriage of theory and practice. Staff members were to gain and regain practical experience by regularly serving with active-duty troops.

Massenbach added that only in this way could commanders make war systematically, calculate its outcome with some probability, and overcome that fatalism which so often undermined military operations. When a campaign ended, the three potential results could then be analyzed. Case 1: the goals of the campaign were fulfilled. This provided evidence for the validity of the operations plan. Case 2: the goals were not fulfilled. This suggested that the operations plan was at fault, or that the plan had been poorly executed, or that other circumstances beyond the control of the commander had intervened. Case 3: the goals were exceeded. This indicated unexpected good fortune. Massenbach described how such a staff could be organized. Its chief, who provided unity and objectivity, needed direct access to the king and supervisory con- trol over military education. Beneath him should be three brigades,

---

4. Christian von Massenbach, "Über die Nothwendigkeit der engern Verbin- dung der Kriegs- und Staatskunde," in *Memoiren zur Geschichte des preußischen Staats unter den Regierungen Friedrich Wilhelm II und Friedrich Wilhelm III*, 3 vols. (Am- sterdam, 1809), 2: 168–82. The earliest work on this topic in North America seems to appear in Dallas D. Irvine's two articles: "The Origins of Capital Staffs," *Journal of Modern History* 10, no. 2 (June 1938): 161–79 and "The French and Prussian Staff Systems before 1870," *Journal of the American Military History Foundation*, 2 (1938): 192–203; Craig, *Politics*, p. 31; Gerhard Ritter, *The Sword and the Scepter*, trans. Heinz Norden, 4 vols. (Miami, 1969–73), 1: 163–64.

divided according to the geographic areas in which Prussian armies might fight: east, west, and south. Officers chosen for this staff were to be selected from all branches of the army on the basis of intellectual capacity, objectivity, creativity, and character.[5]

The transformation of the Prussian bureaucracy began after 1806, as it moved toward standardized regulations governing tenure, promotion, remuneration, and pension rights. The foundation was laid for the gradual transformation of the military service aristocracy into an educated hierarchy of salaried professional experts. By 1824, five years after Moltke joined it, a basic organizational framework had been established. Under the general supervision of the Second Section of the War Ministry, the GGS consisted of a lieutenant general as chief, thirteen field grade officers, and fifteen captains and lieutenants. Outside Berlin a parallel structure existed: each corps and division had a Troop General Staff (TGS) and consisted of a chief of staff and two assistants for each army corps and a chief of staff and one assistant for each division. There were twenty-nine officers in Berlin, twenty-one with the troops.[6]

The GGS initially and for a long time after this period reflected the division of labor suggested by Massenbach. It was one of the two standard forms of nineteenth-century organization: by geographic location and type of activity. In Berlin, for example, the First Section examined future war possibilities for lands east of Germany, including Austria, Russia, and the Scandinavian countries. The Second Section was responsible for the southern war theater, including Switzerland and Italy. The Third Section considered the west: France, Belgium, the Netherlands, and England.[7]

Since the idea of war planning was new, and more important, the GGS as an institution was little known, its span of control and influence was very restricted. In 1822 the kingdom of Prussia was only one of thirty-nine German states. It was one of the two largest but clearly subordinate to Austria, the traditional power-

---

5. Massenbach, "Nothwendigkeit," pp. 168–82.

6. Rosenberg, *Bureaucracy, Aristocracy, and Autocracy*, p. 216; Great General Staff or GGS always refers to the general staff in Berlin. It is used to distinguish between Berlin and the TGSs of corps and divisions. Hubert von Boehn, *Generalstabsgeschäfte* (Potsdam, 1875), pp. 11–12; Bronsart von Schellendorff, *The Duties of the General Staff*, 4th ed. (London, 1905), p. 29; Hansgeorg Model, *Der deutsche Generalstabsoffizier* (Frankfurt, 1968), pp. 11–13.

7. Boehn, *Generalstabsgeschäfte*, pp. 11–12, 43–45; Schellendorff, *Duties*, pp. 25–30.

holder in central Europe. Prussia, raised to great power status only in the middle of the previous century, had been badly humiliated during the early Napoleonic Wars. Moltke had joined the Prussian army in 1819 because it had an historic tradition and was larger and offered a potentially more worthwhile career than the Danish army. But not by much.

The renewed Prussian army of 1808 was characterized by its emphasis on education, the fundamental, modern notion that careers should be open to talent and that formal education was one way to nurture this capacity. The law of 6 August 1808 specified that "from now on a claim to officer rank shall in peacetime be warranted only by knowledge and education." A system of examinations was instituted for promotion to officer rank, presided over by the Military Examination Commission, an institution which lasted into the twentieth century. A higher military school, the General War School, renamed the War Academy in 1859, was established in Berlin. After 1815, a new central authority, the Committee of Military Studies, was set up to coordinate military education. In addition to the War School, an Artillery and Engineering School and eighteen officer preparatory schools also existed.[8]

The founding of the War School was said to be an act parallel to the creation of Berlin University by Wilhelm von Humboldt. The university and the War School both participated in military education. Founded in 1810, they existed in the same intellectual milieu. Professors lectured at both. In curriculum as well the War School resembled the university: both were dominated by the ideal of general education. When Moltke attended the War School in the 1820s, 60% of its courses were general – mathematics, physics, chemistry, German literature, and general history – and 40% were professional – military history and statistics, gunnery, siege warfare, applied tactics, and general staff duties.[9]

These reforms were hotly debated, revealing two sets of competing goals for military education. One set of goals placed general

8. Peter Paret, *Yorck and the Era of Prussian Reform* (Princeton, 1966), pp. 133, 273–74; cf. W. Nottebohm, *Hundert Jahre des militärischen Prüfungsverfahrens* (Berlin, 1908).

9. Peter Paret, *Clausewitz and the State*, (New York, 1976), p. 274; Louis Scharfenort, *Die königlich-preußische Kriegsakademie, 1810–1910* (Berlin, 1910), p. 387; Eberhard Kessel, *Moltke* (Stuttgart, 1957), pp. 32–47; Gustav Hillard, "Epilog auf den preußisch-deutschen Generalstabsoffizier," *Neue Deutsche Hefte* 100 (July–August 1964): 90–99; Cf. Theodore Ziolkowski, *German Romanticism and Its Institutions* (Princeton, 1990), pp. 286–308.

education in opposition to professional education. A Prussian general wrote that the first object of military examinations was to secure a generally well-educated, but not overly educated, officer. The second object was to secure a professionally trained officer. Carl von Clausewitz, a proponent of the latter, criticized the War School. He said it was more a small university than an institute for professional training. His colleague Gerhard Scharnhorst believed that the school had to transmit more than facts: it had to train intelligence and develop judgment. Mathematics and history should form its core because they were essential to the development of reasoning and wisdom.[10]

The second set of goals placed character before intellect. No matter how intelligent an officer was, if he had no heart and could not be trusted, he was useless. Character had always been considered the most important quality in an officer; however, with the new definition of the military as a profession, certain intellectual standards became important. These two sets of goals, general versus professional education and character versus intellect, became the themes in military education debates. In the early nineteenth century, general education and character predominated. By the end of the century professional education and intelligence were in strong ascendancy.[11]

From the beginning military history was central. A separate bureau was created for it, and general staff officers were expected to lecture, research, and write. The results of their study appeared not only in courses at the War School, in war game summations, and in technical background studies; they were published as articles in the *Militär-Wochenblatt* (*Military Weekly*) and as books issued by the Berlin publisher E.S. Mittler & Sons. General staff officers considered themselves part of the intellectual elite of Prussia. Although some considered history the natural bridge joining general and professional work, tensions existed from the start between two visions of exactly how history was to be defined. Some considered it part of universal knowledge, related to politics and oriented toward philosophy. Others believed military history should be dominated by details of practical military life, for example, mathematical knowledge of topography.[12]

10. Huntington, *Soldier and the State*, p. 41; Paret, *Clausewitz*, p. 273.
11. Karl Demeter, *The German Officer Corps in Society and State* (London, 1965), p. 63.
12. Bucholz, *Hans Delbrück*, p. 4; Schellendorff, *Duties*, p. 24.

The issue was joined in 1816 when Berlin publisher Ernst Siegfried Mittler suggested to officers on the general staff that they found the *Military Weekly*. Mittler held to the belief that the end of the Napoleonic Wars heralded a new epoch in the science of war. This conviction was tied to an attempt to bring military affairs under the powerful intellectual methods of Enlightenment science, where knowledge would be debated objectively and critically. From the start, the *Military Weekly* confronted obstacles. Its first editor, Rühle von Lilienstern, later GGS chief, wanted to "militarize the nation and nationalize the army." This was something entirely different from Enlightenment science, referring as it did to nation building using the army, an effort which suited the powerful reactive nationalism of this period. The goal of debating knowledge objectively was soon questioned. A controversy over artillery matters aired in the *Military Weekly* in the early 1820s caused a furor and the removal of the editors.[13]

As a result, in 1823 the new chief of the GGS, Freiherr von Müffling, turned the periodical away from practical or polemical issues and toward philosophical treatises. Dated 3 January 1824, the first issue of the new *Military Weekly* after it was taken under direct sponsorship by the GGS reprinted a lecture, probably by Müffling, advocating the study of military history from a broadly philosophical point of view. From then on it published both general and technical materials. It became the house organ of the GGS, reflecting the internal views of a new military professionalism, the technical experts, the intellectuals of the army. Financially supported by the War Ministry but edited by the historical section of the GGS, articles in serial, particularly whole issues on special topics, often became published books, following accepted scholarly practice.[14]

By 1850 the educational components of war planning had been defined in outline form. With its explicit emphasis on formal education as essential to general staff officers, the ideal range of activities for the intellectual professional included researching,

13. Max Jähns, "Das Militair-Wochenblatt von 1816 bis 1876," in *Max Jähns: Militärgeschichtliche Aufsätze*, ed. Ursula von Gersdorff (Osnabrück, 1970), pp. 301–7; "Über militärisches Schrifttum im preußisch-deutschen Heere von Scharnhorst bis zum Weltkriege," *Militärwissenschaftliche Rundschau*, 4 (1938): 463–82.

14. Jähns, "Militair-Wochenblatt," pp. 307–9; Kessel, *Moltke*, p. 101; Eberhard Kessel, "Moltke und die Kriegsgeschichte," *Militärwissenschaftliche Rundschau* 2(1941): 96–125.

teaching, and publishing. There were disagreements as to whether military education and history were part of general or technical specialist knowledge.

The representational aspect of war planning, mapmaking, underwent a revolution that was almost coincident with Moltke's sixty-year general staff career. Triangulation-based maps, that is, geodetically accurate maps based upon trigonometric numbers, careful topographic recording, and modern printing techniques had appeared in the late eighteenth century, mainly in France, where army engineers aided in completion of the national map survey during and after the revolution. Along the way, they developed standardized methods. Teams of field workers were sent out from mid-spring to mid-autumn; when they returned to the office during the winter months, they analyzed and copied the results, turning them into finished maps accompanied by written commentaries describing the natural resources, economic activities, and topographical features of the given areas.[15] Mapmaking aspired to be an exact science. Military engineers portrayed mountains with such extreme detail that their maps were considered top military secrets. Detailed written reports accompanying them described the "engineer-geographers'" views on defensive and offensive operations.

Although Napoleon's hand-drawn maps covering Europe west of Russia were unusual, the French were very active in representing terrain. From 1802 to 1803 the French army attempted to centralize and standardize cartography for the whole country.[16] A commission adopted decimalization, representative fraction for scales, the metric system, and contour lines. In this process, certain general guidelines were laid down. The use of maps was advocated in the belief that to look at a map was to see patterns that existed in space but were not apparent to an observer standing in the landscape. Maps were used to record observations and data, to analyze and compare the relations between dissimilar natural features. The ability to draw well was considered more than a means of

15. Konvitz, *Cartography*, pp. 38–39. To indicate how primitive cartography was, as late as 1807 the heights of only about sixty mountains had actually been measured; in the seventeenth century the Caucasus Mountains in southern Russia were estimated by some to have an elevation of fifty miles. Arthur H. Robinson et al., *Elements of Cartography*, 5th ed. (New York, 1984), p. 368.

16. Konvitz, *Cartography*, pp. 93, 100. In reviewing Konvitz, Sven Widmalm of Uppsala University referred to the "largely unknown terrain of the history of cartography," *Journal of Modern History* 61, no. 4 (December 1989): 791–93.

expressing an idea: it was critical to the map's very conceptualization.[17]

Defeated by an army with better cartography, Prussia set out to improve itself. For Prussia, mapmaking after 1807 was predominantly a military affair: from 1816 to 1921, the work of land survey in Prussia was in military hands. In fact, up to 1914 four out of six GGS chiefs had worked as topographers and three had written books on the subject. Helmuth von Moltke's 1828 book, *The Military Drawing of the Land*, was a summary of his lectures on that topic presented in a divisional school. Lieutenant Alfred von Schlieffen served as a survey officer for two years and three decades later still began his workday in the GGS map room.[18]

In 1816 there was no comprehensive map survey of Prussia and in that year a Land Survey Section was created. Headed by Freiherr von Müffling, it was divided into the Astronomical-Trigonometric Bureau, the Survey and Drawing Bureau, the map archive, and the Lithographic Institute. Müffling had begun active duty as a military topographer. In 1805 he participated in the triangulation work in Thuringia and in 1808 retired from military life to become director of a land survey office in the duchy of Weimar. After returning to military duty, he worked on the Lecoq map of south Germany and from 1816 to 1820 carried out topographical surveying from the Rhine to Thuringia.[19]

From the start mapmaking was recognized as a technical as well as an artistic endeavor. Tension existed between mathematical accuracy and topographical verisimilitude: one was the result of objective measurement and calculation, the other was derived from the mapper's subjective ability to see and draw. Accuracy began with trigonometric measurement of distance and planimetric measurement of area. Both required the use of mathematical formulas. The next step was the topographical sketch, made while in the field viewing the land. Here the problem was to

---

17. Creveld, *Command*, p. 290; Konvitz, *Cartography*, pp. 94, 104, 137.

18. Georg Krauß, "150 Jahre preußische Meßtischblätter," *Zeitschrift für Vermessungswesen* 94, no. 4 (April 1969): 126; Theo Müller, "Die topographischen und kartographischen Vorschriften für die preußischen Meßtischblätter," *Kartographische Nachrichten* 34 (1984): 174–79; Dr. Thiede, "Das Zentraldirektorium der Vermessungen im preußischen Staate und sein Einfluß auf das preußische Vermessungswesen," *Zeitschrift für Vermessungswesen* 64 (1935): 148–59.

19. Günter Scheel, *Die Entwicklung der deutschen Landesvermessung mit den wichtigsten Daten aus den geodätischen Nachbarbereichen und Fachinstitutionen* (Wiesbaden, 1978), p. 6.

transfer the spherical surface of the land to the plane surface of the sketch to make a transformation known as a projection. Even then the result retained various geometric qualities, for example, the maintenance of angular consistency based upon a rectangular coordinate system. Once measured and sketched, the results were turned into a cartographic image using point, line, and area symbols. Mapping, then, was a complex procedure involving both science and art.[20]

In 1821, four days after his appointment as GGS chief, Müffling, a professional engineer, issued his "Instructions for the Trigonometric and Topographic Work of the Royal Prussian General Staff." In it he established the Prussian polygonal projection as the basis for topographical work. Using this system, every degree of terrain was mapped with sixty plane table sheets. To accomplish this, fifteen to twenty officers on three-year assignment worked in the topographic and trigonometric sections. The first phase of mapping from 1821 to 1830 included the provinces of Brandenburg, Saxony, Silesia, Pomerania, and Posen. The Land Survey Section pushed forward with the ambitious project of completing the mapping of Prussia throughout Müffling's nine years in office. At scales of 1:20,000 to 1:25,000, they were done according to a format of about 10 kilometers square, using 3 to 5 trigonometric points per sheet with hachure lines for contour. Formal instruction, that is, continuing education for officers assigned to trigonometric and topographic work accompanied these efforts.[21]

A second mapping phase from 1830 to 1848, carried out under GGS Chief Wilhelm von Krauseneck, substantially improved upon the scientific basis of mapping by establishing a more accurate trigonometric foundation and adding contour lines to replace colored hachury. Three-year assignments continued, with field survey work, trigonometric measuring, and topographic sketching during the summers and cartography during the winters. Good maps were also important for many civilian aspects of Prussian life, such as

---

20. For this discussion of mapping I consulted Konvitz, *Cartography*, pp. 93, 100; Robinson, *Elements*, pp. 72–161; David Greenhood, *Mapping* (Chicago, 1964), pp. 203–39; F.J. Monkhouse and H.R. Wilkinson, *Maps and Diagrams*, 3d ed. (London, 1971), pp. 13–190.

21. Krauß, "150 Jahre," p. 128; Joachim Schröder-Hohenwarth, "Die preußische Landesaufnahme von 1816–1875," *Nachrichten aus dem Karten- und Vermessungswesen*, Reihe 1: Deutsche Beiträge und Informationen 5 (1958): 12–18; Scheel, *Entwicklung*, p. 7; W. Stavenhagen, "Die geschichtliche Entwicklung des preußischen Militär-Kartenwesens," *Geographische Zeitschrift* 6 (1900): 504–12.

trade, commerce, and economic development, and beginning in 1841 these maps were sold to the general public.[22] Increasingly, various aspects of cartographic production were carried out by civilian specialists. Modern map production developed in the nineteenth century through two techniques, lithography and photography. The change from manual processes to mechanical and then to photomechanical was in line with trends toward making faster, cheaper and higher-quality copies. Intermediate steps were slowly eliminated. In time the Lithographic Institute of the GGS became a modern master printing works.

Not only did GGS officers know how to make maps, but maps were widely available and used throughout the army. They were the starting point for war games, staff rides, and field maneuvers. From Helmuth von Moltke, who in 1832 prepared the general staff ride for Thuringia, to Wilhelm Groener in 1914 telegraphing encoded war games to railroad LCs, the first step was always to prepare the maps. Throughout the nineteenth century, as the size of armies and the range of weapons expanded, as the geographic space in which they fought grew, and as the time required for mobilization shrank, spatial precision was the first requirement for estimating future war requirements. Improved geographic images gave the Prussian army significant advantages.[23]

The innovation that was ultimately to be the most significant was the *Kriegsspiel* or war game, a new way of thinking about war. Its earliest form, a war chess game, was associated with Helwig and Venturini, two tutors at the court of Brunswick in the 1780s. It was played on a chess board consisting of 1,666 small squares, about three centimeters on a side, tinted in various colors to represent terrain features, buildings, villages, and cities. A line across the middle was the frontier, each player had a fort, and equal numbers of troops represented by pawns were maneuvered according to complex rules.[24] The second source for the war game was the thinking of the Prussian military reformers. In 1795 Christian von Massenbach had already suggested how to prepare a

22. Wilhelm Scharfe, "Preußische Monarchie, preußische Kartographie," in I. Kretschmer, J. Doerflinger, and F. Wawrik, eds., *Lexikon zur Geschichte der Kartographie: Von den Anfängen bis zum Ersten Weltkrieg*, (Vienna, 1986), pp. 636–42; Scheel, *Entwicklung*, p. 8.

23. Robinson, *Elements*, p. 432; Kessel, *Moltke*, p. 91.

24. Spencer Wilkinson, *Essays on the War Game* (Manchester, 1887), pp. 7–9; "Foreign War Games," trans. H.O.S. Heistand, in *Selected Professional Papers* (Washington, D.C., 1898), pp. 235–42.

military operations plan. First, find two intelligent officers, each with full understanding of the campaign area. Put one into the role of the commander on one side, the other into the position of the commander on the other side. Then have them maneuver against each other. Neither knew the plans of the other, both used every means to succeed, each tried to understand the other's thinking, and neither neglected any aspect of war, including supply, magazines, requisitions. Finally a third officer of even greater talent, intelligence, and experience evaluated their work, summarized the outcome, and formulated a general conclusion. In this way, Massenbach wrote, war could be conducted systematically and its outcome calculated with some probability.[25]

In 1809 Gerhard von Scharnhorst introduced the "application method" into military education. In the best Renaissance tradition, it meant "learn by doing." In addition to lectures and reading, officers were expected to make clay models and maps of terrain, write papers on the influence of topography on human life, and travel as widely as possible to observe in reality what was studied in the classroom. Scharnhorst's concept revolutionized large-scale field maneuvers. Instead of carrying out prearranged schemes, units were divided into two forces which maneuvered against each other, acting independently as in actual war.[26]

The final evolution of the early war game is associated with two Prussian officers, the Reisswitzs, father and son. In about 1810, the father had put together a war game played with plaster terrain and porcelain models at a scale of 26 inches to the mile. By 1816 his son George, an artillery officer stationed at Stettin, had replaced the plaster terrain with a relief map at 8 inches to the mile, metal pieces to represent troop units, and a set of rules. It was a simulation in which the opposing players decided the course of action on the basis of knowledge of their own and their opponent's situation and intentions. Originally designed for battalion level play, George von Reisswitz expanded it to corps level. The pieces on the opposing sides were colored blue and red. The game was played by single moves during which each commander was allowed to move his forces a distance on the map not greater than that which actual troops could have marched during a fixed time period. All disputes were settled by an umpire who decided the outcome

25. Massenbach, "Nothwendigkeit," pp. 173–77.
26. Paret, *Clausewitz*, p. 278.

of engagements on the basis of dice, a set of rules, and knowledge of military history. Dice represented the element of chance so important in war. That element was applied according to a simple principle. On each occasion when a decision was required, the umpire assigned to each side a certain number of faces on the die. Thus if blue, with two hundred men, attacked red, with one hundred, the chances in favor of blue were two to one. Accordingly, four sides of the die were to be colored blue and the remaining two red. If, when the die was thrown, a blue side turned up, blue had defeated red; if red, the reverse. Having decided which side was successful, the next thing was to settle how many men on each side had been placed *hors de combat*.[27]

In 1824 Reisswitz demonstrated the game to GGS chief Müffling, who saw its potential immediately. It was described in the *Military Weekly* of 6 March 1824, during Moltke's second year at the War School and was associated with Müffling's comment: "It's not a game at all, it's a veritable war school. I shall recommend it most emphatically to the whole army." Soon thereafter the game was played by King Frederick Wilhelm III, Prince Wilhelm (later German Kaiser Wilhelm I), commander of the 3d Corps, and officers of the Berlin garrison. The king directed that all regiments be supplied with the game, and under royal patronage it flourished. War game clubs were established in Berlin and elsewhere. In 1837 Helmuth von Moltke found that Ottoman commander Chosref Pasha in Constantinople wanted to learn it. Ten years later, large garrison cities had clubs organized to play competitively. As chief of the staff to the 4th Corps, Moltke's Magdeburg Club ranked first in 1844.[28]

Whether the war game was recognized as pathbreaking at the time is arguable. With the exception of a few individuals and a few institutional settings, it probably was not. But as the Kriegsspiel concept and method developed, it influenced at some point the ways of thinking about war of the officers who came in contact with it. By midcentury, the war game had thoroughly permeated general staff procedures. Like the general staff organization, mili-

27. Wilkinson, *War Game*, pp. 8–11; "Foreign War Games," pp. 244–46; Alfred H. Hausrath, *Venture Simulation in War, Business, and Politics* (New York, 1971), p. 506.

28. G.H.R. von Reisswitz, "Anzeige," *Militär-Wochenblatt*, no. 42 (6 March 1824): 2973–74; General von Dannhauer, "Das Reisswitz-Kriegsspiel von seinem Beginn bis zum Tod des Gründers, 1827," *Militär-Wochenblatt*, no. 56 (11 July 1874): 524–32; Wilkinson, *War Game*, p. 11.

tary education, and cartographic representation, it influenced many levels of the army. Because it drew upon other parts of the system, it became the central building block of Prussian war planning. As such it served four purposes. (1) It was a training ground for practical decision making, for learning and teaching methods to lead armies. In verbal and written responses to simulated war conditions, often in the actual physical setting of historical battles, officers estimated situations and drafted orders to meet them over a several-day or several-week period. (2) It was a means of testing and evaluating plans in a simulated war situation, of trying out, within the tension of a competitive situation, diverse possibilities ranging from textbook to historical to innovative solutions with immediate results and reaction forthcoming. (3) It was a data bank and research method – a kind of early think tank – from which insights were generated and new military ideas evaluated against historical and contemporary reference points. (4) It was a testing vehicle for personnel by means of which officers were pitted against each other under the eyes of their superiors. Careers were made, put on hold, and accelerated at war games. One can ponder the artificiality of such a situation; however, given the scarcity of actual war experience during the half century following 1815, war games and military history served as essential metaphors.

### Moltke's Career and the Evolution of Prussian War Planning

To illustrate the evolution of the four aspects of Prussian war planning, let us follow Helmuth von Moltke's career. He transferred from the Danish to the Prussian army in 1819 by means of a series of examinations, interviews, and letters of introduction. He was tested in German and French, mathematics, field fortifications, geography, statistics, and world and German history. He became a cavalry squadron lieutenant. Four years later he passed examinations and received recommendations for the War School, which he entered in the fall of 1823 and from which he graduated in the spring of 1826.

The War School at the time was an institution of German Neoclassicism where Enlightenment science and Greek humanistic and artistic ideals came together. It was undoubtedly a great age for German education, even in the military. The students read the literature of Greek, Roman, and medieval military history.

During the three-year course, with about thirty students per class, Moltke came under the influence of a gifted faculty. His best marks were in survey under the instruction of Franz O'Etzel, a graduate of Wittenberg University in chemistry and mineralogy, associate of Clausewitz at Koblenz, and later a pioneer of the telegraph in Germany. Working under Karl Ritter, one of the founders of comparative and historical geography, Moltke became a gifted artist of land study. But military history made the greatest impression on him. His favorite teacher was Karl von Canitz und Dallwitz, the author of a two-volume history of cavalry and well-known interpreter of the Napoleonic Wars.[29]

Upon graduation, Moltke entered a nine-year period devoted primarily to imaging the land, learning military history, and relating the two in war games, staff rides, maneuvers, and lectures. Initially he returned to his division school as a teacher of field drawing and sketching, instructing younger regimental officers preparing for the War School examinations. In 1828 his book, *Military Drawing of the Land*, was published and he joined the topographical section of the GGS.[30] The small GGS section which Moltke joined combined engineering and art. It measured and portrayed the space in which armies were to be active. In a sense space was the most basic fact of nineteenth-century war: it dictated what size of army could move, how, and in what period of time. Like pouring water into a pitcher in which the water takes the shape of its vessel, armies moving or fighting in a space assumed the shape of that space. They were squeezed by mountains, they spread into long ribbons on roads, they were slowed or halted by rivers or lakes along whose banks they spread, hovering like a semiliquid. Their speed of motion was changed by different grades, moving slowly up or down hill and steadily on flat land. Visual education for officers involved learning to see and record the earth's surface in such a way as to figure out these matters and record them in mathematical and cartographical terms.[31]

The measurement of the trigonometrical sections called for

---

29. Paret, *Clausewitz*, pp. 311–13; Kessel, *Moltke*, p. 43; Albrecht Graf Roon, *Denkwürdigkeiten aus dem Leben des Generalfeldmarschalls Kriegsministers Graf von Roon*, 5th ed., 5 vols. (Berlin, 1905), 1: 51–61; Heinrich von Brandt, *Aus dem Leben des Generals der Infanterie z.D. Dr. Heinrich von Brandt* (Berlin, 1868), pp. 8–22.

30. Kessel, *Moltke*, pp. 50–53.

31. For Prussian mapping of this period I consulted F.H.O. O'Etzel, *Terrainlehre*, 2d ed. (Berlin, 1834), pp. 1–5, 417–29; Stavenhagen, "Entwicklung," pp. 506–7; Schröder-Hohenwarth, "Landesaufnahme," pp. 20–25.

covering the whole kingdom with a network of triangles and marking them with stone implacements every square mile.[32] On each stone was inscribed longitude, latitude, and elevation. These coordinates allowed rectangular grid lines to be constructed and from them a triangulation network. The topographical section recorded: using the network, it executed original plane table drawings. Surveying has been called visualizing the land on paper. Prussian military surveys were all conducted within square-mile grid structures at a scale of 1:25,000. Equipment used included a plane table, probably 12 by 17 inches, a spirit level, sight rule, compass, and pencils. The procedure was to sight on a distant object to get a bearing and draw a line along the edge of the rule indicating that bearing on the map at hand. Using the triangulation marking system, such a procedure produced fairly accurate drawings and, in the process, educated the officer in the geography of the land. The cartographical section then made the maps, and the final lithography was based on standard stone printing technology.[33]

Moltke was assigned to Lower Silesia and completed sheets for Schmollen, Oels, and Zerkow in 1828, Grab and Rusko in 1829, and Schwersenz and Miloslaw in 1830, drawing in summer and fall in the field and finishing the sheets in Berlin during the winter months. Moltke's seven ordinance surveys must have been fairly good, for 162 years later his map of Schmollen makes up part of the modern German Ordnance Survey Map No. 4870 for Groß Zöllnitz. Quartered in the homes of Silesian estate owners, he enjoyed conversations on a variety of matters. Moltke's sketches and drawings and his later travel books reveal a keen perception of the land and its inhabitants, as well as a celebrated visual and literary ability.[34]

In March 1832, after three years of topographical apprenticeship, Moltke was transferred to the Second Section of the GGS. Its main job was preparation of the annual GGS ride. When not working on this, he contributed to the current military history project on the wars of Frederick the Great and wrote essays describing the Austrian and Danish armies. Lest it be thought that GGS life was all drudgery, we should note that he rode every day at noon and attended dinners and dances at the homes of official and

32. Görlitz, *German General Staff*, p. 65, Kessel, *Moltke*, pp. 64–68.

33. Greenhood, *Mapping*, pp. 218–22.

34. Kessel, *Moltke*, pp. 64–68; Schröder-Hohenwarth, "Landesaufnahme," pp. 15–17.

social Berlin in the evenings. One January he went to eleven balls in fourteen days and danced every dance.[35]

How did the four aspects of war planning interrelate during Moltke's early career on the Prussian general staff? Graduation from the War School qualified him for the small sixty-man general staff and exposed him to the scrutiny of its leadership. Three years in the topographical section were provisional. He learned what was considered the basic building block of general staff education in his day: the land, the survey, and the sectional map. He was regularly evaluated by the chiefs, Müffling and Krauseneck. By 1833 Moltke had passed muster and formally joined the GGS. His duties combined topographic, historical, and operational work. The then-current general staff historical work dealt with the campaigns of Frederick the Great in 1760-62. Moltke pored over topographical terrain maps, some of which he himself had participated in producing. He prepared indoor sand table and map games and wrote a series of military topographical essays, including terrain presentations, describing the battles. Then, using his topographical and historical knowledge, he prepared the annual general staff ride.

By the mid-1830s the general staff war game schedule had begun to be regularized. Every September there were maneuvers with regiments and divisions in which the king participated. In May the GGS officers spent a month's practical service with a troop unit. During the rest of the year many weeks were spent traveling, taking part in staff exercises. The most important was the GGS ride. Using the precise terrain in which a well-known historical battle had been fought, the GGS chief chose a dozen or more officers and divided them into two groups, blue and red. The sides maneuvered against each other, rode ten to twenty miles per day through the actual terrain of an historic battle, issued orders for division-sized forces, and otherwise conducted themselves as if they were fighting an actual war. The GGS ride was the ultimate war game test. It took place once a year and involved intimate working contact between the chief and a handful of officers. Setting up the whole problem for both sides was a test in itself. In 1833 the ride went through Lusitz, in 1834 to Norbhausen and Kulm, in 1835 to Silesia for Frederick's Liegnitz campaign of 1761.

35. Max Jähns, *Feldmarschall Moltke*, 2d ed. (Berlin, 1906), pp. 39–40; Kessel, *Moltke*, pp. 90–102.

How did these rides integrate military history with current defense problems? The goal was to attain a general idea of what had happened during a specific battle and combine that general idea with painstakingly detailed specific knowledge of the terrain in which the battle had taken place. In other words, historical accuracy was sacrificed to practical terrain and tactical knowledge. Late twentieth-century historians may be amused when they come across repeated examples of nineteenth-century officers working through a particular geographic setting in which several great battles of the past had been fought. The situation described here of Moltke and his colleagues working against each other in the geographic circumstances of the battle of Liegnitz is not an isolated example; it occurred again and again in the professional lives of Prussian officers. In fall 1853 the war game was carried out between Naumberg and Weissenfels on the battlefield of Rossbach, one of Frederick's stunning victories during the Seven Years' War. Later, as potential enemies began to appear in a real time and space context, they were introduced into the games. In fall 1858 the GGS ride took place in northern Silesia against a Russian force and in fall 1860 in southern Silesia against an Austrian opponent. In all these situations, not only were historical and terrain factors considered, but also current intelligence on the size, configuration, capability, and leadership of opposing armies. Officers of the general staff spent a good deal of their working year traveling and war gaming in this way.[36]

War games involve people playing roles in imaginary worlds. Simulation involves an act of collective "let's pretend" among the participants, and the usefulness of such activities depends both on the conviction with which people act and the relationship of such behavior in "simulated" situations to that in "real" situations. We have suggested that the GGS war game, staff ride, and maneuver process was intimately related to (1) knowledge of the land; (2) the military educational system, especially the study of history, military procedures, and current intelligence; (3) the appointment, retention, and promotion system; and most important, (4) thinking about possible future wars. There is no question that these games were taken with the utmost seriousness.[37]

36. Kessel, *Moltke*, pp. 101–4.

37. Michael Nicholson, "Games and Simulations," in Amos Perlmutter and John Gooch, eds., *Strategy and the Social Sciences*, (London, 1981), p. 73; Thomas B. Allen, *War Games* (London, 1987), pp. 21ff.

One final interest of Helmuth von Moltke during these years and one that was to assume importance, later dominance, within the GGS, was the railroads. In 1841, just back from four years in the Ottoman Empire, he joined the board of directors of the new Berlin-Hamburg Railroad Company, whose track construction was yet incomplete. Railroads had begun to be used in Prussia but within the military they were not much understood. In 1839 eight thousand troops had been moved from Berlin to Potsdam for a maneuver and in 1846 twelve thousand men of the 6th Corps were sent by railroad to the border of the Polish state of Krakow. In early spring 1850, as chief of staff of the 8th Corps, Moltke used railroads in the corps maneuver.[38]

These small-scale practice mobilizations were the prelude to a large-scale, real war mobilization which turned out to be a disaster. In May 1850, during the crisis with Austria, the Prussian army used railroads to mobilize 490,000 men. The mobilization itself took over two months to complete. There were no specific plans for military use of the railroads. Transportation was carried out using existing civilian facilities and personnel. Military troop trains were simply inserted into the normal schedule, where they moved in a leisurely pace from station to station on single track lines without careful thought to provisions and supply. There were no military officers or officials in charge, and the entire operation was in the hands of the Commerce Ministry. Everything went wrong. Mobilization orders were inappropriate to the order of battle, unit sequence was erroneous, loading cumbersome. The difference between peace and war strength was too great. There was awkwardness with supply, rear area, and hospital units, none of which existed in peacetime. Artillery and cavalry had too few horses, and military authorities were unprepared to purchase more. All of this contributed to Prussia's diplomatic and political humiliation at Olmütz in November.

For two subsequent chiefs of staff, the May 1850 mobilization was an early warning signal. Alfred Graf Waldersee, viewing this debacle as a regimental artillery officer, noted that the train columns ended up in a "tragic situation." Supply officers, who never had anything to do with horses, "fell all over themselves." Moltke, as chief of staff of an army corps, realized that coordinating separate movements of troops from many different provinces was an intricate

38. Hermann Rahne, *Mobilmachung* (East Berlin, 1983), p. 23; Kessel, *Moltke*, pp. 195–203.

business requiring complicated plans well laid in advance. Here was a problem which needed to be completely rethought.[39]

The years 1848 to 1850 disclosed many gaps in military planning and organization. With a peacetime army of about 200,000, war mobilization strength was roughly 637,500. The GGS itself consisted of a lieutenant general as chief, four colonels as section heads, and fourteen captains or lieutenants. Below this level, in nine corps and eighteen divisions, the TGS was comprised of twenty-seven field grade officers as chiefs of staff with nine captains as assistants. There were sixty-four officers, of whom 28% worked in Berlin. The main agencies responsible for war mobilization were the War Ministry and each army corps. The TGS was larger than the GGS and its relationship to Berlin was rather loose. TGS chiefs were equal in rank to section heads in Berlin and they were under the chief of the GGS for general staff work but subordinate to their own corps or division commanders for day-to-day work. In addition, annual personnel reports were forwarded to the War Ministry over the signature of the local commanding general. Since war mobilization came from the War Ministry and each TGS officer worked for his local commander, the TGS-GGS tie was weak at best. The GGS was out of the war plan command channel.[40]

The war plans of these years, under GGS chief General von Reyher, are described as "timid and confused." As for the task environment, after the dangerous years 1848 to 1850, Prussia was completely dominated by Austria, France, and Russia. Prussia had not fought a war for forty years, and most of those with war experience had died or retired. It was a full-blown peacetime army. Strategy was entirely defensive and based upon control of land and

---

39. Rahne, *Mobilmachung*, pp. 16–18.

40. Ibid., pp. 12–14; Kessel, *Moltke*, p. 231; Jähns, *Moltke*, p. 249. According to the Militärgeschichtliches Forschungsamt, Freiburg (MGFA), West Germany, prior to World War I, various fundamental aspects of general staff work were not written down but were passed along on the basis of custom and experience. For example, one aspect involved the precise legal or bureaucratic responsibilities of general staff officers in relation to their commander. In other words, who was responsible for what in the process of making command decisions? This would presumably apply whether the relationship was that of the chief of the GGS to the king or of a corps or divisional general staff officer to his commander. The MGFA argues that the fundamental right of the general staff officer to disagree verbally and in writing with his commander's decision was a standard, although unwritten, traditional prerogative until its publication in the 1936 edition of Militärgeschichtliches Forschungsamt, ed.,: *Tradition in deutschen Streitkräften bis 1945* (Bonn, 1986), p. 171.

fortress warfare. As for war games, Reyher, a former engineer, thought of the exercises entirely as a reflection of the personality of the officer in charge. Each exercise was unique, with few standard features and no coordination. It was not part of a war planning system. The separate parts of the skeletal framework were disconnected, partly through disuse, partly because of the lack of external pressure, and partly because of a discontinuity between theoretical and practical experience. There was little coordination or cooperation between the GGS and TGS on the one matter which counted most, the war plan.[41]

There are a number of reasons for this lack of coordination. For one thing, there was no one office in the army responsible for writing war plans. The War Ministry was the action office, but its plans were mainly for weapons and logistics. As for the GGS, Reyher's plans were political essays filled with vague generalizations. They contained little on strength, assembly points, or operation lines. The GGS was not organized for this kind of work. None of the existing sections dealt specifically with mobilization, and there were no officers who specialized in drafting war plans. Everyone worked on military history and "operational studies." The GGS was mainly an educational bureau, not the office for mobilization or war preparation. The same was true outside Berlin. The nine army corps were even less prepared, and their linkages to Berlin were spasmodic. There was no sense of timing. During mobilization the civilian train system fit nearly half a million soldiers slowly and intermittently into its normal timetable. The men were lucky to find their regiments at all: their orders were delivered by post or by local officials on horseback. Some officers received their orders five days after mobilization was declared.

Theodor Fontane's description fits this picture well. In May 1848, in the midst of the revolution of that year, he heard General von Reyher speak in the wool loft on Neue Königstraße, Berlin. Old Reyher, one of the "best men," said things that bore hardly any relation to the issue at hand. His comments were curious, often comical, and spontaneously wide of the mark. Fontane called them "dilettantish wheezing." Such was Prussian war planning in the early 1850s.[42]

---

41. Hajo Holborn, *A History of Modern Germany*, 3 vols. (New York, 1969–71), 3: 130; Kessel, *Moltke*, pp. 237–38, 245–46.
42. Kessel, *Moltke*, pp. 245–46; Rahne, *Mobilmachung*, pp. 16–17; Theodor

## *Moltke and the General Staff*

A great change occurred under Moltke's leadership and as a result of the experience of war. He had already served in the Prussian army for nearly forty years, but it was only during the next decade that this service changed military history. Moltke's thirty-one year tenure as chief of the general staff may be divided into three phases. (1) Six years of peace (1857–63) during which the war planning processes evolved slowly and haltingly. Moltke tried to transform and develop the GGS, but neither he nor the GGS had sufficient prestige or independence, and the task environment was not urgent, but only indirectly and unclearly supported change. (2) Seven years of war (1864–71) under whose task pressures the GGS was dramatically and substantially transformed. Three stunning military victories resulted in a fundamental restructuring of the political configuration of Europe, the elevation of Prussia to the role of a dominant partner in a new nation and the promotion of the general staff to mythological status among the institutions of European culture. (3) Seventeen years of peace (1871–88) divided into ten years of active and seven of indirect leadership. During this period the Prussian war planning system, legitimized in war, achieved independent bureaucratic status and began its transition to a more technical professional bureaucracy.

The GGS over which Moltke was appointed head on 29 October 1857 was small, subordinate to the War Ministry, its potential unappreciated, its institutional credibility unvalidated. It had little reputation, real or imagined. After nine years of work, in June 1866, its chief's orders still met with incredulity. Six weeks later this was no longer true: his name and the organization he represented had entered military history. How did this come about?

Moltke took charge of the chaos revealed during the mobilizations of the early 1850s by focusing on transportation and communication. In March 1858 the GGS issued a draft statement on the use of the Prussian railroads for large troop movements. In September the first large-scale railroad exercise in peacetime was conducted. Sixteen thousand troops, 650 horses, and 78 fully war-loaded wagons of the 5th and 6th Corps were transported from

Fontane, "The Eighteenth of March," in Peter Demetz, ed., *Theodor Fontane: Short Novels and Other Works* (New York, 1982), p. 334; Görlitz, *German General Staff*, p. 75.

their maneuver area back to garrisons near Liegnitz. The exercise went off fairly smoothly, revealing that the capacity of the railroads for troop transportation was much greater than had been supposed, that much earlier preparatory work was necessary, and that the activities of the four agencies involved – the GGS, and the War, Commerce, and Interior Ministries – had to be coordinated. Moltke observed that railroads were highly interactive systems. Scheduling had to be precise and timetables met: one late-running train created problems miles away. Moltke began to realize that railroads might allow him to deploy external lines, scattered broadly over a wide area of operations, then concentrate these divided forces at a single point in space and time. This simultaneous extension and decentralization would also alter the commander's relationship to the army, forcing or allowing subordinate commanders to be more independent.[43]

By 1859 Moltke had written to the War Ministry asking for more track to be built in the west, particularly double track lines, so that each corps could be assigned a line with one track going in each direction. In June, with the outbreak of the Franco-Austrian War, Prussia mobilized six corps or 80% of its active army in support of armed mediation. As it turned out, France made peace with Austria before Prussia could do anything; however, the exercise again revealed Prussia's weaknesses. Moltke studied the situation. The campaigns of 1859 were the first to demonstrate the practical importance of railroads in war.

Two weeks after the fighting had ended, Moltke convened a conference of Prussian civil and military officials with railroad jurisdiction. He proposed that GGS and railroad officials cooperate in three standing commissions, a Central Commission in Berlin, below that a series of Line Commissions for each major rail segment, and within these at loading stations a group of Reserve Commissions. The Second Section of the GGS became the Mobilization Section and within it the RRS was created. Mobilization procedures were substantially altered. Orders were henceforth sent by telegraph and notification time was reduced from 120 to 24 hours, an improvement of 500%. A time limit of twenty-one days was set for the completion of mobilization transport. Military transportation and communication were given priority in the railroad and telegraph systems. Army corps would henceforth be

---

43. Kessel, *Moltke*, pp. 240–43; Görlitz, *German General Staff*, pp. 75–77.

transported in their war order of battle. Individual units would not be separated during transport, and the troops furthest away and those ready first would be moved first. The unit train rule was instituted: one war-strength infantry battalion, cavalry squadron, or field artillery battery would be moved by a single train, with no change of railroad cars and no long stops. During field exercises military units practiced on-and off-loading. In July these procedures were put to the test. In twenty-nine days, almost 50% better than in 1850, the 5th Corps carried out a practice mobilization at Frankfurt am Main which became the model for the first generation of modern Prussian mobilization.[44]

In the next year, 1860, came the great army reorganization. Aside from the constitutional conflict which arose from it, the change provided internally that each divisional staff have its own supply section and increase its annual intake of recruits, including volunteers and *Einjährigen*, to about 70,000 men per year. This number was roughly ten times the size of the average industrial organization in Germany at the time.[45] Moltke recognized that the strategic environment for war as a whole was changing. Tactically it appeared that troops could no longer advance across open ground against a well-entrenched enemy. Strategically the overall organization of the army had to be simplified. The commander in chief could no longer do everything himself; too many decisions were required at separate locations. Greater reliance had to be placed on staff officers and local commanders. Geographic dispersion, forced by size and space considerations, meant division and subdivision of labor and a change in communications.

Strategically, Moltke achieved a revolution in Prussian thinking about war along the lines that Clausewitz had described. For one thing, he was no longer primarily concerned with fortresses or with defensive war. Fortresses were essential as a refuge for defeated armies and as supply depots or blocking points along rail lines but they were no longer appropriate strategic goals. The goal of military operations was the destruction of the enemy fighting force. Moltke saw that the size of forces was becoming unique in war history and that only railroads would henceforth allow their full

---

44. Rahne, *Mobilmachung*, pp. 25–27; Kessel, *Moltke*, pp. 272–75.
45. Rahne, *Mobilmachung*, p. 32; Jürgen Kocka, "The Rise of the Modern Industrial Enterprise in Germany," in Alfred D. Chandler, Jr., and Herman Daems, eds., *Managerial Hierarchies: Comparative Perspectives on the Rise of the Modern Industrial Enterprise.* (Cambridge, Mass., 1980), pp. 77ff.

deployment. Railroads were of little use in moving forces into combat, but of great use in mobilization, concentration, and supply. Railroads could strengthen the defense, but they also permitted a new kind of offense based upon moving widely separated forces outside the battle area, then concentrating them on the battlefield.

In 1861 a Railroad Commission was created for the German Confederation. The Austrian delegate was the chairman; Graf Wartensleben, Moltke's railroad expert, was Prussia's delegate. The commission began work by traveling over the railroad lines of central Europe to collect information about the condition and workload of the existing rail systems. Following this, it drew up a railroad mobilization plan for the confederation against France which became the technical foundation for later Prussian general staff plans in this area.

War games, staff rides, and corps maneuvers were used to work out the details of the new strategic thinking. First of all, Moltke redefined the Rhine and Weichsel rivers. Previously they had been lines to be defended. Now they became the axis of operations. In October 1859 elements of the 7th and 8th Corps played through an exercise against the 4th Corps. France had attacked across Belgium, with a secondary thrust aimed through Metz. In October 1860 another plan was war gamed, with one corps protecting along the east border, three corps defending at the Rhine, and six corps attacking at the Main River. In January 1861 a GGS war game simulated an enemy landing in Pomerania, with Danish troops supporting a French force at the mouth of the Elbe River.[46]

The study of military history and current field operations paralleled these exercises. Moltke himself researched and lectured to the GGS on the Bavarian campaign of 1809. The campaign of 1809 had certain similarities to the Franco-Austrian War of 1859 which became a subject of intense interest as soon as it broke out. Moltke followed it closely, using the reports from Vienna filed by the Prussian military observer, Major von Redern, then wrote two essays on Solferino and Magenta and delivered them as talks within the GGS. When the war ended, Moltke sent Colonel Ollech, head of the Military History and Mobilization Sections, to France to observe the demobilization of French forces. Major von Strantz was sent to northern Italy to observe the battlefields at close hand.

46. Kessel, *Moltke*, pp. 240, 281–88; Rahne, *Mobilmachung*, pp. 26–31.

On the basis of their reports and with help from officers responsible for the southern European land area, Moltke wrote an account of the campaign and presented it in the form of a lecture and an essay in a special issue of the *Military Weekly* published in 2800 copies. One historian has called this work good critical military history: it asked important questions and was open ended in its conclusions. The GGS Military History Section was used for other purposes as well. In 1861 and 1862 it was ordered to work on the historical part of the rank and quarter list of the Prussian army and prepare a battle calendar of Prussian military history.[47]

Moltke meanwhile had already begun looking to the north. In December 1862 his first memorandum on the subject of a possible war with Denmark pointed out that the north German railroads could move troops into the duchies faster than Danish ships could. He suggested a twenty-day movement of the Prussian advance guard to the Eider River, then, under their protection, moving troops from Hamburg and Lübeck and echeloning them to Rendsburg and Kiel by the twenty-eighth mobilization day. In this way 61,000 Prussian troops would face a Danish force of roughly 43,000. In 1863 the Military History Section researched the German-Danish War of 1848–49, and a GGS exercise prepared orders and timetables for the concentration by rail of a Prussian expeditionary force around Hamburg and Lübeck. Moltke had also been watching developments in the American Civil War. The Civil War was the first to wage war over great distances largely by means of railroads, and the Union army created separate corps to operate trains and maintain equipment, used armored trains, and hospital cars.[48]

### Three Wars, 1864–1871

During the eighteen-month Danish War approximately 65,000 Prussian troops were mobilized. Although a small force in contrast to the wars which followed, it created formidable transportation

---

47. Kessel, "Moltke und die Kriegsgeschichte," pp. 106–11.
48. Kessel, "Moltke und die Kriegsgeschichte," p. 110; Dennis Showalter, *Railroads and Rifles: Technology and the Unification of Germany* (Hamden, Conn., 1975), p. 49; Craig, *Politics*, p. 182; Jay Luvaas, *The Military Legacy of the Civil War: The European Heritage* (Chicago, 1959), p. 122; Edward Hagerman, *The American Civil War and the Origins of Modern Warfare* (Bloomington, Ind., 1988).

and supply problems. Those called up reported to separate divisions which were only reformed into corps upon arrival in the campaign area. For example, the 13th Division – 517 officers, 15,058 men, 4583 horses, and 379 wagons – was carried in 2,282 railcars divided into forty-two trains of about fifty cars each. These trains went from Minden through Hanover to Hamburg, where the division joined the 2d Corps. A new supply system was introduced. Men were given three-day "iron rations" to carry, provision columns following behind carried supplies for three to four days, and movable magazines were used for heavier supplies. If Moltke's influence was small at the beginning of the campaign, by its end, as chief of staff to the commander, Prince Frederick Charles, he was credited with the planning and direction of the successful operation that brought the war to a close. Henceforth he attended meetings of the king's Ministerial Council whenever GGS matters were on the agenda.[49]

The Danish War revealed weaknesses in several areas, one of which was mobilization. In mobilizing, 66% of the Prussian army was made up of reserves, while the small standing army provided 34%. This meant that mobilization took a long time. A second problem was that of garrison cities. Prussian troops were spread around very thinly. Between 1850 and 1869 the number of garrisons increased from approximately 230 to more than 330. In 1865, for example, of the 81 Prussian infantry regiments, only 29 originated in a single location, 44 were mobilized from two cities, and 8 from three cities. The same applied to cavalry and artillery regiments. Only pioneer and train units were located, for reasons of training and equipment, in a single location. As the war strength of the Prussian army rose above 600,000, garrisoning troops became increasingly unwieldy.

To deal with these problems, decentralization seemed necessary. Moltke suggested to the War Ministry that the general commands, that is, the peacetime corps headquarters, become the focal point of all preparations for mobilization. To accomplish this a new institution, the DC, was created. It was to be the bottom rung of the mobilization ladder with control over reserves, *Landwehr*, and substitute reserves. DC offices became local mobilization centers based upon their connections to the railroad and

49. Rahne, *Mobilmachung*, pp. 42–45; Craig, *Politics*, pp. 194–95; Görlitz, *German General Staff*, pp. 83–84.

telegraph networks. As the leadership and overseeing of this work lay in the hands of general staff officers assigned to the corps and divisions, the GGS for the first time gained some immediate influence over mobilization preparation. Orders, however, still emanated from the War Ministry.[50]

By spring 1866 the Prussian army had significant new organizational strengths. The peacetime army was already formed into the corps, divisions, and regiments with which it would take to the field. With the exception of the Guard Corps, which drew its members from the kingdom as a whole, each corps was stationed in the district from which its reserves came. Within army commands, mobilization preparation was directed by general-staff-trained officers and was delegated within the DC framework. Finally the GGS itself was reorganized and enlarged. During the Danish War there had been a shortage of trained officers. GGS officers had been sent directly from Berlin to serve in the Prussian army in Denmark, leaving the GGS with barely enough men to carry out its duties. The decision was made that there were certain technical and scientific specialties which deserved their own independent departments. In the summer of 1865, therefore, the GGS was subdivided. Half of it was split into a special branch called the Secondary Bureau for Scientific Affairs. Headed by a major general and staffed by fourteen officers and twenty-four men, mapmaking activities were its focus. To preserve continuity in these technical areas, officers assigned to this branch were exempt from the usual rotation to troop regiments.[51]

The Austrian war of 1866 was a more complicated affair. Instead of 65,000 men, more than 280,000 were mobilized. In place of a single theater, 1866 was fought in two widely separated locations, northwestern Austria and north central Germany. Instead of a single trunk rail line, two main lines and six trunk systems were employed. Whereas in 1864 there had been little chance of intervention, even from England, in 1866 Prussia confronted a potential French mobilization as well as local challenges from the smaller German states, who were likely to ally with Austria. Timing and force interdependency became paramount. Bismarck's diplo-

50. Rahne, *Mobilmachung*, p. 33; Erich von Schichfuß und Neudorff, "Der Sieger," in Generalleutnant a.D. von Cochenhausen, ed., *Von Scharnhorst zu Schlieffen, 1806–1906: Hundert Jahre preußisch-deutscher Generalstab* (Berlin, 1933), p. 154.

51. Scheel, "Entwicklung," pp. 504–12; Schellendorff, *Duties*, p. 31.

macy allowed a narrow window of opportunity, a brief time period during which the Prussian armies could fight on two fronts. Should the time frame be exceeded, the window would close and then Prussia would face the possibility of war on a third front against a power stronger than any of those already engaged.

The timing worked because the Bohemian campaign area was technologically favorable for Prussia. There were five Prussian railroad lines leading into the theater of war, while Austria had only one. Beginning in April 1866, Graf Wartensleben, who was stationed in Berlin as chief of the RRS of the GGS, prepared detailed deployment plans. Working in conjunction with the Central Railway Directorate of the Prussian Commerce Ministry, planning was carried out through the three joint military-civil committees set up in 1859 – the Railroad Commission in Berlin, Theater Line Commissions for each of the five axes of advance, and Field Army Line Commissions for each operating army. The gist of the war plan, based on the intermeshing of railroad timetables, was to advance forces separately, then concentrate them at a single point as near to the enemy forces as possible. The whole of Moltke's plan depended on a sense of timing and or an awareness of the necessity of speed in the interest of coordination. It very nearly did not work. Few shared Moltke's sense of timing at the strategic level.[52]

Prior to the start of the Austrian war, the War Ministry had a hand in preparing the overall plans, but the GGS had prepared the railroad mobilization. By 2 June railroad transport had become so critical that Moltke was given authority to transmit orders directly to the field commanders, bypassing the War Ministry. In the short term this development came just in the nick of time. In the longer term it marked a relocation not only of operational orders, but of effective planning control from the War Ministry to the GGS, with railroad technology as the medium of transfer. In June 1866 it took ten preparation days to get the railroads ready. As finally executed, the Prussian advance into Bohemia had four phases. Phase one was the movement of men, horses, and supplies to mobilization centers. Phase two, the concentration of four army corps in Silesia and Lusatia by rail, was completed between May 16 and 23. Phase

---

52. Showalter, *Railroads*, pp. 59–60; Gordon Craig, *The Battle of Königgrätz* (Philadelphia, 1964), p. 47; David Chandler, ed., *A Guide to the Battlefields of Europe*, 2 vols. (Philadelphia, 1965), 1: 22–26; Henry S. Haines, *Efficient Railway Operation* (New York, 1919), pp. 416ff.

three entailed marching from railhead into battle formation. Phase four was the attack. The rail lines allotted to each corps handled eight to twelve trains per day. Each corps was responsible for its own forage and rations and for keeping itself supplied. Quarters and medical care were requisitioned.

That the victory of Königgrätz took place in spite of errors, wrong moves, mistakes, and misadventures is well known. Early in the campaign, on 26 June, Austria missed an opportunity to attack the isolated 2d Prussian Army and by 2 July had been maneuvered into a less favorable position where they waged an essentially defensive battle. This permitted Prussia to attack by bringing up two "masses of maneuver," one of which griped the enemy frontally while the other was deployed in a great flanking movement. Moltke completely lost communication with subordinate units and had to rely on personal emissaries traveling on horseback. Had the war gone on much longer, events might have gotten completely out of hand. At the same time, Moltke had a certain measured confidence in his system. At 11 A.M. on the day of victory, in response to a worried query from King Wilhelm, he is reported to have replied that not only the battle but the campaign would be won that day. Although it may be a simplification of a very capricious situation, nevertheless, viewed in the overall context of the nineteenth century, Moltke's strategic manipulation of size, space, and time by railroads appears strikingly unique.[53]

After Königgrätz Prussia had forty-six months to digest the lessons learned before the final midcentury mobilization, that of 1870. During this time, the war-mobilized army expanded from 288,000 to over 800,000, an increase of 180%. It changed from an army of Napoleonic proportions to one approaching twentieth-century standards. This was the army of the reforms of Albrecht von Roon of 1858, expanded after 1866 into the areas of the North German Confederation. It comprised twelve regional or corps commands – eight for Prussia, with Schleswig-Holstein constituting a ninth, Hanover a tenth, electoral Hesse, Nassau, and Frankfurt an eleventh, and the kingdom of Saxony a twelfth; the Grand Duchy of Hesse furnished a single division to the 11th Corps. Each of these included both active and reserve forces. Each corps enrolled men from its own region. Outside of Berlin, the twelve corps commands contained twenty-seven equal-size infantry and two cavalry divisions.

53. Showalter, *Railroads*, pp. 66–67; Craig, *Königgrätz*, pp. 110–11.

Parallel to this active army, there were 216 Landwehr battalions organized in the DC system.[54]

While army size increased, the army by no means used up all available manpower. Universal military training meant three years' active duty at age twenty, followed by four years' reserve duty, followed by five additional years in the Landwehr. Thus contingents based upon twelve-year cycles constituted the whole force. The army law of 1867 had reduced military service from nineteen years to twelve years. However, of 170,000 liable for service, only 93,000 were called up because the law capped peacetime army size at 1% of the population of the North German Confederation. This limitation was to become a persistent concern in future years.[55]

Although the corps organization allowed the extension of Prussian military methods to the remaining German states after 1866, it was the general staff system which gave a measure of uniformity to the whole thus created. To match increases in army size, the GGS was increased to 101 officers, 46% in Berlin, 54% with the TGS. Following 1866 the GGS and War Ministry issued over two hundred regulations and directives to reorganize the railroad plans and field telegraph and build a field supply and medical system. The relationship between the GGS and the TGS changed, becoming more centralized. The TGS relied upon the GGS for specialized knowledge and materials. To assure continuity, officers stayed in the GGS longer. The Second Section of the GGS became more important: it contained the Mobilization Section and RRS.[56]

The Secondary Bureau for Scientific Affairs, known as the "geographical-statistical" group, was headed by the cartographer Emil von Sydow. Although in Moltke's years as a junior officer the topographical bureau of the GGS had been a mandatory assignment for all GGS officers, after 1867 this was no longer the case. From that time on, only one-third of those selected for the GGS worked initially in the Secondary Bureau. Its officers did not have the same rapid promotion advantages as members of the main bureau and they tended to remain in the Secondary Bureau instead of rotating, thus reinforcing their role as technical experts. Civilian

54. Rahne, *Mobilmachung*, pp. 52–66.
55. Rahne, *Mobilmachung*, pp. 53–66; Michael Howard, *The German-French War* (New York, 1969), pp. 21–22.
56. Rahne, *Mobilmachung*, pp. 52–66; Kessel, *Moltke*, pp. 501–7.

specialists rather than military officers began to dominate the map-making process.[57]

In 1865 Verdy du Vernois, chief of the Military History Section, suggested the GGS publish a complete history of the Prussian wars. *The Campaign of 1866 in Germany* was the first volume in this series. Issued in an initial print run of 13,000 copies, each volume was 720 pages. The forty-one appendixes include the order of battle for the main army corps, special orders for armies, and casualties lists – killed, wounded, and missing in action given by brigade for Austria and by regiment for Prussia. The volumes ended with four pages of corrections, additions, and printing errors. This is tactical or regimental history writ large. Researched mainly with Prussian sources and completed in about eight months, it succeeded in its aim to present the Prussian army in a favorable light. In commenting on it, Moltke said that in publishing a work for the general public the GGS could give the truth but not the whole truth.[58]

As for the War Academy, Moltke recruited a dozen outstanding officers from each graduating class of forty. They were put on probation, working under Moltke's supervision. Those who did not measure up were returned to regimental duty. After assignment to the GGS, they returned to duty with the TGS at each step in promotion – an intermingling of staff and line which kept the staff aware of life with the troops and disseminated Moltke's ideas and standards throughout the army. By 1870, alongside each corps and army commander was a chief of staff who had trained in this system.[59]

In war games, GGS rides, and outdoor maneuvers, there was heightened interest in the western campaign area. Intelligence gathering, an essential aspect of war planning, became more systematized and focused. Alfred Graf Schlieffen was assigned to Paris in November 1866 to assist the Prussian military attaché, Freiherr von Löe, in these efforts. Assignments included specific detailed intelligence aimed at figuring out the French war plan. For example, they were sent to Lyon to observe the transportation of

57. Jähns, *Moltke*, p. 440; Eberhard Kessel, "Die Tätigkeit des Grafen Waldersee als Generalquartiermeister und Chef des Generalstabs der Armee," *Welt als Geschichte* 14 (1954): 208.
58. Kriegsgeschichtliche Abteilung des Großen Generalstabs, *Der Feldzug von 1866 in Deutschland* (Berlin, 1867); Kessel, *Moltke*, p. 505.
59. Howard, *German-French War*, p. 25.

munitions and other military supplies from there to Metz. Another assignment was to reconnoiter the artillery garrisons in the north and to discover the locations of the extra horses positioned along the route of march, to reveal artillery mobilization assignments. A third mission was to find out how French troops stationed in Algeria were linked into war mobilization. Löe wrote that all of this information was collected without any difficulty.[60]

In November 1867 the first detailed mobilization instructions for the corps commands were issued. These provided for uniformity and phase-timed call-up. Reservists were apportioned equally to each army corps. The corps order of battle formations detailed the reserve and Landwehr formations and supply plan for regiments and larger units. By 1870 each Prussian corps was served by a train battalion of 40 officers, 84 doctors, 1,540 men, 3,074 horses, and 670 wagons. These battalions followed the combat troops in three ranks. First came the spare horses, pack horses, medicine cart, and mobile canteen; next the divisional wagons with infantry ammunition, field forces, remaining canteen wagons, troop provision columns, and one field hospital per division. Finally came the heavy baggage, ammunition columns, officers' baggage, field bakery, field hospitals, second echelon ammunition columns, pontoon column, and remount depot. Behind the front the Prussian supply system apparently did not work very well in either 1866 or 1870. It consisted of three tiers. Behind the corps, as described above, was the zone of communications in which heavy transport companies carried materials between the combat tier and the third tier, the railheads. Close coordination was necessary between the combat armies, the RRS of the GGS, and the rear area.[61]

The civil bureaucracy was made responsible for supporting war mobilization. Provincial governments in Prussia were obliged to provide officials for the commissariat and pay office. The Prussian post office operated the field post system, the Commerce Ministry the railroads, the telegraph office the field telegraph system. The Justice Ministry added lawyers and jurists to run the military justice system, the Ministry for Spiritual Matters provided chaplains. District animal doctors became army veterinarians, public health officers became medical and pharmaceutical officers.[62]

60. Freiherr von Löe, *Erinnerungen aus meinem Berufsleben* (Stuttgart, 1906), pp. 130–34.

61. Rahne, *Mobilmachung*, p. 57; Creveld, *Supplying War*, p. 97.

62. Rahne, *Mobilmachung*, pp. 56–58.

Moltke codified mobilization instructions for those thirteen officers with whom he had direct contact, the corps chiefs of staff. A military transportation plan provided the framework for this codification. For the first time the entire mobilization plan, including times and sequences, was laid out. This time military travel took complete precedence over civilian travel: civilian traffic was suspended during mobilization. Permanent LCs existed, three in peacetime, and thirteen in wartime. Each was a joint civil-military undertaking. The main instrument used to achieve uniformity and enhanced speed was the MTP. Hermann von Wartensleben-Carow, chief of the RRS, stated, "Each new railroad line which is opened gives us a chance to speed up the strategic mobilization of the army at the rate of one army corps per week." A travel plan was prepared for each train which traveled beyond the boundaries of a single corps region. The corps GS then coordinated this schedule with regional railroad officials, and this plan was fitted into the overall railroad system. At this time Germany had fifteen state-owned railroads, thirty-three privately owned railroads, and five semi-state-owned railroads. A considerable amount of coordination was needed between these diverse bodies.[63]

The result was a carefully timed and much shortened mobilization. In a November 1867 war game, the MTP took thirty-two mobilization days to position the army to begin its march into the west front of the campaign area. A year later this had been reduced to twenty-four days and by January 1870 to twenty days. The MTP had been speeded up by 60%, which had a correspondingly dramatic effect on the mobilization as a whole. Moltke's strategy was time measured. There was an overall structure provided by the timetables which, if it worked, put the army corps onto the battlefield so that they arrived at roughly the same time. The concept of "war alert" related for the first time to exact numerical designation of troop strength. For the west front, the MTP moved four armies with two or three corps each over six railroad lines, with eighteen trains daily in each direction over double track lines and twelve trains daily in each direction over single track lines. It ran from July 15th for twenty days

63. Kessel, *Moltke*, pp. 537–41; Jahns, *Moltke*, pp. 446–47; Rahne, *Mobilmachung*, pp. 53–63; Wolfgang Petter, "Die Logistik des deutschen Heeres im deutsch-französischen Krieg von 1870–71," in Militärgeschichtliches Forschungsamt, ed., *Die Bedeutung der Logistik für die militärische Führung von der Antike bis in die Neuzeit* (Bonn, 1986), pp. 109–33.

and carried 1,520 trains, an immense flow of traffic for its day.[64]

Moltke continued to use those officers he knew, on the basis of their knowledge and trustworthiness, regardless of where they were on the organizational chart. After 1866, when the GGS assumed responsibility for preparing the war plan itself, trusted officers carried out the essential tasks, bringing him the results of their various specialized labors which he then integrated into the mobilization plan. In July 1870, when the GGS had full power of command, Moltke took only fifteen officers with him into the field against France. He created the "sufficient staff" necessary to do the job, irrespective of the formal structure existing in Berlin. Besides himself and two adjutants, there were three influential section chiefs – Paul Bronsart von Schellendorff (operations), Julius von Verdy du Vernois (intelligence) and Freiherr von Brandenstein (railroad) – and ten other officers.[65]

The 1870 situation was a very complex one. In terms of railroads, the German states had public, private, and jointly owned lines. Even the political and economic relationships within the North German Confederation were such that it was difficult to use the existing "through lines." In contrast, France had in place a large-capacity, unitary railroad system under a single bureaucratic agency of the central government.[66] Learning from the experience of 1866, Moltke had placed Colonel von Brandenstein in sole charge of railway matters. Rail concentration began according to schedule on the eighth mobilization day. By 3 August, the nineteenth day of mobilization, the main force was assembled and march ready. Due to technical railroad incapacity, three army corps could be not included in the initial two and one-half week MTP. These corps, from East Prussia, Pomerania, and Silesia, were

64. Rahne, *Mobilmachung*, pp. 51–63.

65. Walter Görlitz, *Die Junker: Adel und Bauern im deutschen Osten*, 4th ed. (Limburg, 1981), p. 267.

66. Hermann von Staabs, *Aufmarsch nach zwei Fronten auf Grund der Operationspläne von 1871–1914* (Berlin, 1925), pp. 1–3. There is a clear picture of the more than three thousand miles of French railroad track destroyed during the German invasion, then rebuilt and brought back into service in Hermann Budde, *Die französischen Eisenbahnen im deutschen Kriegsbetriebe 1870–71* (Berlin, 1904). Budde was the former head of the RRS Section of the GGS as well as Prussian minister of public works and director of the Prussian railroads. Photographs, sketches, and detailed drawings make clear the engineering skills that were needed to reconstruct over 120 bridges, tunnels, and viaducts. Also provided are details of timetables drawn up and examples of train schedules and traffic breakdown on the French railroads operated by the German military authorities during the Franco-Prussian War.

moved into position beginning 26 July as a second line behind the 2d and 3d Armies. One infantry division and two Landwehr divisions were moved by railroad to coastal defense locations.

When the concentration was completed on the twenty-seventh mobilization day, it was seen by some as an extraordinary piece of good luck that it all fell into place. Measured against the French mobilization it looked impressive. On 4 August, when the German concentration was nearly finished, the French had not yet completed mobilization. The result was that the French professional army was outnumbered three to two in the early phases and three to one later on. On the basis of the French railway network, Moltke had calculated that, in order to mobilize rapidly, the French would have to concentrate in two areas divided by the Vosges Mountains. Knowledge of the peacetime railroad system allowed a clear indication of France's war plans.[67]

As its most recent commentator has written, the Moltke system, not fully complete until 1873, ushered in the modern era of staff work and organization. Within that context, the GGS performed both collective and decentralized functions. In its central role it developed strategic plans and operational methods. Its decentralized functions were handled by the staff officers who were trained in the War Academy and in the GGS and were assigned as chiefs of staff and in other staff roles at army, corps, and division levels. As Theodore Ropp wrote, the Prussian system institutionalized combat efficiency by ensuring that in a given situation different staff officers, educated to a common fighting doctrine, would arrive at approximately the same solution to employ the available forces most effectively. In addition to personnel, this system depended on conformity to a common fighting doctrine and common operational procedures.[68]

---

67. Although these were technically known as Line Commissions in peacetime and only became Line Commands in war, I will use the latter term throughout this work. Howard, *German-French War*, pp. 61–62; Rahne, *Mobilmachung*, pp. 59–66; Staabs, *Aufmarsch*, pp. 1–5. Although it may be argued that the war itself should be treated in more detail because the experience of that war, particularly after the Battle of Sedan, was important to future Prussian strategic thinking, I am not pursuing that question here because I am concerned with planning processes and mobilization. Those interested may consult Stig Förster, "Optionen der Kriegführung im Zeitalter des 'Volkskrieges' – Zu Helmuth von Moltkes militärisch-politischen Überlegungen nach den Erfahrungen der Einigungskriege," in Detlef Bald, ed., *Militärische Verantwortung in Staat und Gesellschaft: 175 Jahre Generalstabsausbildung in Deutschland* (Koblenz, 1986), pp. 83–107.

68. Gunther Rothenburg "Moltke and Schlieffen" in Peter Paret, ed., *Makers of*

J.F.C. Fuller criticized this system by saying that Moltke brought his armies to the starting point and then abdicated his command and unleashed them. In a sense this was true. Moltke deployed his forces strategically, but left the tactical actions to the commanders in the field. Moltke knew that (1) many of them were crusty old men who would do what they wanted anyway, but that (2) each was guided by a chief of staff trained in the Moltke system and (3) that many division commanders and lower-level officers were also schooled in uniform GGS doctrine. Having concentrated superior forces and educated the staff officers in uniform doctrine, perhaps Moltke could afford to let events take their course. The Prussians had a two to one superiority in 1866. In 1870 German forces had approximately a three to one numerical advantage.[69] Viewed cumulatively, the changes in Prussian war mobilization during the seven years from 1864 to 1871 were gigantic: in terms of size, an increase on the order of 1,500%; in terms of space, an increase of about 1,000%; in terms of time, a reduction of about 400%. It is no wonder that much went wrong and the German armies had difficulty digesting the changes. But it is also true that such exponential changes came about only with mechanization, the application of railroads, the engine of the nineteenth-century industrial revolution, to war.

What of grand strategy and the overall purpose these increasingly elaborate preparations had for war in the context of Prussia's political interest? Although it is possible to say, as Gordon Craig does, that in the heat of the moment Moltke and his colleagues were "driven by ideological passions" and that they wanted wars of annihilation against both Austria and France, there is another possibility. Although Gunther Rothenberg does not accept Gerhard Ritter's description of Moltke as a "humanist of the post-Goethe era," he does argue that Moltke was essentially a soldier and what mattered to him was the controlled application of force in the service of the Prussian monarchy. Moltke was a "grammarian of war" who did not engage in abstract speculation like Clausewitz but, like most soldiers of his generation, accepted war as inevitable and looked for ways to conduct it successfully. He was not a theorist, but a pragmatist. Hans Delbrück made a similar point.

*Modern Strategy from Machiavelli to the Nuclear Age* (Princeton, 1986), p. 301; cf. Theodore Ropp, *War in the Modern World* (New York, 1961), pp. 153–57.

69. J.F.C. Fuller, *A Military History of the Western World*, 3 vols. (New York, 1954), 3: 134.

Delbrück wrote that Moltke differed from other great strategists like Alexander, Caesar, Gustavus Adophus, Cromwell, and Frederick the Great in that he was only a soldier, whereas they were also political leaders. Even Scharnhorst and Gneisenau, often compared to Moltke, not only fought in the Wars of Liberation but were also carriers of the spirit of liberation. Delbrück believed this was not simply an exterior accumulation of different circumstances, but a deep inner difference. Moltke was exclusively a strategist: he was neither politician nor troop leader. But the art of war which Napoleon practiced as a naive genius, Moltke practiced systematically. Moltke's theoretical understanding conformed so closely with practical knowledge that his actual war decisions could be relied upon absolutely. Moltke was quoted as having said that mistakes made during the initial concentration of armies could scarcely ever be rectified during the course of a war. However, he relied not only on the large "cosmic" factors such as size, space, and time, but also on the bravery and determination of Prussia's combat soldiers. Seldom in modern history, Delbrück concluded, have theoretical plans been fulfilled by such influential and long-lasting practical success.[70] Although Moltke may look like the philosopher king or evil genius to some, perhaps he was closer to the modern dentist who just fills the tooth, without paying much attention to the state of health of the whole body.

Aided by defeats from 1806 to 1807 and victories from 1864 to 1871, the genesis and early development of modern Prussian war planning processes took place within its institutional frameworks and experiences. In the half century between these events, development slowed and stopped. Initially the representational component flourished because it was important to normal peacetime economic development. The educational and organizational aspects of war planning saw periods of heightened interest, followed by disregard. The analytical component, tied closely to the war plan, remained important in times when the war plan seemed

---

70. Gordon Craig, *Germany, 1866–1945* (New York, 1978), p. 32; Rothenburg, "Moltke and Schlieffen," pp. 297–306; Hans Delbrück, "Moltke," in *Erinnerungen, Aufsätze und Reden* (Berlin, 1902), pp. 546–75; the most recent and balanced account of this period, especially of civil-military relations, is Lothar Gall, *Bismarck, the White Revolutionary,* trans. J.A. Underwood, 2 vols. (London, 1986). In Gall's view, military interference in both 1866 and 1870–71 is seen as less significant. Bismarck, the political leader, was in control and the military is portrayed as an instrument of state policy, not as a force of equal power in a situation which was out of balance.

important. The GGS itself evolved from a few dozen officers grouped patrimonially around the person of the chief to more than one hundred officers organized into a somewhat rational bureaucracy.

The GGS organization grew in size and reputation as a result of its instrumental, functional role in the creation of a new European nation-state. Three components contributed to the growth of the GGS. Representationally it was provided with a clear, precise image of physical reality. Methods to create and revise this image were widely known in the GGS and they informed the planning processes. In the hands of their most gifted practitioneer, Moltke, these methods were both artistic and mathematical. Educationally, the GGS participated in the beginnings of a modern comprehensive military education system. Yet there was tension over whether this system should aim at humanistic and general or at technical and professional education. The split was evident in curricular changes but above all in the practice of history. Military history became more and more important; it was considered the paramount method of learning war in peace. Analytically, the war game, staff ride, and maneuver were the integrating mechanisms. They were at the same time theoretical and practical in specific details, historical and contemporary in framework, rational and speculative in final outcomes. Above all they were exercises in understanding what future problems were likely to occur. Finally, it was the growth of knowledge, specific detailed technical and scientific knowledge, that is evident in each one of these aspects. Prussia was a culture which had honored the life of the mind and unsurprisingly valued knowledge and education in its military system as well.

If feudal, reactionary elements could continue to dominate certain aspects of European armies until well into the 1920s – one thinks of the English chief of the imperial general staff, who in 1927 (!) was "prepared to recommend" the abolition of the lance for cavalry units – this was not true of railroad technology.[71] We have argued that railroads may well have played a more decisive role during the wars of 1864–71 than historians have hitherto conceded. Railroads were the only functioning part of the war plan that could deliver continuous, reliable, and predictable levels of performance. They were the basis for Moltke's revolutionary

71. Harold Winton, *To Change an Army: General Sir John Barnett-Stuart and British Armored Doctrine, 1927–1938* (Kansas City, 1988), p. 84.

strategy of using concentric exterior lines to achieve concentration. Finally, they were the only means to utilize effectively the masses of manpower which became available in the second half of the nineteenth century. Even Bismarck recognized the importance of railroads. During peace negotiations with the governments of Baden, Württemberg, and Bavaria in 1866, he had insisted on inserting into the treaties a clause providing that, in time of war, their railway systems would pass to Prussian control. In fact, the only land that Bavaria lost after 1866 was a small strip that Prussia desired for a railway connection. In the 1871 Treaty of Frankfurt, Prussia acquired over eight hundred kilometers of track from the French Eastern Railroad Company in Alsace-Lorraine. A considerable part of the huge French war indemnity was put into railroad securities. One economist wrote that by way of the indemnity, France finished off the main German railway network.[72]

Military history showed the opposite tendency. Academic history, a dominant nineteenth-century intellectual discipline, was idealistic and national, and so was general staff history. But the study of history in the general staff was even narrower and more limited than in the university. Not only was it limited to "battles and leaders," who were described in the technical language of drill regulations, but it was limited because, as Moltke said, the military could tell the truth but not the whole truth. There were certain values and ideals which had to be upheld and these did not always correspond with reality, historical or otherwise.

72. Craig, *Germany*, p. 6; Clapham, *Economic Development of France and Germany*, p. 346.

# Chapter 2

# Moltke, Waldersee,
# and the General Staff, 1871–1891

After 1871 no one asked any longer who General von Moltke was. Instead, it was said there were five perfect institutions in Europe: the Roman curia, the British Parliament, the Russian ballet, the French opera, and the Prussian general staff. In retrospect, such cultural mythology is astonishing, but it does suggest that the practical accomplishment of creating a new nation in three quick and brutal wars not only validated the institution thought largely responsible, but also raised it to the level of a cultural icon.

Some believed the Prussian system to be a whole new technique of war suddenly thrust upon the world fully formed. From the inside, however, things looked different. The period from 1871 to 1891 saw the GGS evolve from a Prussian to a Reich bureaucracy which digested the changes made in the late 1860s and added to it the lessons learned in 1870–71. During the years 1872 to 1875, Moltke used its newly won prestige to complete the reorganization begun during the war years. By 1877 this had been accomplished and the GGS assumed the full bureaucratic form which it would retain through the late 1880s.

In spite of potentially dangerous revisionist powers east and west, the task environment remained balanced and the decade closed with a remarkable and novel military alliance. As Gordon Craig points out, the Dual Alliance of 1879 between Germany and Austria was a landmark in European history. It called for assistance if either signatory were attacked by Russia but benevolent neutrality if either were attacked by another power. While previous treaties had been concluded during or on the eve of wars or for specific purposes and restricted durations, this one was made during peacetime and turned out to be permanent. Furthermore, it was the first of the secret treaties whose contents were always suspected but never fully known. For the GGS, 1879 fundamentally reshaped the east front. For the first time in a century, Austria was downgraded as a major battlefield opponent in Prussian war plans.[1]

With increasing age, Moltke's concerns narrowed. The *Kaiser-manöver* in the late 1870s, for example, were conducted from carriages, not horseback, with little preparation beforehand and little reflection afterward. The elderly staff officers considered them more of a Sunday outing than a serious military exercise. More effort seemed to be expended on military spit and polish. In September 1873, at the ceremony dedicating the 1871 victory monument, the Siegessäule in Berlin, the 17,596 men, 4,592 horses, 72 guns, and 24 carriages of the guard corps, standing by in eleven streets leading to the square, formed up in full parade formation in thirteen minutes.[2] Victorian Europe had entered the age of splendid superficiality.

Second-generation leadership of the German Reich began tentatively with GGS Deputy Chief Alfred Graf Waldersee in 1881 and received major impetus with Kaiser Wilhelm II in 1888, followed by Chancellor Leo Graf Caprivi in 1890 and GGS Chief Alfred Graf Schlieffen in 1891. The generation of the *Gründerjahre* – Wilhelm I was in his nineties, Moltke in his eighties, Bismarck in his seventies – was passing away. Historiographically and in every other way Waldersee has been overshadowed by his predecessor and his successor. In fact, during Waldersee's tenure a good deal changed. In 1883 there was a fundamental organizational realignment, in 1889 the largest army bill in Reich history up to 1913 was introduced, and in 1890 the task environment began a dramatic alteration. But it was mainly prologue. The vague shadowy outline of the pre-1914 world did not appear. Lacking the impetus of Moltke's wars or Schlieffen's dangerous task environment, the GGS did not evolve dramatically.

## Force Structure

Organizationally the German war system underwent many changes from 1871 to 1891. In the first decade these changes occurred outside the GGS in the army as a whole, while within the GGS changes were consolidated. During the second decade the position,

1. Craig, *Germany*, p. 114; Holborn, *Modern Germany*, 2: 240–41; Ritter, *Sword and Scepter*, 1: 229–35; Kessel, *Moltke*, p. 705; cf. Ferdinand von Schmerfeld, *Die deutschen Aufmarschpläne, 1871–1890* (Berlin, 1929), passim.

2. Hans Mohs, *Generalfeldmarschall Alfred Graf von Waldersee in seinem militärischen Wirken*, 2 vols. (Berlin, 1929), 2: 110; Schellendorff, *Duties*, p. 149.

power, and influence of the GGS within the Prussian government was elevated, and it began to expand in response to increased army size and technical mobilization demands.

The army law of 1867 of the North German Confederation provided for a standing army equal to 1% of the population and an annual allocation of 225 thalers per man. In 1871 this law was extended for three years under the constitution of the German Reich, and when it ran out in 1874 the so-called *Septennat* system began in which army appropriations were granted in seven-year blocks. For the next decade and more, army funding and hence size did not increase noticeably.[3]

An important new concern in late nineteenth-century European armies was that of force structure. It resulted from the creation of several different kinds of civil-military relationships. There had always been active soldiers, the standing army, and reserves, men called to active duty in war for reinforcement and to man fortresses, defend cities, and carry out various tasks at home while the active army was abroad. The idea of a militia had been tried and had failed in the ancient regime. With the wars of the American and French Revolutions and the establishment of a new relationship between the state and its citizenry, a different kind of armed force had come into being. In Prussia, it took the form known as *Landwehr* and *Landsturm*. The Landwehr, "army of the land" first formed in East Prussia, was originally officered by well-to-do citizen volunteers and soldiered by freed peasants. It was used as a backup reserve force. The Landsturm, "protector of the land" officered by feudal estate holders and soldiered by their peasants, remained at home as a defense force. After 1815 both forces were regularized: they formed a backup to the active army.[4]

With growing populations, these reserves grew larger, and this altered the force structure of the army. By 1870 reserves outnumbered actives by three to two. The result was a ratio of active army to reserves, on the one hand, and different levels of reserves, on the other hand. Force structure had to be considered because it was complicated and changing. Second, in terms of effective combat operations, there were substantial differences between various kinds of force. For example, active troops were considered

3. Hans-Ulrich Wehler, *The German Empire, 1871–1918* (Leamington Spa, 1985), p. 146; Michael Geyer, *Deutsche Rüstungspolitik, 1860–1980* (Frankfurt, 1984), p. 51.

4. Alfred Vagts, *A History of Militarism* (Greenwich, 1959), pp. 139–41.

better trained, with greater marching capacity and combat toughness. A larger active army meant that less time was required to mobilize, whereas a larger reserve army increased mobilization time. Reserves were of questionable reliability, especially in dangerous and uncertain situations. Yet summer exercises regularly trained hundreds of thousands of them. The question of how reserves were integrated with active troops in a war mobilization was of prime concern. From the 1870s on, the issue of force structure was always tied to the question of quantity versus quality. Moltke and the army leadership came down decisively on the side of maintaining and increasing quality.

The force structure of the German army by 1875 was the result of a requirement for three years in the standing army, four years in the reserve, and five years in the Landwehr. Beyond that, men between the ages of seventeen and forty-two who were not a part of the army or navy were required to serve in the Landsturm. Thus there were four different kinds of troops: active, reserve, Landwehr, and Landsturm. Depending upon age, men between seventeen and forty-two served in one or the other of these forces. During the 1870s, DCs, the lowest-level coordinating body, were empowered to call up the reserves in their regions once a year and these call-ups were loosely integrated into the mobilization plans. New recruits were called up on 1 November, trained for six months, and joined the regular army on 1 April. Reserve forces were mustered out of the regular army on 1 November. It is no coincidence that a new war plan went into effect each year on 1 April and that war plan revision began in earnest in November.[5]

The system described is that of a defense manning cycle. At various points in the cycle there was high readiness or low readiness, rapid or slow mobilization, an army mainly of actives or of reserves. Only between 1 April and 30 October was the Reich army at maximum peacetime strength. During the winter half year, recruits were in training but not trained, and reserves had to be called up and were not already under muster. Feed and fodder for the huge horse contingent was less available in the winter countryside after harvest time. Thus the supply problem was different depending upon the season. Add to these factors the maneuver schedule: with dates beginning in early and mid-July for small units, progressing to larger units, and finishing with army corps and imperial war games

5. Rahne, *Mobilmachung*, pp. 73–76.

in August and early September. European war planners knew that war was more likely during the window of maximum force and supply and minimum mobilization friction, 1 April through 1 November. Considering the necessity of providing for horses by requisitioning from available field crops – it was physically impossible to carry fodder for many hundred thousand horses – and the window of war expectation in reality narrows even further. For the late nineteenth-century German armies, force structure began to be complicated by large numbers. Peacetime active army size was set in 1874 at 401,659 men. By 1880 this had risen to 427,274. However, the total force, including Landwehr and Landsturm, was much larger. One estimate of this for 1875 is 1,445,318 men, 329,164 horses, and 2,532 guns.[6]

To meld active and reserve forces into a war-mobilized army, three methods were used by nineteenth-century armies. One was to maintain active and reserve units separately and simply bring the reserves into active duty alongside, but quite separated from, the standing army. The French mobilized in this way. A second method was to add equal numbers of reserves to units of the active army. Russia mobilized in this way. A third method was to decrease the number of troop units in the active army but use it as an umbrella or accordian organization to which individual men and officers from reserve units were fitted for summer training exercises and in time of war. Structurally the standing army opened like the skeleton frame of an umbrella and the spaces created were filled. The first two methods had the advantage of more rapid war mobilization, with the disadvantage that the reserves were at a much lower state of training and work capacity.[7] The third variant, chosen by Prussia, enabled a high level of mobilization readiness but only because it was based upon a high quality of training throughout the army. In the 1870s the organization of the Reich army was as follows. Overall there were four high commands, called General Inspections, into which were placed the Reich corps: 1st–11th (Prussian), 12th (Saxon), 13th (Württemberg), 14th (Baden), and two Bavarian corps. The corps was the important unit below the GGS. Although its commander was appointed directly by the Kaiser and therefore the Military Cabinet played a role, it was the chief of

6. Craig, *Politics*, pp. 220, 226; Rahne, *Mobilmachung*, pp. 78–79; Ottmar Freiherr von Osten-Sacken, *Preußens Heer*, 3 vols. (Berlin, 1914), 3: 307.
7. Rahne, *Mobilmachung*, pp. 79–81. Rahne is the only historian to include all force levels and his figures must be used with caution.

staff of the corps and his staff that carried on day-to-day operations. The dynamic between these levels and kinds of forces changed depending, on the one hand, upon who was corps commander and what his relationship to the Kaiser and Military Cabinet was and, on the other, who was chief of staff and what his relationship to the GGS in Berlin was. Personal relationships counted a good deal, but so did plans and procedures.

Within the Reich army an important relationship was that between the Prussian army and the various state contingents, such as those of Saxony, Württemberg, Baden, and Bavaria. The integrator for these diverse units was the war plan. At war mobilization the armies and the railroad systems of these states were subordinated to Prussia, in effect to the GGS mobilization section and RRS. Beyond that there were subtle differences in the relationship. Without going into detail consider, for example, the 13th or Württemberg corps. After 1871 the Württemberg king continued to receive the oath of allegiance and to commission, promote, and transfer officers. Regiments kept their distinctive battle flags and standards. Uniform design was decided by the king as long as the cost of Württemberg's uniforms was no more than the cost of the uniforms worn by other Reich contingents. Units of the Württemberg corps were stationed within the kingdom during peacetime, and other federal troops were not stationed in Württemberg without the monarch's consent.

In 1873, the Württemberg army was expanded to form a self-contained corps in conformance with Prussian organizational norms. All of the units comprising the corps were renumbered according to the federal army's continuous numbering system. The king of Prussia became the supreme commander of the field army, with the right to inspect all Reich contingents. The Württembergian soldier's oath included a pledge to render the Kaiser service. Corps commanders were named by the Württemberg king but with prior consent of the Kaiser. In the event of war the telegraph network and railroad system of Württemberg came under control of the Reich supreme command, which meant the GGS.[8] In 1873 the Reichstag passed legislation extending to the

8. R.T. Walker, Jr, "Prusso-Württembergian Military Relations in the German Empire, 1870–1918" (Ph.D. diss., Ohio State University, 1974), pp. 33–36; the question of Prussia's relationship to the federal Reich and the problems of national versus federal political relations are discussed in Hans Goldschmidt, *Das Reich und Preußen im Kampf um die Führung* (Berlin, 1931). Curiously there does not seem to be much on their military relationships.

Reich certain military provisions long customary in Prussia and important for war planning. With the declaration of war, all counties and cities were responsible for providing quarters, supplies, and transportation to the army. Farms were required to sell their horses for the lowest average price. Each of these provisions – quarters, supplies, transportation, and horses – was a major component of mobilization.[9]

In conclusion, force structure for this period shows many changes. One was the creation of a peacetime Reich army which melded together the armies of Prussia and the other states. Another was the large increase in reserve forces, complicating force structure. A third was the extension of Prussian war support provisions to the cities and counties of the Reich. In each case, federal armies, civilian agencies, and populations were subordinated to the military traditions and system of Prussia.

## The GGS Becomes Independent

To keep up with the general army expansion and consolidation, the period from 1872–1875 marked the beginning of expanded GGS bureaucratization. In July 1872 came a whole new set of army regulations in nine series, dealing with railroads, supply systems, field intendants, sanitation, military telegraphy, and field post. Moltke wrote a series of memorandums on future wars, improving readiness, the organization of the GGS, and weapons in which he outlined the fundamental program for defense of the country. Even though the chief of the GGS saw himself as the trusted personal servant of the king, by 1872 the GGS began to resemble in various ways other Prussian governmental departments. An expanded chief's office, including a chancellery and plan room, became the office manager for the entire GGS organization: it kept the paper flow, set schedules for work, monitored task completion, and logged documents in and out. The Military History Section, with its archive and library, the geographical-statistical section (Secondary Bureau for Scientific Affairs) with its map library, and the RRS all expanded.[10]

9. Rahne, *Mobilmachung*, p. 75.
10. Boehn, *Generalstabsgeschäfte*, pp. 43–46; Schellendorff, *Duties*, pp. 36–38. Osten-Sacken, *Preußens Heer*, 3: 318; Kessel, *Moltke*, p. 502; Kessel, "Die Tätigkeit des Grafen Waldersee," p. 187.

Moltke followed no organizational charts. As the bureaucratic expansion took place, he concentrated on two aspects of general staff work – war plans and military history – and organized his closest colleagues to accomplish them. According to Eberhard Kessel, he worked closely with only two men, Colonel Alfred Kessler, the chief of the Railroad and Mobilization Sections and the two chiefs of military history, first Julius von Verdy du Vernois, then Graf Herman von Wartensleben-Carew. The rest of the work he left to the section heads and to his adjutant. Moltke chose his close associates on the basis of their knowledge and personality and shaped the GGS functionally around them. For example, he had united the tasks of mobilization and the RRS because of Kessler's competence. When Kessler retired, Colonel Franz Oberhoffer, a "pure technician" and land survey officer from the Baden general staff, became head of the RRS. Moltke did not like him, did not get on with him, and therefore shifted war planning to the First Section under Vogel von Falckenstein, thus temporarily separating war planning and the RRS. Moltke maintained the most important tasks in units headed by those he knew and trusted.[11]

By the 1880s the general staff to which Waldersee and Schlieffen were assigned was very different from that to which Moltke had been posted in the 1830s. Instead of obscurity, it was one of the most famous elite institutions in Europe. In place of the few dozen officers, there were several hundred. When Waldersee joined the GGS in 1881, a new position was created for him, that of deputy chief to Moltke. This was a potentially difficult role, turned down by others who questioned whether they would be able to carry out such a subordinate yet independent role. Waldersee got along well with Moltke and had few difficulties with the novel arrangement. Undoubtedly this was aided by the fact that Moltke was out of town a great deal. In fact, he spent only a few months of the year in Berlin. Because it was widely believed that he had virtually been named as Moltke's successor, Waldersee had a great deal of authority as well as influence. Coincident with Waldersee's appointment, GGS section chiefs were upgraded to the same rank as brigade commanders and corps chiefs of staff. This made GGS service more attractive and indicates an expansion and upgrading of the entire organization.[12]

11. Kessel, *Moltke*, pp. 612, 688.
12. Kessel, "Die Tätigkeit des Grafen Waldersee," p. 182; Kessel, *Moltke*, p. 692; Mohs, *Waldersee*, 2: 21–27; Schellendorff, *Duties*, p. 38; Hugo Zeitz, "Der

In 1883, a year after Waldersee's appointment, a momentous structural change occurred: the GGS became an independent office of the Prussian government, roughly equal to the War Ministry, Foreign Ministry, Treasury, and so forth. How this came about is still not clear. As a result of a sudden, unexpected attack on army expenditures in the Reichstag, spearheaded by Eugen Richter, and the weak response of the war minister, Bismarck was forced to ally himself with the military establishment, particularly General Emil von Albedyll, chief of the emperor's Military Cabinet. One interpretation is that independent status was Waldersee's idea, and War Minister Paul Bronsart von Schellendorff was willing to accept it because of his personal relationship to Moltke. In this view Schellendorff's appointment was made contingent on a significant downgrading of the War Ministry. Waldersee was also close to Albedyll, who wanted to disencumber himself from the influence of the War Ministry and increase his own power. The Military Cabinet, instead of the War Ministry, henceforth administered officer personnel matters. The downgrading of the War Ministry worked to all their advantages.[13] The War Ministry and the GGS had jockeyed for position within the Prussian state for half a century. The GGS, because of its war planning capability, had emerged as superior in 1871, and it became increasingly stronger as war planning became more complex. The War Ministry now receded. The Military Cabinet also gained strength, but only in the limited area of appointments. Within a few years this change had been fully solidified. As War Minister Verdy du Vernois put it in 1890, "The new War Minister must make his debut in office as a kind of suicide."[14]

This structural change had many ramifications. One was that the GGS chief or deputy was now included in the schedule of the royal entourage. The GGS had direct access to the king, by means of the *Immediatvorträge*, the personal reports of the chief to the sovereign. Another was that the GGS had more control over its own organizational destiny. The way was now open for Waldersee to push forward his own program. This consisted mainly of ways to

---

Schirmer des geeinten Reiches" in Generalleutnant a.D. von Cochenhausen, ed., *Von Scharnhorst zu Schlieffen: 1806–1906: Hundert Jahre preußisch-deutscher Generalstab* (Berlin, 1933), p. 223.

13. Kessel, *Moltke*, pp. 702–3; Görlitz, *German General Staff*, pp. 191, 108; Craig, *Politics*, pp. 227–32; Ritter, *Sword and Scepter*, 1: 120–21.

14. Craig, *Politics*, p. 231.

enhance, speed up, and broaden the process of war mobilization. Waldersee wanted more cooperation at top Reich levels to coordinate troops, railroad facilities, and fortresses in border areas. He desired the creation of a distinct "war preparation period" prior to the declaration of mobilization. He opened direct communication with military attachés abroad to increase the quantity and quality of information on foreign armies and also to enhance his own political position within the Prussian hierarchy. In addition, he tried to use the attaché system to influence policy. The response to Waldersee's bureaucratic impetuosity often led to more friction rather than results, and many of these changes did not come about.[15] In addition to organizational and procedural changes, there were size increases. The army grew 39% from a peacetime strength of 401,659 in 1874 to 557,093. By 1891, the army's need for new officers had far outstripped the nobility's capacity to supply them.[16]

During the 1880s, the mobilization year time schedule begun in the 1870s was consolidated. It opened on 1 April with the introduction of the new war plan and the completion of training for recruits who then began their period of active duty. This marked the beginning of the highest state of war readiness. During the six summer months, three years' worth of fully trained recruits were under arms, whereas from October to April there were only two years' worth. For example, an infantry battalion at war strength was 1032 men. During the winter its peacetime strength was 378, whereas during the summer it was 567. This difference of almost 200 men or about 18% had important residual impact on all aspects of mobilization: the military transportation plan, supplies, weapons, and horses. By the 1880s, the more than 200 DCs had direct responsibility for over a million reserves and Landwehr. Every January many of these participated in a control assembly, and during the summer approximately 120,000 went out on maneuvers, which also served as a practical exercise in mobilization call-up.[17]

15. Kessel, "Die Tätigkeit des Grafen Waldersee," pp. 194–202; Alfred Vagts, *The Military Attaché* (Princeton, 1967), pp. 21–24; Craig, *Politics*, p. 267; Martin Kitchen, *The German Officer Corps, 1890–1914* (Oxford, 1968), pp. 64ff.; Rothenburg, "Moltke and Schlieffen," p. 313.

16. Görlitz, *German General Staff*, p. 101; Craig, *Politics*, p. 235; Rahne, *Mobilmachung*, pp. 88–92. Professor Ulrich Trumpener maintains that Prussian army dependence on nobles as officers had ended long before the 1890s. He believes that much of the literature on this question is off the mark and that, in reality, nonnoble officers were important both in the army as a whole and in the GGS long before that date. Letters to the author of 22 March and 16 May 1990.

17. Rahne, *Mobilmachung*, pp. 80–85; Osten-Sacken, *Preußens Heer*, 3: 285.

## *Modern Mapmaking*

The second aspect of war planning was representational. In June 1870 a mixed commission of civilian and military officials, the Central Survey Board, had been created to consider all problems of imaging the land in the broadest framework of economic as well as military development. Moltke was its president. One commissioner each came from the Finance Ministry (domanes, forests, and direct tax), Public Works and Commerce (railroads, roads, and waterways), Economics (agricultural improvement, local affairs), the Navy (hydrophy and coastal defense), the Interior, the Geodetic Institute, the War Ministry, and the GGS, especially the Secondary Bureau for Scientific Affairs. As a result of these deliberations, on 1 January 1875 the imaging program of Prussia was combined in a new office, the Royal Prussian Land Survey. Directed by a lieutenant-general who was equivalent in rank to a divisional or corps commander, the three sections – Trigonometric, Topographic, and Cartographic – were headed by major generals equivalent to brigade commanders.[18]

Thus was inaugurated a new era of high-capacity, centralized, bureaucratic mapmaking. Like the railroad LCs, it was a mixed civil-military department, its work was considered scientifically grounded, and it had a very large civilian complement. It was the largest department of the GGS. Although eighteen GGS officers headed the organization as a whole and twenty-three others were assigned to it on a three-year rotating basis, several hundred civilians completed its numerous technical positions. These included trigonometers, topographers, cartographers, printers, photographers, lithographers, and specialists in electroplating. Moltke is credited with endowing the new organization with sufficient funding, more than a million reichsmarks annually, because it was attached to military funding in the budget. Although a Prussian agency in name, its work was national and its funds were Reich as well as Prussian derived.

The Trigonometric Section, with forty-six officers and civilians assigned, was divided into six sections. This included a chancellery and registry which organized and monitored work. Sections were established for main, secondary, and detail triangulation and others for leveling, for printing, and for the archive and library. Each one

---

18. General von Morozowicz, "Die königlich-preußische Landes-Aufnahme," *Militär-Wochenblatt*, Beiheft (1879): 15–16; Scheel, *Entwicklung*, p. 13.

corresponded to a segment of the work done in creating an entirely new set of maps. The main triangulation section created a large, or first order, network with triangles eight miles on a side. Within those the second-level triangulation section built a smaller network of triangles, one and one-half miles on a side, and within that the detail triangulation section planted ten stones per mile to mark the spatial points of distance and elevation. The leveling section then figured the elevation using geometric methods. Triangulation maps noting these points were made available so that each plane table map was based upon twenty-two trigonometric markpoints.[19]

The Topographic Section, with ninety-eight assigned workers, had eight divisions: a registry; a chancellery; a section devoted to planning and monitoring summer work; a section for buying, maintaining, and monitoring instruments and equipment; an archive; a library; a section devoted to reconnaissance; and finally, a very large survey department of five groups. This department's main task was to take the triangulation maps prepared by the Trigonometric Section and produce topographic map sections showing everything of military, political, and economic importance. In contrast to the work done prior to 1875, the work of this period was characterized by significantly enhanced technical quality. Each polyhedron projection sheet covered 10 degrees of latitude and 6 degrees of longitude, showing terrain lines every 5 meters. Teams of officers and topographers went into the countryside between 15 May and the end of October. Each team worked on an area of 2.7 square miles, about the size of one survey section at a scale of 1:25,000. These formed the basis for the lithographed survey sections and grade section maps at 1:100,000. The originals were photographically copied and then photo-lithographed. A separate section carried out continual reconnaisance, correcting and upgrading existing map sections.

The Cartographic Section of almost three hundred was divided into nine groups: a registry and chancellery; an archive and library; a section for terrain grade maps at 1:100,000; a section for state maps at 1:25,000; sections for proofing drawings and for lithographs; a copper etching section; a printing section, and a photogrammetric section.

As the imaging process became technologically more complex

19. Scheel, *Entwicklung*, p. 14; Thiedel, "Zentraldirektorium," pp. 148–59.

and sophisticated, the task cycle lengthened. By 1878 each GGS map set took nine years to produce from the time of trigonometric measurement to the publication of the map itself. Sections were named for the largest town in the segment, and each was numbered to fit into its north and south location for the Reich as a whole. In addition to the creation of new maps, series of older maps were upgraded. For example, in 1874 the GGS purchased the existing Reymann map series at a scale of 1:200,000, and brought it up to date with current topographic knowledge. Stone lithography had begun in 1867, and soon this advanced to color lithography. The printing section published books of formulas, schematas, and tables assembled by the Trigonometric and Topographic Sections as an aid to civil engineering.

Not only did the map quality improve, but the annual work capacity increased. Prior to 1870 the area of the Prussian state took seventy-five years of production work to map. By the late 1880s the whole task cycle was reduced to twenty years, an improvement of over 266%. Every ten years map sheets were newly reconnaissanced and corrected. In addition to new surveys, three times that quantity were inspected, updated, and reprinted. Statements used in Reichstag budget debates to describe the section's work took on the familiar ring of twentieth-century political rhetoric. In 1878, Land Survey Director General von Morozowicz wrote that the work of his section was so technologically complex and so valuable to the state that the section needed double the number of men and supplies and twice as large a budget as it had up until then. For 1876, this amounted to 2,291,634 reichsmarks. His report reads like that of a modern bureaucrat using a sales pitch to convince the Reichstag of the need for additional funding, rather than resembling an audience granted by the sovereign to a subject, the most often quoted traditional model for the Prussian army.[20]

Here is an example of an area of knowledge applied to practical life in which the knowledge became more and more specialized and technical as it came into contact with established areas of science and engineering. By 1891 the representational aspect of war planning had reached a modern level of bureaucratic management and technical accomplishment. It was the largest unit within the GGS system, and it exceeded other sections in funds, civilian

20. Scheel, *Entwicklung*, p. 14; Morozowicz, "Landes-Aufnahme," pp. 16–35.

ties, and geographic extension. It was made up of military and civilian personnel. As with many aspects of war planning, the representational operated in deep-future-oriented task cycles. Five- and ten-year work schedules were routine. Many map series took twenty-five years or longer to complete. The 1:100,000 Reich Map begun in 1878 and completed in 1910, with an integrated scale for Prussia, Saxony, Bavaria, and Württemberg, was the first step toward a unified German cartography.[21] As the Land Survey's tasks were divided and subdivided, so was its organization. Each section became coterminous with specialist knowledge from civil and mechanical engineering, etching, lithography, and photogrammetry. The department became the major supplier of maps to the civilian as well as to the military sector of Prussian-German life. Although funding did pass to it, power did not. This is so because, first of all, it was only tangentially connected to the war plan itself. More important, its product was duplicatable and, once produced, remained basically stable – not much change occurred in terrain over a ten-year period.

21. Morozowicz, "Landes-Aufnahme," pp. 15–29; Scharfe, "Preußische Monarchie," pp. 640–41; Craig, *Politics*, p. 277. A great variety of statistical information was used by Prussian officers. A summary of some of this is provided in the *Festschrift des königlich-preußischen statistischen Bureaus* (Berlin, 1905). It is important to note that the use of mathematical data was by no means limited to the Secondary Bureau of the GGS: in many ways it characterized the Prussian army as a whole. For example, on the basis of this cartographic image of Prussia, plus other demographic and statistical information available from the Royal Prussian Statistical Bureau, three kinds of tables were drawn up for marches, quarters, and rations when the army went into the field. Tables of marches indicated how far and where troops moved, tables of quarters indicated specific villages or towns troops were to stay in and lists of quarters detailing the actual number of men and horses each village and town was to receive, and tables of rations indicated the rations for men and forage for horses and the depots for the sick on a given evening. Each of these tables was cleared with local civilian authorities prior to arrival and each table was based upon detailed army regulations for each rank. For example, a colonel received more food and firewood than a lieutenant, who received more than a private, and so forth. The extent to which the tables, the planning model, depended on specific numerical ratios for every conceivable possibility from the length of a column of march (different for a battalion, battery, squadron, company) to the size of a frontage in bivouac, the length of a given daily march, and the maneuver time of brigades, divisions, and army corps cannot be overemphasized. Each was precisely prescribed and each was a ratio which fit into a structure. In a sense, then, prescribed size, space, and time factors, mathematically laid out beforehand and practiced in war games, dictated everything. As the buttons of an officer's dress coat were to be precisely one and one-eighth inch apart, according to regulations, the same format applied to virtually everything else in the Prussian army. Cf. Schellendorff, *Duties*, pp. 367–412.

## Military Education

The third aspect of war planning was educational. During this period a position in the highly prestigious GGS became a more technical and professional career which began to attract middle-class aspirants. Military education as a whole, especially the War Academy system, was taken under the aegis of the GGS, and there was an intensive effort to raise technical educational standards. Changes came in both the first and second decades of this period.

In November 1872 the War Academy, along with a number of other schools such as artillery and engineering, was placed under the authority of the chief of the GGS. Bureaucratically this removed the academy, the lead institution in the Prussian system, from the control of the General Inspectorate of Military Education and placed it directly under the control of the GGS for curriculum, faculty, and educational matters. It has been argued that this step contributed fundamentally to the changing character of the War Academy: from an educational institution for officers of the army as a whole, the War Academy became a preparatory and admissions school for the GGS. Moltke believed that a good general education was the foundation, but specialist knowledge had to be applied whenever it was needed. Other officers wanted to reform the curriculum in favor of more practical and less theoretical work. In fact the argument was stated in terms of increasing the work capacity of the academy.[22]

Military careers undoubtedly became an attractive choice after 1871. In the 1850s Schlieffen was hard pressed to decide between the army and civil government. After 1871 this seems to have changed. In the 1850s the War Academy had fewer than 130 students. By 1877 it had over 300, and the number of applicants was two or three times as great as those admitted. Other federal states sent officers to train in the Prussian education system. Although Saxony kept its cadet school, Württemberg maintained its school until 1874, and Bavaria had its own military education system, they all sent officers to Berlin.[23]

---

22. Joachim Hoffmann, "Der Militärschriftsteller Fritz Hönig," *Militärgeschichtliche Mitteilungen* 1 (1970): 15; Hubert Rosinski, *The German Army* (Washington, D.C. 1943), pp. 163–66; Kessel, *Moltke*, p. 607; Detlev Bald, *Der Deutsche Generalstab, 1859–1939* (Hamburg, 1972), p. 38; Demeter, *German Officer Corps*, pp. 80ff.

23. Osten-Sacken, *Preußens Heer*, 3: 319–32; Rosinski, *German Army*, pp. 165–67.

Competitive examinations for the War Academy were held annually in January for each year's October first opening day. If Karl Litzmann's account of 1872 is typical, it was apparently the object of some pride on the part of divisions and regiments when their officers passed this examination. After his divisional commander spoke to all officers, enjoining them to take the War Academy entrance test, Litzmann requested permission from his regimental commander. Having passed through the Artillery and Engineering School, he felt confident in all test areas. In history and geography the examination subjects were drawn from the eighteenth century. He studied the wars of Frederick the Great and the physical geography of Germany. A GGS officer arrived to give the examination. Litzmann wrote essays on "the turning points in the Seven Years' War" and on the "river system of Germany." He was among the first to be called to the new War Academy class.[24]

Below the War Academy was the entire military education system comprised of the Artillery and Engineering School, nine War Schools for officer candidates, seven cadet schools, the Military Shooting School, the Teaching Infantry Battalion, the Riding School in Hanover, the Artillery Shooting School in Berlin, and the School for Doctors, Veterinarians, and Officials in Berlin. Nineteenth-century Prussian officer education may have been impressive, but below it was another educational level intended for noncommissioned officers. Each division operated a school offering a three-year course which, by the 1890s, already had four hundred applicants per division for its 150 slots. If there were twenty army corps, each with two or three divisions, roughly 9,000 NCOs would be trained every year. Regimental schools trained NCOs in technical subjects such as artillery, cartography, and engineering. The Artillery and Engineering School in Berlin accepted eight hundred NCOs from the army annually for its course in hydraulic construction, surveying, architectural drawing, military engineering, the history of war, chemistry, and French. Below the NCO level was another level of education represented by the Military Orphan Houses, three of which had educated several thousand military dependents by the 1890s. Their curriculum included academic subjects such as German, natural history, algebra, trigonometry, and history as well as lithography, music, and saddlemaking. Graduates had to serve six years in the army but

24. Karl Litzmann, *Lebenserinnerungen*, 2 vols. (Berlin, 1927), 2: 59–65.

could enter as NCOs.

One should not overemphasize either the strength or the extent of the Prussian military education system. However it is possible that this system was quite different from the civilian educational system of its time. In contrast to civilian education, military educational was free, secular, and national in focus, open on a competitive basis, and its curriculum was oriented toward practical subjects, especially science and technology. It is worth speculating on the extent to which the strength of the nineteenth-century Prussian army may have resided as much in the lower level of the army, the small unit and its NCOs, as it did in the top level of the army, the GGS.[25]

The decade of the 1880s introduced the second stage of change in military education. Waldersee, the man who depended on contacts and personal relationships, seems to have spurned this method in his own evaluations. On the contrary, in choosing assignments for lower-ranking officers, he relied heavily upon written reports by his section heads. He seems to have been concerned with textbook form in evaluating the way in which his officers performed. For example, it mattered to him that they used correct grammar in drafting orders. Waldersee also wanted to raise the educational level of GGS officers as a whole and by the end of his term 50% of each class had the *Abitur*. Rigorous admission examinations continued, testing the candidates in theoretical and applied tactics, weapons, fortifications, history, geography, mathematics, and French.

By the late 1880s the Military Cabinet rebelled against what it believed were excessively high requirements for admission to the War Academy. Waldersee and the War Ministry felt these requirements were too low and in any event were being loosely applied. The Military Cabinet won and the attempt to tighten entrance requirements further failed. Thus character, or "leadership abili-

25. Little sustained research has apparently been devoted to the education of the Prussian NCO corps or, for that matter, the Prussian soldier. It is possible that it was significantly different from civilian educational opportunities available to the same social classes. See, for example, Bernhard Poten, *Geschichte des Militär-Erziehungs- und Bildungswesens in den Landen deutscher Zunge*, 4 vols. (Berlin, 1889); Freiherr Ferdinand von Ladebur, ed. *Die Geschichte des deutschen Unteroffiziers* (Berlin, 1939); Richard Nelson, "Notes on the Constitution and System of Education of the Prussian Army," *United Service Magazine*, (1839): pt. 3, 497–522; Henry Barnard, *Military Schools and Courses of Instruction in the Science and Art of War*, 2 vols. (Philadelphia, 1862), 1: 336–55; Julius von Hartmann, *Lebenserinnerungen, Briefe und Aufsätze* (Berlin, 1882), pp. 68–84.

ties" as they were defined on the personal recommendation forms, continued to play a crucial role even as technical education became more and more important. By 1891, of those admitted to the War Academy, 210 were infantry officers, 35 cavalry, 56 artillery, and 11 engineer. They were between the ages of twenty-three and thirty-eight, with five to sixteen years' active duty.[26]

With the curriculum of 1888 an era of educational humanism ended and a period of philosophical materialism and positivism began. The goal was to produce the pure military specialist. Even the terminology changed: courses previously called the art of war, *Kriegskunst*, were changed to the science of war, *Kriegswissenschaft*. Required courses increased, electives were reduced. Aside from the required "military science" courses, students had only to choose between a foreign language, initially French or Russian, later also English or Japanese, or a natural or mathematical science, a category that included physical geography, chemistry, physics, or geology. The enriched science curriculum centered around mathematics. It included stereometry, spherical trigonometry, analytical geometry, and differential calculus. Physics included heat, electricity, acoustics, and optics. Chemistry was two-thirds inorganic, one-third organic.

Tactics became the major academic subject within the dominant war science curriculum. We recall that GGS history also focused primarily on the tactical level, and since it was the major source for War Academy lectures, this curricular shift is not surprising. Courses began with a summary of the historical evolution of the order of battle and tactical forms, including the study of field service regulations and ordinances. Military history began with the campaigns of Frederick the Great, followed by those of the French Revolution and of Kaiser Wilhelm I. In 1890 ancient and medieval history were purged from the curriculum. Third-year students no longer studied history at all. History courses which remained were abbreviated, following Waldersee's direction, to allow time for more science. Yet practical emphasis continued. Once admitted, War Academy students began immediately to be trained in the general staff tradition of "work study." During the school break, from July through October, officers were cross-branched for summer training, with infantry officers assigned to

26. Mohs, *Waldersee*, 2: 39; Demeter, *German Officer Corps*, pp. 86–87; Poten, *Militär-Erziehungswesen*, 4: 306.

field artillery regiments, for example. Military surveying and general staff work, the latter including an extensive examination of railroads and supply services, concluded with a three-week field exercise conducted exactly like the GGS ride.[27]

For many of the newer "war science" disciplines, serving officers in each specialty were brought in because older officers assigned to the GGS were not trained to teach them. For example, military doctors taught military medicine. Although Moltke's stated curricular and pedagogical goal for the War Academy continued to be a combination of specialist and general education, it is clear that War Academy education was changing. General education was still considered the best foundation for professional soldiers but, because most War Academy students were now secondary school graduates, it was assumed that this basic level had already been mastered.[28]

Admission to the GGS after War Academy graduation also changed. During the 1870s it had followed the time honored traditional method of personal selection by the chief. Each year Moltke, on the recommendation of his colleagues and associates, chose lieutenants and captains from the graduating class for GGS duty, fifteen for the Secondary Bureau, 35 for the Main Bureau. In fact by 1881, the selection had devolved down to section and even to branch heads because Moltke no longer had effective contact with younger officers. Moltke or Waldersee signed the papers. Their subordinates, generals or colonels in their forties and fifties, made the decisions. New GGS officers assigned on probationary status competed with those already assigned and with those officers called up each year from the TGS and from front commands to participate in the war games and GGS rides. War game participation, based upon these four candidate pools – probationary and assigned GGS officers and TGS and front officers – was said to be the ultimate criterion upon which GGS selection was based.

It is evident that changes in personnel policies during the 1880s were based primarily on technical and bureaucratic factors. Older officers had relied upon men they knew personally. In fact up

27. W. Lexis, *Die Hochschulen für besondere Fachgebiete im Deutschen Reich* (Berlin, 1904), pp. 229–40; Bald, *Der Deutsche Generalstab*, pp. 440–46; Poten, *Militär-Erziehungswesen*, 4: 295ff.

28. Kessel, "Die Tätigkeit des Grafen Waldersee," p. 189; Poten, *Militär-Erziehungswesen*, 4: 204, 298; Kessel, *Moltke*, p. 608; Bald, *Der Deutsche Generalstab*, pp. 142–46.

through the 1860s, the Prussian king apparently knew all the generals personally and did not have to rely on official personnel records. Older officers still placed great emphasis on parades: leading an army corps on parade appeared to them to be the consummate test of an officer's skill. Many "heroes" were to be seen on the Tempelhof parade field. Waldersee discounted maneuvers and parades believing that the real assessment of an officer was to be found in official personnel documents and written work. Instead he favored intellectual and technically oriented officers.[29]

## Military History

It has been argued that one way institutions survive is by using information processes. They gain legitimacy by providing their members with a set of analogies to explore the world and justify the naturalness and reasonableness of institutional rules. Ultimately, the institution begins to control the memory of its members, causing them to forget experiences incompatible with its correct, legitimate image and emphasizing events which sustain views that are complimentary to itself. In the end, the institution provides the categories of thought, sets the terms for self-knowledge, and fixes identities.[30]

One of the central building blocks of Prussian war planning had always been military history. The Military History Section, including the library and archive, was basic to the GGS from its foundation. Officers assigned there also taught in the War Academy and published books and articles. The Berlin publisher E.S. Mittler and the GGS edited the *Military Weekly* and carried these activities forward in numerous publications. Military history, like mapping, was becoming a technical specialty.

In 1871 the chief of the Military History Section was Verdy du Vernois, one of Moltke's assistants at military headquarters during the war against France. As soon as the staff returned from the campaign, its members began to write its history. To some extent it was a new kind of project. No longer was it to be purely Prussian

---

29. Kessel, *Moltke*, p. 614; Mohs, *Waldersee*, 2: 39–42; BAMA, Nachlaß Hans Hartwig von Beseler, N30–46, Lebenserinnerungen, pp. 32–48. Waldersee impressed Kaiser Wilhelm I on a GGS ride by leading it without ever using a map, whereas other participants were glued to theirs. Mohs, *Waldersee*, 2: 168.
30. Mary Douglas, *How Institutions Think* (London, 1987), pp. 102, 112.

history as in 1867. This time it was to be Reich history, the first "German national historical monument," as Verdy described it. Many officers worked on these bureaucratic volumes. For each army, a single section was created. Graf Wartensleben worked on the operations of the 1st Army, Freiherr von der Goltz on the 2d Army, and General von Hahnke on the 3d Army. It was a difficult project because there were gaps in the sources. Various war diaries, official documents, orders, and telegrams were missing. In 1872 Verdy, who had served as department head for seven years, was replaced by Graf Wartensleben, who continued the project for more than six years. During this period Moltke apparently did not work on the volumes himself. In 1877, when Wartensleben retired, Moltke took the project back and from then to its completion was dedicated to it. Although the Military History Section went forward with various other projects, for example, its histories of the German regiments and of eighteenth-century Prussian wars, this was the one to which Moltke was devoted. The first volume was published in 1874, the final one in 1881.[31]

Gazing at this set today, one is struck by its quantitative and book art aspects. It comprises eight large volumes, five of text and documents plus three of maps, sketches, and charts. Stacked one on top of another they weigh twenty-five pounds and contain 2,786 pages. Tactical actions are described down to the level of company with mention of individual soldiers from the rank of field marshall to lieutenant. The vocabulary used is technical military: terms used in issuing orders, writing war games, and army regulations. There are 1,147 pages of appendixes listing orders, order of battle, and royal, army, and corps proclamations. Each of the volumes of tactical battle descriptions contains single-page maps at scales down to one inch to three hundred paces. The three map volumes are monumental in themselves. They contain seventy-five maps in all, each 28 by 25 inches in eleven different scales from 1:20,000 to 1:3,666,666. Frequently the scale is given both in meters and in paces and most of the maps are done in four colors. Many have two measurement scales: one for distance, measured as the crow flies, and one for grade. Contours are shown in great detail: often each contour line is specified at the map edge, in addition to elevations for mountains, hills, and escarpments. Individual plates often use separate colors to indicate changes during a single day of combat,

31. Kessel, "Moltke und die Kriegsgeschichte," p. 117.

for example, to illustrate changing troop positions from 10 A.M. to 3 P.M. or 5 P.M. of the same day. As examples of cartography and lithography, these surely rank with the best artistic and technical productions of the nineteenth century. Toulouse-Lautrec's printer would rightly be jealous. As publishing feats, these volumes in editions of 13,000 copies each are something with which to conjure. Thirty six million two hundred thousand pages is a substantial production for the nineteenth-century book world.[32]

As an historical encaenia, it is not surprising that the first volumes won the Verdun Prize for German History awarded by the Prussian Academy of Science in 1878. As works of history, it is instructive to compare these volumes with twentieth-century accounts. Take for example the battle of Spichern, 6 August 1870. The GGS history, volume 1, number 1, published in 1874, deals with this battle in one hundred pages of text plus five maps and several sketches. The discussion begins with a "terrain overview" of the entire battle area. This is a straightforward technical account of physical reality. The region is broken down into two sections – one area between the Rhine, the Saar, and the Vosges and the other Lorraine. The available transportation paths are described. Basel to Mainz is a 200-mile stretch, 15 to 23 miles wide, with specific topographic features such as river crossing points and major strongholds highlighted. The Vosges Mountains pathway is 147 miles long and 18 to 23 miles wide. Distance is measured both in miles and in marches. For example, moving troops from the Rhine area to the Saar averaged five to seven one-day marches. Rivers are described in terms of crossing possibilities: for example, the Mosel from Frouard to Didenhofen averaged 150 to 200 paces wide and could only be forded during dry weather. However there were bridges at Frouard, Marbache, Dieulouard, Pont à Mousson, Corny, and Ars.

Beyond close attention to terrain features, a second aspect of these histories that is significant is their treatment of railroads. Six through-going rail lines are described for transporting forces to the area between the Mosel and the Rhine rivers. Mobilization was declared on 23 July, transportation by rail began the next day. On the tenth mobilization day the first units debarked over the French border, and by the thirteenth day combat forces from two army

---

32. Kriegsgeschichtliche Abtheilung des Großen Generalstabs, *Der deutsch-französische Krieg, 1870–71*, 8 vols. (Berlin, 1874–81).

corps were assembled there. By the eighteenth day German forces numbered over 300,000, and in three weeks the offensive moved forward with half a million men.[33]

In contrast to the objective and technical description of terrain and railroads, the influence of the Prussian school of history – idealist and national – is dominant in dealing with the human actions. Beginning with overall troop disposition, the battle description of Spichern leads off as the 3d Prussian Uhlan Regiment commanded by Captain Hammerstein came under fire moving from St. Johann to Saarbrücken on the evening of 5 August. From then on, major movements of troops down to brigade and regiment are noted by the hour. Ninety pages later the work concludes that the attack of the 14th Division against strongly entrenched, well-positioned, and overwhelmingly superior French forces was "instinctively" correct, the decision everyone "felt" had to be made at the time. It was not contrary to orders because it sent forces to attack a retreating enemy, an action "completely in the spirit of the German offensive." The use of the future conditional tense is emphatic, just as it is in war games, tactical exercises, and maneuvers. Even if the attack had failed, the defeat of a small part of the army in the face of overwhelmingly superior forces "would not have had" much impact on the whole operation. "Even if" the French had not been attacked at Spichern, they might have retreated anyway; however, in that case they "would have" reached the Mosel River without any losses. How to explain the bloody loss of life which gave the battle its character? This was due to the closed unit tactical forms used by the German troops plus the fact that reserve forces did not arrive until nightfall.[34]

For GGS historians the "decisive victory" of Spichern came about because German commanders timed their independent actions to support one another. Although the material value of the battle was less than that of the battle of Wörth, the moral value of the great triumph at Spichern had impact far beyond the battlefield. The completely unexpected news of the simultaneous defeat of French forces in Alsace and Lorraine worked "as a thunderclap sent from heaven" on the war aims of the leadership in Paris. At French headquarters the staff temporarily gave up all idea of resistance. In the course of the following week, all of France as

33. Ibid., 1: 126–32.
34. Ibid., 1: 297, 377, 379.

far as the Mosel River fell into German hands. So impressive was the battle of Spichern that streets and squares all across Germany were named in its honor.[35]

Twentieth-century historians generally view this battle as a disaster from beginning to end. The 14th Division attacked without orders at the only place in the French line where German troops were guaranteed to meet superior forces, with reinforcement nearby. They lacked surprise and adequate cover. From 11 A.M. to 5 P.M. German forces moved methodically forward, completely exposed. The French fired downhill, with superior weapons, inflicting enormous casualties on the closely ordered German units. Finally, at 7:30 P.M., the French, who were about to be outflanked, withdrew. As even the GGS work admitted, the French probably would have been forced to withdraw sooner or later as a result of the German flanking movement. Artillery, hardly mentioned in the official account, was crucial in avoiding a worse disaster. Thirty Germans batteries held the ground and prevented a more punishing French attack. Casualties were very high. Of roughly 42,000 Prussians engaged, 12% were killed or wounded.[36]

All in all *The German-French War* was a fitting memorial to the Prussian school of history, which preserved a correct and honorable view of the army. It is general staff history, bureaucratic and patriotic. The attack is the correct form of war. Spiritual qualities dominate material factors. Moltke wrote that what appeared in military history was window dressing; however, it was a duty of piety and love of fatherland not to destroy this because the victories of Prussia's armies depended on its association with certain distinct impressions and personalities.[37] As this history was reaching completion, the first postwar generation of GGS officers began to assume important roles. In 1878 Adalbert von Taysen was appointed to the Military History Section, and at Moltke's suggestion the section began updating and revising its series on the wars of Frederick the Great begun in 1863. It is worth considering this series.

Prior to about 1870, the GGS and the universities had an unwritten division of labor for military history. The universities dealt with war in what they understood as the humanistic framework, emphasizing political causes and consequence and leaving out or mini-

35. Ibid., 1: 380.
36. Howard, *German-French War*, pp. 86–119.
37. Kessel, "Moltke und die Kriegsgeschichte," p. 124.

mizing military actions. The GGS dealt with war as a technical study, emphasizing tactics, battles, and leaders. The purpose of GGS history was threefold: first to underline a desired image of the army in society; second, to provide practical military training; third, to assist in future war planning. In order to carry out these purposes GGS history was written under certain conditions. First, it was bureaucratic: there was no single author responsible but instead collaborative volumes were issued under the stamp of the GGS. In fact no individuals were mentioned and complete anonymity was preserved. Second, it was narrowly technical in the sense that it focused on battlefield tactics, following single units in the style of what is known as regimental history. Third, it omitted the broader context of campaigns and wars, especially the political and social framework. Fourth, it was written not by trained historians but by trained officers, by those who had practical experience either in war itself or at least in military service. What qualified them to write military history? Their experience as soldiers. They could best understand the military past because they experienced the military present. Fifth, it was written under the aegis of the single most successful military institution in modern European history, the GGS. Who better to write about the military past than those associated with its most successful contemporary institution?

Finally and most important, beginning in the late 1870s, GGS history began to superimpose a single uniform strategic theme over all past wars. This theme is clearly evidenced in the GGS series on the wars of Frederick the Great. The first volume, published in 1879, was a reissue of Frederick's *Military Testament* of 1768. The original in French had been written long after the close of the most difficult war years of Frederick's monarchy, during the final ten years of his reign. The testament, which was intended as the king's instructions for the next war, presented Frederick as conservative and defensive, advocating the cautious choice of strong positions and the avoidance of battles in open country and attempts to gain small advantages here and there which, taken together, might yield an overall successful outcome. Frederick did not recommend total and unlimited warfare carried out by battles of annihilation: in fact he advocated the exact opposite; limited war carried out by blockade, maneuver, and seige.

To this original document the GGS attached a commentary in German emphasizing that this limited strategy was an aberration and exception to Frederick's usual strategic ideas. It emphasized that normally Frederick called for total war carried out by battles of annihilation. When this view of Frederick's strategic fundamentals was questioned by a young lecturer at Berlin University, a whole bevy of officers came to its defense, provoking a conflict between the lecturer, Hans Delbrück, and officers of the GGS then teaching at the War Academy which lasted for the next twenty years. Delbrück invoked Clausewitz and cited Frederick's other wars and writings to support his case. The officers questioned Delbrück's qualifications as a military historian – the problem was appropriately dealt with by practitioners, not theorists – and argued that in any event a strategy of limited war was illegitimate. Frederick had understood the truth that the destruction of the enemy fighting force in battle was the single legitimate strategy for all time. Any other conception contradicted the very nature of war. Material factors such as the size of armies and supply systems were important, but they did not constitute the essence of any historic period. Frederick's genius, his will to battle, was so great that it enabled him, with much smaller material resources than Napoleon and Moltke, to implement the same strategy in the eighteenth century that these commanders, with much greater material resources, carried out in the nineteenth. Frederick the Great was the spiritual progenitor not only of the new German Empire but of nineteenth-century strategy. He was the true originator of the strategy of total war.[38]

Coincident with this emerging image of Frederick the Great, Clausewitz was being rediscovered and reinterpreted. To the GGS it seemed that Moltke's strategy had been perfectly described by Clausewitz half a century before. The strategy of total war was the single correct and legitimate form, as proved by Frederick, Napoleon, and Moltke. The melding of this interpretation of Clausewitz with the historical interpretation of modern wars meant that within the GGS a single image of war history and historical strategy was developing. It aimed to interpret the military past in terms of a single strategic concept. Whether in past, present, or future, war was an act of violence carried to the utmost limits. The only legitimate strategy was the offensive carried out in battles of annihilation.[39]

38. Bucholz, *Hans Delbrück*, pp. 1–44.
39. Ibid., pp. 8–15; Michael Howard, "Men against Fire: Expectations of War in 1914," and Stephen van Evera, "The Cult of the Offensive and the Origins of the

*The German-French War* initiated a series of GGS publications which continued until 1914. The first dealt with the wars of Prussia beginning in the eighteenth century. The second, entitled Military History Monographs, ultimately included more than forty volumes dealing with individual battles from nineteenth-century wars. The third was Studies in Military History and Tactics, and it included a dozen volumes on army movement, fortresses, and supply. A fourth series contained the published writings of well-known Prussian generals, for example, Moltke's military correspondence, his tactical and strategic essays, and his history of the Franco-Prussian War. Outside the GGS, accompanying the appearance of these books was a surge in publication of new military journals aimed at both professional and popular audiences: *Jahrbücher für die deutsche Armee und Marine, Loebell'sche Jahresberichte, Neue Militärische Blätter*, and others began publishing during these years.[40] In sum, the GGS sponsored a veritable library of military history publications during the next half century. One general, a contemporary of Schlieffen, snickered that even as the great mass of paperwork grew, its real value shrank and ultimately it would end up in the trash bin as wastepaper.[41]

Deep-future-oriented war planning confronts a fundamental problem in human knowledge which is how to plan for future war, a social phenomenon which cannot be closely simulated because of its relationship with death. This problem is exacerbated during periods of rapid technological change. As Galbraith argues, the information requirements of organizations involved with technology tend to increase. In the case of the GGS, this specialization of labor resulted in the creation of the technical expert, the basis of whose power position within the state was knowledge. One area of that knowledge was history. Within the GGS the writing of military history became a technical competence. It was institutionalized with specialized methodology, lectures, seminars, practical laboratory exercises, and publications. History conferred legitimacy. The GGS harnessed information in support of itself, its rules, procedures, and ideals.

First World War," in Steven Miller, ed., *Military Strategy and the Origins of the First World War* (Princeton, 1985).

40. Howard, *German-French War*, pp. 464–65.

41. Egon Freiherr von Geyl, *General von Schlichting und sein Lebenswerk* (Berlin, 1913), p. 388.

## War Gaming

The fourth aspect of war planning is analytical. By the late 1870s different levels, methods, and kinds of war games had developed. As for levels of play, there was the tactical and the strategic. And as for kinds of war games, there were indoor war games, played on paper or around a map or sand table, and outdoor games, including the GGS ride and the troop maneuver. The basis for everything was the tactical war game, learned by officers assigned to regimental duties during their first years of active duty.

Before 1864 the tactical game had evolved into a kind of mathematical gambling contest in which umpires, lacking war experience, consulted minute, voluminous, and complex rules, then threw the dice to determine final outcomes. The decision of the umpires had to conform to a set of fixed rules which always produced numerous imponderables. Tactical knowledge was hardly used at all; instead, it was memory of the drill regulations that counted. The whole process was considered tedious and unimaginative.[42]

Colonel Jacob Meckel, a Hanover War School instructor in the 1870s and GGS department head in the early 1890s, wrote that prior to 1871 the emphasis had been on theoretical studies, especially of the works of Clausewitz, but that the wars of unification had proved that the study of pure theory was insufficient. Officer instruction demanded practical means for its development. Officers had to study concrete cases, single tactical problems drawn from the experiences of war. Following 1871, a flurry of new books sought to redefine and reinvigorate war gaming. Their central idea emancipated the umpire from complicated written rules and emphasized the application of tactical experience. The war game was to be conducted on the same principles as the staff ride. In both exercises, no one thought of deciding the success of an operation by the throw of the dice; the umpire made his decision based upon his own judgment.

What were the components of Meckel's game? It began with maps that were appropriate to the level of play. Detachment war games were played on a map drawn to a scale of 1:6,250, brigade games on a scale of 1:12,500, strategic games on a scale of 1:100,000. Maps were chosen of land suitable for troop movements, land offering a variety of features such as villages, farms, and

---

42. "Foreign War Games," pp. 257–59; Cf. Wilkinson, *War Game*, pp. 52–54.

wooded patches but without vast open plains, dense forests, or mountainous regions. Once maps were selected, they were divided into squares of from 30 to 35 centimeters. Pawns representing the different arms were used. The unit of time per move, the duration of a round, was fixed at 2.5 minutes for the tactical game and ten minutes for the strategic game. The speed at which troops marched under normal conditions was based on the regulation gait, measured out on strips of sheet brass. The actual conduct of the game proceeded with five officers in each of two rooms with the third room used by the umpire. Each side received the hypothesis or general situation a few days ahead of the match, and each had a commander and four subordinates. Generally each side played with one or two battalions of infantry, plus appropriate cavalry and artillery. Orders were transmitted to the umpire in writing. The umpire announced the first round, his assistant noted the time, and the match began. Communications were given to the umpire by each commander in such a way that his adversary could not read them. At decisive moments, the duration of a round was subdivided into periods as short as desired to facilitate the study of detail. An umpire could base his decision entirely on tactical considerations, if by reason of rank or recognized experience his authority was received with respect.[43]

The period of war gaming after 1871 was founded first, on war experience; second, on the historical image of that experience; and third, on field service regulations. In other words it was based on various kinds of knowledge. All officers were expected to be familiar with weapons, the handling of troops, supply, various forms of movement, and so forth. No one wanted his ignorance of military details to be revealed. Not only the players but also war game conductors were evaluated in these terms. There were three degrees of war game leader corresponding to three levels of knowledge. The best director, whom the Prussians called "the conductor," was one who had the most war experience, who had witnessed or participated in combat so that, confronted with a specific game situation, he could say, "I saw an advance exactly like this under similar conditions at the battle of Gravelotte and here is what happened. . . ." Obviously such directors were few and far between, and they became scarcer as time went on. The second-best conductor was one who had studied in detail the

---

43. "Foreign War Games," pp. 258–84.

history of so many battles as to be able to base his decisions on an analogous instance from modern military history. The third and weakest director, lacking combat experience or historical knowledge, based his decisions on tactical textbooks and field service regulations.

But a critical bottleneck remained, how to estimate casualties. Following 1871 it became possible, perhaps for the first time in military history, to provide reasonably accurate casualty statistics. Between 1866 and 1870, the Prussian army created medical and hospital units on a massive scale. Part of their task was keeping track of killed and wounded. If GGS histories could blur the specifics of a battle, providing only limited truth, there was no way to blur the number of casualties. Sooner or later the true number of dead and wounded would become public knowledge. The series *Military History: Single Examples*, begun in 1883, meant that individual regimental histories tried for accuracy at least in statistics of killed and wounded, if not in how these injuries were sustained.

From the GGS history of the Franco-Prussian War came a new casualty formula for regimental war games. Lieutenant von Naumann of the Saxon army used the GGS description of the battle of Spichern to construct mathematical casualty tables. Why he chose this battle is an interesting question in itself. Spichern was later described by a French military historian as the supreme example of moral force in war. The French general, though undefeated, thought he had been defeated and therefore he was. The Prussian general, half-defeated, refused to believe it and therefore he was not. Spichern was characterized by point-blank rifle and artillery fire at lethal ranges. It pitted some 54,000 French against 42,000 Prussians over a twelve-hour period. It was an example of modern weapons technology confronting traditional tactical doctrine. Almost twelve thousand of those engaged became casualties.[44]

The essence of Naumann's system was an attempt to answer the question, why do troops retire before an enemy? Aside from the case where every man was killed or wounded, he posited three answers to this question. Either they were exhausted or in confusion, or they were frightened. In many cases all three conditions existed together. A potent cause of alarm and confusion was surprise. The sudden appearance of the enemy where he was not expected or where his presence was dangerous seemed always to

44. Howard, *German-French War*, pp. 85–89.

have a disturbing effect. The effect of a flank attack upon troops in its neighborhood was well known. But the main cause of the alarm or panic that preceded defeat seemed to Naumann to be the losses caused by the enemies' firearms. The impact of killed and wounded comrades on their fellow troops' morale was the most severe. The question therefore became, at what point would men be induced to change their minds about attack and retreat? Naumann concluded, first, that the effect of losses upon a company varied considerably according to whether the "general conditions" of the company were favorable or unfavorable. Favorable conditions were that the company was attacking; that it was on the side which in general had been more successful in the war; and that its losses were spread over some span of time, an hour or more. Unfavorable conditions were that the company was on the defensive; that it was the side which, during the war, had been the loser; and that the losses were suffered in a short time, a quarter of an hour or less. In every case attacking troops were given an advantage: their morale was assumed higher merely by virtue of their participation in an attack.

Naumann based his formula on the German company of 250 men, confined his figures to active troops, and used the battle of Spichern as the basis for his calculations. Naumann argued that a company in favorable circumstances would lose 40 men without flinching. A company in all but very exceptional cases had to be considered shaken if it had lost, under favorable circumstances, 90 men, under unfavorable circumstances 60. A loss of 120 men even under the most favorable circumstances put a company out of action and a loss of 150 men was equivalent to its complete destruction. Based upon these considerations, a table was constructed showing the effect upon the morale of a company of any given percentage of losses. When called upon to decide the result of an engagement or to decide at some point during an engagement whether a particular company would advance, halt, or retire, the umpire asked himself three questions: Were the troops tired? In war games this meant, had they been moved for any length of time at more than their normal pace? Hardly anything exhausted infantry so much as hurrying the pace of march. Second, were the troops in good order and was their general morale good? In war games this meant a handicap for all troops who had received contradictory orders, following the military tradition of "order, counterorder, disorder." Third, what was the effect upon these troops of the enemy's fire?

Captain Naumann's answers to this last question were described on a scale. The results of firing depended upon the number of firing units, the range, the time occupied in firing, the condition and situation of the target, the number of units fired at, and their degree of protection or cover. Thus the average result of firing by one squad of infantry for one minute at various force densities, ranges, and coverages was indicated using a set of tables. On the basis of these tables, which numericalized tactical war games, regimental exercises attained new popularity. More important, since young lieutenants learned this method during their first regimental experiences, the officer corps of the 1880s began active duty emphasizing a mathematical, slide-rule approach to war.[45]

Presumably officers of the Prussian army were familiar with the tactical war game from their first tour of duty. At the War Academy and later in the GGS, they were introduced to several additional kinds of war games. In winter, early in January, the GGS presented its final problem. This was a tactical exercise lasting a few days, handed out to all assigned lieutenants. No teams were selected, and each officer competed against the others. In each case the format was the same. A tactical military situation, applicable to regimental or squadron actions, was described. Each officer was asked to estimate the situation and issue orders. This was followed by a second situation, a continuation of the first. Again, estimates and orders were requested. Responses were written out and handed in. Finally the chief and a senior general and department head criticized the responses verbally and in writing. The verbal discussion was carried out before the assembled officers, presumably with individual responses being discussed anonymously. This critique was anticipated by the officers like a final examination and was discussed for weeks before and afterward.

A third war game was the GGS ride. In late spring the chief of the GGS chose about thirty officers from the GGS, TGS, and active units for a three-week outdoor exercise ride. This was a strategic war game. Aided by a small staff, the chief himself acted as conductor. The participants were divided into blue and red armies,

---

45. Wilkinson, *War Game*, pp. 46–52; Julius Verdy du Vernois, *Beitrag zum Kriegsspiel*, 2d ed. (Berlin, 1881), pp. 1–2; Charles A.L. Totten, *Strategos* (New York, 1880), pp. 170–73; John Keegan reaches much the same conclusion in *The Face of Battle* (New York, 1976), chap. 5.

each of which was commanded by a field grade officer. The sides competed against each other in a problem at the army corps level. There was a general situation common to both sides and a special situation unique to each army. Each side was asked to estimate the situation, then issue orders. Often there was a follow-up to the first problem. GGS rides familiarized officers with terrain, especially in the border areas where many of these rides were conducted, provided experience in issuing orders for large forces, and enabled the chief of the GGS to get to know these officers well, for they traveled and worked together for several weeks. A certain amount of military comradeship was clearly involved. But the staff ride was also related to the current war plan, its problems and possibilities.[46]

The fourth kind of war game was the outdoor large-scale maneuver. Maneuvers were conducted in staggered series throughout the summer beginning in early June, gradually escalated from regiments to divisions during July, and finally culminated in the Kaisermanöver, a large-scale affair planned, judged, and critiqued by the GGS in early September. Even in this game, formal communications standards were high. Divisional and corps commanders were expected to keep war diaries. At the day's end written and verbal reports and sketches were completed on enemy positions and strengths, disposition of marches and lines of battle, and orders for march and rest. When time permitted, an officer opened the exercise day with a formal lecture concerning an event from military history "scientifically researched" and related to the specific terrain of the surrounding maneuver area.[47]

War gaming changed operational planning. It conditioned Prussian officers to think in terms of a bipolar war situation, to think in terms of the opponent. During the long peace from 1871 to 1914 – forty-three years without great power European wars – the more distant war experience became, the greater was the dependency upon war gaming.

For the gaming aspect of Prussian war planning, a useful distinction can be made between pure and applied research. Pure research begins with a blank sheet of paper, whereas applied research begins with an actual problem. The GGS was engaged in applied research. It was in this sense that the officers repeatedly questioned whether the practitioner or the theoretician was best

46. Mohs, *Waldersee*, 2: 38–39, 109–14.
47. Schellendorff, *Duties*, pp. 124–216.

qualified to deal with military history questions. The officers had no doubt that they, the practitioners, were best qualified and that it was their experience as soldiers that qualified and lent authority to their opinions. Historians lacking that experience had no business trying to answer military history questions, especially since those questions were pointed in a single direction, that of future military operations. The "application method" was the bridge between the past and future. GGS military history and war gaming was essentially technical applied research. The "practical problem" appeared in both past and present, and it was, in a sense, the same problem, whether defined as a war game or as an historical image. As one officer stated, they wanted to take what had happened at a past time and make it happen again. Considerations of change – technology, organization, tactics – were not at the forefront of their thinking. Considerations of sameness – size of forces, number of weapons, geography, and the technical aspects of armies – were foremost. The dominant factors of similarity and continuity in military history, war games, and war plans were nonmaterial: heroism, self-sacrifice, team play, character. The will to victory conquered all. It was the main theme of success, or at least of honor, in war.

Beginning in the 1870s a gap opened between the GGS image of past military experience and its plans for future war. This gap remained open for about two decades until Schlieffen effectively closed it in the late 1890s, finally bringing war plans back into a congruent relationship with the GGS image of the military past. War games served as the active intermediary between past and future, that is, war games employed historical examples to test out possible future contingencies. Up until about 1892 both games and plans emphasized the defensive-offensive strategy. By that time, however, the image of the military past represented in GGS history had been almost purely offensive – the strategy of annihilation carried out by great battles – for nearly two decades.

The relationship between history, war games, and strategic plans and the gap between past image and future preparation are already evident in the thirteen war plans drafted between 1 April 1871 and January 1881. On many counts, war games of this period contained elements from the active war plan. In the case of intelligence estimates, the then-current estimate for French forces in the southwest was around 100,000 men in four corps around Belfort, corresponding exactly to their strength and force disposition in war games. Both war plan and game estimated French mobilization time at thirteen days. The importance given to railroads in games corresponded to actual plans. Officers recognized that the initial movement of these large forces depended on railroads; therefore the rail lines indicated beforehand the probable large-scale disposition of troops. Appropriate concern was expressed in both plan and game not to mobilize forces too near border areas where they might be prematurely overrun. Game forces were, as in the plans, generally assigned to receive a French attack in a favorable terrain position, then counterattack. Implied in both was the changing size dynamic – the attackers losing strength as they advanced, the defenders gaining strength as they withdrew. It must be emphasized that Moltke constantly changed his thinking about the form and location of a possible French attack, considered many different locations, and tried them all out in exercises and games but remained constant in his defensive-offensive approach. Moltke's fundamentally conservative but also highly expedient and realistic philosophy may be illustrated by his passion for the game of whist.

In whist four players competed against each other. The cards were dealt out one at a time, and the last card turned up became trump. Players followed suit and tricks were taken by the highest card of the suit lead or by the highest trump. For each trick over six, players score one point. Because there was no bidding beforehand, the game just began. The knowledge of the opponent and the preparation of the players were always incomplete. Each hand was a surprise, revealing information that the players did not have before. To play successfully the players were forced to adopt a series of expedients.[48] Whist is an appropriate paradigm for Moltke's strategic philosophy when it is defined as a "series of expedients." Although this view may overstate Moltke's lack of control and undervalue the quantity and quality of his preplanning, the wars of 1866 and 1871 could nevertheless be won by these expedential methods. Thereafter it became progressively more and more impossible. Industrial mass war with million-man armies could not be played like whist. Bridge became the new game paradigm. Intricate bidding revealed long-range strategies based on carefully built-up, competitive strengths. It was a game based upon detailed rules and well known conventions. Known quantities dictated long-range planning. Skilled players had the entire game in their minds as the first card was played. Although expedients still

48. Kessel, *Moltke*, pp. 737–38; Litzmann, *Lebenserinnerungen*, 2: 62–63.

played some part, it was mainly a game which, once underway, followed the preprogrammed schema of the opposing plans, unless there were serious errors committed by one side or the other.

## The Transition of 1888

In the only honors list that Kaiser Friedrich III approved in late spring 1888, Waldersee was advanced to general of cavalry, which he considered a good promotion for his age of fifty-six. Meanwhile Prince Wilhelm drilled the guards on the Tempelhof field, sometimes inviting Waldersee to the exercises. The crown prince and deputy chief would then ride back into Berlin at the head of the troops, with bands playing and crowds cheering along Unter den Linden. It was a heady experience. On 15 June Kaiser Friedrich died. On 10 August Moltke retired and Waldersee became chief.[49] His selection was welcomed within the army. He was seen as the military mentor of the young Kaiser, a well-known personality and accomplished bureaucratic infighter. According to some, Waldersee had an immediate impact when he sent his old ally, Albedyll, chief of the Military Cabinet, packing in favor of General von Hahnke and got rid of the war minister, Paul Bronsart von Schellendorff, in favor of Verdy du Vernois. Whether Waldersee also considered incorporating the War Ministry into the GGS, as was rumored, is difficult to say. Whether true or not, it indicates the relative value of the two institutions, as seen by observers at the time, and suggests that the swell of power and influence enjoyed by the GGS following the military triumph of 1871 and the bureaucratic victory of 1883 continued unabated.

It was at this time that German defense philosophy began a fatal transition. The last Septennat defense law had run out on 1 April 1888. Bismarck used the defense issue as the central point in his domestic political platform. As he phrased the question, should the German Reich be defended by an imperial army or by a parliamentary army? This coincided with large increases in the French and Russian defense budgets and created a great political brouhaha. In the midst of anxiety and fear, the Reichstag voted. Moltke realized it was old-fashioned merely to increase size. He understood that a new age had come. He argued against massive army increases, but

49. J. Alden Nichols, *The Year of the Three Kaisers* (Urbana, 1987), pp. 254–55; Görlitz, *German General Staff*, pp. 113–14; Hull, *Entourage*, pp. 208ff.

in favor of improved technology. Rather than simply increasing the size, Moltke wanted to upgrade the existing army's work capacity by equipping it with the best weapons.[50]

Verdy du Vernois, who under Waldersee's influence became war minister in August 1888, struck a different note in armaments policy in contrast to Bismarck's bluster. As we have seen above, because of army increases, a shortage of officers had developed. The general staff wanted changes in the military service law to open up reserve officer status to the middle class. In contrast, during Bismarck's chancellorship there had been a certain aristocratization of the officer corps. This now came to a halt. By the end of this phase of high defense spending, the officer corps was over 50% middle class in origin. More important was an overall change in defense philosophy. Vernois made clear that the whole Septennat system was foolishness. What the army really needed was the possibility for flexible, accelerated rearmament. The Septennat only allowed Germany a step-by-step, follow-its-neighbor defense policy. This produced a patchwork quilt pieced together with men and materials; it was out of date. In its place, Verdy put forth a comprehensive program to be developed in long-term stages. It was to be written in such a way that, once passed, it enhanced the possibility of giving the military a free hand in its implementation.

First of all, the program freed the defense budget from annual approval by putting it into a long-range rather than short-term spending context. From this time on defense spending in five- to ten-year planning increments was presented as the first priority of the Reich budget. Verdy's second goal was to bring every man of military service age and ability into training. This in effect amounted to an attempt to amend the Reich constitution of 1871, which limited peacetime strength to 1% of the population. Vernois proposed abandoning this policy in favor of a more flexible approach which advocated training all the war-qualified power of the nation in direct response to the French and Russian defense systems. Germany was falling behind in military preparedness because it did not train all its available manpower, whereas France did. Statistically these ratios began to look ominous by the early 1890s.

Coupled with the new defense budget was an attempt to reorganize the peacetime active army. The concept of average

---

50. Geyer, *Rüstungspolitik*, pp. 54–56; Johannes Werdermann, "Der Heersreform unter Caprivi" (Ph.D. diss., University of Griefswald, 1927). The author used GGS and War Ministry papers destroyed in World War II.

strength before war, followed by significant enlargement when war was declared, was replaced by that of a larger, mobilization-ready organization better trained and faster in its response. The peacetime cadre was expanded, but above all, the war army was ready to mobilize and fight more rapidly. Troop education, summer training, and the Kaisermanöver became more important.

Finally, the relationship between material and personnel began to change from a "personnel-intensive" to a "material-intensive" policy. This trend, although largely unrecognized, continued unabated right up to 1914. Material buildup not only opened the door to private industry currently in the defense business, but it encumbered the Reich budget with huge funding increases. When the war minister proposed figures of 240 million marks altogether, with a 147-million-mark one time increase for the first five-year defense period, this sum put the already hefty increases of the period 1889/1890 into the shadows. The years 1875 to 1886 had not been years of large defense growth. Even in 1882, there had been only a 5% increase. However, from 1886 to 1898 there was a 100% increase in the army budget, which in three instances exceeded 100 million marks and once exceeded 250 million. The peacetime standing army increased from the 427,274 of 1881 to 1887 to the 557,093 of 1893 to 1899. Michael Geyer believes that two comparable periods are those of 1862 to 1867 and 1912 to 1914.[51]

But it was not the size increases that were most important. It was the reshaping of the social and political position of the army in the Reich which made Verdy's approach so novel. The Bismarckian military tradition was based on the idea of exclusivity. The military was considered an elite outside the constitution and above society. The chancellor himself led the politics of the military state. In 1888, at least part of the military was ready to give up the special position of the army in society in return for the strengthening of fighting power. The new formula meant that future defense budgets depended not only on the growth of population and material wealth within the German Reich, but were also related to the military budgets of other states. In other words, foreign defense budgets were to be used as a measure of German defense preparedness. A new interdependency was established between the armies of Europe. Interlocking defense spending

51. Geyer, *Rüstungspolitik*, pp. 53–62.

ultimately served as an indication of the upward spiral that later came to be known as the arms race. Interdependency in defense budgets, army size, weapons, and technology in the 1890s foreshadowed interdependency in war plans after the turn of the century.

All these changes signaled a new relationship between domestic and foreign policy, between the economy and the society. Of necessity, the military began to interact directly with the Reichstag and with big business. This change, impossible to imagine in a military-state army, Prussian and noble-dominated, was enhanced by a national or Reich army, one with middle-class leadership at especially critical points. The period of elite limited war had ended. The era of modern mass war had entered a new phase. This new defense policy, it has been argued, coincided with the "refounding" of the German Reich under Kaiser Wilhelm II, which was characterized by three elements: first, concentration on the central European power block, accompanied by an aggressive anti-Russian foreign policy; second, a defense policy whose goal was to use the whole power of the people, a "people in arms" concept; third, an attempt to separate the workers from social democracy and fuse them into the monarchical state in a new mixture of power and subordination.[52]

A final factor of environmental change which affected the GGS under Waldersee was the selection in March 1890 of Leopold Graf Caprivi as chancellor. Caprivi had his own agenda. He concurred with Verdy that the army needed long-range strengthening. Following the ideas of Heinrich von Gössler, director of the General War Department in the War Ministry, this meant a systematic upgrading of the reserves. Caprivi wanted an army of the people, but also a force disciplined by military training. He believed that high-quality troops were critical at the beginning of a war, but that later the quantity of troops became dominant. In other words he came down on the side of a quantity army overall, with emphasis on a large trained reserve force in a high state of readiness. Although the army bill passed in July 1893 was a compromise, nonetheless in one stroke it raised the size of the army by more than all the previous increases since 1871 put together. Perhaps of greater import was Caprivi's lack of impact on foreign relations. Friedrich

52. Ibid., J. Alden Nichols, *Germany after Bismarck: The Caprivi Era, 1890–1894* (New York, 1968), p. 214; Stig Förster, *Der doppelte Militarismus: Die deutsche Heeresrüstungspolitik zwischen Status-Quo-Sicherung und Aggression, 1890–1913* (Stuttgart, 1985), pp. 28–74; Craig, *Politics*, pp. 238–47; Craig, *Germany*, pp. 170–79.

von Holstein appears to have taken over the reins of decision making from Bismarck, with ominous results for Germany. In June 1890, the Russian-German Reinsurance Treaty was dropped and soon thereafter Germans saw an iron ring beginning to close around them.[53]

Finally, two technical changes occurred as Waldersee assumed his post. The new exercise regulations for infantry were promulgated on 1 September 1888. These regulations, mainly from the pen of General von Schlichting, replaced the standard attack orders with mission type orders delegating greater authority based upon the unique situation and estimate of the commander. Mission type orders required greater uniformity of thinking and reliability of action based on common education and training. A year later, artillery piece no. 88 was introduced. It was a 7.9 centimeter caliber gun which used a smokeless shell and was accurate to 7,000 feet. A gradual increase in the power of available artillery support to field troops, aimed at local fire superiority, coincided with an increase in the degree of flexibility for divisional and brigade commanders. Neither the old exercise grounds nor the old shooting grounds were sufficient any longer. The new combat regulations required larger maneuvering space, and the new field gun required more room for practice firing. In response, between 1888 and 1914 a whole series of large-scale maneuver grounds were established, one per army corps. Thirteen of these, or about half, were located in border areas.[54]

In March 1889 Waldersee expanded and reorganized the GGS. The offices that reported directly to the chief were an enlarged chancellery, the Central Section, a significantly upgraded and enlarged Military History Section and the Land Survey Section. To

53. Geyer, *Rüstungspolitik*, pp. 56–61.

54. According to some, *Auftragstaktik*, was an old tradition in the Prussian army developed by Helmuth von Moltke the Elder and first recorded in the field service regulations of 1885. Lt. Col. Walter von Lossow, "Mission Type Tactics versus Order Type Tactics," *Military Review* 57 (June 1977): 87–91; MGFA, *Tradition in deutschen Streitkräften*, pp. 87–91; Kurt Jany, *Geschichte der preußischen Armee vom 15. Jahrhundert bis 1914*, 2d ed., 4 vols. (Osnabrück, 1967), 4: 297; *German Army Handbook*, trans. War Office (reprint of *The Handbook of the German Army in War*, London, 1918; London, 1977), p. 164. Some of these maneuver grounds remained constant after World War II. The author, serving with the U.S. Second Armored Cavalry Regiment during the early 1960s, went on several occasions to the maneuver area it shared with Bundeswehr units, called Grafenwöhr, located northeast of Nuremberg in rugged and isolated terrain near the Czechoslovak border. In 1914 Grafenwöhr was the training area for the 3d Bavarian Corps.

replace the single deputy chief, his old position, he created instead three deputy chiefs of staff, lieutenant generals with adjutants, and placed them directly under the chief. The most senior of the three acted as deputy chief in Waldersee's absence. The men appointed to fill these slots were Albert von Holleben and Grafs Gottlieb Haeseler and Alfred Schlieffen. In effect, the second level was multiplied by three, creating an entirely new tier just below the chief and chancellery. The third level consisted of six section heads, of the rank of colonel, and subordinate to these were nineteen branch chiefs, either lieutenant colonels or majors. Thus a four-tiered organization was created. The Secondary Bureau for Scientific Affairs, with over 450 men, continued its size advantage during these years. The GGS was becoming a substantial bureaucracy, yet it remained small in relationship to the forces for which it planned. GGS officers in Berlin now totaled nearly two hundred. Chief quartermaster I directed the Railroad and Mobilization Sections; chief quartermaster II dealt with military education and fortresses; chief quartermaster III handled intelligence on foreign armies. Waldersee did not believe that GGS intelligence was very good, and he sought to improve it.[55]

By September Waldersee had created a fifth working level between himself and the three chief quartermasters: Schlieffen was released as deputy chief and assigned to work directly for Waldersee, a position formalized six months later. Waldersee seems to have concentrated on outside relationships between the GGS and the exterior domestic environment, while Schlieffen took care of matters within the GGS. The geographic organization, which had characterized the GGS from its inception, had now fallen away. It was replaced by a purely functional and technical management structure. The addition of adjutants indicate expanded staff responsibilities. These men routinely took care of promotions, appointments, general orders, and reports, and their role indicates that the office management function of each level of the GGS had expanded.[56]

---

55. BAMA, Nachlaß Beseler, Lebenserinnerungen, p. 39; Eberhard Kessel, *Generalfeldmarschall Graf Alfred Schlieffens Briefe* (Göttingen, 1958), p. 319; Görlitz, *German General Staff*, p. 116; Schellendorff, *Duties*, pp. 38–39. It remains obscure how good this intelligence ever became. The most recent analysis does not deal with this period. Holger Herwig, "Imperial Germany," in Ernest May, ed., *Knowing One's Enemies* (Princeton, 1984), pp. 62–97.

56. Görlitz, *German General Staff*, p. 116; Kessel, *Moltke*, p. 705; Kessel, "Die Tätigkeit des Grafen Waldersee," pp. 194–95; idem, *Schlieffens Briefe*, p. 283; Schellendorff, *Duties*, p. 225.

In 1890 the Kaisermanöver took on new life. Wilhelm II decided to take command of one side or the other in these large outdoor exercises. Waldersee noted that, as a result, this war game became much more important than it had been before and he responded in characteristic fashion. Waldersee built the Kaisermanöver into a massive outdoor spectacle, a stage on which Wilhelm could perform. The outcome proved very mixed. Wilhelm often failed to understand the maneuver plan or which side was stronger or weaker. Misunderstanding was enhanced by blunders. In the September 1890 exercise, after a series of dangerous mistakes, the Kaiser managed to get the river Neisse between two of his divisions and his corps was soundly defeated. He was incensed.

Waldersee saw himself as an historical teaching leader. In the summary comments of the last GGS ride that he led in early 1890, Waldersee concluded his remarks to the assembled officers by thanking them for their attention, hard work, and intelligence. If one of you is motivated to further study, if any of you have learned even one thing, then the exercise was a success, he said. "Each of you must study and understand military history for it is the master teacher which works not with theory but only with the power of actual events." Waldersee seemed confident that the image of past wars, as he read it in military history, corresponded exactly with what had happened on the battlefields.[57]

## Waldersee and Mobilization

In March 1882, at Waldersee's suggestion, Moltke had discussed mobilization problems with Kaiser Wilhelm I and had persuaded the Kaiser to issue a cabinet order authorizing accurate and rigorous testing of mobilization procedures. What worried Waldersee when he briefed Moltke was that increased size and speed could lead to disastrous confusion. Waldersee wanted to begin testing for the breaking points of the war mobilization system. By the late 1880s four mechanisms were placed in operation by means of which the GGS vertically integrated its war plan throughout the Reich army. These mechanisms were the railroad LCs, the chief of staff system, the DC system, and standardized procedures.

By 1890, the German railroad system was divided for military

---

57. Kitchen, *German Officer Corps*, pp. 17–21, 87; Mohs, *Waldersee*, 2: 17, 231.

purposes into twenty LCs. Each had peacetime responsibilities for overseeing the construction of new rail lines, for maintaining and upgrading existing lines and stations, and beginning in the 1880s, for practicing mobilization exercises. In 1883 the LCs had been reorganized and the whole system decentralized. Communication and coordination between the various federal railroads was still incomplete, yet the possibility of joining all the LCs with the RRS in Berlin via telegraph and telephone suggested that the national rail network could be technologically unified even if the system was still organizationally separate. But many difficulties still remained because there were so many different railroads operating within the German states. In addition, there was another problem which made integration difficult. The MTP was written in local time. It had to be translated into unitary time and thus reconciled for all of Germany. There were five different time zones in the Reich: in north Germany and Saxony, Berlin time; in Bavaria, that of Munich; in Württemberg that of Stuttgart; in Baden, that of Karlsruhe; and on the Rhine Palatinate that of Ludwigshaven. Thus the railroad traveler found that at each new railway station there was a different time which did not accord with his watch. Independent railroads and separate time zones created problems for military mobilization.

A second integrating mechanism was the DC system. The two hundred DCs were responsible for mobilization orders for over a million reserves, substitutes, and Landwehr. During the year, over 120,000 of these were called up for maneuvers and "control assemblies" to test out communication, addresses, and so forth.[58] A third integrating mechanism was the chief of staff system, which tied together the GGS in Berlin with each TGS in the corps and divisions. Each of the fourteen corps and thirty-seven divisions had its own general staff, modeled after the GGS in Berlin and staffed with officers educated at the War Academy and trained in the GGS. The line and staff format meant a constant rotation of officers in and out of Berlin. One way to monitor this interchange is by examining the lists of officers who participated in the GGS rides each year. For example, for the nine rides from 1882 through 1890, of the 276 officers who took part only six reappeared in successive rides. There is no indication that Waldersee called together all chiefs of staff for periodic conferences, but at least in the war mobilization

---

58. Rahne, *Mobilmachung*, pp. 88–89.

plan, in summer maneuvers, and through the MTP, all chiefs of staff had to respond to the same rules, regulations, and time frame.[59]

Thus a fourth integrating mechanism was that of bureaucratic procedures. The office procedures of the GGS established a standard which was replicated at corps and division headquarters. Since the administrative unit of the Prussian army prior to 1914 was the army corps, the corps staff was the unit through which the administrative information flow of the division passed. What did these staff officers do as chiefs of staff of corps and divisions? The so-called 1a was completely in charge of marches, quarters, movements of troops, drills and maneuvers, mobilization, roads, railways and telegraph, frontier and political questions, the strength, condition and distribution of neighboring foreign armies, bridging and pontooning, and maps. In other words, they replicated at a lower level many tasks that were also carried out in the GGS in Berlin. But like the GGS, their main job was to be sure the corps and its subordinate components were ready to execute the war plan.[60]

In peacetime, the chief of staff was also the office manager for the corps command. He carried out the same job that the adjutants and chancellery carried out in Berlin. For example, officers serving as corps adjutants, judge advocates, and commissariat, medical, and chaplains had to report first to the chief of the general staff before they reported to the commanding general. It was the 1a who decided if they needed to report directly to the commander or if matters could be handled according to standard regulations. During the weekly interviews or "audiences" with the commanding general, modeled on those of the GGS chief with the Kaiser, only the 1a remained when other officers transacted their business. It was the chief of the TGS who made sure that work assigned to officers and units within the corps was carried out correctly and within the time frame specified.

The office procedure of the corps was highly formalized, like that of the GGS. Every letter addressed to the commander was opened by either the general himself or by his 1a and was marked with the date of receipt, together with the section to which it was referred for action. A registry of consecutively numbered incoming and outgoing correspondence was kept which included the name of the official from whom it was received, the date of

59. Mohs, *Waldersee*, 2: 121–244.
60. Schellendorff, *Duties*, pp. 110, 122; Boehn, *Generalstabsgeschäfte*, pp. 107–17.

receipt, a précis of the contents, the number of enclosures, if any, and the number of the section to which it was referred. There were numerous other kinds of records kept by corps commands. All of them had to do with control, direction, and routing of internal information. There was the chief index, a book indexing the registry by date, person, office, and action. Other examples include the order book containing the originals of royal orders received by the headquarters; the work schedule kept by each subsection of the headquarters, which described the time allotted for the completion of each piece of assigned work; the time calendar showing the periods of time allotted for transaction of business on documents received or sent out; and finally, three ledgers cataloging in detail the army corps books, service regulations, and maps. The massive correspondence generated by the corps was duplicated at lower headquarters.[61]

In contrast to this large paper flow, an active Prussian corps of approximately 12,000 men was led by a staff of perhaps twenty-five officers. Active divisions of around 6,000 men were headed by a similarly small general staff of about ten officers. Expansion to war mobilized strength, approximately doubling these numbers but preserving the ratio of staff to troops. As we have argued above, this lean tooth-to-tail ratio is characteristic of the Prussian army – and of Prussian monarchical society. The few commanded the many. This had important and positive ramifications in terms of management efficiency and organizational decision making.[62] Each of these mechanisms, the railroad LCs, the DCs, the general staff system, and the bureaucratic procedures allowed a degree of decentralization but preserved standardization and uniformity throughout the army.

By 1889, Waldersee's second year as chief, four trends in war planning are visible. The first was for the speedier transition to an operations-ready army. This meant increased speed of mobilization and enhanced interlinking of active army, reserves, Landwehr, and Landsturm. The second was for a heavier first strike resulting from the increased use of artillery and larger concentrations massed in the first attack.[63] A third trend called for secrecy of information. By

---

61. Schellendorff, *Duties*, pp. 110–22.
62. M. von dem Bergh, *Das deutsche Heer vor dem Weltkrieg* (Berlin, 1934), pp. 27–46; Walter Elze, *Tannenberg: Das deutsche Heer vor 1914: Seine Grundzüge und deren Auswirkung im Sieg an der Ostfront* (Breslau, 1928), pp. 13–15.
63. Rahne, *Mobilmachung*, p. 104.

the early 1890s a document classification system was introduced. "For official use only," "confidential," and "secret" markings begin to show up on GGS war planning documents. Neither the War Ministry nor GGS gave any information about active duty strength, collecting points for the war plan, length of time of mobilization, or numbers of reserve forces away. Within the GGS, information on mobilization was given out on a strict "need to know" basis. Only a few officers in the mobilization and railroad sections knew all there was to know about the war plans. A fourth trend was in premobilization action. This concept is reflected in Waldersee's use of the term "preparatory measures," meaning actions taken before the actual public declaration of war. He apparently feared that in a crisis situation the government would lose foreign policy "freedom" if steps were not taken prior to an actual war declaration. He wanted to insure the speedy transition to an operations-ready army that would appear on the field earlier and with larger forces. Test mobilizations of the army corps, begun in 1890, complimented the emphasis on speed. Portions of the corps went through simulated mobilizations when notified by the GGS. The tests were monitored, the units debriefed, and the results compared with earlier tests.

Coincident with these, Waldersee in about 1890 considered the first change in actual mobilization plans. Three years prior to this, he and Moltke had already disagreed on strategic thinking. Moltke planned a strategic defense in the west, a limited offensive in Poland. Waldersee wanted offensive action aimed at victory in both Poland and Lorraine. To do this he strengthened the west front by two additional army corps moved from the east and put in a request for a new corps, the 17th.[64]

### War Games and War Plans

In spite of all these changes, neither the strategic war games nor the actual war plans were substantially altered. On the contrary, they retained the same form and content, balanced and cautious, that Moltke had given them a decade before. To demonstrate this, let us compare one of the GGS exercises during Waldersee's tenure with the then-current war plan. The GGS ride conducted in

---

64. Ibid., pp. 104–9; Kessel, "Die Tätigkeit des Grafen Waldersee," p. 202.

East Prussia on 13–30 June 1888 is instructive in many ways. Waldersee laid it out and directed it on the first day, but had to return to Berlin that evening for Kaiser Frederick's funeral. Schlieffen became conductor. Aiding Schlieffen were five officers of the "conductory." Teams consisted of eleven officers for east (Russia) and thirteen for west (Prussia). The exercise began with the officers arriving in Gumbinnen by train with horses on 13 June. During the next eighteen days they made nine rides, covering 180 miles at the rate of about 15 to 20 miles per day, which is about one day's march for war armed troops, simulating a campaign between two armies of roughly 100,000 men, in a real space of about 4,200 square miles, and in a real time about half as long as the exercise. The general situation was that Germany had mobilized in response to dangerous actions by Russia and Russian mobilization followed.[65]

The specific situation for west created a new army with headquarters at Insterburg and forces distributed south to Goldap and southwest to Angerburg. Its mission was to protect East Prussia and to secure the left flank of the main army astride the Weichsel River. Forces available were two army corps, two reserve divisions, and two cavalry divisions. Standing "mobilization ready" in Königsberg were railroad companies and artillery batteries. West's forces were to be "operations ready" on 1 August. Fortresses at Königsberg, Pillau, Memel, and Boyen were placed in a state of war readiness. The specific situation for east created a new army along the Narew and Niemen rivers with forces distributed along the line Kowno-Vilna-Grodno-Bialystok. Its force consisted of three corps and three cavalry divisions. The invasion of East Prussia was ordered beginning 1 August on two fronts: from the east an advance was made to set and hold defending German forces and from the south a stronger, deeper drive was made toward Königsberg, separating East Prussia and cutting west's supply and communications line. Each commander was ordered to assess the situation and issue general orders and specific rail transportation lists. The outcome was that west, finding itself between two major east concentrations, using railroads for rapid movement, inflicted a defeat on one of these forces at the Narew River, then pulled back to the north, rejoining the main army which then attacked the

65. Mohs, *Waldersee*, 2: 199–203.

invading east forces moving northwest from Russia.[66]

The summer 1888 GGS ride played out one-half of the war plan contained in Moltke's memorandum of February 1888 then in effect, and it envisioned a two-front-war, a campaign against Russia fought simultaneously with a war against France. German east front force level was seven corps, plus twelve Austrian corps. With forces of 935,000 (German-Austrian) against 757,000 (Russian), two German corps were sent to Gumbinnen and Lyck, the eastern border of Prussia, to confront the Russian Niemen army. The other five were stretched along a 140-mile front from Hohensalza to Ortelsburg to defend against the Narew army. The war plan estimated that the Russian main force at Warsaw would take at least four weeks to mobilize. From there the distance to the border of Silesia was 140 miles. Changes were made in the war plan in March 1888 because two new Russian armies had been moved into position opposite the Prussian east border, on a line Kowno to Kischinew, a 375-mile front. This force of 240,000 might turn south against the Austrian main force or move directly toward Berlin. Space and time factors became very important. The route to Berlin was 375 miles and it was considered unlikely that the Russians would make a direct push against the German capital city. To conquer the Province of East Prussia, the war plan estimated that the Russians could attack Gumbinnen with 186,000 men against the 115,000 of the Prussian 4th Army, a superiority which was to be compensated for by reinforcing with Prussian Landsturm from Königsberg and by the careful use of terrain. If the 4th Army retreated, Prussia would then have 351,000 men operating on inner lines between two enemy armies.[67]

There are a number of correlations between the 1888 GGS ride and war plan. For one thing, both employed a defensive-offensive strategy based upon conservation of power in the face of superior forces. Prussian forces were to wait for Russia to make the first moves, then react, capitalizing especially on Russian mistakes. Such a strategy depended upon good intelligence and wise use of terrain. Strategic movement by railroads enabled Prussia to take advantage of the differential timing between Prussian and Russian mobilization and geographic locations. The expectation was that a

66. Ibid.
67. Mohs, *Waldersee*, 2: 203; Ludwig Freiherr von Gebsattel, *Generalfeldmarschall Karl von Bülow* (Munich, 1929), pp. 22–23. Schmerfeld, *Aufmarschpläne*, pp. 154–55.

smaller Prussian force would be able to beat a larger Russian one by movement and timing, using inner lines.

Interestingly enough, two features of the 1888 general staff ride reappear twenty-six years later during the opening weeks of the Great War. One is personnel. In 1888, the sixth ranking officer on west side was a forty-one-year-old major named Paul von Beneckendorff und von Hindenburg. A second is terrain. Quarters during the ride, begun at Gumbinnen on 13 June 1888, were Goldat, Darkemen, Angerburg, Rastenburg, Bischopsburg, Passenheim, and Allenstein. The final three reappear at the Battle of Tannenberg, 22 August 1914; the first six at the Battle of the Masurian Lakes, 12 September 1914. During the following twenty-six years, general staff, corps, and divisional rides and exercises played over this ground and this exercise area a dozen times, intermingling officers from lieutenant to general who had been there before and would be again. Seldom in military history have such deep-future-oriented strategic planning and exercises been attended by such a degree of good fortune in final execution.[68]

During Waldersee's tenure as chief, three war plans were promulgated, of which two were dated 1 April 1889 and 1 April 1890. The third of 1 April 1891 was also his, as Schlieffen had only been appointed on 7 February and it is unlikely that he had made any substantial changes by 1 April. We should note that no historian has devoted descriptive power to Waldersee as a strategist. As Eberhard Kessel emphasized, Waldersee was much more the practical troop leader and much less a true general staffer.[69]

In reviewing Waldersee as a strategist, Kessel concluded that he had three main characteristics. First, although at times he appeared to stray away from the Moltke war plans, in fact he did not. In May 1890 Waldersee had an audience with the Kaiser in which he apparently discussed a complete change in the mobilization plans for the east front. The Kaiser agreed and Waldersee discussed the ideas with the deputy chiefs and with Moltke. But nothing was done. The general lines remained the same through 1891. Second, Waldersee, like Moltke, was concerned with the defense of southwest Germany. Several GGS rides, exercises, and maneuvers dealt with a French invasion through Switzerland. Third, Waldersee worked with Germany's allies, Austria and Italy. Following the

68. Mohs, *Waldersee*, 2: 203.
69. Kessel, "Die Tätigkeit des Grafen Waldersee," p. 206.

signing of the Triple Alliance in 1882, he tried to integrate Italy into German war planning.[70] Waldersee believed, above all, that France wanted Alsace-Lorraine back and that, in a war, it would invade Lorraine. In that case there was insufficient space across the border to oppose a mobilization. The French, however, would not just sit behind their fortresses; public opinion would force them into an offensive across the German border. When that happened, many opportunities were created. GGS rides, exercises, and maneuvers often enacted precisely this scenario.[71]

Waldersee's strategic goals are not found in the war plans. It was in his correspondence with Moltke and in his conclusions to GGS rides and exercises that he put forth his radical ideas for a victory on two fronts. But he did not implement these ideas. After listening to his discourse for seven years, it is proper to ask what impact this had on Schlieffen, who took over in February 1891. In strategic thinking Waldersee was influenced by Moltke and Schlieffen by Waldersee. However, both the domestic and foreign task environment were dramatically different after 1891. Waldersee's bellicosity found little response either at home or abroad. Up until March 1890 German domestic leadership was stable and consistent, German diplomacy carefully calculated to maintain the balance of power, particularly vis-à-vis Russia. The reinsurance treaty and the Austrian alliance helped to guarantee a single-front war. Bismarck fought Waldersee's intrigues in favor of preventive war successfully.[72] Waldersee's contribution within the GGS was to give it independence, very high technical and intellectual standards in appointments, education and exercises, and a substantial bureaucratic reorganization. At the same time, outside the GGS the whole defense environment was beginning to change.

At 6 P.M. on 18 March 1890, with Bismarck gone, the young Kaiser gathered his military leaders together in the Berlin Schloß: the chief of the general staff, the army inspectors, and the commanding generals, a select group of two dozen high officers. His

---

70. Ibid., p. 205; Mohs, *Waldersee*, 2: 331.

71. BAMA *Nachlaß Beseler*, Lebenserinnerungen, p. 49.

72. Mohs, *Waldersee*, 2: 232–342; Konrad Canis, *Bismarck und Waldersee: Die außenpolitischen Krisenerscheinungen und das Verhalten des Generalstabes, 1882–1890* (East Berlin, 1980), pp. 250–78; idem, "Bismarck, Waldersee und die Kriegsgefahr Ende 1887," in Horst Bartel and Ernst Engelberg, eds., *Die großpreußisch-militaristische Reichsgründung 1871* (East Berlin, 1971), pp. 396–435; Kitchen, *German Officer Corps*, pp. 64–95; Schmerfeld, *Aufmarschpläne*, pp. 99–166; Craig, *Politics*, pp. 266ff.

purpose was to lay out Verdy du Vernois's defense plan. To give it a properly theatrical context, Wilhelm began by stating that "since the Seven Years' War, Prussia has never been in such a dangerous position!" It was a theme which was to be echoed with increasing stridency during the next twenty-four years. Although substantially false in 1890, within a decade the Reich leadership itself had done much to make this statement credible.[73]

Shortly after this meeting the Waldersee-Wilhelm II relationship fell out due to Waldersee's political intrigues and also to GGS war gaming. In 1890 Wilhelm launched a broad criticism of a solution to a War Academy examination. It was so harsh that Waldersee, who had written the problem and its solution, felt he had to resign. His resignation was not accepted. Months later in full hearing of a roomful of officers, Waldersee criticized Wilhelm's solution to a problem at the conclusion of an exercise. Four months later, in February 1891, Waldersee was appointed commander of the 9th Corps in Altoona.[74]

Meanwhile the strategic situation confronting Germany was changing. This situation was summarized by Field Marshall von Moltke in a famous speech to the Reichstag in March 1891. When this war that has been hanging over our heads like the sword of Damocles for more than ten years comes, he said, neither its length nor its ending can be foreseen. The great powers of Europe confront each other for war armed as never before. None of them can be so completely annihilated, in one or two campaigns, that they will declare themselves defeated. This war may last seven years, it could last thirty years.[75]

73. Kessel, *Moltke*, p. 746.
74. BAMA Nachlaß Beseler, Lebenserinnerungen, p. 42. Cf. Lamar Cecil, *Wilhelm II: Prince and Emperor, 1859–1900* (Chapel Hill, 1989), pp. 182–87.
75. Generalleutnant a.D. von Zoellner, "Schlieffens Vermächtnis," *Militärwissenschaftliche Rundschau*, Sonderheft (January 1938): 12.

# Chapter 3

# Schlieffen and the
# New Strategic Era, 1891–1896

Alfred Graf Schlieffen has remained an enigma since that January day in 1913 when he died, supposedly after uttering the fateful words: "It must come to a fight. Only make the right wing strong enough!" His statements became army mythology. "What is thinkable is attainable!" "Say little, do much. Be more than you appear." This is the same man who, according to colleagues, began his day at 6 A.M. in the general staff map room, worked regularly until eleven at night, and then completed the evening by reading his daughters to sleep with military history. He was called "master teacher," "genius," and the "sphinx who encloses the secret of victory" by general staff officers of the next generation.[1] It is strange that Schlieffen was so venerated for he was only the author of a plan that failed. He did not win great victories like Moltke the Elder. He was not around to put the plan into action as Moltke the Younger was. As Eberhard Kessel noted, what would we think of Moltke the Elder if we had only his campaign plans, but not their successful outcome?[2]

## *Schlieffen: Hutterian and Uhlan, 1833–1884*

Schlieffen's identity was anchored in his family. Born on 28 February 1833 in Berlin, his mother stemmed from a preeminent noble family, the Stolbergs from Wernigerode, one of the five largest landowning families in Prussia. On the court order of precedence of 1878, Schlieffen's uncle occupied the first place,

---

1. Hugo Rochs, *Schlieffen: Ein Lebens- und Charakterbild für das deutsche Volk*, 2d ed. (Berlin, 1921), p. 90; "Viel leisten, wenig hervortreten – mehr sein als scheinen," in MGFA, *Tradition in deutschen Streitkräften*, p. 6. Schlieffen apparently got this from Goethe, whom he read assiduously. Goethe borrowed it from Tycho de Brahe, "appears as nothing, but be all."
2. Kessel, *Schlieffens Briefe*, p. 23.

his grandfather's family the twenty-first, far ahead of the Bismarck family at forty-second place on a list with sixty-two rankings. His father, a captain in the 2d Foot Guard, had been raised to the *Grafenstand* in 1812. The third born of eleven brothers and sisters, Alfred met his double first cousin Gräfin Anna when she was eleven and married her a decade later on his parent's wedding anniversary.[3]

3. Arno Mayer, *The Persistence of the Old Regime* (New York, 1981), p. 26; Fedor von Zobeltitz, *Chronik der Gesellschaft unter dem letzten Kaiserreich*, 2d ed., 2 vols. (Hamburg, 1922), 1: 327. His mother's family was part of the *Standesherren*, those high nobility deposed by Napoleon. The Stolberg-Wernigerodes were *Reichsunmittelbare*: they were technically subject to the emperor alone and were addressed formally as *Durchlaucht*, illustrious, whereas ordinary Grafs were *Hochgeboren*. Graf Christian Friedrich had left Westphalia when it was ruled by Jerome Bonaparte and had migrated to the Silesian mountains. He settled on two estates, Peterswaldau and Kreppelhof, which between them contained thirteen villages and more than ten thousand inhabitants. Alfred's mother was born in 1809 at Peterswaldau. Joachim von Dissow, *Adel im Übergang: Ein kritischer Standesgenosse berichtet aus Residenzen und Gutshäusern* (Stuttgart, 1961), p. 74; Dr. Carl Prinz Radziwill, *Entwicklung des fürstlich-Stolbergischen Grundbesitzes* (Jena, 1899). For the economic background see Johannes Ziekursch, *Hundert Jahre schlesischer Agrargeschichte*, 2d ed (Aalen, 1978); Clemons Wischermann, "Zur Industrialisierung des deutschen Braugewerbes im 19. Jahrhundert: Das Beispiel der Reichsgräflich zu Stolbergischen Brauerei Westheim im Westfalen, 1860–1913," *Zeitschrift für Unternehmensgeschichte* 30 (1985): 143–80.

At the foot of the Riesen Mountains in Moravia, not far from Groß Krausche, was Kreppelhof, estate of Graf Anton von Stolberg. Nearby was Fischbach, the estate of the prince and princess of Prussia, who were old friends; Anton had been the prince's adjutant at the Battle of Belle Alliance. Field Marshal Graf Gneisenau lived nearby at Erdmannsdorf. The Stolberg-Wernigerodes, as one of the ranking Prussian families, were close to the throne. In 1830 Anton, youngest of the four brothers, was appointed governor of the Rhineland and adjutant to Prince Wilhelm and in 1842 became minister of state and head of the privy council in Berlin. Arnold Wellner, ed., *Anne Countess zu Stolberg-Wernigerode* (London, 1873), pp. 22–75. Otto Furst zu Stolberg-Wernigerode was the first Prussian *Ober Präsident* of Hanover, vice chancellor under Bismarck, and *Oberst Kammers* for Kaiser Wilhelm I. He was the reigning Graf in Prussia throughout the century. Graf Udo Stolberg was president of the Reichstag in 1900; John Röhl, "Hof und Hofgesellschaft unter Kaiser Wilhelm II," in Karl F. Weaner, ed., *Hof, Kultur und Politik im 19. Jahrhundert* (Bonn, 1985), pp. 230–69; Wolfgang Zorn, "Unternehmer und Aristokratie in Deutschland," *Zeitschrift für Firmengeschichte und Unternehmerbiographie* 8, no. 6 (1963); Heinz Gollwitzer, *Die Standesherren: Die politische und gesellschaftliche Stellung den Mediatisierten, 1815–1918*, 2d ed. (Göttingen, 1964), p. 44; Rochs, *Schlieffen*, p. 13; Kessel, *Schlieffens Briefe*, p. 300; Stephan von Stradonitz, "Über die Zuständigkeit des preußischen Heroldsamts," *Archiv für öffentliches Recht* 18 (1903): 191ff.

As Fritz Stern has written, nobility of this rank and kind were honored because their position combined personal freedom with a strict moral code. They were thought of as people of honor and service, correct and incorruptible. One admired their moral certainty, their often impoverished but proud existence; the cold, steely eyes that did not cast an envious look upward. One sensed and often envied their

His mother's branch of the Stolberg-Wernigerodes was defined and organized by Hutterian Pietism. These evangelical nobles participated in the Prussian "great awakening" during Schlieffen's childhood. The Herrenhuter community at Gnadenberg stood on estate land. Schlieffen's mother, mother-in-law, and wife were fervent Hutterians, who spent their summers entertaining circuit-riding evangelists and their winters at home and in country churchs. There were settlements at Niesky, Lobau, Muskau, all around the estate. Johannes Gossner, one of the great Hutterian preachers, was a regular guest in Schlieffen's home. Hutterianism supplied religion, entertainment, education, and social life. It defined Alfred's world, providing vocabulary, images, and a worldview.[4] In periods of change there are sometimes bridges from one life-style to another. For Schlieffen, one such bridge was Hutterian Pietism. Philosophically transcendental but infused with the practical modern work ethos, Hutterianism uniquely prepared Schlieffen for the emerging bureaucratic world of the GGS, which combined conservative life values with progressive ideas about work and planning. Paradoxically the fit between Hutterianism and the general staff was surprisingly close. In both, time, space, and size were measured and utilized along the daily path. But only as the means to the end. For the individual, just as for the organization, the purpose

---

rootedness in the land, their proximity to nature, their familiarity with life as it had been lived for millenia, dependent on the exigencies of climate and crop. They were on easy terms with the common folk. They knew their peasants and loved their animals; they were, or so it seemed to the outsider, unbrokenly themselves, less affected, less afraid. Something of an older and purer world clung to them. Much more than a mere product of military triumphs and ideals, their respect derived from voluntary subordination to a more persistent ideal. Stern, "Prussia," p. 61; Ferdinand Tönnies, "Deutscher Adel im neunzehnten Jahrhundert," *Neue Rundschau* 2 (1912): 1041–63; Otto Graf zu Stolberg-Wernigerode, *Die unentschiedene Generation: Deutschlands konservative Führungsschichten am Vorabend des Ersten Weltkrieges* (Munich, 1968), p. 159.

4. Herman Dalton, *Johannes Goßner: Ein Lebensbild aus der Kirche des neunzehnten Jahrhunderts*, 3d ed. (Berlin-Friedenau, 1898), p. 346; Rochs, *Schlieffen*, pp. 13–14; Kessel, *Schlieffens Briefe*, p. 13; Mary Fulbrook, *Piety and Politics: Religion and the Rise of Absolutism in England, Württemberg, and Prussia* (Cambridge, 1983); Martin Brecht, "Der Spätpietismus: Ein vergessenes oder vernachlässigtes Kapitel der protestantischen Kirchengeschichte," *Pietismus und Neuzeit* 10 (1984): 124–51; Holborn, *Modern Germany*, 2: 137ff.; Robert M. Bigler, *The Politics of German Protestantism: The Rise of the Protestant Church Elite in Prussia, 1815–1848* (Berkeley, 1972); Robert M. Berdahl, *The Politics of the Prussian Nobility: The Development of a Conservative Ideology, 1770–1848* (Princeton, 1988), pp. 247–53. Few have dealt with religion and nineteenth-century modernization, although for earlier periods the connection has been made. Cf. Richard L. Gawthrop, "Lutheran Pietism and the Weber Thesis," *German Studies Review* 12, no. 2 (May 1989): 237–48.

of life was directed by a higher law toward an ancient transcendent purpose.

Hutterites participated in both sacred and secular time. Sacred time related to beliefs about creation. Secular time measured events that took place on earth. Sermons, read from German script, were exact copies of sixteenth-century texts. Each person was reminded that God's time was measured by eternity, in contrast to the swift flow of hours during the busy workweek. Between sacred and secular time were history and dreams. History was seen as a dimension of the presence of God in the world. It was a source of strength to the faithful, not a dated sequence of events. There was a blending of the deep past and recent events: miracles of the sixteenth century were fused with those of the nineteenth, since the worldly time sequence was unimportant. History was a dimension of secular time that was recalled primarily because it illustrated eternity.[5]

Daily life was broken into small units that formed a correct, although not rigid, schedule. This severe patterning meant that individual members of the colony had little free choice and few decisions to make. Since material objects were not owned by the Hutterite, he also had little concept of private time. The time that was needed for the completion of an operation, for example, building a goose shed, not the time contributed by the various individuals, was given careful thought. The speed with which an individual worked within the community, however, gave him status. A woman knew how long it took her to make an article of clothing, and both adults and children set up tasks in such a way that the speed with which they finished was obvious. There was a great emphasis on practical work completed, following a daily, weekly, and annual schedule. The basic plan varied with the time of year. It was modified by weather or adjusted to accommodate special tasks. When colony work was pressing, evening church could be cancelled. Work stood above all else as a measure of service.

Authority was at the same time divine and corporate. All authority, whether inside or outside the colony, was believed to originate with God. Governmental authority over the secular world was also said to be so ordained. Baptized members were believed to have received supernatural gifts through obedience and submission. The corporate group had the power to exclude and to accept

5. John Hostetler, *Hutterite Society* (Baltimore, 1974), pp. 153–66.

members. The preacher was elected by lot and ordained to full power only after several years of proven leadership.[6]

As in all distinctive subcultures, the sense of belonging was enhanced by signs and symbols that distinguished members from nonmembers. For Hutterites the symbols included their manner of dress, gestures, leisure, and nonverbal forms of communication. Gestures were subdued and severely limited according to a stylized, not individualized, pattern. Modesty and restraint characterized conversational patterns. The young were expected to show respect, take orders, and avoid reference to personal opinions. Meaningless talk was frowned upon and foolish remarks brought reproach. Singing, reading, visiting, and going for long walks were acceptable forms of leisure. It was a culture of austerity, a way of living more frugally and doing so with dignity and purpose.[7]

This was the model in Schlieffen's family and early life: the influence of the Herrenhuter community was dominant in forming his character and personality. Austerity, strictness, order, submission – ancient rural virtues of traditional Prussia. History infused with God's mission, recent events intertwined with ancient ones. From divine and corporate authority it was an easy transition to royal and regimental. At Easter 1842 Alfred went off to grammar school at Niesky, joining his older brother Theodor who had entered the year before. Niesky was Pietistic in general and Hutterian in particular, one of the best-known schools for sons of the country nobility, officials, and officers.[8]

Niesky was communitarian and intellectual. It was not organized in school classes in the modern sense, but instead each member ate, slept, and prayed in the comradeship of the community. They were a large family, set off from the rest of the world. Herrenhuters believed in high standards. Strong in old German literature as well as the best modern German writers, the school was also good in science and math. Schlieffen studied Latin, French, and mathematics and engaged in football, sledding, and ice skating as well as gardening. Niesky was also military and Prussian. The Niesky regiment elected its own officers and dedicated itself to God and Prussia. First Corinthians 6:20 was their model: "You do not belong to yourself but to God, he bought you for a price, so use your

6. Ibid., pp. 195–201.
7. Ibid.
8. Helmuth Kittel, *Alfred Graf Schlieffen: Jugend und Glaube* (Berlin, 1939), p. 14.

bodies for God's glory." The ideal of competition was fostered, whether in sports or schoolwork, in marching and swimming in summer or sledding and skating in winter. Everything worked competitively, nurturing a knightly manner and making great demands on the individual. This must have been difficult for Alfred, for his school record showed that the main tendency of his character was shyness. He had talent, but a phlegmatic, apathetic exterior, and was often slow in his work. The Niesky regiment conducted war games modeled after historic Prussian victories. It celebrated the sovereign's birthday with parades and exercises and in June 1844, Prussian king Frederick Wilhelm IV greeted the school during its final exercises.[9] Finally, Niesky was aristocratic. Alfred's classmates comprised a dictionary of the old noble families of the kingdom of Prussia. When he was at Niesky, members of the Dönhoff, Lüttwitz, Bonin, Bülow, Schlippenbach, Dohna, Gneisenau, Falkenhayn, Schwerin, Wartensleben, Reuß, Richthofen, Schweinitz, and Stein families also attended. Many lived on country estates and did not have access to city schools. Comradeship such as this is said to have marked its members for life.[10]

In September 1847 at age fourteen, Schlieffen went to live with his uncles in Berlin. Since the Niesky Pedagogium did not give the secondary school certificate, Theodore and Alfred entered the Joachimsthal Gymnasium. Established in 1607, it was known for its solid humanistic education and Christian character formation. At Niesky it mattered less that you were of the nobility; what was more important was your participation in the "comradeship" of the community. Schlieffen, as a young adult in Berlin, became part of the social world of the high nobility there. In Berlin the nobility lived apart. They believed that their special privileges were based upon their professional relationship to the state: those who served as officers or high officials fulfilled the role designated as the duty of their class. Many relatives lived in Berlin and Potsdam and the brothers grew up in this powerful family circle. For the next six years his family world was shared with the classical gymnasium, from which he took his Abitur at Easter 1853. In Berlin Schlieffen went his own way. He read a great deal of history and geography, took an extra half year to finish, and then simultaneously enrolled at Berlin University as a law student and as an *Einjährig-Freiwilliger* in

9. Ibid., p. 30.
10. Ibid., p. 24; Stolberg-Wernigerode, *Unentschiedene Generation*, pp. 182ff.

the 2d Guard Uhlan Regiment.[11]

In Berlin his conservative political views were confirmed. During the "March Days" of 1848 violent demonstrations erupted as students with sabers seemed to control the city. Outside his windows a shoemaker and a papermaker were killed, and a man lost an arm in a military charge. An uhlan, knocked off his horse, was beaten to death by the mob. Speeches were made, barricades erected, the military fired into the crowds. The mob was bayoneted out of the second-story windows of the Kölnisch Rathaus. His uncle Carl, commander of the 2d Guard Regiment, brought the news of the troop withdrawal from the city to the cheers of the crowds, and on 20 March in the afternoon the city was empty of line regiments. Students with cavalry swords loafed about. On the 21st, the day the king toured Berlin wearing the revolutionary tricolor, his uncle's family packed away their silver and clothing and fled to the town of Potsdam, well outside the city limits. Other Stolberg-Wernigerodes were already there, and the house was full. "When the Berliners come, we don't know what will happen," they muttered. In Potsdam everything was quiet. By 30 May things had quieted down. On his way to the gymnasium, Schlieffen encountered Landwehr battalions, with flags and music. Revolutionary activities lasted through October, when barricades and flags were still visible as he walked the city streets.[12]

By September 1853 Alfred had completed the first half of his service year, and the time was approaching when he had to decide if he should remain. His father suggested that he talk to a cousin, who at that time was adjutant to the commander of the Guard Cavalry, to find out if he could go directly into the regiment or if the father should write to the regimental commander, as was the custom. In October 1853 Schlieffen was accepted as *Avantageur* with the 2d Guard Uhlan and was promoted to *Portepee-Fänrich* in December and to lieutenant a year later. Colonel von der Goltz, commanding, wrote to Alfred's father that he was happy to receive Schlieffen into the regiment.[13]

During his *Leutnantzeit* (1854–58) Schlieffen and his brother Theodor were called the "crazy Schlieffens." Quiet, reserved, and self-deprecating, Schlieffen was a man whose humor and sarcasm

11. Kittel, *Schlieffen*, p. 42; Kessel, *Schlieffens Briefe*, pp. 37–38.
12. Kessel, *Schlieffens Briefe*, pp. 72, 43–47, 80.
13. Ibid., p. 85.

were highly valued. It is said that he introduced Friedrich von Holstein, at the time a young civil servant in Berlin, to society and established a relationship with him that became important three decades later, when Schlieffen was chief of the GGS and Holstein was arbiter of German foreign policy. Even though the evidence for this is slim, the relationship with Holstein is likely. If they became friends in the 1850s, crossed paths in Berlin in the 1880s, and met again in the 1890s, both in positions of influence based on professional reputations of thirty years, it is less difficult to accept the method Schlieffen is said to have used to present his war plan to the small elite in Berlin that mattered in these affairs. Both men had grown up in the high nobility, on country estates, both tended to be shy and withdrawn. Both took their Abitur in 1853 and entered Berlin University to study law. In spite of Norman Rich's skepticism, a Schlieffen-Holstein relationship in the 1850s makes sense.[14]

During the first twelve years of his military career (1853–65), Schlieffen went through a great deal of doubt and questioning. At times he believed he would have been better off as a civil bureaucrat. He was always in competition with his brothers during the early years. Training recruits, he approached them as future defenders of the fatherland, not as tools of the inner mission, as one of his colleagues suggested. Why had Prussia had so much military misfortune? He asked his parents for money for a horse and lamented about his debts.[15] Schlieffen's view of "Travailler pour le roi de Prusse" was that modern life demanded certain changes. His father's family had settled in Pomerania in the twelfth century and had resided in Kolberg, where they had been members of the Kolberg city council. Once upon a time the relationship of the state official to economic society was a practical compromise in which nobles and nonnobles mixed together, with nobles dominant. In the city council of Kolberg this was explained by the fact that councilors received such small salaries. Kolberg shopkeepers were content to make money and leave city government to the

14. Wilhelm Groener, *Das Testament Graf Schlieffen* (Berlin, 1930), p. 2; Norman Rich, *Friedrich von Holstein: Politics and Diplomacy in the Era of Bismarck and Wilhelm II*, 2 vols. (Cambridge, 1965), 1: 7–10, 2: 725–27; cf. Peter Rassow, "Schlieffen und Holstein," *Historische Zeitschrift* 173 (1952): 297–313; Kessel, *Schlieffens Briefe*, p. 54. It has been argued that until the 1860s both the industrial middle classes and the higher civil service families disdained military careers for their sons. Thereafter both looked on the army with more respect. cf. Gillis, *Prussian Bureaucracy*, pp. 203–4.

15. Kessel, *Schlieffens Briefe*, pp. 93, 95.

nobility. Schlieffen believed this system would no longer work. It had to be changed. Implied here are both a feeling that government office should be carried out by everyone and the view that those who did it ought to be reasonably well compensated.[16]

Schlieffen set his sights on attaining what he called a "scientific-military education." Chosen for the War Academy in fall 1858, he joined "forty young warriors" in his class. The War Academy at midcentury was quite different from when Moltke had attended in the 1820s. As we saw in chapter 2, it had begun the transition from broad, humanistic education toward narrower professional training. Everyone studied the engineer-geographer courses: mathematics, land survey, and fortifications, with heavy emphasis on military history. Yet, whereas Moltke had read Shakespeare and Goethe and studied French and English, Schlieffen studied the science and art of command and army leadership. Even the language describing the courses had changed. Schlieffen uses both *Feldherrnkunst* – the art of command – and Kriegswissenschaft – the science of war – in describing his courses. The traditional art of war was being supplanted by modern war science.[17]

Upon completing his term at the War Academy in 1861, Schlieffen spent five years in uncertainty. Prussia was in the midst of a military reorganization and constitutional crisis of the first magnitude. He was temporarily assigned to the Topographical Section of the General Staff. The summer of 1863 found him in Lithuania, Vilna, and Gumbinnen, close to the Russian border. He talked with Russian officers about the Polish Revolution. All the railroad stations had been protected against threatening possibilities. By July 1864 Schlieffen had failed to be assigned to the Danish War theater. In the Topographical Section things were slow. Summer maneuvers found him among the Masurian Lakes, staying with an estate owner in a one-story house roofed with straw near Rastenburg. He had once thought of taking over Groß Krausche, the family estate, but realized now that this was impossible. His father had died. At age thirty-one, he was the oldest first lieutenant in his regiment. His chance to be appointed to the general staff was gone. Schlieffen concluded, "I'm at the end of a faulted career."[18]

16. Friedrich von Boetticher, *Alfred Graf Schlieffen* (Göttingen, 1957), pp. 11–12; Rochs, *Schlieffen*, p. 88.
17. Kessel, *Schlieffens Briefe*, pp. 98–100.
18. Ibid., pp. 163, 170.

Soon his fortunes changed. In August 1865 he received his first invitation to participate in a three-week GGS ride in the Rhineland and Westphalia. In spring 1866 he was posted as military attaché to the Prussian Embassy in Paris and in March his engagement was announced. Six weeks later the war against Austria began.[19] By 3 May mobilization was decided upon. Four Schlieffen brothers went to war in 1866. Alfred knew by 19 May that he would be assigned as a staff officer to Prince Friedrich Karl, commander of the 1st Corps. Not much was known about this corps or where it would be assigned in the war. Schlieffen, however, knew every one of the officers leading it either personally or by reputation: the chief of staff was Colonel von Witzendorff, adjutant to Friedrich Karl and riding school director at Schwedt – energetic, determined, and moody; the first general staff officer was Major von Alvensleben, elegant, a bit caught up in himself, a well-known steeplechase rider; adjutants Rittmeister von Borres of the 11th Hussars, formerly adjutant to the Hohenzollerns at Düsseldorf and very skillful with superiors, and Rittmeister von Krosigk of the 5th Dragoon Regiment, extraordinarily able, very dependable, an excellent rider; the personal adjutants to the prince were Schlieffen's relative Rittmeister von Radecke of the 1st Lithuanian Dragoons, very clever and ebulient, whose second wife had a bad case of consumption, and Rittmeister Graf Hardenberg of the 12th Hussars, formerly of the GGS. Finally, there would be assorted minor princes and sovereigns along to curry Prussia's favor.[20]

The war actually began on 14 June. Twenty days later Prussia had defeated the Hanoverians at Langensalza and the Austrians at Königgrätz. Schlieffen participated in the latter conflict. The battle was concentrated in an area of about ten square miles, stretching from Sadowa on the northwest of Bistvitz Creek to Königgrätz in the southeast on the Elbe River. The Austrians stood on the high ground east of the Bistvitz and were pushed across the Elbe, retreating southeast of Könnigrätz. Schlieffen was not a combat officer. He often lamented only seeing the white flags and singing the victory hymns when it was all over. His cavalry corps arrived near Sucha at 8 A.M. to link up with the Elbe army expected to arrive on their right flank. They rode steadily, anticipating that the Austrian main force was somewhere to the rear. When the

19. Ibid., p. 174.
20. Ibid., pp. 191–92.

battle began, they thought they were facing only an advanced guard. In reality it was the Austrian main force of three armies, concentrated together. The staff held fast during an artillery barrage which lasted most of the morning. At 11 A.M. Schlieffen was sent to the prince for instructions and met him at Dub after passing through artillery fire at Mzan. His regiment had been attached to General Herwarth's 2d Division and it was ordered to draw up behind the defile of Sadowa. There they remained the whole afternoon, watching the high command up on the heights, musing over the virtual stalemate of the Prussian troops in front of them, and waiting expectantly for the arrival of the crown prince's army from the northeast.

At 4 P.M. that army appeared and the battlefield situation altered dramatically. At that point Schlieffen's division was ordered forward. His brigade moved across the Bistritz River and over the main road between Lipa and Chlum. At Langenhof a nasty cavalry fight developed as the Austrians made one last charge, playing for time to withdraw. Schlieffen watched the 3d Dragoons and the Curaisser Regiments Wrangel and Prince Karl of Prussia fighting bravely. His own brigade commander Graf Groeben was wounded. Schlieffen noted that fortunately it rained the whole day – as the heat would have affected the tired Prussians much more if it had been dry. The sun finally came out at evening, illuminating the battlefield. In the distance could be seen the Elbe River and the white walls of Königgrätz. Hurrahs were raised and the "Hohenfriedberger March" played – everybody was full of peace and joy.[21]

Schlieffen's marriage in October 1868 returned him to intimate contact with Hutterianism. In Hanover his life settled into a routine. He rode every day at 8 A.M., earlier in the summer. The cavalry practiced speed rides between 10 and 12, with Alfred urging them on. At noon he went to the office. The presence in Hanover of Prince Friedrich Karl meant reviews and banquets which never ended. Schlieffen found the quantities of food and drink that such a commander could consume extraordinary. Someone of my stature, he wrote, would be quite exhausted by it all.[22]

Two years later on 19 July 1870, France declared war on Prussia. French ships were rumored to be nearby at Eckernförde off the Hamburg coast. Troops under the command of the grand duke of

21. Ibid., pp. 192–95; Craig, *Königgrätz*, pp. 157ff.
22. Kessel, *Schlieffens Briefe*, p. 238.

Mecklenburg-Schwerin were mobilized. Throughout the summer the staff waited in Hamburg. Schlieffen's youngest brother meanwhile died of wounds received at the battle of St Privat. Finally in mid-August Friedrich Franz went to the Prussian headquarters and received the 13th Corps, which was reinforced and sent to support the attack against the fortress at Metz, the seizure of Toul and Soissons, and finally the Loire campaign. By November Schlieffen had been promoted to major. His combat experience during these months was less than in 1866. What was heightened was his circle of acquaintances. Relatives abounded. General Albrecht Stosch arrived to take over as chief of staff. Others on the staff included Waldersee, whom Schlieffen already knew from two years in Paris. After the armistice, he moved to the general staff of the new 15th Corps.[23]

It was in Straßburg a year later that his second daughter Marie was born; four days later she was baptized and then her mother was given communion and died. Schlieffen returned to Gnadenberg for the burial. In July 1874 his younger sister Catinca died. Thus Schlieffen's life through the first half of the decade of the 1870s was filled with the tragic deaths of his wife, the dominant force in his life, and two younger siblings. Schlieffen went into a period of grief and withdrawal. His annual personnel reports describe this. Graf Moltke wrote that in spite of many good qualities, the general staff was not Schlieffen's element: he lacked "liveliness, fresh imagination," and his "overly great quietness" permitted his consciousness to make these deficiencies permanent. He would make an honorable and brave troop leader. In December 1872 Moltke reaffirmed that Schlieffen was not suited for the highest place in the general staff. His fine character and military abilities would be better used in *Frontdienst*. In November 1873 Moltke wrote that Major Graf Schlieffen lacked the intellectual ability and initiative that a commanding general needed from his chief of staff.[24]

In the summer of 1875 Schlieffen again took part in a GGS ride in Pomerania, and by December Moltke had changed his mind. He wrote that during that year's exercise ride Graf Schlieffen demonstrated such clear understanding and correct decisions that he was now fully qualified to be chief of the GGS. He displayed resolute grace and an outstanding scientific education.[25] But the die had

23. Ibid., pp. 251–257.
24. Ibid., pp. 259–60; Kittel, *Schlieffen*, p. 14; Boetticher, *Schlieffen*, pp. 32–34.
25. Boetticher, *Schlieffen*, p. 33.

already been cast. Schlieffen and his brother Theodor were appointed to command Guard Cavalry regiments in Potsdam – Alfred the 1st and Theodor the 3d Guard Uhlan. For Alfred, a lieutenant colonel, this post lasted almost eight years. When Kaiser Wilhelm II was asked during the first year of his reign which regiment had pleased him most, he said the model was the 1st Guard Uhlan under Graf Schlieffen.[26]

An uhlan regiment in peacetime was five squadrons of about 150 men plus 40 recruits each, or about a thousand men. Winter service (1 October–1 April) began at 4 A.M. in the stalls, *Stalldienst*, followed by riding, shooting lessons, lance practice, and tactical moves which ended at 5:30 P.M. and included short breakfast and lunch breaks. Einjährige were instructed every evening from 6 to 7 P.M.. Often there were month-long exercises for the entire regiment. A high point of autumn and winter duty for officers was the trail hunt, the *Schleppjagden*, in which the officers began by jumping obstacles and fences and ended by chasing a live fox. There were two hunts per week during the fall, with the biggest taking place on 3 November; called the Hubertus Hunt, over a hundred riders participated on the estate of a former regimental member. At day's end, coffee was served in the manor house, followed by the officers' dinner in the casino. The regiment celebrated the Kaiser's birthday and the founder's day. Winter service included war games and the so-called winter work, a military research problem in which *Fachliteratur* was used to examine an historically based tactical problem. Regimental dances were held during the ball season. Summer service was much more varied and included squadron and regimental exercises, tactical war games with large units – eight regiments or approximately eight thousand riders – at a troop exercise place, and finally, the late summer corps maneuver. The regiment often bivouacked in a maneuver area for shooting practice. As in barracks, trumpeters opened the day at 4 A.M. and closed it at 9 P.M. with a military retreat. During the night watch posts were set out.

The officer corps of a cavalry regiment consisted of twenty-nine men – the colonel commanding, a major and captain as staff, five captains as squadron commanders, six first lieutenants, and fifteen lieutenants. Of these only eight were available in the regiment at any one time. The other twenty-one were off attending school –

---

26. Rochs, *Schlieffen*, p. 20.

the War Academy, the Riding Schools in Hanover and Soltau, the War School, Telegraph School, Blacksmith School, and so forth. This is a low tooth-to-tail ratio of 1,000:8 or .001% in peacetime and 1,000:29 or .029% in war. The regiment was always intertwined with the society. Everywhere it lived, traveled, or worked there were retired or reserved members of the army, *Korpsbrüder* serving as local officials, tax assessors, judges, and estate owners.[27]

Eight years leading the 1st Guard Uhlan introduced Schlieffen to peacetime military life, Frontdienst, in a way that no chief of the GGS from 1819 to 1914 would experience it. It was his combat experience. At the same time it reproduced, in various ways, his experiences at Niesky. Schlieffen set the style of the regiment: at 4 A.M. the first morning he was in the stables of the 5th Squadron, following every detail closely. He got to know the horses and the men, the NCOs and corporals, and most of the privates as well. He mastered details of every job. From the paymaster's office, for example, the books were brought to his quarters each evening and he checked them over, making marginal notations. He bought pigs, raised them himself, and served them to his men every eight to fourteen days, thus greatly improving rations. On holidays married NCOs received sauerbraten. Reserves were said to look forward to returning to the regiment during summer duty for "the good life." He changed horse management. Previously an outside contractor collected the manure for a specific sum each month. By contracting with a local fruit grower who leased regimental meadow land, the squadron had its manure spread over this land and received a few thousand reichsmarks more than before. Schlieffen took care of those NCOs who had served the regiment, watched over them in civilian life, helped them get jobs, and took care of them in the regimental hospital. In December 1912, fourteen days before he died, Schlieffen participated in the Christmas celebration of the 1st Guard Uhlan in the Potsdam casino.[28] At the same time this particular Frontdienst was carried out in Potsdam, the seat of several Hohenzollern palaces. The court duty and service of the

---

27. Otto Livonius, "Erinnerungen eines alten Blücher-Husaren," in Gerd Stolz and Eberhard Grieser, eds., *Geschichte des Kavallerie-Regiments 5* (Munich, 1975) pp. 198–237; On the relationship of estate owners and cavalry regiments cf. Görlitz, *Die Junker*, p. 27.

28. Rochs, *Schlieffen*, p. 18; Hugo Freiherr von Freytag-Loringhoven, "Introduction." In Großer Generalstab, ed., *Alfred von Schlieffen: Gesammelte Schriften*, 2 vols. (Berlin, 1913), 1: 12–14.

regiment, its officers and especially its commander, were always an important priority. Likewise, "service" by the royal family in the regiment was constant. In 1883, Prince Wilhelm accompanied the 1st Guard Uhlan on an exercise ride.[29]

## Schlieffen in the GGS, 1884–1891

In 1884 Schlieffen's thirty-year apprenticeship was completed. Hutterian Pietism had introduced him to the modern world of work efficiency and the 1st Guard Uhlan schooled him in the traditional world of peacetime command. On 25 March he was appointed chief of the Third Department of the GGS. Deputy GGS chief Waldersee knew Schlieffen well. For the next four years, Schlieffen worked as Waldersee's understudy. In a short time he became the latter's chief assistant.[30] Schlieffen immediately began to play a dominant role in the major integrating vehicle of the GGS, the war game, specifically the annual general staff ride. While still commander of the 1st Guard Uhlan, Schlieffen lead east army in the 1883 ride in Thuringia and Franconia. He lead a side in 1884 in Württemberg and Baden and in 1885 in Posen and West Prussia. In 1886 in Silesia he assisted Waldersee as conductor. In 1887 in Rhine province and the Pfalz he commanded the German side. In 1888 in East Prussia he was ride conductor. After Waldersee was appointed GGS chief, Schlieffen became one of three deputies. Appropriately, the 1889 ride pitted two of these deputies, Grafs Haeseler and Schlieffen, against each other as leaders of east and west respectively. In 1890 in Silesia Schlieffen again served as aid to Waldersee, the conductor.[31]

29. Kessel, *Schlieffens Briefe*, p. 27.

30. Mohs, *Waldersee*, 1: 357; it is arguable whether Schlieffen was actually chief of the Mobilization Section. Kessel argues that mobilization shifted to the Third Section, headed by Vogel von Falckenstein, in 1882; *Moltke*, p. 688. Schlieffen became head of the Third Section on 25 March 1884. Kessel, *Schlieffens Briefe*, p. 319. Others have said that Schlieffen initially became chief of the "French section," implying one of the so-called language sections dealing with intelligence, but that later he headed the Second Section, mobilization and planning. Helmuth Otto, "Alfred Graf von Schlieffen: Generalstabschef und Militärtheoretiker des imperialistischen deutschen Kaiserreiches zwischen Weltmachtstreben und Revolutionsfurcht," *Revue internationale d'histoire militaire* 39, no. 3 (1979): 74–88; it seems clear that he was concerned mainly with war plans and mobilization and the backup work done for these – military history, the GGS exercises and rides, war games, maneuvers, and railroad coordination.

31. Mohs, *Waldersee*, 1: 127; 2: 161, 167.

On 10 August 1888 Waldersee had been appointed chief of the GGS. On 19 September Schlieffen was assigned to be one of his three deputy chiefs. On 4 December he was promoted to lieutenant general, the level of division commander, which placed him among the top hundred officers in the kingdom of Prussia. Although Waldersee and Schlieffen worked closely together, officers who came in contact with them noted sharp differences in their personalities and working methods. Schlieffen was much more self-contained and nearly unapproachable. Often he was a silent observer but one who, with a single word or gesture, could say more than others with many words. Nonetheless, for most Schlieffen remained a complete mystery.[32]

Schlieffen's arrival in the GGS coincided with the beginning of a change in its strategic thinking. Although the war plans themselves were not altered, Waldersee had begun to question, rethink, and ponder various options. These included: (1) a victory in the west, (2) a victory in Poland and in Lorraine, and (3) heightened preparatory buildup in the period immediately preceeding war declaration. To test out his novel ideas, Waldersee used them as the basis for GGS rides. What are the lessons of these rides and how do these lessons relate to the war plans? Procedurely the rides followed a familiar pattern. Approximately twenty-five to thirty officers were assembled under the leadership of the chief and his staff. They entrained to their exercise starting point, then rode for two or three weeks, usually staying in six to ten different locations. As we saw in chapter 2, the problem routinely created two new armies immediately subordinate to Berlin and allocated to them various existing units. These armies were then placed into the midst of a war. The point of insertion depended upon the purposes that the ride served. Generally game time and real time coincided. At intervals of every other day ride participants were asked for their specific responses to the developing combat situation. They were asked to estimate the situation, to issue orders for specific units, time, and location, and, now for the first time, to issue railroad transportation orders. At the close of the exercise the chief of the GGS gave an extended lecture, the final critique, commenting on everything that had happened.[33]

32. Kessel, *Schlieffens Briefe*, pp. 283, 319; BAMA, Nachlaß Beseler, Lebenserinnerungen, p. 39.
33. Kessel, "Die Tätigkeit des Grafen Waldersee," p. 202.

Time, space, and size were the critical ingredients of these rides. Space was emphasized repeatedly with constant reference to several size maps: 1:8,000, 1:25,000, and 1:100,000. Size was relatively constant: these officers were moving imaginary forces of a hundred thousand men, including infantry, cavalry, and artillery. Intendants from the War Ministry participated on both sides and supply problems were inserted and discussed. Time was always something to be used carefully. To gain time for reinforcement was always a valid reason for troop movement. Nothing was done suddenly, without thought, but once a decision had been reached forces were expected to execute it rapidly.

Strategically, the employment of railroads was the most important theme running through the exercises. At the start of the game, it was sometimes stated: equal forces, equal railroads. In other words, railroads were as important as the size of the forces employed. Railroads were essential to the dominant strategic concept employed, the defensive-offensive. The German or blue side generally waited for an enemy advance, then attacked a vulnerable portion of it. In doing so, it was railroads which suggested and allowed for possibilities. For example, in 1885 along the Polish border in East Prussia, railroads permitted the blue side to conduct limited offensive actions because they enabled a more rapid, denser concentration than did the Russian railroad lines. All reinforcement depended on railroads. As early as 1885 Waldersee considered the movement of three army corps from the west to east front: this was only possible within the available time frame using railroads. Railroads were the key to the defense. In East Prussia the GGS constantly asked for more rail lines in order to defend the lower Weichsel River area adequately. Finally, railroads were the key to mobilization at the start and resupply during the course of the exercise. In 1885 there was only one double track line connecting Berlin to the east border regions. In his final critique Waldersee specifically requested four additional lines.[34]

During this time the army as a whole was growing. In 1887, as army size increased during the war scare, the number of train battalions was raised to simplify future mobilization, and artillery was added so that every infantry division had a field artillery regiment. The February 1888 law provided for large increases in

---

34. Mohs, *Waldersee*, 2: 147–68.

reserve forces, including (1) reinstatement of the second Land-wehr levy, whereby Landwehr duty was extended to age 39; (2) extension of the substitute reserve duty from ten to twelve years; (3) extension of Landsturm duty to age forty-five and its usage in field and reserve units. This allowed the creation of an entirely new Landsturm organization. The result was that an additional 700,000 trained men were available in time of war. Even preceding the huge army bills which came in 1889, re-serve forces had begun to mushroom.[35]

Railroads continued to grow as the dominant vehicle in war planning. As we have seen, they had become part of the order-issuing process within war games. Each side was expected to include in its orders the most basic quantitative measure, the number of trains per day per line. Railroad troops, inspection companies, and building companies became prominent among tactical units. In 1889, the railroad system was "in a state of war readiness" as an assumption of the ride. For the 1890 exercise in Silesia a whole accordianlike army was backed up behind the field forces on the railroad lines running to Berlin: the Guard Corps, two reserve guard divisions, and the Guard Cavalry Divi-sion were standing "mobilization ready" along the tracks. Rail-road maps became central to strategic decision making. In the final critique of the 1890 exercise, Waldersee chided the of-ficers for using maps too large in scale. They could not see the whole picture. In the exercise just concluded several times commanders had made the wrong decisions because they con-sulted a large-scale detail map and, in so doing, had misplaced an army corps. Whenever Field Marshal Moltke makes an important decision, Waldersee told the assembled officers, "he uses the *Reichskursbuch*" – the German railway guide![36]

In 1889 Schlieffen drafted a series of memorandums on the use of railroads in war. For no army are railroads as important as they are for ours, he wrote. Germany's geographic position is that of a country on inner lines between east and west. Vulner-able when confronting two opponents, we can only achieve superior strength on one or the other battlefield through the use of railroads. Railroads were becoming far more important than for-tresses. Victory could depend on rapid rail movement, defeat could

35. Rahne, *Mobilmachung*, pp. 90–91.
36. Mohs, *Waldersee*, 2: 211, 226.

result from deficient rail capacity. It was not enough to prepare the army, provide the troops with weapons and munitions, and order the mobilization. The transportation plan had to be laid out faultlessly.[37]

In February 1890 he drafted two memorandums, "War against France" and "War against Russia." On the subject of France, he pointed out that the relationships in the western campaign area had changed unfavorably for Germany. France had built a line of fortifications and hoped to lead a successful war against Germany from there. Initially it would be prudent for Germany to relinquish the offensive to the French, who wanted to recover Alsace and Lorraine. As the French mobilized, Germany, with the larger part of its forces committed against Russia, would concentrate along the railroad line Bolchen to Saarburg, with weaker forces placed further south in Alsace which would withdraw to Straßburg or to the east bank of the Rhine in the face of heavier French forces. In April 1888, even though aid from Italian forces was not expected to be important, Schlieffen traveled to Rome to negotiate a railroad agreement with the Italian general staff. In fighting Russia the goal was a decisive battle as soon as possible. Schlieffen suggested a concentration of German forces along the southeast border of East Prussia and then an attack across the line Lomscha to Kowno against Russian forces backed up in front of the Niemen, Bobr, and Narew rivers. Such an attack depended on the building of a double track railroad line connecting Thorn and Korschen. Schlieffen wanted to concentrate the German forces as far east as possible. This depended on increasing rail capacity in East Prussia.[38]

## Schlieffen as Chief, 1891–1896

On 7 February 1891 Schlieffen was appointed chief of the great general staff. If we can believe what he wrote to his sister and brother-in-law, he dreaded it: "A difficult task has been given to me, yet I am imbued with the firm conviction that the Lord . . . will not forsake me in a situation into which He has placed without my effort or desire." Exactly how this appointment came about is

37. Boetticher, *Schlieffen*, pp. 39, 40.
38. Ibid., pp. 42–45.

difficult to say. Sixteen years earlier Schlieffen had been unsuited for general staff duty. Seven years before he was regimental commander. Three years earlier Waldersee had seemed well established for a long tenure. Several factors intervened.[39] Apparently Waldersee's public criticism of the young Wilhem II during a military exercise in the autumn of 1890 had been a serious mistake, souring a relationship which always depended upon how the Kaiser felt at a given moment. But there were other reasons why Wilhelm's entourage felt uneasy about Waldersee. His constant political intrigues upset everyone. He was too much like the Kaiser, impetuous and undisciplined, too much of a character full of divergent enthusiasms to be on the loose at the highest levels of the Second Reich. It was much better that he was removed from center stage to Altona. Two such characters in Berlin was one too many: damage control might become impossible.[40]

Certainly Schlieffen had many more relatives and friends and perhaps fewer enemies at court and in the Military Cabinet than did other candidates. A close relationship was probable with Friedrich von Holstein, which then gave access to Philipp Eulenburg, the fulcrum of the Kaiser's entourage, who was then at the peak of his influence. Clearly Waldersee himself, although very different in personality and temperment, valued Schlieffen highly. Schlieffen, after all, held the same position in relation to Waldersee that Waldersee had held in relation to Moltke. There had been other candidates, but at that moment late in the autumn of 1890 and early in the new year of 1891, they were not available. Some had died. Others were unknown or were openly disliked by Wilhelm II. No officer had had as much experience in the GGS and its main business, war planning, as had Schlieffen. Few were better or more immediately known to the sovereign.[41]

Gerhard Ritter has called Schlieffen a "pure courtier." This may be a bit unfair. It may also be inaccurate. As Eberhard Kessel argues, it is likely that Schlieffen appeared to be the typical

39. Friedrich von Boetticher, *The Schlieffen Problems* (Fort Leavenworth, 1925), introd.; Kessel, *Schlieffens Briefe*, p. 292.

40. John C.G. Röhl, ed., *Philipp Eulenburgs politische Korrespondenz*, 4 vols. (Boppard am Rhein, 1976–86), 1: 620–32. Although Wilhelm II had many serious psychological quirks, Waldersee also had his eccentricities. He often took his two dachshunds out on GGS rides in a basket and when they went after a deer, the whole general staff took after them. Mohs, *Waldersee*, 2: 112.

41. Röhl, "Hof und Hofgesellschaft unter Kaiser Wilhelm II," pp. 262–67; Röhl, *Eulenburgs Korrespondenz*, 1: introd., 9–37, 631.

underling the Kaiser so treasured, tractable and pliant. When the Kaiser remarked in 1891 that the new chief of the GGS had to be a sort of amanuensis to himself, Waldersee remarked: "He wants to be his own General Staff chief. God preserve the fatherland." However a different view is possible.[42] Schlieffen understood and lived by the conventions of his time, yet he did not do so uncritically or without understanding. Publicly he paid deference to the traditional verities: family, social class, the church, the monarchy, Prussia. Privately his ridicule and sarcasm were unbounded. He criticized individuals regardless of their positions. At the beginning of the reign Schlieffen was openly disrespectful: within the family the Kaiser was referred to as "Willy." Later he dropped this, but never held back from criticizing Wilhelm's most ridiculous actions. The way the young Kaiser removed Waldersee from his post as chief of the GGS must have shocked Schlieffen, doubly so when Schlieffen was then unexpectedly named as successor. Although not intimate or close friends, Schlieffen's career from 1884 on had depended on Waldersee.

Schlieffen soon concluded that the Kaiser was an obstacle to be circumvented, so he had to keep his opinion to himself. He learned this in his very first GGS war game, the New Year's exercise final summary in 1891. Following Schlieffen's presentation, the Kaiser gave a detailed criticism, finishing up with his own conclusions, which were diametrically opposed to Schlieffen's. The situation was only saved by Field Marshal Moltke, who praised both solutions as correct. Moltke's authoritative and diplomatic response quieted Wilhelm's enthusiasm, and he changed the subject and launched into an extended discussion of the recent Russian maneuvers that he had attended.[43] For Schlieffen the Kaiser was a "given," a God-willed reality. Making himself conform to the framework of the monarchy through his office and career was for Schlieffen a religious duty. He was convinced that the history of the world and the given order of things with all its faults, as seen by humans, was willed. But he did not want to be someone whom the monarch called by snapping his fingers. At the same time he fulfilled the essential demands of the office and tried for Wilhelm's respect as much as he could. It was a moral obligation. The conventions he understood and valued were not mere formalities or superficialities

42. Kessel, *Schlieffens Briefe*, p. 29; Kitchen, *German Officer Corps*, p. 88.
43. Kessel, *Schlieffens Briefe*, p. 294.

but matters of vital importance.[44] For Schlieffen's generational peers the Prussian military ethos combined a Christian fatalism, the service of the nobility to the sovereign, and the duty of the professional officer. Self-surrender to the will of God was the means by which the individual gained power over his destiny. There was a strong sense of predestination. War was neither tragic nor extraordinary. It was not necessarily mixed with national feelings. It was normal – a vocation to which the military nobility had responded for centuries.[45]

Schlieffen's personal leadership style differed sharply from that of many in the imperial government and entourage. Here Hutterian training became dominant. The Kaiser changed uniforms eight times daily and traveled to and fro among his seventy-five castles and palaces, unable to work at first, uninterested later. As Fritz Stern has written, he was the very model of the insecure modern man: anxious, impulsive, fitfully aggressive, simultaneously emperor by divine right and yet desperately yearning for popularity despite his alarming arrogance and his very un-Prussian preference for appearance over reality. His entourage sought to provide what damage control they could, all the while jockeying for those plums of appointment, advancement, and decoration that Wilhelm controlled.[46]

Schlieffen ran the GGS as a combination Hutterian Bruderhof and cavalry regiment. From Hutterianism came a work orientation emphasizing careful use of time and attention to personal relationships, rank, and precedence. Regimental were the knowledge of detail, the early morning to late night schedule, the concern for individual members. Schlieffen was often at his service desk at 6 A.M. and rode in the Tiergarten at 8. After a light breakfast, he conferred with the bureau chief of the Central Section and with his adjutants: they kept the daily and weekly office schedule of appointments, interviews, and appearances. From then until 4 P.M. followed a series of uninterrupted interviews with his deputy chiefs and section heads. After tea, he worked alone until dinner at 7,

---

44. Ibid., p. 30.

45. Hostetler, *Hutterite Society*, pp. 141–43; Dissow, *Adel im Übergang*, p. 90; the standard manual for young officers which described this ethos in detail is Camill Schaible, *Standes- und Berufspflichten des deutschen Offiziers: Für angehende und jüngere Offiziere des Stehenden Heeres und des Beurlaubtenstandes*, 3d ed. (Berlin, 1896).

46. Fritz Stern, *Dreams and Delusions* (New York, 1987), p. 60; Some of the atmosphere of smaller court life during the Wilhelmian era is well portrayed in Thomas Mann's *Königliche Hoheit* (Berlin, 1919).

followed by work, often with an adjutant, until 10 or 11 at night, then an hour with his daughters. On GGS rides he drove himself and his officers hard: up at 4:30 A.M., with breakfast followed by two hours of map study, nine hours of riding over the terrain, rest, and a dinner break until 9 P.M., followed by three hours of critique and discussion.[47]

He was probably not a very pleasant person for whom to work. He took little pride in work and profession. Schlieffen took neither himself nor others very seriously: as humans they were all faulted because they were tainted by original sin. Schlieffen's standards were high but he was prepared for disappointment. Irony tinged with sarcasm buffered him from the outside world.[48] The exchanges between Schlieffen and his GGS subordinates which illustrate these traits are legendary. Asked by a young major if he had slept well, the master replied that he would have slept better if he had not read the major's report just before going to bed. Having left the chief's office upon completion of a lengthy oral report during which Schlieffen had said nothing, the reporting officer hurriedly returned. He had made an error. He apologized and corrected the point wrongly presented. Schlieffen replied that he had not believed that point either. Schlieffen heard many presentations without a word or sign of any kind, his features unchanged. Presenters did not know if he had understood or not. It was believed that he always understood, for he was a brilliant questioner who always asked unsettling questions. Many were uneasy in his presence. They lost their composure. Some generals went out of their way to avoid spending a minute alone in his presence. Schlieffen's rank and position in the organization exaggerated the impact of his personality. The contrast with the Kaiser's working methods, lifestyle, and garrulous identity could not have been greater.

Schlieffen was considered a master of technical fundamentals and rational thinking, but he clothed his judgments and criticisms in sharp, often sarcastic language, occasionally using scorn and ridicule. When dealing within the GGS, it was said he never took account of the person, only the argument. His closest associate wrote that although some were wounded by this, whoever recognized that Schlieffen's judgments were influenced solely by factual,

47. General von Stein, *Erlebnisse und Betrachtungen* (Leipzig, 1919), p. 115; General von Einem, *Erinnerungen eines Soldaten, 1853–1933*, 6th ed. (Leipzig, 1933), p. 49.
48. Kessel, *Schlieffens Briefe*, pp. 31–33; Stein, *Erlebnisse*, p. 30.

technical fundamentals was not hurt but was instead thankful for the many new ideas which developed during the discourse.

In dealing with the task environment beyond the GGS, Schlieffen customarily moved out of the way of opposition. Like Moltke, he did not have a fighting nature. In confronting resistance, he sought the peaceful middle ground. For example, the Kaiser, like his grandfather, wanted to protect southern Germany from attack with heavy fortifications. Schlieffen believed that south Germany had to bear the burdens of war like any other region of the Reich. Therefore he wanted only simple defensive escarpments which the army could build with little effort and expense. To think through solutions to the problem, Schlieffen took a few officers and rode through the upper Rhine River valley. Although he did not expect to reach any compromise, in fact he found a solution which suited the Kaiser.[49]

Unpolitical in his activities, Schlieffen nevertheless had a wide range of relatives and friends placed throughout the court and bureaucracy. Like his contemporary in England, Lord Salisbury, Schlieffen could always gain access to and careful hearing in the Prussian and Reich power structure. Schlieffen buffered himself from the outside world. Within his own sphere, the GGS and army, this was easy. Within the imperial hierarchy it was more difficult, but was facilitated by the Kaiser's inability to concentrate, his sporadic interest in the substance of military affairs, and ultimately, his respect for the technical expert. To hear better and not be distracted by appearances, Schlieffen in later years often closed his eyes during meetings and audiences, even with the Kaiser. It was said that the sleeping Schlieffen heard more than one hundred men awake. His recognition of the difference between appearance and reality, between promise and fulfillment, implies an attitude of emotional detachment. Learning from Waldersee's troubles, he avoided politics yet, when the political scene became unclear, he would visit Holstein to receive guidance from a man intimately aware of court and bureaucratic affairs.[50]

Outside the GGS he was not well known. In public he held back, rarely revealing himself. In September 1905, at the ceremony unveiling the Moltke memorial on the Königsplatz, Schlieffen delivered an oration which left listeners spellbound. One state

49. Freytag-Loringhoven, "Introduction," 1: 16; Stein, *Erlebnisse*, p. 35.
50. Rochs, *Schlieffen*, p. 67.

secretary was so surprised that he wanted to know who had written Schlieffen's speech. Members of the GGS were not surprised. Schlieffen did not react, as it were, conventionally. He mystified his colleagues.[51] Yet Schlieffen fit easily into the aristocratic leadership of the Prussian army. The degree to which the top posts were held by the old military nobility is still fascinating. For example, the military entourages of the Kaiser and Prussian princes, the army inspectorates, and the twelve Prussian corps commands were filled with old family names. On active duty at this time were sixty Bülows, fifty Arnims, Bredows, Goltzes, Kleists, Puttkamers, Schwerins, and Wedels; twenty to fifty Belows, Bonins, Borcks, Dewitzs, Knesebecks, Massows, Schulenburgs, and Zitzewitzs; twenty to thirty Alvenslebens, Bismarcks, Dohnases, Finckensteins, Kamekes, Marwitzes, Natzmars, and Zastros. A well-connected small family could have four general officers in two generations. The Massows had nine generals in two generations, the Brauchitschs twelve generals from 1800 to 1941. In this respect, Schlieffen fit the mold well.[52]

In only two places was this noble domination intruded upon, in the War Ministry and the GGS. In the War Ministry the cavalry departments were headed by nobles, but many middle-class officers held positions in the infantry, artillery, and technical departments. As for the general staff, 63% were noble in 1900, but by 1914 this had fallen to 40%.[53] In both cases many of the most sensitive jobs, those that had to be done well, were held by middle-class officers,

51. Staabs, *Aufmarsch*, p. 34; Rochs, *Schlieffen*, pp. 25–26.

52. Görlitz, *Die Junker*, pp. 298–99; Detlev Bald, speaking of the Prussian army as a whole, emphasizes a well-known theme. The role played by the old nobility can scarcely be overestimated. It was unique in Europe. The same families that had settled in Mark Brandenburg and Pomerania in the thirteenth and fourteenth centuries, who had fought in the battles of the first Hohenzollerns, the Great Elector, and Frederick the Great, were the leaders in the nineteenth-and twentieth-century army. The homogeneity of values, social consciousness, and professional orientation of this group permeated the officer corps as a whole. *Vom Kaiserheer zur Bundeswehr*, pp. 35–41. Various attempts have been made to quantify noble and middle-class membership in the Prussian army at various levels. For example, von dem Bergh lists the top thirty-seven regiments in terms of percentages, *Das deutsche Heer*, p. 104, as do Manfred Messerschmidt for the years 1850 to 1890 and Wilhelm Diest for the period 1890 to 1918. Manfred Messerschmidt, "Das preußisch-deutsche Offizierkorps," in H.H. Hofmann, ed., *Das deutsche Offizierkorps, 1860–1960* (Boppard am Rhein, 1977), pp. 21–38; Wilhelm Deist, "Zur Geschichte des preußischen Offizierkorps, 1890–1918," pp. 39–57 in the same work.

53. Ulrich Trumpener, "Junkers and Others," pp. 29–47.

not feudal nobility. One clearly visible trend, then, is a "careers open to talent" approach in the GGS which saw Erich Ludendorff, Max Hoffmann, Herman Kuhl, Wilhelm Groener, and others appointed to key positions on the basis of ability, not nobility. Schlieffen recognized the necessity to bring the "best minds" of the officer corps into the GGS, irrespective of family background. How he defined best mind became in the course of time very significant for Prussian Germany.

## The New Strategic Era and Organization

Just as Schlieffen came to office there was a unique, dramatic volte-face in the task environment. As John Röhl has shown, Imperial Germany, like many modern states, was governed by an oligarchy, a handful of men. They determined internal and foreign policy, initiated legislation, and controlled appointments. After 1888, a cyclical development from autocratic rule through collective leadership back to autocratic rule occurred. When it was all over, by about 1897, Kaiser Wilhelm II was firmly in charge. Wilhelm wanted to be Reich Kaiser, not just Prussian king. Whether one interprets this as a Prussianization of the German states or as a nationalization of hitherto separate regional sovereignties, the process took time. Although the black, white, and red flag – the symbol of national sovereignty – was first proclaimed as the German flag on 8 November 1872, it was not until March 1897, a quarter century later, that Wilhelm II decreed that it was to be carried by all German troops.[54] As noted above, Bismarck's replacement had immediate and dramatic impact on foreign policy, creating within weeks the loss of the Russian-German Reinsurance Treaty, within eighteen months the first Franco-Russian alliance in forty years, and within a decade and a half the alienation of England and the Triple Entente. What had been for Moltke and Waldersee merely a bad dream, a two-front, three-opponent war, became a reality for Schlieffen. Soon Prussian officers could realistically talk of the reoccurrence of the military circumstances of the Seven Years' War.

Initially Wilhelm wanted to upgrade the commanding generals,

54. Röhl, *Germany without Bismarck*, pp. 171ff.; cf. Nichols, *Germany after Bismarck*, passim; Theodore Schieder, *Das Deutsche Kaiserreich von 1871 als Nationalstaat* (Cologne, 1961), p. 74.

giving them prominence above the GGS. He soon lost interest. As early as 1888, he had begun to change the fall maneuvers into a personal spectacle. Although his interest in the maneuvers seldom waned, the maneuvers themselves remained a valid exercise in spite of his interference. His appointment power, carried out through the Military Cabinet, meant that personal favorites and old family names held many of the corps commands; however, the critical leadership posts through which the GGS had to work in the event of war were the chiefs of staff. The Kaiser staked out the two most feudal elements of the army – the guard corps and the exercise rules – as the center of his activities, leaving the GGS alone. Specialization based on knowledge went forward. As an organization, the GGS was left to Schlieffen to develop.[55]

To some extent the activities of the GGS, and especially its chief, were tied to the imperial schedule. As stated above, Wilhelm II was the first ruler who tried to be a Kaiser as well as king. This resulted in a larger court calendar and royal schedule into which the GGS fit at certain times of the year. Although Schlieffen was chary of court life he had lived in Potsdam for fifteen years and had learned that one could not be absent from court and still maintain one's place in the entourage: influence was based on one's personal relationship with Wilhelm. For the first three or four months of the year, from 1 January through the end of May when the Kaiser was in Berlin, the chief of the GGS met with Wilhelm on Saturdays. The rest of the year the Kaiser was out of Berlin. He sometimes returned for the Spring parade in Potsdam. The summer months were spent yachting or traveling, with a return in early September for the military parade at Tempelhof followed by two weeks of army and navy maneuvers. After that until Christmas was the hunt season; except for a few weeks, the Kaiser was on the official court hunts at Liebenberg or Donaueschingen, followed by the Silesian hunts. Returning in December, the family celebrated Christmas in Potsdam and seven days later moved to Berlin, where the whole cycle began again.[56]

Professor Hull's account makes clear, however, that although

55. Hull, *Entourage*, chap. 1; John C.G. Röhl, *Kaiser, Hof und Staat: Wilhelm II und die deutsche Politik* (Munich, 1987), chap. 3; Geyer, *Rüstungspolitik*, p. 70; *Militär-Adreßbuch*; Trumpener, "Junkers and Others," pp. 29–47.

56. On the court calendar there were four functions which we may assume Schlieffen attended. The first was the *Ordensfest* held on 18 January and attended by some eight hundred people, presumably those already honored with an order and

Wilhelm II began his reign in 1888 by trying to follow the routine and schedule of his grandfather, within two years he had ceased doing any serious or consistent work, instead filling up his days with a flurry of innocuous activity. For the GGS this meant that there were four imperial interfaces which counted. One was audiences. A second was high personnel appointments. The third was the Kaiser's participation in the fall maneuvers, and a fourth was his participation in GGS lectures, war games, and staff rides. Assuming Schlieffen saw Wilhelm on all of those Saturdays that he was in Berlin, this amounted to at least sixteen times per year or over two hundred audiences. There is very little evidence on which to base comments here. As we shall see, the Kaiser was a regular and important player in the annual fall maneuvers. And as for Wilhelm's participation in GGS activities when he was in Berlin, again the evidence is thin. However, there are hints and suggestions here and there that he participated often, if sporadically, that he was thoroughly familiar with the war plans, and that, like his grandfather, he took his role as soldier seriously, and occasionally even deferred to those military experts whose knowledge of military affairs was greater than his own.[57]

---

those decorated each year. It took place at the Berlin Schloß and included a formal receiving line, a church service, dinner, coffee, and "conversation." Second was the *große Defiliercour* at which those accredited to the court itself – the *hoffähig* – presented themselves as a body. This group included members of the princely houses, ladies and gentlemen of the court, foreign diplomats and their wives, and officers of the guard regiments. Third, on 27 January the Kaiser's birthday was celebrated. This event opened with reville played by the music corps of one of the guard regiments, continued through formal birthday congratulations to the sovereign, delivered in the Rittersaal, which were then followed by a church service, a military parade at the Zeughaus, and a show in the opera house. After that the ball season opened and there were usually at least two court balls. These affairs began promptly at 9 P.M. with the arrival of the Kaiser and ended formally at 1:30 A.M. with the polonaise. The final ball of the season was the *Fastnachtsdienstag* held on the last Tuesday before Lent in the spring. After that no more balls could be held in Berlin. Herzogin Viktoria Luise, *Im Glanz der Krone: Erinnerungen* (Munich, 1967), pp. 203–14; Karl Hammer, "Die preußischen Könige und Königinnen im 19. Jahrhundert und ihr Hof," in Karl F. Wenner, ed., *Hof, Kultur und Politik im 19. Jahrhundert* (Bonn, 1985), pp. 94–97; E. Schröder, ed., *Zwanzig Jahre Regierungszeit: Ein Tagebuch Kaiser Wilhelms II von Antritt der Regierung 15. Juni 1888 bis zum 15. Juni 1908* (Berlin, 1909). For the daily routine, cf. Martin D. Sagebiel, "Alltag bei Hofe zur Zeit Fürst Leopold II zur Lippe," *Lippische Mitteilungen aus Geschichte und Landeskunde* 53 (1984): 207–27.

57. Hull, *Entourage*, pp. 27–41. For example, the schedule diaries of the Kaiser's adjutants, located in the Merseburg Archives, DDR, apparently list those who came for audiences, but make no comment on the nature of the interviews; cf. Zoellner, "Schlieffens Vermächtnis," p. 45.

The most basic aspect of the war planning process was organizational. The history of the defense budget into which the GGS fit during these years indicates clearly that from 1888 to 1898 there were dramatic increases in army funding. From 1899 to 1912 army funding was put on hold, while Tirpitz's "risk" fleet was constructed. Thus in approximately one decade prior to 1898 the army's peacetime strength had risen by over 160,000, the number of active corps from eighteen to twenty, the number of divisions from thirty-seven to forty-three. War-mobilized strength was 2,746,300 (including active army, reserve, substitute reserve, Landwehr I and II, and Landsturm I and II).[58]

The GGS structure Schlieffen inherited in 1891 was as follows. Beneath the chief were a Central Section and four deputy chiefs. Three deputies directed the Main Bureau, which had six sections and nineteen branches. One deputy directed the Secondary Bureau for Scientific Affairs, which had five section chiefs. The full general staff was well above six hundred men, separated first into the GGS, those serving in Berlin, and then the TGS, those serving with the army corps and divisions. It was further divided between the GGS itself and the Secondary Bureau. The Central Section included the chief, his deputy, and a number of adjutants and secretaries. This section was the office manager: it controlled the flow of paperwork, set the calendar due dates, and monitored work completion. The Second Section included the Mobilization and Railroad Section. The Fourth Section directed GGS rides and the War Academy. The First and Third Sections essentially handled intelligence, examining foreign armies east, west, and south of Germany. The Fifth Section dealt with military history.[59]

The GGS system remained consistent. First of all, this meant that a procedure for separation and rotation existed between the GGS and TGS. Several mechanisms served to relate the TGS to the GGS. The chiefs of staff at corps and division levels had been trained at the War Academy and in the GGS, and they were often upgraded in GGS procedures through participation in rides, exercises, and maneuvers. In spite of size increases in the whole army,

---

58. Geyer, *Rüstungspolitik*, p. 52; Osten-Sacken, *Preußens Heer*, 3: 371; Rahne, *Mobilmachung*, p. 92. The problem of Rahne's estimation of army numbers is a complication here; however, he is the only one who deals consistently with all the various levels of manpower from ages seventeen to forty-five.

59. Osten-Sacken, *Preußens Heer*, 3: 491; Schellendorf, *Duties*, p. 39; Jany, *Preußische Armee*, 4: 294.

the command and control factors were in the hands of a small group of GGS officers who knew each other. Second, general staff personnel were handpicked from each War Academy class and tested against each other in war games. They taught in the military education system, and their thinking on war was continually redirected back to a common framework, that of the war game system of analysis. Third, the GGS reflected structurally the problems with which it dealt, tempering its organization through a predilection for giving the most complex and critical aspects – the war plans and everything which contributed directly to them – to a select few especially valued by the chief. At base, everything related to the war plans. As Paul Bronsart von Schellendorff demonstrated in his *Duties of the General Staff*, the functioning of the GGS and each GS at corps and division levels was orchestrated by modern bureaucratic procedures: highly formalized, hierarchical, and centralized.

The Prussian army was a lean organization. At the top were a few men considered extremely able, even unique. They were given great latitude and independence of action. Michael Geyer gives the peacetime strength of the army in 1893 as 557,000.[60] This force was directed by a general staff of roughly 600, or .001%. This same ratio prevailed at corps, divisional, regimental, and company levels. Such hierarchy was reflected in language customs. As Alfred Vagts once described it, officers in the German army in 1914 talked to their men using the German word for children. Unsurprisingly, the Kaiser sometimes spoke to his generals and entourage using the same term. In this elite society, the few counted among the many. They were marked out at birth, trained during youth. When they became adults, their uniqueness continued in the organizations they led. The lieutenant was unique in his company, as was the colonel in his regiment, the general in his corps, the *Graf* on his estate. In a traditional society, "special" single individuals counted a great deal. In a sense each member of the hierarchy used his delegated authority to act on behalf of the monarch and this personification was transferred downward, animating the entire structure. Curiously enough, in a large, modernizing bureaucracy such uniqueness was an advantage. It meant that the organization was unlikely to become top-heavy or to acquire too many managers in relationship to workers. The organization may have been overburdened with paperwork, but it was not filled

60. Geyer, *Rüstungspolitik*, p. 52.

with extra levels and layers of people. In this respect traditional Prussian society fit effectively with modern management techniques.

There were several integrating mechanisms utilized by the GGS to coordinate the mobilization plan. We have already described the chiefs of staff and the LCs. A third was the DCs. The DCs had been instituted in the 1870s, and by 1899 there were over three hundred districts implanted into the Reich army corps structure. For example, the DCs of Berlin were comprised of approximately 4,000 retired officers, 4,000 inactive officers, 900 medical officers, and 250,000 NCOs and men. The main work was done by a few active-duty lieutenants and captains whose job was to keep lists of the men in the districts and their mobilization assignments and to carry out a practice call-up each year. Depending on age, each man was assigned to either the active army, reserve, Landwehr, or Landsturm. Units were in turn echeloned into the war mobilization structure. The beginning of two-year service in 1896 meant that the army grew rapidly, drawing especially on trained reserves. To meet this increased size, the mobilization process was simplified. Orders were prepared during peacetime and updated annually, that is, every 1 April, with the date, time, and place that each reservist was to join his troop unit. At war mobilization, these orders were sent out through the post by messengers or runners, and each year the system was tested.

At mobilization a number of new armies were created. In 1899 there were six, each one containing a mixture of active and reserve corps. For example, when war-mobilized the 3d Army contained four corps: three active corps, the Saxon 12th and 14th and the Prussian 11th; and one reserve corps, the 12th. Linkages between these were personal as well as structural. In 1914 the general officer called out of retirement to command Communications Zone Inspection 3 was attached directly to the high command of the 3d Army. Before reporting to his own headquarters in Dresden, the sixty-four year-old general reported to the commander of the 3d Army in Berlin, General von Hausen. In doing so, he discovered that he knew all the key players: von Hausen was known to him from GGS service; the chief of staff of the 3d Army had been his general staff officer in the 39th Division in 1901; and he knew each of the chiefs of staff of the four army corps. Thus even in this large organization, which valued above all anonymity and interchangeability among the small leadership cadre, everyone knew each other.[61]

The second aspect of war planning was educational. At least in the early 1890s, it has been argued, advanced theoretical training was derided. When Wilhelm Groener attended the War Academy, it enjoyed neither imperial favor nor broad army respect. In the first years of his reign, Kaiser Wilhelm II wanted to increase the power, authority, and influence of the corps commanders, those men technically under his direct command in peacetime. Concurrently he wanted to decrease the authority and influence of the GGS. This suggests that there was a period of perhaps several years, before Wilhelm became bored, when the War Academy had to maintain a low profile. Schlieffen, it was said, understood this and simply chose the best War Academy graduates and completed their education in the GGS. Schlieffen outlasted the Kaiser; when Wilhelm's attention span had passed, Schlieffen was still in office. A few years later, the Kaiser had forgotten all about his antipathy and was giving lectures on Japanese naval history in the War Academy.[62]

Through it all the general staff retained a strong intellectual cast. Schlieffen was called the "master teacher." We are not suggesting that he ran the GGS like a small, very patriarchical university, even if he was given an honorary doctorate by Berlin University and called himself Dr. Graf Schlieffen in his correspondence with a university professor. The point is that he thought of himself as an intellectual, and he admired the supposed erudition of Moltke and previous generations. Verdy du Vernois wrote in 1903 of the immense intellectual leadership of the chief of the GGS. The War Academy curriculum during these years continued in the direction of pure technical training and away from general education. Military science disciplines were required – tactics and general staff service, military sanitation, weapons, military law, forts and fortifications, military geography, mathematics – everything else was optional. A recent commentator says that this concentration on professional courses produced military technocrats with starkly limited views.[63]

In the educational system tension continued over officer recruitment standards. The Kaiser repeatedly emphasized that young

61. Litzmann, *Lebenserinnerungen*, 1: 114–17, 184–87.
62. Helmut Haeussler, *General William Groener and the Imperial German Army* (Madison, 1962), p. 16; Litzmann, *Lebenserinnerungen*, 1: 104.
63. Bald, *Der deutsche Generalstab*, pp. 44–53.

officers needed technical and scientific competence. For the War Ministry, however, the more important consideration was social homogeniety. The battle was finally won in favor of technical education and in 1902 the crucial regulation was passed that opened up the position of career officer to all those who possessed the Abitur without requiring the two supplementary tests, the testimonial of character by the commander (*Dienstzeugnis*) and the judgment of worth by regimental officers (*Würdigkeitsurteil*). Between 1890 and 1912 the number of secondary school graduates among new officers increased from 35% to over 65%, and this figure was reflected even in the modernization of the curriculums of the cadet academies, the preparatory schools from which approximately 40% of young officers came.[64] Enlarging the officer corps meant introducing men deemed by some to be socially unacceptable. Schlieffen, in so far as it was under his control and in contrast to his own aristocratic predilections, gathered around him the "best and brightest" irrespective of their social origins and class standing. By the late 1890s the central core of the GGS, the Railroad and Mobilization Sections were heavily populated by middle-class officers. Ten years later, on the eve of the Great War, 70% of the GGS was middle class, and the core technology, planning and railroads, was solidly in their hands. Schlieffen seems to have made an important distinction between his own family, whose marriage alliances he guarded zealously, and the needs of the GGS, a technical professional matter judged by different standards.[65]

Unsurprisingly, military history in the GGS had expanded so that there were now two sections, one for ancient and one for modern history. Schlieffen gave a great boost to this aspect of the GGS. Under Moltke in the 1870s instruction had concentrated on Prussian wars. Schlieffen argued that the GGS should concern itself with all European military affairs. A few years later, he created a second vehicle alongside the *Military Weekly*, the *Vierteljahreshefte für Truppenführung und Heereskunde* (*Quarterly Journal for Troop Leadership and War Science*). Its purpose was to focus on modern and contemporary military affairs.

During these years the use of military history in war games, tactical exercises, and maneuvers took a bizarre turn in the direction of

64. Manfred Messerschmidt, "Schulpolitik des Militärs," in Peter Baumgart, ed., *Bildungspolitik in Preußen zur Zeit des Kaiserreichs* (Stuttgart, 1980), p. 249.
65. Bernd Schulte, *Die deutsche Armee, 1900–1914* (Düsseldorf: Droste Verlag, 1977).

scientific methodology. Strategic thinking was measured against historical examples. Vernois describes the "testing of strategic ideas for their correctness" by applying military history. As one leading practitioner wrote, the goal was not only to describe various strategic ideas advocated by leading military circles but, hand in hand with the discussion, to test their correctness. How was this done? By exercise rides and military history. Current doctrine was compared against an image of past practice, an image dominated by a single conception, the strategy of annihilation.[66]

The third aspect of war planning was representational. A GGS officer's map training still began in the War Academy with the basics of survey and drawing, triangulation, leveling, and measurement. Students used pocket range finders, similar to those used on 35-mm cameras. They drew sketches and maps and worked on scales from 1 inch = 1 mile to the standard 1:100,000 map base. The representational system of the GGS was more sophisticated, more tightly integrated into the analytical system, and larger than it had been prior to 1890. Although the Secondary Bureau enrolled only a quarter of War Academy graduates for their initial tour of duty, the section itself was larger than any other section, its head was a major general who reported directly to the chief of the GGS, and its work output continued to be prodigious. Between 1877 and 1914, over 3,300 entirely new plane table drawings of Prussia at a scale of 1:25,000 were produced. From these, 6,000 square miles were topographically and cartographically worked up each year. The new map of the German Reich at a scale of 1:100,000 was created in copper engraving and was published in 542 sheets five years after Schlieffen left office.[67]

The final aspect of war planning was analytical. By the 1890s the war game was a universal method of "learning war during peace" in the Prussian army. As noted in chapter 2, war games took many forms. During the winter half year from 1 November to 1 April, these problems were given mainly as written exercises. Problems were handed out to assigned lieutenants and captains several times a year. Section chiefs collected them, the GGS leadership – the

66. Julius Verdy du Vernois, *Studien über den Krieg* (Berlin, 1902) 3, no. 1, p. 12. "Weiterhin ist es die Kriegsgeschichte, welche bei unserem Vorhaben in Betracht kommt; sie ist für uns die wichtigste Quelle, Erkenntnisse zu schöpfen und durch erneutes und vielseitiges Studium bereits erlangte Erkenntnisse zu reguliren . . . Am wichtigsten aber bleibt für uns die Verwerthung der Kriegsgeschichte als eine Handhabe zur Prüfung."
67. Poten, *Militär-Erziehungswesen*, 4: 30; Krauß, "150 Jahre," p. 132.

chief and his main advisors – read the solutions, and then everyone was called together, probably around a large sand table or in the GGS map room, for a final critique at which the best solutions were discussed. The final problem of the year, completed in May–June, continued to influence the next year's assignments for younger officers. By 1899 the RRS conducted extensive written war games. In the War Academy gaming was used extensively, especially for the final test at the close of the third year. Below GGS level, TGSs replicated these exercises at corps and divisional levels. Regimental officers, even those in the cavalry, were given war game problems to solve as part of the "winter work."[68]

During the summer half year from 1 April to 1 November, war games moved outdoors. The GGS chief led two rides a year. It seems that a single ride had been customary up to 1891, but by 1899 two a year was typical, with one scheduled in June and one in October. A few years later a new outdoor war game was instituted; the administrative staff ride was an extensive supply, support, and transportation war game. Schlieffen also added the GGS fortress ride. The best-known and most visible war games were those large-scale maneuvers conducted during the summer. These continually grew. More units participated, and the games themselves became larger.[69]

In 1891 some officers within the GGS had regarded Waldersee's removal as a sad day. Schlieffen was an unknown: they did not know how he would perform. Schlieffen's first Kaisermanöver in September 1891 solidified opinion in his favor. The maneuver demonstrated skill in execution and a completeness which up to then had hardly ever been attained. Outside the GGS, Schlieffen was criticized for the Kaisermanövers. It was said he allowed the Kaiser to run roughshod over them, creating a spectacle which had little or no military value. Schlieffen had given the matter considerable thought. His conclusion was that one could question whether it was a good idea for the "all highest warlord" himself to participate. However there could be no doubt that if the Kaiser played, he had to win.[70]

---

68. Cf. Livonius, *Erinnerungen*, p. 218.
69. BAMA, Nachlaß Beseler, Lebenserinnerungen, p. 59. Hermann von François, *Verwaltungs-Generalstabsreisen* (Berlin, 1910), introd.; Stein, *Erlebnisse*, p. 30; Jany, *Preußische Armee*, 4: 298.
70. BAMA, Nachlaß Beseler, Lebenserinnerungen, p. 152; Stein, *Erlebnisse*, p. 35.

It seems likely that what Schlieffen did was self-conscious and had several purposes. One was to continue the Kaisermanöver as an outdoor military show rivaling the naval fleet maneuvers which usually followed them on the imperial schedule. It was a once-a-year public display and Wilhelm could do what he liked. Schlieffen set it up so that unless the sovereign made drastic mistakes, he would win. Second, Schlieffen recognized the public relations value of the maneuvers, as demonstrated by his treatment of foreign military observers and of the foreign press. It is possible that Schlieffen had in mind a kind of "deterrence by demonstration," publicly displaying the powerful and efficient German army to European military observers. This is in marked contrast to the passion for secrecy of his successor, Helmuth von Moltke the Younger. Third, Schlieffen recognized that strategic war relationships could in any event not be fully portrayed in an exercise. Cost and consideration for the maneuver area limited what could be accomplished. Yet many essential aspects of the war mobilization could nevertheless be tested.

The most important game for war planning was the GGS ride. Schlieffen led thirty-one of these: sixteen along the west front, fifteen at the east front. They were the most intimate testing ground for men and ideas at the top of the Prussian war planning process. By 1894 one can see a new spirit in the rides. Schlieffen's concluding remarks sharply reflect the changes he perceived in war and in the task environment. In commanding armies today, he said, one can see fundamental differences when compared with earlier periods. A commander can no longer direct the battle with help from a few adjutants and ordinance officers. The army is far too large. The march order has replaced the attack order, and indeed it is not the march order which leads to the battle but the march order which sets the army into initial movement and finally leads to enemy contact. Things do not normally go smoothly and methodically, they happen only with difficulty. Sudden changes arise from new circumstances. For these situations orders from the high command are impossible. Lower-ranking officers therefore must of necessity reach independent decisions.[71] We no longer

71. Generalstab des Heeres, Kriegswissenschaftliche Abteilung, ed., *Dienstschriften des Chefs des Generalstabs der Armee Generalfeldmarschall Graf Alfred von Schlieffen*, vol. 2, *Die Großen Generalstabsreisen-Ost aus den Jahren 1891–1905* (Berlin, 1937), pp. 48–50; cf. Generalstab des Heeres, Kriegswissenschaftliche Abteilung, ed., *Bestimmungen über Generalstabsreisen* (Berlin, 1908).

live in the period of the cabinet wars, Schlieffen said, when one knew exactly how many battalions and squadrons each general had. We live in an era of the army of the people. Behind the peacetime standing army, which can be generally known, stand reserve corps and reserve armies. How shall one know which part of this million-man army one has in front of one? The general who marches against the enemy must be superior to him in quantity or quality. Mathematical certainty that he is stronger in numbers is seldom known. Schlieffen emphasized that every military situation was the result of mistakes made by both sides. Commanders must perceive and use the mistakes of the enemy and understand how far they can overstep "scientifically given laws" in any situation.[72]

During the 1890s Schlieffen restlessly turned east and west, southwest and northeast, trying to master Prussia's strategic dilemmas. From 1892 he recognized that a two-front war would be necessary, with England very possibly fighting against Germany.[73] By the middle of the decade it was clear that whatever chaos the Kaiser might work throughout the Reich leadership, aside from the corps commanders, he would leave the GGS alone. Aside from Wilhelm himself, Schlieffen became one of the longest surviving major figures in the Prussian and Reich leadership.

### Railroads and the War Planning Process

By 1894 the RRS was becoming dominant in war planning. By then Russia was defined as a slow-mobilizing power. France was considered a rapid-mobilizing power. Both conclusions depended on railroads, France's modern radial system contrasted with Russia's poor, incomplete one. In the interval or "window" between the rapid-mobilizing French and the slow-mobilizing Russians, Prussian war planners began to consider whether there might be enough time first to defeat the French, then move east to defeat the Russians. The vehicle on which this consideration rested was the railroad system.

By about 1897 the Reich railroad system envisioned by Bismarck

---

72. Generalstab des Heeres, Kriegswissenschaftliche Abteilung, ed., *Dienstschriften des Chefs des Generalstabs der Armee Generalfeldmarschall Graf Alfred von Schlieffen*, vol. 1, *Die taktisch-strategischen Aufgaben aus den Jahren 1891–1905* (Berlin, 1937), pp. 16, 123.
73. Rochs, *Schlieffen*, p. 34.

in the early 1870s was approaching completion. It included 32,000 miles of track. To be sure, this system was still comprised of a diverse mixture of public and private, Prussian, Bavarian, Saxon, and Württembergian lines. In 1893 a new set of regulations governing the railroad system was published. These regulations gave the chief of the RRS influence over the building of track and purchase of equipment. At the same time the Reich railroad itself was reorganized into twenty-one directorates, each with a good deal of independence. This decentralized the entire system. The joint military-civilian LCs were also located in the same places as the Railroad Directorates and, in most cases, were also the headquarters of the corps in that region. The chief of the RRS appeared at Reichstag budget commission hearings to discuss the strategic role of the railroads, since these were included in defense bills. Month-long sessions during the early 1890s resulted in a whole series of railroad building programs. Important connecting lines, especially in the border areas, new track systems, bridges over the Rhine and Weichsel rivers, and additions to existing track were put on the drawing boards. Electric signal and telegraph service was installed along the main lines. By 1904 the existing track had increased to 35,000 miles. More important, Germany had 20,000 locomotives, in contrast to 12,000 for France and 10,000 for Russia, which gave the German system a larger work capacity. By then the GGS considered itself to have overtaken France and to have achieved a many-day advantage over Russia as measured by the railroad system's ability to concentrate forces at the border for war.[74]

Schlieffen knew something about railroads because, as we have seen, he had been involved in setting up large-scale maneuvers during the 1880s. However, he had never been directly involved in railroad planning. By 1894, the third year of his tenure as chief, both the domestic and foreign task environments had altered drastically. Judging from his letters, he was already beginning to feel the pressure to move in the direction of what he later called a "new stage in the evolution of war." The change was intended to gain a decisive technological advantage.

During the 1890s several innovations inclined him in that direction. One was the introduction of standard time throughout Germany. The MTP was customarily written in local time, which then

---

74. Staabs, *Aufmarsch*, pp. 18–20.

had to be translated into service timetables by railroad officials so that the whole system worked together. To avoid confusion in war mobilization, the military asked the Reichstag in 1889 to legislate standard time throughout Germany. The Reichstag refused. In 1891, a few weeks before he died, Field Marshal Moltke addressed the plenary session of the Reichstag on time reform. Moltke told the Reichstag that the five different German time zones created difficulties in the event of war. Mobilization timetables had to be detailed in the time used in each locality. Naturally the reserves called out could only judge by the clock at the place of their assembly. As the north German authorities only reckoned by Berlin time, all the arrangements and tables had to be in Berlin time. This same procedure, repeated elsewhere, easily became a source of error. A change in the arrangements, a stoppage or accident on the railway very much increased the difficulties. To arguments that the introduction of common time would cause confusion in daily life, Moltke replied that time was already manipulated. The agricultural worker did not pay much attention to the hour. He looked around to see if it was already light and knew he would soon be called to work by the court bell. When the court bell clock went wrong and chimed a quarter of an hour too fast, then certainly the worker arrived a quarter of an hour before it was time to work, but by the same clock he left a quarter of an hour before it was time for work to end. The duration of work remained the same. Seldom in practical life was punctuality required in respect to minutes. In many places it was customary for the school clock to be put ahead ten minutes so that the children were present when the teacher arrived. In villages which lay near the railways, the rule was to put the clock forward some minutes so that local people did not miss the train. Indeed, this difference often became a quarter of an hour or more. Moltke concluded by saying that the legal proclamation of standard time was needed for the security of the most important traveler, the defender of the fatherland traveling to the border. The Reichstag agreed.[75]

A second change was the reorganization of the GGS Railroad Section. Even though in 1891 the RRS was the highest military authority for the use of railroads in war, its chief was only a major and thus not equal in rank to regimental commanders. Officers who

---

75. *Documents Relating to the Fixing of a Standard Time* (Ottawa, 1891), pp. 25–28.

wanted to be promoted had to be reassigned. The LCs, moreover, were often staffed by young lieutenants on temporary duty from the Secondary Bureau. In 1894 Schlieffen began to change this situation. The RRS was upgraded, given more men, and reorganized. The chief, now a lieutenant colonel, sat at the top of an organization of LCs, each of which comprised one region of the civil railroad administration. Each LC was directed by a military officer and a civilian official of equal rank, both technically trained to deal with railroads, plus a staff of subordinates. In a relationship paralleling that of the GGS and the TGS, RRS officers were vertically integrated into the Reich railroad bureaucracy. They worked outside Berlin at the regional rail headquarters, where a joint military-civil office supervised the railroad aspects of war planning, helped to facilitate maneuver and exercise transportation, and cooperated in planning the future development of the rail system.[76]

Since at this point railroad technology begins to dominate war planning processes, it is necessary to describe briefly its main characteristics. Three factors controlled rail planning: size, space, and time. The track system defined size, train scheduling controlled space, and signaling defined time. At the most basic level was the track system. From the 1830s on, rail technology progressed from cast to wrought iron, then to steel. Rail segments lengthened from 24 to 110 feet. Track weight increased from 95 to 120 pounds per yard or more. Laying of track changed: formation drainage, ballast points, and crossings improved. Instead of serving as a fixed geometric structure, track became a flexible complex that relied on its resilience for varying degrees of control: it had to be rigid enough to ensure safe passage of trains, but flexible enough to adapt progressively to the forces acting on it and thus avoid the buildup of excessive strains. All of this was mathematically measurable by weight and speed. The outcome was that by the 1890s concentrations of heavy and high speed traffic became possible for the first time. In the years 1892 to 1905 European and American trains set speed records that were not broken until the 1960s. What had been technically impossible in the 1860s became practical in the 1890s.[77]

76. Schellendorff, *Duties*, pp. 39–41; Staabs, *Aufmarsch*, p. 21.

77. *History of Railroads*, 2 vols. (London, 1972), "Tracks for Tomorrow," 2: 545–48. Preußischer Minister der öffentlichen Arbeiten, Bayerischer Staatsminister für Verkehrsangelegenheiten, Eisenbahn-Zentralbehörden anderer deutscher Bundesstaaten, *Das deutsche Eisenbahnwesen der Gegenwart*, 2 vols. (Berlin, 1911), vol. 1, chap. 3; Haines, *Efficient Railway Operation*, pp. 214–45.

The second factor was space. Space was controlled by railroad timetables that evolved into a complex, mathematical plan. Its task cycle had several stages. First came the preliminary stage, which took into consideration train loadings, frequency of service, times of first and last trains, intermediate stops, average speed, journey time, and train formation. The first draft considered the power of the locomotive, overall train weight, maximum speed on each track segment, and the signaling system that governed the headway or signal blocks between trains. Train timing was a problem of pure mathematics based on the power-to-weight ratio of the train as a whole, signal capacity, station allowances, and principle connections. Train schedules are interactive systems: they must synchronize to work. Interconnection and synchronization are based on accurate numbers. Even locomotive power capacity was based on technical factors such as the quality of coal. Higher-quality coal meant larger work capacity. The principle of timetable building was that a great number of trains could be run over a section of track if they all traveled at equal or near equal speed. Therefore trains were grouped in flights called the "correct speed mix." Timetables were often so complex they had to be devised a year in advance. Once set, they could not be altered easily or quickly. A third factor was time. Time was controlled by the signal system. Each rail line was divided up into a series of block sections running from one signal box to another. The general rule was that no more than one train ran in one block section at a time. In the late 1840s the telegraph helped to control these. By the 1890s telephones were introduced.[78]

In all of these matters, standardization and uniformity were employed to bring order. Achieving this was the result of organization. To run railroads efficiently required preplanning and very long lead times. One to five years was not unusual. Ten-year periods were common. By 1900 the Prussian State Railroad was the largest bureaucratic organization in Germany with the greatest number of employees, broadest span of control, and largest amount of investment capital. As railroad technology became central to the GGS, railroad procedures began to influence GGS ideas. The modern GGS ethos, defined as continuous, reliable, predictable

---

78. *History of Railroads*, "Planning the Time Table", 1: 425–28, "Signalling," 1: 173–75; Preußischer Minister der öffentlichen Arbeiten, *Das deutsche Eisenbahnwesen der Gegenwart*, vol. 1, chaps. 5, 17; Haines, *Efficient Railway Operation*, pp. 257–70.

service regardless of which GGS officer was in charge, began to derive from this technology.

An example of how size, space, and time came together in railroad planning is provided by Wilhelm Groener. On 1 April 1899 Groener joined the RRS to work in the west front section. His assignment was to lay out the technical railroad plan for the war mobilization. He was assigned to Line Command C, encompassing the region of railroad direction for Frankfurt am Main. His wife helped him to work out the series sketches showing echelon differences between flights of trains in correct speed mixture. For the MTP each line was divided into a series of stretches, with arrival and departure times all dependent upon the first train, the so-called lead train. Behind it all the others followed at designated intervals. Each line was laid out in tables and charts. If one was off schedule, the whole line and everything which followed was thrown off. Once one train was accidentally left out, and Groener and his wife had to work all day Sunday to redraw the series sketches. In addition to line C, the other nineteen LC echelon charts were worked up. Slowly Groener became aware of the whole west front war plan. Because railroads were interconnected systems, knowledge of one LC's transportation plan gave insight into the whole war plan. This is undoubtedly why RRS war games were all classified for official use only and were often "secret" by the late 1890s.[79]

By this time the war plan was divided into four parts. Phase one, mobilization, designated the movement of reservists, horses, weapons, supplies, and munitions to single mobilization points, their military units. From there the units moved to a railroad on-loading point or military collection stations. There were thirty-one of these by 1914. Phase one transportation went across, around, and through Germany. Various war materials such as equipment or weapons were stockpiled at collection points, an activity requiring close coordination with the War Ministry and the corps commands. Phase two, the MTP, involved a uniform movement of trains through the single LCs, all of which were tightly interconnected with larger stretches called transportation paths. Once loaded onto a train, troops, materials, weapons, munitions, and horses remained on board until transportation was complete and only debarked some

79. Freiherr Hiller von Gaertringen, *Wilhelm Groener: Lebenserinnerungen*, ed., (Göttingen, 1957), pp. 66–67.

distance from the border crossings. Schlieffen recognized that moving the off-loading point ahead was one way of placing the entire mass forward. At the frontiers the main force was preceded by special advance attack groups, that is, reinforced cavalry and infantry, which protected the border area rail lines, towns, and fortifications. The timing of this force had been Waldersee's special concern: he wanted to speed it up. Phase three called for the concentration of the armies from the railhead to the borders, followed by phase four, the deployment itself. As Groener learned, the proof stone of the whole mobilization came when the RRS laid out its transportation plan: from it they were able to ascertain whether the war plan could be carried out in the time and space provided. The MTP was the sine quo non of the war plan. It was the only phase which, if it worked properly, was thought to guarantee reliable, predictable, and continuous execution.[80]

Like Moltke, Schlieffen drafted most of the war plan himself, working closely with two sections of the GGS, Railroad and Mobilization. The task schedule went as follows. At the beginning of winter, on 1 November, Section IIA of the RRS received a single sheet of paper titled "Directive for Deployment" on which the chief wrote in clear, precise language the strength of the army and its proposed concentration areas at the borders. Based on this information, the chief of the RRS prepared the railroad technical proposal. The technical feasibility of Schlieffen's ideas were worked out, using specific transportation paths, on- and off-loading stations, and timetables. Included were proposals for movement of army corps from one LC to another. These specifics then went back to Schlieffen with details so precise that he could plan his operational goals around them. From this study further ideas, new thoughts, or entirely different plans might originate. From December through February a series of war games were conducted. Those within the RRS, for example, were in series, were cumulative over a several-week period, and usually included many additions to the initial problem. On the basis of these, changes in the plans might be made. At the same time Groener and his colleagues were continually going over the MTP, tightening the rail schedules to achieve maximum load and minimum speed. The capacity of each rail segment was scrutinized. Normal civilian traffic speeds

80. U.S. National Archives, Washington, D.C., Groener Papers, roll 8, no. 35, letter to Reichsarchiv of 11 November 1923.

on main lines were thirty kilometers per hour, on secondary railroads twenty-five. The speed set for the MTP was a uniform twenty kilometers per hour. The whole war plan depended on maintaining that speed for fifteen to twenty-five consecutive days. After these war games, feasibility studies, and revisions, the war plan itself was set during March and went into effect on 1 April. Then portions were tested out during the summer in staff rides, exercises, and field maneuvers. In order to master all of the intricacies of the new transportation plan, RRS officers were assigned to one of the twenty field LCs for three months during the summer.[81]

By 1900, a great many additions and alterations to the German railroad system had been completed, in particular, the building of double track stretches in the east to transport a number of corps from the Rhine to the Weichsel and the improvement in the west Prussian lines and the lines to Metz. A new Rhine River bridge at Mainz was planned. On the basis of this expanded rail system, there were attempts to put greater flexibility into the MTP. For example, Groener conducted a war game with a few colleagues to determine whether it would be possible to turn the army about and redirect it right in the middle of a phase two railroad movement. At this time Schlieffen was searching for a solution to his strategic puzzle. He tried everything: in many studies he tested out the possibilities for a defense in the west using abrupt, unexpected army movements by railroad. Groener's war game suggested that the railroads held unexpected possibilities and that they could be developed into a flexible means for moving a very large army. No longer were railroads limited to rear area supply: they could now have a decisive impact on the operations of a battle. Groener wanted the railroad plans to have greater flexibility. Schlieffen in one of his studies worked out a small west front war plan in which only the border corps were given *fixed* MTP. The other corps were assigned certain train connections but no exact time schedules for mobilization days or fixed unloading stations. The unknown time factor was figured in the exercise as "X." Groener and Schlieffen realized that such an arrangement would be very difficult for corps commanders accustomed to the fixed and

---

81. Groener Papers, roll 12, no. 34, "Der Eisenbahn im Weltkrieg," p. 15; Staabs, *Aufmarsch*, p. 25; Groener Papers, roll 8, no. 35, letter of 7 March 1924 to Reichsarchiv. Gaertringen, *Groener*, p. 72; Haeussler, *Groener*, p. 33; Adolf Sarter, *Die deutschen Eisenbahnen im Kriege* (Stuttgart, 1930), p. 42.

rigid timetables of the war plan.[82]

Prussian war plans were continually changing, depending as much on the foreign military situation as on Prussian size and configuration. In the 1870s Moltke had believed that France was not only the most dangerous enemy but the one which could mobilize first. The Russians, he believed, would take many weeks to reach the Weichsel River. His war plans were aimed at fighting a defensive-offensive campaign against the French for several weeks, then turning these forces east against the Russians. On neither campaign field did Moltke expect as decisive a victory as happened in 1870. It was to be a limited battle, responding to a French or Russian attack, then falling upon them, piece by piece. In the 1880s Moltke's war plans changed. The reorganization of the French army and the new fortifications along the German border convinced him that rapid military successes in the west were no longer possible. The Austrian alliance of 1879 was in place. Instead the war plans called for an active defensive action in the west and a limited offensive against Russia, aided by Austrian forces. The Italian alliance of 1882 added the possibility of friendly forces on the upper Rhine. The war plans of the late 1880s included a sustained west front defensive and a rapid offensive on the east front in coordination with the Austrians. By 1890 strategic thinking almost balanced force sizes. Greater flexibility was introduced so that even strategic troop movements could be changed depending on how the opening battles came out. Against this, however, was the ever-increasing size of the forces and the inherent conservatism of the commanding generals, some of whom did not trust the railroads.[83]

During the nineteen years from 1871 to 1890, there had been no Franco-Russian alliance or military agreement. France remained isolated and Bismarck worked to maintain French isolation. Although a west front foe was expected at the start of hostilities, the entry as well as the timing of a potential east front enemy remained uncertain and problematic. Very late in this period, through provisions of the secret Russian-German Reinsurance Treaty of June 1887, the two powers promised each other neutrality in the event either became involved in war with a third

82. Gaertringen, *Groener*, p. 77; Groener Papers, roll 8, no. 35, Groener letter of 11 November 1923 to Reichsarchiv.
83. Staabs, *Aufmarsch*, pp. 12–14.

power, provided neither signatory was the aggressor. In March 1890 the reinsurance treaty came up for a renewal. Bismarck and N.K. Giers, the German and Russian foreign ministers, both favored it. But Bismarck was removed from office, and on 18 June the treaty was discontinued, probably due to Holstein and his friends. In the following three years, this lapse fundamentally and dramatically altered the diplomatic as well as the military task environment. By August 1891 a Franco-Russian military agreement had been accepted in principle and in January 1894 a secret military alliance was completed.[84] The exact nature of this changed environment was already becoming clear when Schlieffen described it as follows in November 1892. The French military law of 1889 gave France, with only thirty-eight million inhabitants, a larger army than Germany, with forty-seven million. This size diffential between the armies of the two countries would grow larger in time and, Schlieffen believed, could become as great as a million men. At the same time, the German army was of better quality and younger than the French. On the east front Germany also confronted a much larger enemy. In war Russia would send the largest part of its forces against Germany, the smaller part against Austria. Therefore Germany's enemies outnumbered it in a ratio of 5:3. It was clear that Germany had to enlarge its army. The art of the commander was easily defined; he is numerically stronger on the battlefield. Prussia's victories in the nineteenth century – 1813–15, 1864, 1866, and 1870 – were won at least partially for this reason. Everything is now in flux. The only certainty is the fundamental that our army must be as strong as possible.[85]

Initially Schlieffen did not change the war plan, although the GGS rides, war games, tactical exercises, and maneuvers indicate that his ideas were quite different from Moltke's. From the start, he thought in terms of timing a two-front war. As the French increased the size of their army, built their fortifications, and quickened the speed of their mobilization, he concluded that an immediate French attack was planned. France was the larger and more dangerous enemy and some response to this danger had to be made. By the late 1890s, confronted with the fact of the Franco-

84. George Kennan, *The Fateful Alliance: France, Russia, and the Coming of the First World War* (New York, 1984), p. 20; D.C.B. Lieven, *Russia and the Origins of the First World War* (New York, 1983), pp. 15,155–56; Nichols, *Germany after Bismarck*, pp. 53–57.

85. Kessel, *Schlieffens Briefe*, pp. 296–97.

Russian alliance, Schlieffen used the war games, GGS rides, and maneuvers to search for a way of dealing with this problem. He looked for a momentary time advantage against one enemy or a temporary time lag against another. He must have sent members of the GGS into Belgium and northeastern France to examine their railroad systems, just as he sent members of the RRS on a tour of the western Russian provinces in 1899. They reported that the Russian railroads in these areas were ten years behind Germany.[86]

As a result of the European railroad systems, purely technical considerations began to suggest certain strategic possibilities. By 1900 the thickest railroad network in Europe was that of Belgium, whereas in Germany the thickest railroads were in the northwest quadrant of the west border. Although the average for Germany was 11.31 kilometers per square kilometer, there were great variations. The Rhine province had 17.59, Hesse 19.43, Baden 13.88, and Alsace-Lorraine 12.66. East Prussia had the lowest, 7.83, and of the other border provinces West Prussia had 8.89, Posen 9.77, and Silesia 11.84. As for the east front, in 1892 Schlieffen wrote that the "almost railwayless vastness of Russia" created great technical difficulties to be overcome both in deploying troops and in advancing through Lithuania. In 1894 Schlieffen expected a rapid French attack in the west and considered detraining German forces further forward to meet the attack with a German initiative.[87]

Schlieffen's search for the solution to his strategic puzzle led him to military history, where he tried to identify precedents for the strategic problem with which he was confronted, as he had done all his life. He had determined that Germany could no longer utilize a passsive or defensive approach. Following GGS historical writing of the previous quarter century, the lesson of the past was that the only legitimate strategy was to attack in battles of annihilation. Time and size disadvantages created by the rise of the Triple Entente dictated that the initiative had to be seized. By the late 1890s, questions to be resolved concerned the essential details:

86. Staabs, *Aufmarsch*, p. 31.

87. Sarter, *Deutsche Eisenbahnen*, p. 34; Kessel, *Schlieffens Briefe*, pp. 34, 38. In addition to a lack of good railroads, there were other factors influencing Schlieffen's thinking regarding the east front. Cf. Lothar Höbett, "Schlieffen, Beck, Potiorek und das Ende der gemeinsamen deutsch-österreichisch-ungarischen Aufmarschpläne im Osten," *Militärgeschichtliche Mitteilungen* 12 (1984): 7–30.

whether to go first to the east or to the west, what size and structure of forces to send, and above all, in what manner to carry out the attack. Gerhard Ritter, noting the decisive difference between the German war plans of 1892–99 and that of 1905, says that the period after 1899 marks a sudden and radical change which points to the central issue in the historical understanding of the Schlieffen Plan. The answer to Schlieffen's strategic conundrum seems to have come from history. In about 1900 he read an account of the famous battle of Cannae in 216 B.C. In it a Carthaginian army, outnumbered almost two to one, virtually annihilated a larger Roman force by moving around the flanks and into their opponents' rear. The Romans panicked and were destroyed almost to a man.[88]

Schlieffen's description of this battle, which marked a turning point in his strategic thinking, is instructive. He wrote that both armies advanced against each other. Hasdrubal, Carthaginian second in command, overpowered the weaker hostile cavalry on the right flank. The conquerer then turned the front of the hostile infantry and advanced against the Roman cavalry on the wing. The Romans were completely routed. Upon destruction of the hostile cavalry, Hasdrubal turned against the rear of the Roman phalanx. The Romans were pushed back, encircled, and crowded together. Hannibal, the Carthaginian commander, his heart full of hatred, circled the arena of the bloody work, encouraging the zealous, lashing out at the sluggish. Hours later his soldiers desisted. Weary of slaughter, they took the remaining three thousand men prisoners. In a narrow space, forty-eight thousand corpses lay in piles. Schlieffen believed that a battle of complete annihilation had been fought. In spite of all theories, it had been won by a numerically inferior army. Weapons and modes of combat had undergone a complete change during the intervening two thousand years. Still the fundamentals of warfare remained unchanged. A battle of annihilation could be fought today according to the same plan elaborated by Hannibal in that long-forgotten time. The hostile front was not the point of the attack. The essential problem was to crush the flanks. The wings should not be sought at the advanced points of the front, but along the entire depth and extension of the hostile formation. The extermination would then be completed by

88. Ritter, *The Schlieffen Plan: Critique of A Myth* (London, 1958); Bucholz, *Hans Delbrück*, pp. 58–63.

an attack against the enemy's rear.

Schlieffen then went on to describe how Frederick the Great, Napoleon, and Moltke had achieved similar successes, using nearly the identical strategy. Although he admitted that a complete battle of Cannae was a rare event in the history of war, Schlieffen believed that Moltke had come very close. Just as Napoleon had turned the front of the Prussian army assembled north of the Thuringian forest by rapid marches in 1806, Moltke, by means of railway transportation, had turned the front of the French on the upper Rhine and appeared at the central course of the river between Karlsruhe and Koblenz. If the Germans in 1870 had crossed the Meuse with their right wing and had forced the French in a southerly direction against the Rhine and the Swiss frontier, this would have corresponded to the Napoleonic strategy of 1806 and to Frederick's attack at Rossbach. Schlieffen concluded that only the incomplete railway system of forty years ago failed to allow for such an operation.[89]

89. Generalfeldmarschall Graf Alfred von Schlieffen, *Gesammelte Schriften*, 2 vols. (Berlin, 1913), 1: 27–30, 221–35.

# Chapter 4
# The Schlieffen Plan
# 1897–1905

The foreign task environment for the Second Reich continued to darken. With the first naval bill of 1897, Germany began a sustained high-technology arms race with England which, aided by the first Moroccan crisis, gradually and fundamentally alienated their relationship. In 1904 the Anglo-French Entente was signed.[1] The Franco-Russian military alliance had been in existence for ten years. The German leadership saw an iron circle closing around its country.

After fourteen years' work in the GGS and seven years as chief, Schlieffen in 1897–98 effected a major reorganization which coincided with the maturation of the Reich railroad system and the beginnings of a complete transformation of the war plan. The war plan and the GGS were linked by railroad technology: changes in one brought changes in the other. This is evident in each of its planning processes: organizational, educational, representational, and analytical. Technological linkages which allowed control of size and space in war did so only by increasing pressures of time. To move the size across the space required sufficient time. A seventy-two hour lag behind an opponent meant, in the minds of the GGS, possible compromise of the opening west front battles. Success in the west front war of forty days hinged, in timed sequence, on the east front campaign of thirty days' duration. The GGS was beginning to come to the same conclusion which the French general staff arrived at later: each loss of twenty-four hours of mobilization time to an opponent meant giving up ten to twelve miles of terrain space.[2] In war planning, time meant space.

---

1. Zara Steiner, *Britain and the Origins of the First World War* (New York, 1977), p. 30.
2. quoted by Stephen van Evera, "The Cult of the Offensive," p. 73. Such thinking was not new; the GGS, War Ministry, and other agencies had long thought in terms of the specific duration of a future war. Cf. Lothar Burchardt, *Friedenswirtschaft und Kriegsvorsorge: Deutschlands wirtschaftliche Rüstungsbestrebungen vor 1914* (Boppard am Rhein, 1968).

Schlieffen's changes in the war plan were completed by December 1905, in the midst of war crisis and uncertainty. After that date the draft of what became known as the Schlieffen Plan remained as his legacy to his successors. It was described as the most ambitious project ever undertaken for controlling the immediate future of so many people.[3]

## Schlieffen Reorganizes the GGS

The first aspect of war planning was organizational. Between 1890 and 1905, the GGS increased in size from fewer than three hundred to more than eight hundred – including those in Berlin, those assigned to the TGS and the Land Survey Department, and the increasing number of staff members attached from the War Ministry. During the same period the peacetime army strength increased from fewer than 500,000 to more than 600,000, an increase of about 20%. As for the war plan, mobilization in 1891 required thirty-seven divisions for the west front, twenty-two for the east front. Later Schlieffen prescribed thirty-three and a half corps for the west front alone. By 1905 the west front warmobilized army was seven times as large as the attack force of 1891.[4]

The overall size of the regular army grew in several ways. As the normal population grew, so did the army. And as foreign armies added men and especially funding, the German defense budget increased. Finally, as overall army size grew, the field army was regularly subdivided; new army corps were added and the whole structure enlarged. During Schlieffen's tenure five army corps were created: in 1890 the 16th (Metz) and 17th (Danzig); in 1900 the 2d Bavarian (Nuremberg), the 19th (Leipzig), and the 3d Bavarian (Nuremberg). At that time the entire Reich was reorganized into twenty-two army corps regions. From then until the First World War only two more were created, the 20th (Allenstein) and the 21st (Saarbrücken).[5]

---

3. Stephen Kern, *The Culture of Time and Space* (Cambridge, Mass., 1983), p. 284.

4. François, *Verwaltungs-Generalstabsreisen*, p. 18; Schellendorff, *Duties*, p. 42; Osten-Sacken, *Preußens Heer*, 3: 366; Jany, *Preußische Armee*, 4: 326; Ritter, *Schlieffen Plan*, pp. 25, 143; MGFA, *Handbuch*, 3: 55–57.

5. MGFA, *Handbuch*, 3: 55; on the technical details of adding new army corps cf.

On 1 April 1898, Schlieffen abolished the old distinctions between the Main and Secondary Bureaus, creating one centralized organization, as had been the case prior to 1867. The GGS was becoming a substantial bureaucracy. It directed what was, from the standpoint of German public and private organizations as a whole, the largest single institutional entity in the country. Grouped together with the government railroad and telegraph offices, with whom the GGS conducted an increasing volume of work, these organizations dwarfed civilian agencies. There were sixteen sections encompassing all assigned, attached, temporary, and permanent officers. The First, Third, and Ninth were the so-called language sections. The First dealt with Russia, the Balkans, and East Asia; the Third with France, Belgium, the Netherlands, and Luxembourg; the Ninth with Austria and Italy. The Fourth and Seventh Sections dealt with foreign fortresses and fortifications. The Second was the Mobilization Section. The Fifth and Eighth Sections dealt with educational matters, especially with continuing education and the War Academy. The Sixth Section was in charge of preparation, execution, and evaluation of the Kaisermanöver. There were two sections for military history, ancient and modern. The Land Survey Section, the RRS, and the Central Section oversaw the work of the whole organization. The final components of the GGS were the map library, the general library, and the archive.[6] The permanent cadre consisted of over two hundred

---

BHSA, A1–165, *Organisations-Bestimmungen aus Anlaß der Bildung zweier neuer Armeekorps* (Secret) (Berlin, 1889); BHSA, M. Kr. 1126 "Übersicht der Neuformationen bzw. Etatserhöhungen." In describing war planning processes, it is important to consider the various answers to the question of how large the Reich army was. Because of the question of reserves, the numbers given by different sources are often at variance. Active army corps have more men then reserve corps, and the same goes for divisions, regiments, and so forth. Some writers include civilian officials, some do not. It would appear that in 1890 there were twenty-eight army corps (with a wartime strength of 1,080,800, or fifty-nine divisions and a peacetime strength of about 468,409) and by January 1906 there were thirty-eight army corps (war time strength of 1,466,800, peacetime strength of about 600,000). Ritter, *Schlieffen Plan*, pp. 25, 143; Geyer, *Rüstungspolitik*, p. 53; Elze, *Tannenberg*, p. 3. Rahne's figures are different: he includes all potentially mobilizable men ages seventeen to forty-five. Thus by 1888 Rahne's war-mobilized army is 2,746,000 and in 1914 it is 3,983,950, including the navy. Rahne, *Mobilmachung*, pp. 92, 143. Both figures are reasonable given Rahne's framework of including reserves of all age groups. His 1914 figure, for example, is very close to that of the MGFA's *Handbuch*, 3: 57.

6. Schellendorff, *Duties*, pp. 39–41; cf. Kocka, "The Rise of the Modern Industrial Enterprise in Germany," pp. 77–116; Rainer Fremdling, "Germany," in Patrick O'Brien, ed., *Railways and the Economic Development of Western Europe 1830–1914*

captains, majors, and colonels. The temporary cadre, who served one- to three-year probationary stints, consisted of approximately 160 first lieutenants. A third group, about seventy per year, consisted of those officers who participated in GGS rides. A fourth group, the TGS, which served with the corps and divisions, comprised about 175. During their tour in Berlin, officers were regularly rotated to troop units during the summer and also to the TGS for "front" experience every three to five years.[7]

Large, formal paper flow processes continued to burgeon. Take for example the intelligence collection effort. Knowledge of foreign armies became more detailed and specific. Intelligence collected in the language departments included pure military data on topics such as organization, mobilization, education, tactics, weapons and shooting capability, knowledge of the leading personalities, and ship movements of the navy. But it also encompassed such matters as railroad and other transportation construction, governmental budgets, and politics. Each assigned officer was responsible for a discrete body of knowledge and briefed the section chief weekly. Section chiefs assembled the most important details from these individual reports and presented them as a sector analysis to the chief of the GGS. In addition to oral reports, expanded memorandums, and essays, books dealing entirely with intelligence began to be published. The GGS work, *The French Army*, a three-hundred-page description and analysis that included organization, mobilization, tactics, education, the horse provision system, colonial troops, and naval and coastal fortifications was by no means unique.[8] This enhanced collection drive resulted from an extensive effort which may have produced better information than historians have thus far recognized. Knowledge was accumulated from the scientific and general press, army regulations, service publications, and military literature. Officers read the leading newspapers and magazines and collated information from official and classified sources such as military attachés. There was a covert intelligence section which had close relationships to corps intelligence officers on the east and west borders, who sent "trusted

(New York, 1983), pp. 121–47; Bergh, *Das deutsche Heer*, pp. 168–70; MGFA, *Handbuch*, 3: 69–72.

7. Bergh, *Das deutsche Heer*, p. 170.

8. Ibid., p. 171; Generalstab des Heeres, Kriegswissenschaftliche Abteilung, ed., *Die französische Armee* (Berlin, 1909).

persons" across the border in times of political tension.[9]

As we have seen, the GGS utilized various mechanisms to integrate the war plan at all levels of the Reich army. Although some of these were utilized for normal peacetime operations, the bottom line in all cases was mobilization. These mechanisms included line and staff rotation, the chief of staff system, Horse Purchase Commissions, DCs, and above all the RRS. We have already described these mechanisms and therefore need deal here only with those features which were new in this period.

The million-man armies of the early twentieth century created new problems in the area of horses. In 1870 the ratio of men to horses was 4:1. In 1914 this ratio was 3:1. This may not appear to be much of a change; however, it was significant because horses needed ten times as much food as men. In July 1870 the Prussian forces used 250,000 horses. Thirty years later, over 715,000 horses had to be purchased at mobilization to augment the existing peacetime complement, which was approximately 100,000. Although there were sufficient horses in Germany, they were mainly available from East Prussia. In many of the industrial areas in the western border regions, corps could not supply their own requirements. At mobilization, therefore, a great movement of animals in an east to west direction was necessary. For military purposes, horses were divided into four categories according to usage: the best were reserved for the cavalry, second best for the trains, third best for the field artillery, and fourth best for the heavy artillery. As late as 1900 each troop unit purchased its own. By the law of 1871, horse dealers throughout the Reich were required to offer animals to military authorities for examination and purchase. In spite of the regional organization of the forces, there were problems. For example, corps commands had difficulty estimating exactly how many horses were available in their areas during peacetime. As a result of this inaccuracy, the railroad LCs were handicapped in making detailed plans for horse transport. Above all, the complicated and time-consuming health examination of horses conducted by army veterinarians and the complex purchase procedures, entailing much paperwork, impeded rapid mobilization.[10]

In the fall of 1900, the horse purchase system was completely

9. Bergh, *Das deutsche Heer*, p. 173; Herwig, "Imperial Germany," pp. 62–97; Ulrich Trumpener, "War Premeditated? German Intelligence Operations in July 1914," *Central European History* 9 (March 1976): 58–85.

10. Bergh, *Das deutsche Heer*, p. 178; Militärgeschichtliches Forschungsamt, ed.,

reorganized. The entire horse population of the Reich was to be examined periodically by army inspectors, the number of horses determined, their military usefulness verified, and their availability for purchase at mobilization certified. Each corps command organized a Horse Muster Commission. At first these were part of the reserve DC system, after 1903 of the active cavalry brigades. The muster commissions gave out orders for mobilization horse purchase in peacetime. Although it might be argued that the horse purchase system was a War Ministry and not a GGS matter, in fact it was a precondition of the war plan. Horse purchase had to be accomplished prior to full implementation of the MTP. For this reason, the horse purchase program was an important concern of the GGS.[11]

The DC had been established in 1867. On the surface, its function was mainly to coordinate reserve activities such as courts of honor and summer duty. In fact, its essential purpose was mobilization. By 1898 there were 295 DCs, each one responsible for an average of 85,000 soldiers. Berlin, for example, was divided into four districts. The 18th Corps headquartered in Frankfurt am Main had fourteen districts, the 11th Corps headquartered in Erfurt had twenty-two. Their main duty was to keep track of all men who lived within them and to call them up once a year in an exercise which, in various ways, simulated a mobilization.

By 1898 doubts were raised about the effectiveness of this system. The force was very large and the time and security constraints daunting. The annual test mobilization itself was arduous. DC One in Berlin, for example, had to send out 160,000 mobilization orders within a few hours. Great numbers and four levels of forces – field, reserve, Landwehr, and *Ersatz* – made for a broad differentiation among these forces. The possibilities for errors and problems were great, and the whole process was considered risky.

In 1899 a new system was tested out on the 7th Corps (Westphalia), whose DCs had the largest population in the Reich. It consisted of handing out mobilization orders during peacetime. Each order specified the day and hour at which the individual was to report to the collection station or kaserne as soon as mobilization was announced through the press or by notices placed in public

---

*Die Bedeutung der Logistik, für die militärische Führung von der Antike bis in die Neuzeit* (Bonn, 1986), p. 136; Rahne, *Mobilmachung*, p. 105.

11. Rahne, *Mobilmachung*, p. 123.

locations. Beginning 1 April 1901 this system was extended to all districts and thereafter was continually refined as numbers increased and time decreased. This large body of men was separated into two groups and given two kinds of orders. The first kind, known as a "war commanded pass," was given to those reservists called up during the first six days of mobilization who were to be inserted into the war-mobilizing army. The second kind, called the "war readiness pass," was given to trained and untrained recruits who were to be called up after the first six days to fill reserve units. After 1900 conservative generals raised concerns about the secrecy of this system. They feared its compromise or nonfulfillment by members of the political left. The war articles from the constitution were read to recruits and reserves. They were enjoined never to give mobilization information to anyone, to keep it secret, and to give only their DC number and active troop unit to officials when requested. Later a code was developed for further protection: war mobilization information was published in the form of letters and numbers which stood for locations and units.[12]

As we saw in chapter 2, the problem of integrating active and reserve forces was complicated. Reserve forces tended to be created in this period more rapidly than regulars. The period from 1887 to 1897 had marked a new stage in the development of the Prussian army during which reserve forces burgeoned, and now they continued to grow. Under the influence of Heinrich von Gössler, director of the General War Department in the War Ministry, Chancellor von Caprivi systematically increased reserves. Here again the fundamental controversy between a quantity or a quality army surfaced. GGS Chief Waldersee and Kaiser Wilhelm II wanted a high-quality army above all. Caprivi wanted full mobilization, a quantitative approach. The army increases in 1888–1897 changed the whole system. The result was a larger active army, elongated funding, and a more rapid increase in reserves. After Caprivi fell from power in 1894, everyone tried to protect themselves from the consequences of these changes. But the basic framework of the 1914 war-mobilized army had come into existence.[13] German men of ages seventeen to forty-five

12. Ibid., pp. 120–21; cf. BHSA, M. Kr. M 27, Bezirke des IV, XI and XVIII Armeekorps vom 1 April 1899.

13. Craig, *Politics*, pp. 242ff.; Ritter, *Sword and the Scepter*, 2: 209–10; Schulte, *Deutsche Armee*, pp. xviii–xxxxv which introduces this problem; Förster, *Der doppelte Militarismus*, pp. 28–43; Geyer, *Rüstungspolitik*, p. 69; MGFA, *Handbuch*, 3: 48–57; Werdermann, "Heeresreform," pp. 57–64.

were liable for military service as follows: ages twenty to twenty-one: active duty; ages twenty-two to twenty-seven: reserve duty (two drills every two months or two weeks' duty during the summer); ages twenty-eight to thirty-one: service with Landwehr I (reduced drills); ages thirty-two to thirty-nine: service with Landwehr II (further reduced drills); ages seventeen to nineteen and forty to forty-five: no service requirement except in war, when called upon to serve in the Landsturm for home defense or, in case of extraordinary necessity, to increase the size of the field army.[14]

Schlieffen's war planning of the 1890s recognized the distinction between active and reserve forces and called for using reserves only in secondary roles. The War Ministry in October 1899 had wanted to use some reserve forces in the front line opening offensive, mixing them with the regular army. Schlieffen disagreed: this had not worked in the past and it did not usually work in war games and maneuvers. The whole matter could be demonstrated mathematically, Schlieffen argued. Line battalions, he said, could march twenty kilometers a day, reserve battalions fifteen kilometers per day, therefore a division made up of this mixed force was reduced to marching at the rate of its slowest element. Furthermore, reserve forces did not have the same artillery as line troops. Line infantry had twelve or fourteen batteries, reserve infantry only six to eight batteries; therefore they could not fill a place on the front line because this would reduce the firepower. Finally, he argued that reserves were not as well trained as regulars and could not shoot as accurately or as rapidly.[15]

### Railroad Technology and GGS Processes

The RRS was becoming the GGS's most important integrating mechanism for war planning and mobilization, and it was intimately connected to the two large and dominant Reich bureaucracies for transportation and communications, the railroad and telegraph systems. The relationship between the GGS and the German railroads is well illustrated by a story from Max Hoffmann's memoirs. In 1900, as a GGS captain, he forgot the passports for his department

14. Elze, *Tannenberg*, p. 1; Osten-Sacken, *Preußens Heer*, 3: 25; MGFA, *Handbuch*, 3: 5.
15. Freiherr Ludwig Rüdt von Collenburg, "Graf Schlieffen und die Kriegsformation der deutschen Armee," *Wissen und Wehr* 8 (1927): 614–24.

head, General von Lindenau, during a trip to Poland. Telling his chief that he would meet him in Warsaw, Hoffmann on his own authority ordered up an express train, returned to Berlin, got the passports, and reported back to Warsaw just in time to greet the general as he was getting off at the station the next morning. After an appropriate reproof, Schlieffen paid for this junket out of GGS funds. The point is that a GGS captain had a certain leverage within the railroad system.[16]

By 1900 the Reich railroad system envisioned by Bismarck in 1873 finally reached near completion, and in that same year a new bureaucratic organization was put into place for the military railroad system. By 1904 it encompassed the RRS in Berlin and twenty-three LCs outside Berlin. Each LC was made up of officers from the GGS and officials of the railroads. Linked to the railroad system through the LCs, with which it communicated in writing, by telegraph, and by telephone, the RRS had by far the longest, most rapid, and technologically most sophisticated span of control of any GGS department. LCs each had control of a specific segment of the railroad. In peacetime they coordinated knowledge and planning. Knowledge of the current status of each segment was passed along to the RRS Map Section in Berlin for cartographic reproduction of each five kilometer stretch by type of track and degree of grade and curve. On the basis of these detailed railroad charts the work capacity of each segment – how much traffic it could bear, of what size, and how fast – was estimated mathematically. Each LC also knew the time schedule for trains in the current war plan. In 1900 there was concern that the French transportation plan had a time advantage during the first two days. It was believed that the French could move trains more quickly through their network, partly because each corps was assigned one whole line. In response the RRS tried to upgrade the work capacity of the German system, striving for increases of forty-eight to seventy-two trains per day on double track lines, and twenty-four to thirty-six trains per day on single track lines.

The mobilization year began on 1 April, when new time schedules were sent out to the LCs and regular exercises were introduced to train them to execute the MTP. In fact, learning and practicing the MTP was a major, continuing task. In winter, under the code word Kriegsspiel, LCs received short telegraphic mess-

16. Max Hoffmann, *War Diaries* (London, 1921), p. 12.

ages regarding various changes or important disruptions during execution of the MTP. Each LC was to respond with new orders and schedules for the segments of track under their control. Responses were returned to Berlin by express train.[17]

The RRS was the only unit of the GGS which had a close ongoing relationship with the German fleet, which was based on the fact that the MTP transported coal and men during the premobilization period. To "coal the fleet" was a large job which had to be done several days prior to the actual declaration of war. By 1900 the chief of the RRS had become a regular participant in the great summer fleet maneuvers in the North Sea, the naval equivalent of the Kaisermanöver.[18]

Joint military and civilian planning went forward in five- and ten-year cycles of laying new lines, double tracking existing routes, and upgrading bridges, tunnels, and equipment. Up to 1890 railroad construction had centered in Alsace-Lorraine and southwestern Germany. Thereafter it shifted to the northwest, where six additional Rhine River bridges were constructed. Equally important was the trans-Eifel railroad network of approximately 161 miles, stretching west from the Rhine to the borders of Luxembourg and Belgium between Aachen and Trier, which added the final infrastructure needed to link up with the high-density rail systems of Belgium and France. The result was that by early in the twentieth century, four armies, with twenty active and reserve corps and five cavalry divisions, could be assembled there.[19] As pointed out in chapter 3, Germany had a large and sophisticated rail system only exceeded by that of Belgium. In 1910 this system included 566,000 freight wagons with an average capacity per wagon of 13.68 tons. By March 1914 the number of freight cars had increased to 689,000, with 29,520 locomotives and 65,186 passenger cars. As previously noted, German railroads had a much lower ratio of locomotives to wagons than did the French and Russian railroads. This power ratio allowed capacity to be increased immediately.[20]

By 1900 the technology of railroads had begun to penetrate deeply into the war planning processes, creating at the heart of the

17. Staabs, *Aufmarsch*, pp. 30–33.
18. Ivo Lambi, *The Navy and German Power Politics* (Boston, 1984), chap. 13.
19. Staabs, *Aufmarsch*, p. 36; Haeussler, *Groener*, p. 33.
20. Philip Burtt, *Principal Factors in Freight Train Operation* (London, 1923), p. 98; Sarter, *Deutsche Eisenbahnen*, p. 263.

war planning system a core technology – the MTP – around which everything else was assembled. This core technology encompassed both plans and procedures. Technology here is defined as the systematic application of scientific knowledge to the practical task of war planning, in this case the engineering of railroads, which permeated throughout the military bureaucracy.

Railroads operate on the principles of physics, that is, in terms of overcoming resistance in moving a given size through a prescribed space in a fixed span of time. The tractive ability of a high-capacity locomotive, for example, to move one thousand tons at twenty miles per hour, depends upon overcoming three types of resistance, of grade, curve, and friction. Grade resistance, plus or minus from level, is the most severe. Curve resistance, left or right from straight, and friction, overcoming the inertia of bodies at rest, are less severe. However, all three are cumulative. That is, each single source of resistance of grade, curve, and friction is added together to give the resistance as a whole. For example, every axle of a railcar offers resistance and the resistance of each when totaled equals the cumulative resistance of the train. Thus the longer the train, the steeper the grade, and sharper the turn, the greater the resistance. This in turn affected speed. Each block within an LC had a maximum and minimum speed set according to the kinds of resistance contained within it.[21] For war planning,

21. Burtt, *Freight Train Operation*, pp. 36–57. The influence of technology in nineteenth- and early twentieth-century German economic and social history is an important area which requires research. A general introduction is Wilhelm Treue, ed., *Deutsche Technikgeschichte* (Göttingen, 1977). Discussions of the impact of technology on management and the beginning of modern organization in Germany include Heidrun Homberg, "Anfänge des Taylorsystems in Deutschland vor dem Ersten Weltkriege," *Geschichte und Gesellschaft* 4 (1978): 170–84; cf. Sidney Pollard, *The Genesis of Modern Management* (Cambridge, Mass., 1965). For the question of technology transfer, an important but unexplored area in general, but especially within military management and leadership, there is Melvin Kranzberg and Patrick Kelly, eds., *Technological Innovation: A Critical Review of the Literature* (San Francisco, 1972); Hugh Aitken, *Scientific Management in Action: Taylorism at Watertown Arsenal, 1908–1915* (Princeton, 1985). It is possible that in Germany certain modern management techniques were pioneered in public sector organizations, possibly even within the military, particularly the GGS and RRS. Jürgen Kocka's comments on the relationship between the development of the telegraph and military institutions are suggestive. The same may apply to the railroads. Werner Siemens, for example, was originally an artillery officer, 1816–38. Jürgen Kocka, *Unternehmensverwaltung und Angestelltenschaft am Beispiel Siemens, 1847–1914* (Stuttgart, 1969), pp. 48, 55, 175. It appears that historians of Germany in this period have persistently misunderstood the influence of the military in civilian economic and social life. In the historiographic battles spawned by the two world wars, some

however, perhaps the most important aspect is that all of this was mathematically calculable. Formulas provided for minimum speed and this in turn determined timetables. Earlier we argued that tracks defined size, scheduling controlled space, and signaling defined time. All of this was numerical, interactive, and required deep-future-oriented planning. To bring it about various control mechanisms were introduced: standardization, uniformity, interchangeability, and discipline. Based upon these considerations, the laws of physics impose certain operating rules upon railroad systems.

One rule is that of uniform speed. It is more efficient to keep trains moving and keep them moving at as high a speed as possible. Thus the fewer stops, slowdowns, speedups, and brakings, the more efficient the railroad. The goal is a uniform speed as high as possible. Traffic is organized in "correct speed flights" following the principle that greater volume can be achieved when all trains travel at equal speed. Overtaking is avoided by increasing the speed of slower trains or by segregating trains of the same speed on the same track. To control speed and enforce safety, railroad networks are divided into signal blocks. Each block has a general speed limit and, within individual segments, permanent speed restrictions at various points, based upon grade, curve, and traffic.

A second operating rule is interdependency. Almost everything in an active railroad network influences, rather immediately and directly, everything else. For example, one late-running train can result in four potential reactions: (1) the trains following on the same track must slow down; (2) the trains preceding on the same track must be shunted aside to let it pass; (3) the connecting trains at junctions must wait; (4) the trains will conflict at junctions when a late train must be given priority. All of these problems radiate out

---

realities have become clouded. Like many other forces in history, the influence of the military is mixed. For example, a recent analysis of the needs of the military for the health care of German soldiers is Timothy Lenoir, "A Magic Bullet: Research for Profit and the Growth of Knowledge in Germany around 1900," *Minera*, 26 (Spring 1988): 66–88. It has some surprising points. Kees Gispen's *New Profession, Old Order: Engineers and Germany Society, 1815–1914* (Cambridge, 1989) contains no mention of army engineers nor a hint that military engineering education existed. In another area the measurement of practical work capacity (Leistungsfähigkeit) within the GGS appears strikingly advanced and modern compared to its measurement by pioneer industrial psychologists in Germany, 1885–1910. Cf. Joan Campbell, *Joy in Work, German Work: The National Debate, 1800–1945* (Princeton, 1989), pp. 73–85.

in many directions from a single moving train. It is a dynamic interdependency which continually changes as single trains change position through the system.[22] A third rule is that of discipline. Railroad transportation, in contrast to road transportation, calls for highly disciplined movement. It is so because of the two operating principles discussed above. Uniform speed and interdependency require 100% mechanical discipline of speed and time synchronization. To maintain this discipline requires information about the system, the line, and the block. Everything must be predictable and follow prearranged, written directives. Discipline depends upon timely and accurate information.

These principles – uniformity of speed, interdependency of parts, and discipline of movement – resulted in a specific kind of organization for railroads. One of its foundations was the block signaling system introduced in about 1889, which divided railroads into regions, divisions, lines, and blocks. The most basic segment was the signal block into which one train was allowed at a time. As one block received a train, the block behind protected it and the block ahead was asked to receive it. The position of each signal post within a block was electrically known twelve to fifteen miles in both directions. To achieve the continuous movement which was the optimally efficient goal of railroad transportation, the maximum number of movements had to be planned in advance.[23]

Above the block was the line, the basic organizing unit of a railroad, defined according to its "line" capacity, or the number of trains which could pass through it in a given period of time. Line capacity was the unit within which size, space, and time was measured by (1) the time individual trains took to pass through; (2) the difference in speed between the slowest and fastest trains; (3) the arrangement of trains traveling at different speeds; (4) the length of the block sections within each line; and (5) the type of signaling employed, which determined the headway, or number of block sections between trains. The goal was continuous movement or "flow through" technology. Continuous process required control based on continuous information.

Beyond the organizational principles of blocks and lines, two other factors also affect railroad operation. One is the track pattern, which influences size, space, and time factors. The goal of

22. H. Samuel, *Railway Operating Principles* (London, 1961), pp. 11–26.
23. Philip Burtt, *Control on the Railways* (London, 1929), p. 47.

the pattern is to reduce stops and slowdowns, to aim for continuous movement. For example, instead of flat or horizontal junctions at which one train had to slow down or stop to allow another to pass, bridges or tunnels were used because over time the cost of train delay was greater than the cost of building track fixtures. At various points in the track pattern, marshaling yards organized trains by (1) sorting cars according to destinations; (2) combining cars into trains; and (3) forming trains so as to facilitate detaching sections along the way. Within the track pattern there were terminal accommodations, including a marshaling yard at each track end, loading and unloading areas, and finally, feeder lines to outlying areas. The whole system in some ways resembled an umbrella.

Finally, railroads are delimited by timetables. Building a timetable depends on (1) the utilization factor or average speed achieved on all lines within the system; (2) the point-to-point running time, based on the type of locomotive, the load, and braking distances, gradients, and curves in each direction, plus the permanent speed restrictions in effect in each line section; (3) line occupation, or how many trains can run on a line at one time; (4) recovery time, the turnaround time for cars and locomotives; and (5) sequences of planning. A railroad timetable is thus a complex system of moving interpenetrations. Each single moving train relates to all trains on interconnected lines of the system.[24]

As a result of the need for uniformity, discipline, and interdependency, railroads depend heavily on information. In fact, by 1905 German railroads paid a great deal of attention to information control techniques: regularity of data collection, formalization of information processing and decision rules, and standardization of communication feedback.[25] The principles of physics and the discipline of mechanical engineering specified the basic operating rules of railroads. These principles for control of size, space, and time were also those by which the MTP was defined. These axioms – uniformity, interdependency, and discipline, the hallmarks of railroad technology – gradually began to assume a place within the GGS, becoming its unwritten ethos. The "anonymity" of the GGS officer – Hans von Seeckt's term of the 1920s – may well have

---

24. Samuel, *Railway Operating Principles*, pp. 29–35, 131, 154; Emory J. Johns, *Railroad Administration* (New York, 1910), p. 57.

25. What the railroads and the RRS were doing in Germany in the period 1890–1914, railroads had done in America in 1840–90. Beniger, *Control Revolution*, pp. 221–27.

originated in the industrial processes of an age of mass transportation.[26]

How did this ethos develop? John K. Galbraith argues that technology – the systematic application of organized knowledge to practical skills – results in the division and subdivision of labor into components so that tasks become coterminous with established areas of scientific and engineering knowledge. From this basic division of labor by knowledge seven consequences follow: a longer cycle time for tasks; more complex procedures, which lead to greater functional inflexibility; more specialized manpower; a more complex organizational structure; a continuing need for more information; and finally, the transmission of power to those subsections possessing the knowledge for decisions important to the organization as a whole. In sum, Galbraith argues that twentieth-century organizations depend on knowledge in important ways and that dependency shapes their structure, processes, and personnel.[27]

By 1900 evidence indicates that the impact of technology was already being felt within the RRS of the GGS. As for structure, it is interesting to consider the organizational relationship between the Prussian Ministry of Public Works, the Prussian railroad, and the RRS. The Prussian minister of public works was simultaneously the director of the Prussian railroad and was intimately connected to the general staff RRS. In fact, two long-term heads of the RRS, Hermann von Budde (1897–1904) and Wilhelm Groener (1911–26), moved from the general staff to the state directory of public works and railroads. The RRS and the railroads were both organized by region and line. Each decentralized a good deal of decision making yet retained major control in Berlin. As we have seen, they coordinated at the LC level, where joint civil-military authority had broad powers and influence. As the railroads were organized, so

---

26. General von Seeckt, *Thoughts of a Soldier* (London, 1930), p. 111. Like so many other aspects of industrialization in the belated nation, modern business management techniques came late to Germany. Some of the earliest management theories were those of Frederick W. Taylor, who had begun to introduce his system of time study, standardization, and routing in 1893 and who published his first paper in 1895. Only about ten years later did Taylor's ideas begin to be studied in Germany. Aitken, *Scientific Management*, pp. 19–35; Lothar Burchardt, "Technischer Fortschritt und sozialer Wandel: Das Beispiel der Taylorismus-Rezeption," in Wilhelm Treue, ed., *Deutsche Technikgeschichte* (Göttingen, 1977), pp. 52–98; Homberg, "Anfänge des Taylorsystems in Deutschland vor dem Ersten Weltkriege."
27. Galbraith, *New Industrial State*, chap. 3.

was the RRS. It is no accident that the Army Corps command headquarters and the RRS Line Commands were placed where the Reich Railway Directorates were located. In 1905 there were twenty-one directories, and in the locations of eighteen of those the two command posts were also found.[28]

As a result, there was a relationship of structural interdependency between the railroads and the GGS. Three kinds of interdependency are illustrated here: pooled, sequential, and reciprocal. Pooled interdependency means that the work performed was interrelated in that each element or process contributed to the overall goal. At a minimum, a certain standardization characterized all the procedures, exercises, and plans of the RRS and its subordinate LCs. Thus standard operating procedures sent out to chiefs of staff and LCs were common. The beginning of German standard time in 1891 was a step in this direction. To execute the war plan and to practice parts of it in war games, units using the railroads had to conform to that time. A second kind of interdependency was sequential: some activities had to be performed ahead of others. Each echelon of the MTP depended on the speed and departure and arrival times of the lead train. One echelon depended upon another, and so on through the LCs and from one LC to another. Even Schlieffen was dependent upon the RRS's technical assessment before he could determine if his most recent ideas might be feasible. A third kind of structural interdependency was reciprocal. In this aspect, elements or activities related to each other as both inputs and outputs. The input in one LC became the output of an adjoining one. By 1905 feedback mechanisms were built into the MTP and into all the exercises used to test it. As LC block thresholds were entered by military trains, the LCs were given specific messages to telegraph or telephone back to Berlin. Even the content of these messages was written out in advance. These three levels of interdependence, all found in the MTP, RRS, and LC, formed a Guttman-type scale: elements or processes that were reciprocally interdependent were also sequential and pooled. Thus the impact of technology on organization not only made the RRS the core unit within the GGS, but reformed the RRS internally so that it displayed certain organ-

28. Ernest S. Bradford, "Prussian Railway Administration," *Annals of the American Academy of Political and Social Science* 29 (March 1907): 66–77; Roy Morris, *Railroad Administration* (New York, 1910), pp. 156–61; Groener Papers, roll 19, no. 34, "Eisenbahn-Abteilung des Grossen Generalstabes, Linienkarte."

izational and procedural characteristics of the railroad system.[29]

A major task of the RRS was to write, revise, rethink, practice, and distribute the MTP. It was written at three levels. First was the Reich rail plan, which was included as phase two of the war plan. This specified that certain corps were to be on certain transportation paths, with times and locations. There were the LC time schedules, which indicated traffic by time and location on each segment within the LC. Finally, there were the echelon charts, which detailed the traffic within each block of the LC. To assemble the MTP required enormous amounts of paperwork. In 1897 two people working all day could revise the echelon charts for one LC. By 1913 an increase in the speed of the MTP from twenty to twenty-five kilometers per hour took over a year to work out for all LCs within the Reich. As the knowledge demands rose, so did the cycle time for changes and revisions.

To deal with all of the technical details, personnel became more specialized. This is reflected in the increasingly technical curriculum of the War Academy, in the addition of more and more specialists to outdoor war games, and in the increasing attention paid to continuing education within the RRS. Prior to 1905, officers and officials from the War Ministry supply sections participated in GGS rides. Thereafter the War Ministry began to run its own outdoor war games concerned mainly with the massive supply problems of the million-man field army. The average cavalry officer was not trained to provide two thousand sheep or five thousand shells for a division at a specific day, time, and place. Although he might imagine that his equestrian or general military training might equip him to deal with the horse purchase situation, in fact it was far beyond his capabilities to organize 700,000 horses – the number which had to be purchased by 1914. This was a task for a specialist, someone who had done the job before and who did it over and over in field maneuvers, GGS rides, map exercises, and indoor war games.

Finally, the theory that power passes to those who have the knowledge for important decisions is illustrated by the RRS's relationship within the GGS as a whole. Every 1 November, as the chief of the GGS revised the war plan after the summer work of testing out its various components, his first step was to write down general numbers – where he wanted which army corps – and pass

---

29. Scott, *Organizations*, p. 212.

that single sheet of paper to the RRS. The RRS's technical assessment of whether the chief's general idea was feasible in terms of the MTP and, if so, exactly how and within what time framework, was the basis for the rest of the planning process.

Another way to understand why the RRS contained the core technology of the GGS is to examine its internal connections within the GGS and within Prussian war planning processes as a whole. It is argued that bureaucratic power flows from exchange relationships and is rooted in the exchange partner's dependency. In other words, the units whose reciprocal position is essential within the network of the organization become more important, adding responsibilities, personnel, influence, and power. This dependency principle operates in four ways. First, a bureaucratic unit which successfully copes with an important uncertainty within the organization as a whole gains power. Second, a unit whose task cannot be delegated to other units, that is, for whom there is no substitute, gains power. Third, a unit whose task cycle is pervasive, whose work effects other units within the organization, gains power. Fourth, a unit whose work most rapidly effects others gains power.[30]

The RRS touched all these bases. It successfully coped with uncertainty by providing the only consistent, reliably uniform segment of the war plan, the MTP. No other department could do its task in the war planning work cycle. It was pervasive, its product was used by a wide variety of offices, not only in Berlin but in every Army Command, every Line Command, and so on. Changes in the MTP immediately affected all other parts of the war plan. Other units, both in Berlin and throughout the Reich, had to take its most recent work into account. Furthermore, this immediacy was technologically enhanced. Whereas the normal daily written communication volume for any war planning office, including the general staffs of the twenty-five corps, was large, RRS communications were not only large but were amplified through the telegraph and telephone network. Its communication flow was electric as well as written. To protect this technological core from environmental perturbations, the RRS pursued a number of strategies. To buffer itself and reduce uncertainty, it coded its MTP, attempted to use forecasting for long range planning, and created a bridge with the Reich railroad by exchanging information. Also, it increasingly

30. Ibid., pp. 267–70.

limited its internal information flow by a document classification system and rigorous "need to know" accountability.[31]

Clearly by 1905 a division of labor by knowledge had taken place within the RRS, resulting in its differentiation from the rest of the GGS. It contained the core technology of the GGS because its knowledge-based system promised to deliver speed, volume, regularity, and dependability within one segment of the war plan.

## The Thickest Railroad Net in Europe

How did railroads fit into strategic planning? The superior German-Belgian rail network, plus the French line of fortifications in the south, gradually drew Schlieffen's attention to the northwestern sector of the west front. The German railroad network on the lower Rhine fed into the Belgian rail system, which connected directly into the railway network west of the Meuse River and on into France. In contrast, the Russian rail system was much more difficult to use. Not only was it very poor in quantity, but the rails were of a larger gauge than those of the German railroads, requiring extensive modification of roadbed or rolling stock. It took Schlieffen a long time to figure out how the war plan could be adapted to these technical circumstances. His thinking depended on many different kinds of specialist judgments, political as well as military. In 1900 he began to obtain the necessary technical opinions, proceding methodically and carefully to work through the necessary procedures. Many parts of the puzzle were still missing and only gradually fell into place. The first step was to sound out the Reich political leadership as to the feasibility of going through Belgium.[32]

Beginning in May 1900 Schlieffen apparently gave the political leadership – Chancellors Chlodwig zu Hohenlohe-Schillingsfürst and Bernhard von Bülow – an early opportunity to object to the politically risky portion of his military thinking. In an account repeated by half a dozen Wilhelmian memoir writers and accepted by Gerhard Ritter, Fritz Fischer, and Norman Rich, he sought to determine what the Reich political leadership thought about violation of Belgian and Dutch neutrality. In May 1900 Schlieffen

31. Ibid., p. 200; Gaertringen, *Groener*, p. 70.
32. Haeussler, *Groener*, p. 26.

asked Graf Hutten-Czapski, confidential advisor and private secretary to Chancellor Hohenlohe, to visit him. He asked Hutten if he would sound out Holstein and the chancellor confidentially. In the event of a two-front war, Schlieffen advised, success might depend on Germany's not allowing international agreements to restrain strategic operations. Schlieffen apparently did not name the country to which he referred, but Graf Hutten immediately thought of Belgium. Hutten-Czapski broached the matter with his friend Holstein, the influential political advisor to the Foreign Office. Holstein reportedly responded, "If the chief of the Great General Staff, and particularly a strategic authority such as Schlieffen, thought such a measure to be necessary, then it would be the duty of diplomacy to adjust itself and prepare for it in every possible way." A few days later Holstein arranged a social gathering at his house to which the chancellor and the chief of the GGS were invited. After dinner the two retired into an adjoining room where they had a long and lively conversation, presumably on the question of Belgium. Schlieffen apparently carried out the same procedure with Chancellor Bülow.[33]

Schlieffen got a different reaction from Herman Freiherr von Eckardstein, German counsellor in London. Eckardstein had just had a lengthy discussion with English foreign secretary Joseph Chamberlain, a report of which was circulated, with the Kaiser's marginal notations, within the Reich bureaucracy. In October 1902, at an evening social occasion, Schlieffen caught sight of Eckardstein and approached him. He said that he had read the ambassador's account, which portrayed the Reich's international position as not exactly rosy. If you are correct in terms of our relationship with England, Schlieffen reportedly said, I will have to change my entire campaign plan. Schlieffen went on to say that it was impossible for him to think Eckardstein correct. His assessment was far too pessimistic. The ambassador replied that he wished he could think otherwise, but that unfortunately he was

---

33. Ritter, *Schlieffen Plan*, pp. 79, 91–92; Fischer, *Illusions*, p. 391; Rich, *Holstein*, 2: 697; Bogdan Graf Hutten-Czapski, *Sechzig Jahre Politik und Gesellschaft*, 2 vols. (Berlin, 1935), 2: 371ff. It is interesting to speculate about Schlieffen's position in Berlin court and bureaucratic society. The essential point is that he appears to have been looked at very differently than the Kaiser; he was almost a polar opposite. Cf. Marie von Bunsen, *Zeitgenossen, die Ich erlebte, 1900–1930* (Leipzig, 1932), pp. 85–88. There is apparently an important reevaluation currently underway in regard to the six-year chancellorship of Hohenlohe. Cf. Cecil, *Wilhelm II*, p. 249.

very pessimistic. Eckardstein remarked further that if, in the event of war, Germany marched through Belgium, we would, as things appeared then, have England on our neck immediately. At this Schlieffen fell silent. He broke off the conversation and used the first opportunity to excuse himself. When Eckardstein asked about the Belgian question in the Foreign Ministry, he got the impression that they had given it no serious thought.[34] All of this makes sense in terms of subsequent events. Two themes stand out in German thinking. One is the division of labor. The Foreign Ministry did not concern itself with the technical plans of another department within the Prussian bureaucracy. Specialization, document classification, and need to know rules compartmentalized knowledge. By the same token, each specialist respected the technical judgment of his peers. The second is the lack of concern for Belgium, not only at the start, but throughout World War I.[35]

If this validation process can be accepted, what does it mean? For one thing it certifies Schlieffen's influence and reputation as a technical expert among his own generation and social group. Although as high nobility he had easy access to these men as one of their own, it was not that aspect to which they responded, but to his position as chief technical expert of the Reich army. If the chief of the GGS, the authority on these matters, believed it necessary, it was the duty of diplomacy to adjust and prepare. As Max Weber wrote, the power position of a fully developed bureaucracy was always overwhelming. The political master found himself in the position of the dilettante who stood opposed to the expert, the trained official within the administration. More and more the specialized knowledge of the expert became the foundation of power. Added to this was the dependence of one specialist on another. In an age of high specialization of labor, each one depended upon the other's knowledge. German respect for the specialist stood above everything else.[36]

As has been noted, the entry of men like Wilhelm Groener, Erich Ludendorff, Max Bauer, Max Hoffmann, Gerhard Tappen,

---

34. Herman Freiherr von Eckardstein, *Lebenserinnerungen und politische Denkwürdigkeiten* (Leipzig, 1920), pp. 399–400.

35. Ritter, *Sword and Scepter*, 2: 209–10; Ritter argues that the war minister had no clear picture of the GGS war plan and that it was only the Moltke-Ludendorff memorandum of 21 December 1912 which finally lifted the veil. For Austria, the veil surrounding German war plans was not fully lifted until 30 July 1914.

36. Quoted in Scott, *Organizations*, p. 305; Frederick Sell, *Die Tragödie des deutschen Liberalismus* (Stuttgart, 1953), p. 365.

and Hermann Kuhl into the GGS signaled the arrival of the bourgeois technical soldier in that office. They regarded the Reich army as a national, not a dynastic, institution, and their service was directed more to the German, rather than to the royal, interest. The rise of the technical expert has often been commented upon in modern industrial societies. Imperial Germany was one of the first states in which this particular phenomenon came to dominate and it operated up and down the scale. If the nominal political leadership deferred to the military expert, Schlieffen's own plans were in turn dependent on the expert opinion of those specialists beneath him in the GGS. Upon the RRS's knowledge of what the railroads could do in a specific circumstance of size, space, and time depended the whole second stage of the war plan. The only pathway from stage 1 – mobilization of several million civilians – to stage 3 – combat-ready status by the Rhine and Weichsel rivers – was highly technological. It depended on machines, plans, and specialized knowledge.

## Hardware Technology

Since the period under discussion, specifically the final quarter century prior to 1914, is considered an era of rapid technological change, it is appropriate to consider what impact this technology, that is, hardware technology, weapons, equipment, and inventions in contrast to the bureaucratic and knowledge technology we have been addressing, had on war planning. A number of commentators have suggested that the Prussian-German army prior to 1914 was uninterested in the new military hardware and disdained up-to-date weapons and equipment. This view was put forward especially after 1918, often by retired combat officers. The Prussian army, it was said, had a general prejudice against anything technical, including a conspicious disdain for the machine gun and a downplaying of modern communications tools such as the wireless and telephone. Older officers were said to have had an unalterable mistrust of artillery. Prussian officers were romantics in an industrial age. Their social isolation, their belief in the mystique of cold steel, and above all, their belief in the supremacy of man as opposed to machines led them to underestimate the impact of industrial weapons. For them war was an act of will in which man, not machine, was the master of the battlefield. Was there a

179

reluctance to consider modern industrial technology in war? If one examines the record carefully, especially in comparison with other European armies, the result is quite mixed. In fact it appears that the GGS was cautiously in favor of these modern inventions, whereas other elements in the war planning process, for example, the War Ministry and certain corps commanders, were more reticent.[37]

Three categories of equipment come to mind. Most important is transportation equipment; second, weapons; and third, communications. As for transportation, we have already argued that the railroad profoundly transformed war plans and war planning at the highest or strategic level and that it had begun to affect second-level or intermediate operations as well. For example, the creation of field railroad regiments to follow combat troops and repair and build railroad track was well advanced by 1905. Rail transportation methods forced changes in deep-future-oriented planning procedures, altering the way the GGS thought about the next war. Uniformity, discipline, and interchangeability were hallmarks of railroads and of GGS procedures and goals. By 1905 two other transportation machines began to be relevant. One was the automobile for land transportation, the other involved use of the balloon and airplane for observation. Schlieffen himself wrote of receiving reports of enemy troop distribution by balloon and airship and of dispatching orders by motorcycle and automobile. During the summer of 1905, as Schlieffen lay ill with a broken leg, Moltke used an automobile to attend a cavalry exercise and tested out an airplane for observation purposes. Both were added cautiously and in small numbers to German war equipment. Neither one became significant before 1914, probably because of the problem of communication: in spite of what one might see from the air or from an advanced land position, there was no rapid and secure way to convey messages back to headquarters, where such intelligence could be passed on and used. But if this were true in the German army, it was also the case in other European armies of the day.[38]

37. Generalmajor a.D. von Gleich, *Die alte Armee und ihre Verirrungen* (Leipzig, 1919), pp. 21–25; Hermann Teske, *Colmar von der Goltz* (Göttingen, 1957), p. 52; Vagts, *Militarism*, p. 156; John Ellis, *The Social History of the Machine Gun* (Baltimore, 1975), pp. 49ff.

38. Helmuth von Moltke, *Erinnerungen, Briefe, Dokumente* (Stuttgart, 1922), pp. 325–34. There is a good discussion of Schlieffen and new weapons, especially

There are several categories of weapons to consider, the first of which is the machine gun. Although in the years leading up to the First World War the German army was brought up to a higher level of machine gun strength than other European armies, in the final analysis the difference was only marginal. In terms of theory, the Germans were somewhat advanced, but in terms of actual proportion of guns to infantry, they equaled the British army. In 1899 a four-gun Maxim battery was assigned to each Jäger battalion, in 1902 each cavalry brigade on frontier duty received a six-gun battery, and in 1903 all artillery batteries were given six machine guns. The point is that these machine guns were considered to be part of the artillery equipment, rather than primarily an infantry weapon. This employment philosophy meant that prior to 1914, machine guns were used at artillery or intermediate distances greater than six hundred yards rather than as rifle or immediate fire. Especially after 1905 this is curious because Prussian observers during the Russo-Japanese War had commented on the results of machine gun fire; however, other European armies used machine guns similarly.[39]

The second category of weapons is artillery. Artillery during this time began to pass through a profound three-stage transition from direct firing to indirect firing to predicted firing. This development depended on accurate maps to calculate range and bearing and on forward observers, either on the ground or in the air. The German army had good maps of its own lands and fair maps of adjacent foreign lands but lacked communication. Both indirect and predicted firing depended upon close observation of the initial rounds, with rapid communication back to the battery for adjustment. Telegraph lines were cumbersome and radios were not effective for this purpose prior to 1914.

Artillery weapons may be divided into three categories by range: guns, howitzers, and mortars. Field artillery units carried mainly guns and a few heavy howitzers. Foot artillery carried lighter howitzers and mortars. It has been argued that speed and surprise were the keynote of Prussian strategic planning; therefore artillery, which was slow, cumbersome, and unavoidably noticeable,

---

artillery, in Collenburg, "Schlieffen," pp. 622–28. Cf. Helmut Otto, "Die Heraus-bildung des Kraftfahrwesens im deutschen Heer bis 1914," *Militärgeschichte* 28, no. 3 (1989): 227–36.

39. Ellis, *Machine Gun*, pp. 20, 115–16.

was not central to the war plans. During Schlieffen's time, however, steady if slow changes were made. When he assumed office, the number of guns in artillery batteries had just been increased from four to six, a 50% increase. During his tenure, the number of field artillery batteries rose from 434 to 574, foot artillery batteries from 31 to 40. Guns and ammunition were also lightened for greater mobility.[40]

Schlieffen is often cited for his encouragement of the use of artillery and is given credit for trying to increase direct artillery support in tactical combat. During this time, guns were gradually being subtracted from corps and added to divisions to provide close support for smaller units. The field army was given heavy mortars. Gradually divisions were given more control. From 1892 on, the question of rapid-firing artillery became a concern. The problem seems to have been mainly technical: how to control the recoil so the gun did not have to be resighted after each shot. The goal was to achieve eight shots per minute. In 1897 the French "75" was introduced. It fired fifteen aimed shots per minute, and this innovation put great pressure on the Germans, for it was superior to the German "88" gun.[41] Soon Schlieffen wrote to the War Ministry. "Up to now we stood against the numerically superior French with a small advantage in number of artillery. Now this situation has changed. . . . We are faced with a larger infantry and better-quality artillery. After one or two marches on the other side of the border, our forces will push against fortifications which cannot be completely encircled, but must be attacked. For this we must have the new twenty-one-centimeter howitzer. In addition we need to increase the size and quality of artillery and modernize the foot artillery." The War Ministry was slow to react and during the first Moroccan affair there was a crisis over this very point. Reich leadership feared French technological superiority on the battlefield.[42] As in the case of the railroads, Schlieffen wanted to push

---

40. Shelford Bidwell and Dominick Graham, *Fire Power: British Army Weapons and Theories of War, 1904–1945* (Boston, 1985), pp. 1–27; Osten-Sacken, *Preußens Heer*, 3: 527; Jany, *Preußische Armee*, 4: 291; Geyer, *Rüstungspolitik*, p. 58. Cf. Dennis Showalter, "Prussia, Technology, and War: Artillery from 1914 to 1918," in Ronald Haycock and Keith Neilson, eds., *Men, Machines, and War* (Montreal, 1987), pp. 115–51.

41. Osten-Sacken, *Preußens Heer*, 3: 531.

42. Collenburg, "Schlieffen," p. 622; cf. Förster, *Der doppelte Militarismus*, pp. 147–49.

technology forward to the tactical level. In doing so, he was trying to increase firepower at the leading edge of combat, to enhance the killing zone by mechanical means. He sought to achieve a modern Cannae with its 48,000 bodies lying in piles and heaps. This meant greater firepower and control further up the line, toward divisions and regiments and away from corps. Such developments also meant increased weight, both in machines and their accoutrements, ammunition, carriages, and so on. Rapid-fire artillery had already increased supply requirements. By 1914 the trains for an army corps stretched twelve miles behind the corps. All these considerations had to be calculated into the war plan and the equipment transported on the railroads.

Third, there was the question of communications. Although it has been written that the telegraph was instrumental in the victories of 1866 and 1871, this was only true to a very limited degree and it applied only to the initial orders and the largest strategic outline. In 1866 field telegraph detachments do not seem to have worked well at all. After the initial orders, Moltke stayed in contact with subordinate commanders mainly by mounted courier. The 1866 war was fought close to the border so that regular Prussian telegraph lines could be used until quite late in that conflict. In 1871, as soon as the troops crossed the French border, they used what French telegraph lines were left intact, but as the attack progressed the telegraph was not used much.[43]

In 1887 the first Prussian military signal company had been created as a part of the Guard Engineer Battalion. Telegraphy was taught at the Artillery and Engineering School and was included in field engineering training under physics and electrical education, mainly as a four-day field exercise. Between then and 1899, when an independent signal corps was first formed, experimental signal companies and a "teaching" company were created, all within the Guard Pioneer Battalion. 1899 saw the founding of the signal corps in the Prussian army. Three battalions were created, one each in Berlin, Frankfurt an der Oder, and Koblenz. An inspectorate of transportation coordinated transportation and communications. The next year the radio telegraph was tested out in the Kaiser-manöver, and in 1901 a fourth signal battalion and a wireless telegraph teaching regiment were established.

By 1905 the GGS used two methods to transmit field infor-

---

43. Howard, *German-French War*, pp. 1–4, 73.

mation: (1) the imperial post and telegraph system, and (2) the field telegraph, by means of which the army and corps telegraph detachments connected the armies and corps with headquarters and with each other. The telegraph was the instrument par excellence for field communication. It required a small current for operation and its signals could be relayed for several hundred miles. However, it depended on wires and these had to be carefully and laboriously laid. The field telegraph was unable to keep up with a rapidly moving front. The telephone was also used, but prior to 1914 its practical transmission limit over field lines was approximately fifteen to twenty-five miles. On well-built permanent lines, transmission range could be extended to three hundred miles, but the two devices which extended the talking range, the loading coil and the amplifying repeater, were not in commercial use before 1914.[44]

In sum, rapid technological change did take place prior to 1914. Specific inventions such as the telegraph, telephone, machine gun, and airplane were introduced. However, with the single exception of the railroad, they did not have a decisive impact on war planning. The generalization which seems most appropriate for peacetime armies is that new technology is fitted into existing structures and procedures. The organization and operating processes of armies do not change to accommodate them. Within months after World War I began, hardware inventions started to have dramatic impact. In 1914 the German army had fewer than 3,000 machine guns. By 1918 this number exceeded 250,000.

The second aspect of war planning was representational. The Land Survey Section, under centralized GGS control, grew in size and technical production during this time. With a total staff of over five hundred officers, civilians, and technicians, the Trigonometric, Topographic, and Cartographic Sections each contained ten subsections. Military officers fit into an ongoing civilian-dominated bureaucracy of great technical specialization. The smallest section, the Trigonometric, was the one to which the largest number

---

44. Poten, *Militär-Erziehungswesen*, 4: 457; Jany, *Preußische Armee*, 4: 319–20; Paul W. Evans, "Strategic Signal Communications: A Study of Signal Communications as Applied to Large Field Forces, Based upon the Operations of the German Signal Corps during the March on Paris in 1914," *Signal Corps Bulletin* 82 (1935): 33–36. The Prussian Army had a number of teaching units called *Lehr* companies and regiments. They were apparently organized and designated to teach and learn new military procedures and to test out new equipment and organization. The origin and development of these teaching units seems to have escaped historians.

of officers were assigned for field work during the summer months. The Topographic Section also had room for officers. The Cartographic was the most technical, with the fewest officers and largest number of civilians – cartographers, printers, and lithographers. There were also half a dozen purely technical sections, such as photogrammetry and stereophotography. Map production was prodigious. There were seven map series in production, in scale from 1:8000 to 1:100,000, issued in editions large enough for an officer corps of over twenty thousand. If every army unit was issued a map for war games and outdoor maneuvers, the production was sizable. Add to this production for civilian purposes – the major role for Land Survey maps – and the whole production was substantial.[45]

The Land Survey Section and the RRS were the departments in which the highest degree and greatest quantity of specialized knowledge were used, bringing task cycles closest to discrete areas of engineering, physics, and chemistry. However, by 1900 the major technological transformations of the Land Survey Section had already occurred. Maps produced in the 1870s and 1880s could not be dramatically improved. In spite of the annual remapping program in which thousands of square miles were retraced each year, the limit had been reached in terms of incremental improvement. Existing maps were adequate for war planning purposes, new ones were only marginally better. Therefore the whole department reached a plateau in terms of its contribution to the war planning processes. In contrast, substantial refinements of knowledge and technique were still to come in the RRS.

## The Science of Military History and the Schlieffen School of Strategy

The third aspect of war planning was educational. The goal of GGS education in the final two decades prior to 1914 was professional specialization. This is evident in the War Academy curriculum, especially in its lead subject, military science, and in its use of history as an introduction to the study of tactics. The War Academy, although originally intended to educate officers for the entire

---

45. Georg Krauß, "150 Jahre," pp. 132–34; cf. Theo Mueller, "Die topographischen und kartographischen Vorschriften für die preußischen Meßtischblätter," pp. 174–79.

army, had become the most important means of access to the GGS by the turn of the century. By 1905 there were five candidates for every one that could be accepted. War Academy size had increased to more than 150 officers per class. Classes, which were selected annually by examination from lieutenants and captains, were getting older, and those chosen generally had four to fourteen years' active duty. For each of the three classes there were three lecture halls, each one holding fifty students. War Academy director Litzmann believed that this class size was too large for the necessary teacher-student relationship. Once admitted, the competition within the academy was so keen that after three years only 30% of those seeking initial appointment to the GGS for a probationary period of two years qualified. The combination of a large applicant pool for admission and stiff competition after graduation was considered so serious that the kingdom of Bavaria expanded its own war academy. Just prior to Litzmann's assignment as judge of the Kaisermanöver in 1904, he tried to convince Schlieffen to do something about the situation. Schlieffen replied that there was nothing that could be done because the Kaiser was not interested in the War Academy.[46]

Some War Academy faculty believed it had lost its soul. Training had narrowed down to the teaching of pure staff technique. More important, it no longer seemed to play a leading roll in the army as a whole: its necessity was recognized, but not its importance. Teachers were unenthusiastic, other assignments were considered more influential and prestigious. Many officers considered practical experience more valuable than scientific knowledge.[47] The War Academy curriculum emphasized professional military training. First-year courses were distributed equally between tactics, military history, weapons training, mathematics, physics, and language study. In the second and third years the balance shifted sixteen to nine in favor of technical work. The spread of the science of war curriculum meant that whole new courses with technical content could no longer be taught by a nonspecialist GGS officer. Specialists taught topographical surveying and cartography, military medicine, military law, and even aspects of general

46. Quoted in Eugen Bircher and Walter Bode, *Schlieffen: Mann und Idee* (Zurich, 1937), pp. 159–60; Litzmann, *Lebenserinnerungen*, 1: 128.
47. Litzmann, *Lebenserinnerungen*, 1: 127–28; Manfred Messerschmidt, "Militär und Schule in der Wilhelminischen Zeit," in *Militärgeschichtliche Mitteilungen* 1 (1978): 51–75.

staff work. Medical, communications, and engineering officers all taught their specialities. Regularly assigned GGS officers had insufficient knowledge in these areas.[48]

The "science of military history" was the basis for the study of tactics. The first-year curriculum dealt with the campaigns of Frederick the Great, the second year with those of the French Revolution and Napoleon, the third year with nineteenth-century campaigns, including those of Kaiser Wilhelm I. A single first-year course dealt with ancient military history, everything from the Greeks to the seventeenth century. All emphasized tactical actions and the details of specific battles, their origin, conclusions, leadership, and above all, contemporary significance. Faculty were directed to bring the past alive by giving their own opinions, provoking specific decisions from their students, and bringing their listeners into partnership with them. They aimed to introduce students to the three methods of using military history – the retrospective, application, and geographic methods – and to give them a fund of details focused on tactics and terrain.

A rigorous system of written personnel appraisals followed students throughout their War Academy career. At the end of the three-year course, after a series of war game problems and the final ride, the academy's top graduates were distributed among the GGS (about forty-two) or they were assigned as adjutants to high officers (twenty-five) or as faculty for military schools (seven). The rest became troop officers.[49]

Although some contemporaries regarded Schlieffen as an historian of note, this is incorrect, at least according to the way in which we generally think about history and historical work. The key to GGS history during this period is provided by Freiherr von Freytag-Loringhoven, Schlieffen's long-time aid and editor of the *Military Weekly*. He wrote that Schlieffen always tried to illustrate the ideal in his writings in order to establish clear guidelines for the officer corps. Another contemporary, General von Schlichting, wrote that Schlieffen's historical writings were intended to create a uniform teaching.[50] GGS historical reconstruction was not intended

48. Bald, *Der Deutsche Generalstab*, p. 46; Poten, *Militär-Erziehungswesen*, 4: 293.

49. "Der Lehrer muß seine Hörer durch Inanspruchnahme ihres Urteils, welches sich in die Form bestimmter Vorschläge für Maßnahmen und Entschlüße zu kleiden hat, zu lebendiger Mitarbeit anregen." Poten, *Militär-Erziehungswesen*, 4: 299–307.

50. Freiherr von Freytag-Loringhoven, "Introduction," in Alfred Graf Schlieffen, *Cannae* (Berlin, 1925), pp. vii–ix; Geyl, *Schlichting*, p. 350.

to detail exactly what had happened in a particular war, only to give the general outlines so that officers referring to it could spend their time in acquiring and using specific knowledge of the terrain in which the general war situation had occurred. Military history was didactic in purpose, general in presentation, and subordinated to terrain usage.

What sort of uniform teaching did Schlieffen aim for? As he said at the hundredth anniversary of the War Academy: "Before everyone who wishes to be a commander lies a book, military history. In it one attains the actuality, the inspired reality, of war and understands how it has happened, how it must happen, and how it will happen again." Military history was only an intellectual stimulus, a starting point for ideas, not an end in itself. Schlieffen did not aim for historical accuracy; he was not trying to use the best primary sources, to find out what really happened. Rather he wanted a general outline as a teaching vehicle for practical military exercises and future war planning. For Schlieffen it did not matter if army corps moved down roads which did not exist. He aimed for operational teaching – personalities and events powerfully portrayed to illustrate operational views.[51] The generation of officers whom he represented had not experienced war. Schlieffen often reminded his listeners that "today we must return to history for the practical knowledge which the present refuses to grant us." Yorck von Wartenburg, a promising GGS officer who died during the China campaign, explained that "we study military history not to recapture the historical events, nor to use the opportunity to repeat past happenings, so to speak, in written form, but to select what is valuable to us and to say how it went and why." Such was its purpose. How was it taught?[52]

Several methods were used to join military history to tactical exercises; the most important of these were the retrospective and application methods. The former called for reviewing a battle overall in a general way, then analyzing it by going back over it action by action, decision by decision. Strict comparisons were made between (1) the orders given and actions which resulted, and (2) specific paragraphs in various Prussian field service books, infantry drill regulations, and tactical instructions. The latter sus-

51. Heinrich Aschenbrandt, *Kriegsgeschichtsschreibung und Kriegsgeschichtsstudium im deutschen Heere* (Königstein, 1953), pp. 12–13.
52. Schlieffen, *Gesammelte Schriften*, 2: 447; Yorck von Wartenburg, *Napoleon als Feldherr*, 2 vols. (Berlin, 1901), 1: i.

pended the action of an historical battle in the middle and sought to place the officers into the roles of the commanders at that point. On the basis of the knowledge available to the commanders, the officers judged the situation and issued orders for further action. Finally, the orders given by the exercise participants and those issued by the officers at the time of the actual battle were compared with the historical outcome. War Academy student Heinz Guderian noted in 1913 that the application method was widely practiced.[53]

These case study methods were used to illustrate a few general operating principles. One was that the only valid strategy was annihilation, to attack with the goal of virtually destroying one's enemy. Within this general framework, the favored method was to hold the enemy front and attack with one's largest force against one or both wings. The Schlieffen school believed that all successful commanders in Western military history, from the Greeks to Moltke, had followed this strategy. This doctrine was exemplified in the 1903 GGS book, *Success in Battle: How Is It Achieved?* It reviewed the actions of a number of historical commanders and concluded that each one's greatest victories were achieved by means of the strategy of annihilation carried out by the flank attack. The strategies of Frederick, Napoleon, and Moltke, which spanned a century and a half, were seen as fundamentally the same.[54]

By 1904 there was a reaction developing against Schlieffen's single-minded strategic teachings. A split became apparent within the officer corps over visions of military history. Officers reacted against the uniform view of past and future. Their criticism was summarized by General August von Caemmerer in his book, *The Development of Strategic Science in the 19th Century*, written explicitly in opposition to *Success in Battle*. It is significant that Caemmerer was no longer on active duty and that his work was not published by the official GGS publisher, E.S. Mittler.[55] Caemmerer believed that Napoleon employed strategy correctly in his time, but that were he alive in 1904, he would have adjusted it to the new realities. In comparing Napoleon and Moltke, Caemmerer pointed

53. Model, *Deutscher Generalstabsoffizier*, p. 16.

54. Bucholz, *Hans Delbrück*, pp. 63–70, 77–78; Generalstab des Heeres, Kriegswissenschaftliche Abteilung, ed., *Der Schlachterfolge, mit welchen Mitteln wurden sie erstrebt?* (Berlin, 1903).

55. *Die Entwicklung der strategischen Wissenschaft im 19. Jahrhundert* (Berlin, 1904).

out changes in three areas: transportation, communications, and weapons. He concluded that Napoleon, Frederick the Great, and Moltke had used different strategies based on changed material circumstances. He admitted that some factors, such as terrain, did not change and that it was very important to study them. But advances in roads, railroads, the telegraph, telephone, and weapons had now altered the circumstances of war. No experienced commander was simply an improvisor who tackled immediate problems using only the conditions of the moment. On the contrary, commanders relied upon their knowledge of tactical evolution and especially on engineering and artillery science. They used knowledge of military history. And they had to take into account those thousand circumstances – their own character, the nature of their troops, the weapons, the time of the year – which made each situation different from others in the past. The square of the hypothenuse was always equal to the sum of the squares of both sides, whether the right wing was large or small or pointing east or west. But one must ask in every new situation exactly how such standard knowledge applied.[56]

A second reaction to the Schlieffen school of strategy came in the area of officer education. Defined philosophically, this was a split between men like Schlieffen who thought that GGS officers were best trained in strategic operations; that is, how very large troop units should act and react in war; and a second group, led by Graf Haeseler, who believed general staff officers should be trained above all in tactical methods for small unit combat, what to do in specific tactical situations at the regimental and brigade level, for example, in compiling artillery, march, and supply orders. One commentator familiar with both approaches to war compared them. He described Schlieffen's as geometrical and analytical, Haeseler's as functional and operational. Haeseler told his officers they could learn more in three years of troop duty than in three years at the War Academy. Very few officers, he said, would ever be in a position to issue operational orders for army corps. What counted were technical questions of combat for small units.[57]

Here was the old division between theory and practice, but

56. Ibid., chap. 6, pp. 165, 211, 212.
57. Generalleutnant a.D. Marx, "Über Schlieffen Geist und Haeseler Geist," *Militär-Wochenblatt*, no. 12 (1934): 444–48; cf. the same author's *Die Marne – Deutschlands Schicksal?* (Berlin, 1932); another who compared Schlieffen and Haeseler was Erich von Manstein in *Aus einem Soldatenleben* (Bonn, 1958), p. 27.

defined in a new way. No longer was it so much a conflict between general and professional education because by this time everyone assumed that officers were to receive the latter. Rather it was a conflict between two kinds of professional training, staff as against troop education. This distinction had always existed; however, neither one was so specialized that the one excluded the other. Through regular rotation between staff and line duties, GGS officers were presumed to have both. Beginning around 1900, however, the distinction between staff and line work grew larger. It was partially based upon differences in knowledge, partially on differences in experience. In peacetime the gap never became so wide. During the First World War a serious discontinuity developed between combat and staff officers, a divergence in which both knowledge and experience differed so greatly that it virtually produced two kinds of mentalities. After 1918 this difference was widely reflected in the bitter and protracted conflict over the history of the war.[58]

## Learning War during Peace

The final aspect of war planning was analytical. By 1900 war gaming activity was widespread throughout the Prussian army and utilized a model supplied by the War Academy and the GGS. As we have seen, each War Academy class participated in a variety of indoor and outdoor games during the three-year curriculum. Upon graduation, whether assigned to staff or troop duty, war gaming continued. Each year the chief of the GGS led rides that lasted two to three weeks, with thirty officers from different branches participating. By 1905 Schlieffen conducted two rides a year along the formal lines laid down in army regulations. In the years 1899 to 1903, six went to the west border areas, two to the east border.[59]

Every week during the winter half year an older GGS officer gave the younger assigned officers in every department a tactical exercise in the form of a problem for an infantry division. Officers were asked to estimate the situation, decide what to do, and issue operational orders. On the morning of the exercise, officers dropped other duties and completed it. A few days later, in the

---

58. Bucholz, *Hans Delbrück*, pp. 130, 134.
59. BAMA, Nachlaß Beseler, *Lebenserinnerungen*, p. 59.

presence of everyone, the solutions were laid out so that after a while, a fair judgment of the officers' knowledge could be made. Toward the end of the winter the department chief and the supervising quartermaster gave out a series of exercises in the form of problems dealing with a corps or an army. Finally, in the spring, the chief of the GGS himself put out two or three exercises for assigned officers. Called the "chief's exercises," in them Schlieffen concentrated on west and east front strategic problems, often dealing with the relationships in East Prussia, where a weak German force had to engage superior Russian armies along the Niemen and the Narew rivers. In addition, Schlieffen often led indoor evening war games. In the afternoon he would direct a number of officers to report to him. Captains and lieutenants from all of the departments played the roles of commanders on either side, estimating the situation, deciding what to do, and issuing orders.[60] Thus general staff exercises, indoor and out, provided one level of war gaming. Whether conducted in the War Academy, or by the GGS, or at the TGS levels of corps and divisions, they followed a similar format.

A second category of war games were large-scale outdoor maneuvers that included both the active army and the active army plus reserves. Among other purposes, these games were used to integrate reserves called up for duty with an active unit. Every active unit went into the field on a rotating basis once every two years. Although the Kaisermanöver lasted only about two weeks, the entire summer was in fact devoted to outdoor maneuvers. The progression was from small units to large, from regiments and brigades to divisions and finally to corps. If the tactical games and strategic rides were the critical test of who should be assigned to or promoted within the GGS, the outdoor maneuvers served the same purpose for the units of the army corps.[61]

What kind of training was carried on during the war games? As we have suggested, at the beginning and regimental level, the training included the three methods discussed, the retrospective, application, and geographic. Each of these relied upon intimate knowledge of military history and in effect demanded that the officers replay a moment in time. At higher levels, these procedures were also uniform. At the War Academy, GGS, and TGS

---

60. Bergh, *Das deutsche Heer*, pp. 174–78; German Army, *Regulations for Maneuver*, translated by the War Office General Staff (London, 1908).

61. Jany, *Preußische Armee*, 4: 298; Groener Papers, roll 18, no. 175.

level, they entailed the repetition of a two-step formula: estimate the situation and issue orders to deal with it. GGS officers were all expected to be molded of the same cloth, interchangeable parts within the larger system.

One example of this was in written communication, the technique of issuing orders. Once the military technical vocabulary had been mastered, orders were to be clear, precise, complete, and brief. Clarity required logical arrangement, short sentences, expressions universally understood, and time given in the railway timetable mode. In defining precision, a distinction was made between strict orders, which limited the choices of the receiving officer, and discretionary orders, where the receiving officer had more freedom. Completeness meant including by name all units or fractions called upon to perform. Brevity implied that orders should never contain one word the omission of which would not immediately affect their meaning. Two standard kinds of orders were those for march and for battle. March orders, by far the more common, instructed troops to move from one area of quarters to another. Battle orders were based on more intimate knowledge of the situation, especially the enemy's strength and intentions. They omitted a great deal, leaving more choices to the commander. Training in the art of issuing orders was one goal of war games.[62]

Another goal was to exercise the military knowledge of participants. By 1905, there is some evidence that war games had become occasions for applying textbook regulations in a pedagogical manner. An example is provided by Karl von Bülow, commanding general of the 3d Corps from 1903 to 1912. Bülow was highly regarded. Not only was he seriously considered as a replacement for Schlieffen in 1905, but more important, in August 1914 he was given command of the 2d Army, the second element in the right wing execution of the west front war plan. Therefore he was an important player.

Bülow, born in 1846, had spent most of his active duty years with the TGS. Assigned to the GGS between 1887 and 1890 and again in 1902, he dealt with intelligence for southeastern Europe and worked on a commission rewriting the tactical artillery regulations. Bülow combined a gruff exterior with a studious, scholarly mind. As commander of the 3d Corps, he approached his troops as if they were students in a classroom. His biographer describes the

---

62. Schellendorff, *Duties*, pp. 286–91; Bergh, *Das deutsche Heer*, p. 174.

corps as a "school for discipline, exercise, and parade drill." Its commander was nicknamed the "old exercise master." During his first year of command, Bülow put into effect his own set of rules, which emphasized "technical education for attacks" and "leadership functions on the battlefield." Soldiers were trained so that they carried out their obligations on the shooting line in purely mechanical ways. Formal theoretical and tactical preparation was everything. Bülow's training was called a "system of absolute correctness," and his corps demonstrated this in the fall maneuvers, the final examination for the year. Year after year 3d Corps put on splendid tactical shows, winning the coveted "battle tactical stripes" award. To avoid the "unwarlike" situation of having to confront strange terrain during maneuvers, exercises began with an extended map exercise. His commanders gradually worked themselves into the real setting from this theoretical preparation. We are reminded of Hans von Seeckt's story from August 1914. As the staff officers of the 3d Army were approaching the Belgian frontier, the commanding general called them together in his car to prepare them for the war ahead by reading them a military-geographic description of Belgium.[63]

Bülow's remarks on the fall 1905 maneuver reveal what kind of officer the GGS system had created. By age fifty-nine, at the rank of corps commander, he was a pedant who stressed technical rules and procedures and was concerned with carrying out textbook operations. In his maneuver commentary, several themes stand out. In critiquing regimental and divisional field artillery units, Bülow's comments are extremely detailed about what should and should not take place according to army and corps regulations. He often cited company level actions as examples and constantly referred to printed documents: army regulations, corps notices, letters, commentaries, and remarks. In advising his subordinate commanders that going over to a period of rest, that is, taking a break, should be done in an orderly and "warlike" way, he quoted the authority of six field exercise regulations. The army command filing system allowed cumulative comments to be made on different exercises. Thus each of his forty-three maneuver comments was footnoted with the appropriate regulation and in many cases with several of his own previous directives, listed by date and

63. Gebsattel, *Bülow*; Groener, *Testament Graf Schlieffen*, p. 13; Seeckt, *Thoughts*, p. 124; cf. Hans Meier-Welcher, *Seeckt* (Frankfurt, 1967), pp. 39–41.

number. At the end of every maneuver day, a sketch and written report were filed by each commander. Bülow often criticized the form and grammatical language used in orders and reports. A detachment should not be ordered to *eingreifen*, cavalry should not be ordered to *Hand an den Übergang legen*; instead the detachment *greift an* and the squadron *besetzt den Übergang*. Finally, the maneuver commentary itself, ten pages in length with forty-three separate comments, was distributed to a total of 405 recipients in the 5th and 6th Divisions. Over four thousand pages were circulated in all, each hand reproduced by secretaries with distribution lists equal to or exceeding those of our own photocopy days. With such a flow of documents, war was no longer an affair of the sword, but of the pen.

Finally, Bülow's critique reveals that he diametrically opposed the Schlieffen school doctrine that the flank attack was the essence of military history. He believed that deep columns and combined arms, brought together in the classic frontal attack, gave success in war. Bülow criticized officers for going against his explicit written instructions in employing the frontal assault. Many officers, he wrote, tried to surround their opponent. He admitted it was possible, but advised against it. The enemy would prematurely discover the position, open a new front for counterenvelopment, and the objective would be lost. The whole thing was a waste of time.[64]

## The First Moroccan Crisis and the Schlieffen Plan of 1905

The first Moroccan crisis of 1904–5 was the context in which the Schlieffen Plan of December 1905 evolved. It is probably important to reemphasize that, at least up until 1906, Prussian war planning was a dynamic process in which any given war plan published and valid on 1 April of a given year was then subject to constant reevaluation, revision, updating, and alteration. Although each war plan was technically in effect until 1 April of the following year, the process of revision based on the summer's war games, updated intelligence, new railroad lines, and so on, was

---

64. Gebsattel, *Generalfeldmarschall Karl von Bülow*, pp. 14–40; BAMA, Nachlaß von Moltke the Younger, N78–22 Armee Kommand XX, Sekt. 1a, Nr. 1439, 9 März 1906. "Bemerkungen zu den Brigade- und Divisionsmanöver 1906," 24.1.1907.

ongoing. From 1 April through 1 November, the period of summer work, segments of the war plan were tested in the field. Each part was carefully evaluated. During the winter half of the year, 1 November through 1 April, the testing process went forward with indoor war games, GGS map exercises, and RRS exercises. As Groener wrote, each specific war plan was the product of many war games, staff exercises, and maneuvers. It was the momentary best effort amidst a continuing process of hypothesis, testing, evaluation, and new ideas. Each plan was a specific response to a single set of circumstances which appeared at a given point in time. The Schlieffen Plan of 28 December 1905 was created for a specific context, taking into account precise details of the moment. No one in the GGS assumed that it was the final war plan, fixed and immutable for all time.[65]

In April 1903 Hermann Staabs returned to the GGS as a major to head the RRS. On the morning of his return, prior to reporting to Schlieffen, he glanced over the west front MTP, in particular the transportation path maps and the time schedule overview. He found them much the same as in 1899, when he had left for TGS duty. Schlieffen's first question was, what do you think of the war plan? He replied that he didn't like it. The right wing of the concentration reached only to Gerolstein and the off-loading points were still far from the border. In Alsace, south of Straßburg, many off-loading ramps had yet to be built. During the conversation Schlieffen said he had always been told that more than six corps could not be off-loaded north of the Mosel River. Was that correct, Schlieffen asked? Staabs replied that with certain alterations, the number of corps north of the Mosel could be doubled. As a result of this conversation, a whole series of changes were begun.[66]

A clue to what was coming is provided in January 1904 when Kaiser Wilhelm, in a conversation with the Belgian king, Leopold, demanded a written declaration to the effect that in case of war, Belgium would take the German side and that, to this end, the king would guarantee to Germany the use of Belgian railways and fortifications. In effect, the all highest warlord had given away the fulcrum of the west front war plan.[67] The Russo-Japanese War

65. Groener Papers, roll 8, no. 9., Groener letter of 5 November 1932.
66. Staabs, *Aufmarsch*, pp. 26–28.
67. Paul Kennedy, ed., *The War Plans of the Great Powers, 1880–1914* (Boston, 1985), pp. 206–7, Gerhard Ritter asked if this story had any basis in fact, and Gordon

broke out in February, and Russia was soon on the brink of a defeat that considerably reduced its effectiveness as an ally in Europe. In April 1904 came the Anglo-French Entente, which marked the beginning of a major new alignment of the European powers. Earlier the RRS had believed that the French military travel plan allowed the French army to become operations ready forty-eight hours earlier than the German army. Various modifications were being made to meet this challenge. For every two army corps, a single transportation path was to stand ready at the start of the MTP. The Guard Corps was only to draw upon fringe districts located around Berlin for its increase to war size, instead of drawing on areas all across Germany, as had been customary until then. Thus the speed and capacity of mobilization was slowly upgraded.

While these developments were taking place, the Reich leadership began to consider its options. On 19 April Reich Chancellor Bülow requested a strategic assessment from Schlieffen. The request was formulated as a question: could a Franco-German war be conducted without Russian intervention? Schlieffen replied that Russia had transferred many officers and reserves to East Asia and that, if a crisis came, it would probably do everything possible to avoid war with Germany. If war came nevertheless, Russia would hardly be in a position to put up a serious fight. The German military attaché in London, Graf von der Schulenburg-Tressow, was reporting monthly to Schlieffen during this period on the likelihood of English intervention in a possible Franco-German war. Schlieffen seems to have begun to consider whether it was a propitious time for a war against France. Undoubtedly he was thinking of 1866 and 1870–71 when German diplomacy, as well as unique circumstances, had allowed Prussia to fight two brief single opponent wars.[68]

In this context the April 1904 GGS ride took place. Its purpose was to examine west front troop dispositions, especially the strategic use of the northwest quadrant. Schlieffen had been dealing with this problem since the 1898 GGS ride. As we have seen, he had already clarified the potential political problem with the Reich leadership. It was assumed that in a war France would also be

---

Craig concluded that it was unreliable. Whether founded on documentary evidence or not, given the people and the circumstances, the story makes sense. Ritter, *Schlieffen Plan*, pp. 93–94; Craig, *Germany*, p. 317.

68. Fischer, *Illusions*, pp. 53–54; Lambi, *German Power*, p. 242; Rich, *Holstein*, 2: 698.

considering a move through Belgium. France had enhanced its railroad system in the northeast and had constructed new fortresses. More recently Belgium had begun to fortify Liège and Namur heavily. In the April 1904 ride the German attack was split, with the right wing advancing between Trier and Aachen and the left wing attacking between Metz and Straßburg. The result was that the left wing defeated the French, who had come out of their fortress chain, but the right wing proved too weak and got bogged down in frontal battles. In his final critique Schlieffen suggested that one possibility was to move the whole operation north, attacking along the front Verdun to Lille and going as far northwest as necessary to find open space for penetration. He remarked that although this had certain disadvantages, generally the route had smaller fortresses which could be by-passed. Schlieffen concluded that it was by means of Belgium that a connection could be found between the German and French rail systems.[69]

In September 1904 in response to a War Ministry request, Schlieffen wrote that in the event that England mobilized against Germany, France would follow suit. In that case Germany should use the first or English declaration as the signal to mobilize against France, if necessary anticipating French mobilization. He cautioned that any partial mobilizations would be fatal. Meanwhile a general staff officer, Albrecht von Thaer, traveled throughout the garrisons of western Russia to inspect the Russian cavalry horse supply. After several months, he returned to Berlin and reported to Schlieffen that the Russian garrisons were almost completely bare of infantry and artillery and that the border was only protected by a thin screen of cavalry.[70]

Although there is little evidence for collaboration between Schlieffen and Holstein, many commentators have surmised that they worked closely together during the crisis. For one thing, their response to Germany's overall strategic situation at this time was defined in terms of the same metaphor. Schlieffen believed that Germany was surrounded by an enormous coalition, just as Frederick the Great had been before the Seven Years' War. Now, he wrote, we can escape from this noose. The whole of Russia's western border area was stripped of troops. It would be years before Russia could take action, and meanwhile we could settle

69. Zoellner, "Schlieffens Vermächtnis," pp. 42–43.
70. Lambi, *German Power*, p. 244; Albrecht von Thaer, *Generalstabsdienst an der Front und in der O.H.L.*, ed. S.A. Kaehler (Göttingen, 1958), p. 7.

accounts with France, our bitterest and most dangerous enemy. Holstein, writing at the same time, was convinced that before the ring of great powers had closed around it, Germany should endeavor with all its might to break out. The Reich should not step back even from the ultimate decision.[71]

Although during the summer of 1904 the military situation in East Asia was unclear, Schlieffen apparently believed from the start that Russia would be defeated. In the autumn the Dogger Bank crisis brought England and Russia to the brink of war. Germany tried to negotiate a Russian alliance with France as a secondary signer; however, this effort failed. In January came the march against the Winter Palace and the first risings of the Revolution of 1905. By March the decisive battles in Manchuria had caused heavy losses and beyond doubt had lost the war for Russia. In the face of Russia's weakness, Bülow and Holstein persuaded their hesitating monarch to land at Tangier on the 31st of March. Did they intend to provoke a war with France, as Fritz Fischer argues? Historians will probably never know with full certainty; however, there are indications and tendencies to strongly suggest that they did.[72]

France at this time was unprepared for war. Prime Minister Revier feared a surprise German attack would lead France "to defeat and to the Commune." The French recognized that the crisis came at a particularly unfavorable movement when its ally Russia was at war with Japan. Almost immediately after the Tangier landing, Delcasse indicated in public and through unofficial contacts that he was willing to make a settlement. In Berlin, meanwhile, Schlieffen, Bülow, and the war minister were summoned to see the Kaiser. The subject of the discussion was a war against France. According to one report, Einem, the war minister, expressed doubts based on a single technical factor, the superiority of the French artillery. This would have been exactly the kind of point which might have given the Kaiser reason to hesitate, technical details from a military expert.[73]

During this period Schlieffen led his last GGS ride. In it virtually the whole German army was concentrated along the west front.

71. Rochs, *Schlieffen*, p. 40; Ritter, *Schlieffen Plan*, p. 112; Fischer, *Illusions*, p. 58; Rich, *Holstein*, 2: 699.

72. Zoellner, "Schlieffens Vermächtnis," pp. 11–13; Fischer, *Illusions*, p. 54.

73. John F.V. Keiger, *France and the Origins of the First World War* (New York, 1983), pp. 21–22; Rich, *Holstein*, 2: 704–5; Heiner Raulff, *Zwischen Machtpolitik und Imperialismus: Die deutsche Frankreichpolitik, 1904–1906* (Düsseldorf, 1976), pp. 131–32; Lambi, *German Power*, p. 258.

Russian forces were not even considered in the game. Five armies mobilized between Wesel and Diedenhofen, prepared to carry out the great flanking movement, while a sixth army stood between Diedenhofen and Metz to receive the expected French attack. A seventh army covered the fortified positions between Metz and Straßburg, protecting that area against enemy actions from Nancy and the upper Mosel.[74] No special situation was given for force blue: Schlieffen led it himself. France had fortified its borders against Germany. Supported by Switzerland and Belgium, the border from Belfort to Montmedy stood closed. We could attack this position in front, Schlieffen noted, or we could hold the front and fall upon the northern flank. But the corner of the position was not turned and would result in a division of the German forces, so that the French could fall upon each one individually. Therefore the entire front line had to be circumvented. That could only be accomplished by violating the neutrality of a state. Politically, he said, this may be prohibited, but academically we can discuss the question. While holding firm between Metz-Diedenhofen, the whole north wing would swing northwest like a pivot or swinging door, passing Liège, Namur, and Antwerp to fall on the French between Lille and Maubeuge. What would the French response to this be, Schlieffen wanted to know? Red force was given a free hand to do whatever it wanted. Among the participating GGS officers, many solutions were put forward. Three were singled out for extended discussion. Colonel Freiherr von Freytag-Loringhoven moved his red forces one army width north, placing his left flank at Lille, with his main force attacking west of Metz along the line Luxembourg-Namur-Brussels. He also planned to attack between Metz and Straßburg if no German moves were made there. Schlieffen said this was valid but criticized its execution. The outcome would be that, since the Germans did not attack east of Metz, they would have to step aside as French forces moved in the direction of Saarburg. The French main force would then be surrounded on its right flank by a German attack from Metz. On its other fronts forward of the Meuse River, indecisive fighting would go on until the Germans broke through the center of the French front. The eastern part of this front then would retreat behind the Meuse, while the separated western part would have a difficult

74. The account of this war game is from Zoellner, "Schlieffens Vermächtnis," pp. 48–52.

time against the numbers and quality of the German troops. It would be surrounded on its left flank, cut off, and destroyed.

Colonel von Steuben believed that the German turning movement could not be attacked in a decisive way, and therefore the French main attack had to be made between Metz and Straßburg, against the German left wing. He sent weak forces, mainly reserves and territorial divisions, to oppose the German flanking action. Schlieffen did not think this would bring success. The attack between Metz and Straßburg was very difficult to carry out, and he doubted that the French would do it in the face of an ongoing German march through Belgium. If they did, they faced difficulties. The German 7th Army would move against the line Bitch-Straßburg and win the front to the west, then move south into the Vosges Mountains with reinforced Landwehr troops from Upper Alsace. The 6th Army would take defensive positions on a line Metz-Nied-Saarbrücken. Both armies would be very strongly reinforced, but the German troops would have an easy time because the French forces opposing them were composed of reserve and territorial divisions. Schlieffen then turned both forces around and led them, together with the 6th Army, against the flank and front of the French main force east of Metz. Part of the 3d Army, on the south wing of the flanking group, was carried by railroad to Alsace to reinforce the 7th Army for an attack against the French east flank. If all of these complex movements were successful, Schlieffen argued, the fate of the French main force between Metz and Straßburg was sealed.

The third red solution by Major Kuhl allowed the Germans to make their attack, and then called for a counterattack. He surmised that the German right wing north of Liège-Namur was so strong that the German forces between Metz and Straßburg could not be very strong. He divided his forces into two equal groups. One to the east and one to the west of the Mosel, and attacked in a northernly direction. One army group would attack between Metz and Straßburg, the other against the south wing and middle of the German surrounding army, using reserve and territorial divisions for reinforcement. Schlieffen remarked that the attack west of Metz was very risky because it fell upon the main German force. It would soon come to a halt, and the French would find themselves in a very dangerous position in the ensuing battle. The French east group would also confront problems between Metz and Straßburg because the assumption that the Germans were weak there was wrong. These forces, in the meantime reinforced, could mount an extremely effective attack against the French flank and rear.

While the exercise was being played out, but prior to Schlieffen's final comments, the commanders of red were about to declare themselves defeated when Schlieffen drew their attention to the possibility of improving their apparently desperate situation. By quickly transporting all troops which could be spared and all forces behind the front to the French left wing, Schlieffen suggested forming a new army group to counterenvelop the German right wing, the actual French response by General Gallieni in September 1914.[75]

The success of the blue attack in this ride depended upon the size, speed, and unexpectedness of the German advance through Belgium. In fact, the enormous pressure of time was an essential feature. Crossing the Meuse River rapidly was crucial, for only north of the Meuse, via Aachen and the Netherlands, were there enough railway lines. Seizing Liège became the sine qua non for such a plan because it was the junction of four rail lines. The capacity of the Belgian railroad was very great, sufficient for two additional army corps to be brought up from Lorraine and inserted into the right wing. The problem of Paris remained. Paris was the center of the French rail system; how could it be isolated or eliminated? The radial French rail system offered many opportunities to envelop incoming German forces, as the final phase of the ride demonstrated.

Meanwhile the RRS of the GGS played through an almost continuous sequence of serial war games dealing with segments of the war plan. Beginning 12 January, they continued through the fall months and on into 1906. There were ten problems in all, each one a continuation and extension of the previous one. Often the time limit for solution was very short, with immediate response required. They all dealt with the problem of a war against France and England on the west front.[76]

On 19 August, Bülow again asked Schlieffen for a strategic assessment. Schlieffen reiterated that Russia had denuded its west front: ten of its twenty-six European army corps and five of its eight rifle brigades as well as other personnel and material had either arrived in East Asia or were en route there. Russian forces

---

75. From an article by Wilhelm von Hahnke in the *Berliner Börsenzeitung*, 6 May 1930, quoted in Ritter, *Schlieffen Plan*, p. 60.
76. Groener Papers, roll 18, no. 168.

had been greatly weakened not only in quantity and quality, but also in organization.

During November–December 1905 Schlieffen handed out to the hundred or so lieutenants assigned to the GGS his final winter problem. It was a simultaneous war game against Russia, England, and France. Belgium and the Netherlands were neutral and Germany paused in the northwest, giving both states the opportunity, in the event their neutrality was first violated by the Franco-English army, to ally with Germany. Italy was not included. It was expected that Austria-Hungary would restrain a substantial part of the Russian army on its east border. The German field army was made up of twenty-five active army corps, plus a number of reserve corps and divisions, as well as a large group of Landwehr brigades.[77] Germany's opponents marched as follows: Russia attacked with the Niemen and the Narew armies against East Prussia. France attacked along the entire border from Upper Alsace to the North Sea, using several alpine brigades against Italy. England attacked with six divisions on the north flank of the French army in Flanders. The Belgians and Dutch were not highly valued, nor were the English. The Haldane army reforms had not been completed, and the British had little experience leading large forces. Even Field Marshal Lord Roberts, the victor of the Boar War, Schlieffen said, had admitted that British troops were unprepared to fight a war on the continent of Europe.

German actions were as follows. Half of the forces were sent to the east front, where they were slightly outnumbered but were considered operationally and tactically superior to the Russians, who still suffered under the negative impact of their enormous losses against Japan. Because of the limited work capacity of the East Prussian railroads, German forces could only retard or delay the Russian advance. Along the west front, the border from the Netherlands to Upper Alsace was secured with cavalry and Landwehr and reconnaissance forces were readied. Only in the fortress area of Metz-Diedenhofen and in the gap between Metz and the Vosges Mountains were active and reserve forces found. Behind them were assembled heavy reinforcements. Around Cologne was a group of three active and three reserve corps, and in south

---

77. Lambi, *German Power*, p. 259; Schlieffen Papers, roll 3, no. 32, "Kriegsspiel" November/December 1905, Schlußbesprechung, geheim, dated 23 December 1905. Cf. Zoellner, "Schlieffens Vermächtnis," p. 53; Ulrich Liss, "Graf Schlieffens letztes Kriegsspiel," *Wehrwissenschaftliche Rundschau* 15 (1965): 161–67.

Germany the main force of army corps was located around Mainz and Straßburg and in Württemberg and Bavaria. All were standing ready at railroad collection points. Thus Germany allowed both opponents the initiative: in the east because of the railroad situation, in the west to encourage the possibility of Belgian and Dutch neutrality.

The war game began on the twentieth mobilization day, the start of offensive operations for both opponents, and ended on the fortieth mobilization day. In the east there was border fighting, with German partial attacks against the Russian Niemen and Narew armies along a north-south front from the Deime River east of Königsberg to the border of the Masurians. One German force went over the Deime north of the Pregel and attacked deep into the Russian north flank so that the Niemen army retreated, badly hurt. At the same time a deep German breakthrough occurred between the Niemen and Narew armies. The Russians had neglected to destroy several bridges at the center of their front, a tactical error which cost them dearly. The German forces spread out and attacked the Narew army. It was forced to yield and was surrounded and finally destroyed in the swamps south of the Masurian Lakes. The Russian armies in East Prussia were so badly hurt that they ceased to be a threat. On the fortieth mobilization day, a large part of German east front strength was available for transportation to the west front.

On the west front, the game began with combat of both sides along the entire line. French forces moved strongly through the Burgundian *Pforte* and over the Vosges Mountains passes into Alsace above Straßburg. German troops moved out from the fortress Straßburg and across the bridgeheads Hüningen and Istein on the upper Rhine to mount a counteroffensive between Kolmar and the Hart Forest. Between Metz and the Vosges Mountains there was a strong French attack. The main attack came through Belgium, where the mass of French regular troops attacked on a wide front from Luxembourg to Antwerp. As soon as French operations became clear, a German counteroffensive was initiated. The ten Belgian and Dutch divisions allied with Germany protected the fortress Antwerp and the area east of the Demer. Germany reinforced the Belgian town of Liège with active troops. The attack group Cologne crossed the border south of Liège, a second force attacked to the north from the fortress area Metz-Didenhofen, and both surrounded the French between Liège and the central Mosel. Using the Dutch and Belgian railroads, a newly created army group moved west of Antwerp, attacked the French-English army in the flank and rear, surrounded them, and forced them to surrender.

In his final critique, Schlieffen began by saying that the situation was improbable but at least it was not boring. The red commanders had made a series of errors which primarily accounted for the blue success. Fighting against the entire French army, all of the European land forces of England, and a substantial part of the Russian army was a great challenge. Not the least interesting question was how England would divide its forces and whether they would land in Jutland or at a channel port. In this game the question was decided in favor of Dunkirk and Calais. The red west front force comprised of the English and French had a line and reserve infantry of 1,300,000 troops. On the east front the red force was 500,000 Russian infantry. Clausewitz, Schlieffen said, called such a situation "strategic consumption." The initial situation and problem – an offensive through the swamps and forests of Poland and Lithuania or an attack against the forests and defensive positions of France – required so much time and power, that a defensive suggested itself.

Many would go east, beat the Russians decisively, and then turn west. But to transport sufficient force by means of the inadequate road and railroad system reduced the chances of success. Furthermore, 456,000 blue infantry against 500,000 red infantry gave red a small superiority. In this situation blue could neither defeat red decisively nor fight as in Manchuria, for months and months. Blue needed to defeat one enemy quickly so as to have a free hand to defeat the other. In the east there were two advantages to be used carefully, Schlieffen said. One was the Masurian Lakes, a forty-seven-mile-long obstacle and Angerburg, to the south of Johannisburg, with its string of three fortresses at Lotzen, between Lowentin and Spirdingsee, and between Spirdingsee and Niedersee. The Russians, with an army of eighteen divisions on the Niemen and an army of 14.5 divisions on the Narew could only unite the two west of the Masurians. A second advantage was the fortress Königsberg and the defensive line Diems-Pregels-Frischings, a fifty-mile stretch built by engineers. Using both of these, perhaps Germany could hold until the twenty-seventh or twenty-eighth mobilization day, then allow the Russians to move forward and attack their separate forces. If, Schlieffen said, we were able to determine the main lines of the Russian attack, we could move

German forces by rail. He noted that the possibility of heavily fortified lines holding off attacks had been demonstrated in the Russo-Japanese War.

On the west front, Schlieffen argued, Germany did not have the luxury of such a war. The machine with its thousand wheels supplying millions, cannot stop for long. We cannot fight twelve-day battles from position to position for one or two years until the leadership is exhausted and both sides seek peace. We must seek to destroy quickly and entirely. We must aim for a battle of annihilation by attacking the flank and rear. First, secure the borders and, much more important, the railroads. Second, position the German forces from the Meuse to the Mosel, with the cavalry divisions up front and behind them, around Cologne and Aachen, three northern army corps and their reserve corps ready to be transported. During this time we must keep watch along the Belgian-French border for a strong army at Lille, for the English force of three corps at Dunkirk and Calais, and for armies along the Belgian border between Verdun and Maubeuge on the upper Mosel and near the Vosges Mountains.

An invasion of Belgium was fraught with difficulties. If the French invaded along both banks of the Meuse, they would find themselves hemmed in on two sides by the Rhine and on one side by the Mosel, an unpleasant situation. If the right wing of the German force north of Metz pushed the enemy forces behind the Mosel and brought the whole right bank of the Mosel into German hands, we would be in position to move directly against Paris. Under these circumstances, Schlieffen said, we might ask if, instead of waiting to counterattack, the German force might attack? It is possible during the French advance march to attack the French left flank using the space between Antwerp, the Meuse, and the Rhine. The further west the better was the point to attack by sending as many army corps as possible by railroad to Antwerp and the rest to Cologne.[78]

Throughout this period of the Moroccan crisis, a variety of strategic plans, possibilities, and ideas was continually being tested. If we draw any conclusions from them, it is that Schlieffen had reached no final opinion as to what the best plan would be. His major dilemmas, whether to go east or west first and exactly how to operate on each front, were all fraught with difficulties. Each

---

78. Liss, "Graf Schlieffen," pp. 161–67; cf. Schlieffen Papers, roll 1, no. 57.

option was explored, discussed, and critiqued. After December 1905 the situation quieted down. On 1 January 1906 Kaiser Wilhelm II assembled his generals for the traditional New Year's reception. First he announced Schlieffen's retirement and the appointment of Helmuth von Moltke the Younger as his successor. Second, he told the assembled officers that although the Moroccan question had caused great tension in Germany, he had no intention of going to war over it.[79]

It seems clear that in the decision-making process of 1904–5 four factors prevailed. First was that at this period in his reign the Kaiser allowed Chancellor von Bülow to make some important policy decisions. Wilhelm had told Eulenburg as early as July 1901 that he let Bülow rule. "Since I have him, I can sleep peacefully. I leave things to him and know that everything is all right." During the Kaiser's Mediterranean cruise of March 1904, he closed his eyes to Germany's gloomy situation and left it all to "his Bülow" to sort out. However, Bülow was only allowed to make policy up to the point where a decision for war was called for, a decision which the Kaiser reserved to himself. Decisions which Wilhelm reserved to himself, however, were apt to be dependent upon his mood. How he decided any given issue often depended on how he felt at a specific moment, and his mood had to coincide with the advice of those with whom he talked last about the issue at hand.

Second, Holstein and Schlieffen worked closely together. Based upon the testimony of men who discussed the affair with Bülow in later years, and of subordinates of Schlieffen who were in close contact with Holstein, it is highly probable that Holstein was interested in forcing war upon France, based on Schlieffen's technical estimate that Russia was in no position to come to France's aid. Yet in this case Bülow and the Kaiser were in charge, not Holstein and Schlieffen.[80]

Third, it has been argued that the military was not involved at all in foreign policy decision making during this time and those who were involved, such as War Minister Einem, counseled against war. Both Schlieffen and Holstein were ill and unable to be

79. Einem, *Erinnerungen*, p. 114; Craig, *Germany*, pp. 318–20.
80. Katherine Lerman, "The Decisive Relationship: Kaiser Wilhelm II and Chancellor Bernhard von Bülow, 1900–1905," in John Röhl, ed., *Kaiser Wilhelm II: New Interpretations* (Cambridge, 1982), pp. 239–41. Cf. Katherine Lerman, "Bernhard von Bülow and the Governance of Germany, 1897–1909" (Ph.D. diss., University of Sussex, 1984); Gordon Craig, *From Bismarck to Adenauer: Aspects of German Statecraft*, rev. ed. (New York, 1965), p. 31.

influential at the critical period during the summer of 1905. In early August 1905 Schlieffen was badly kicked by a companion's horse. He was unable to walk or ride for weeks and did not attend the Kaisermanöver in September. Holstein was also taken ill and was on leave in August and September. Thus the two leading advocates of military action were not involved in the decision-making process. When Schlieffen came back in late September, he told the Saxon military attaché in Berlin that a war against France and Britain continued to be regarded as a possibility. The general staff and admiralty had been ordered to begin preparing a joint plan of campaign.[81]

However Holstein provides the essential clue. He recognized that he was wrong in his estimates of the Reich leadership. Prince Bülow was reluctant and the Kaiser unwilling to make war by themselves, without a European context. The Kaiser's decision was probably critical. When confronted with the question of whether to make war on France, he responded, "No, I shall never be capable of such action!" In other words, at that particular point in his cycle preventive war was unacceptable. He needed a different kind of rationale. Thus the fourth factor, the decision-making context, was important. Wilhelm II had, under most circumstances, a strong personal reluctance to assume responsibility. This is curiously reminiscent of the pushing and urging Moltke and Bismarck had to do in both 1866 and 1870 to obtain a declaration of war from the Prussian king. In 1905 Kaiser Wilhelm II did not agree to a war against France. It was too much of a risk for this unstable, uncertain man, especially in the face of the conflicting opinions of technical specialists.[82]

Keeping in mind that the actual war mobilization plans for the year 1905–6 were destroyed in the Potsdam Army Achives in April 1945 and that their reconstruction is based on fragments which survived, not on the original document itself, the Schlieffen Plan,

---

81. Rich, *Holstein*, 2: 598; Rochs, *Schlieffen*, p. 75.

82. Fischer, *Illusions*, pp. 54–56; Lambi, *German Power*, pp. 241–58; Richard Ned Lebow, "Windows of Opportunity: Do States Jump through Them?" in Steven E. Miller, ed., *Military Strategy, and the Origins of the First World War* (Princeton, 1985), pp. 160–62. Peter Winzen, "Der Krieg in Bülows Kalkül," in Jost Dülffer and Karl Holl, eds., *Bereit zum Krieg: Kriegsmentalität im Wilhelminischen Deutschland, 1890–1914* (Göttingen, 1986), pp. 171–78; Oscar Freiherr von der Lancken-Wakenitz, *Meine dreißig Dienstjahre, 1888–1918* (Berlin, 1931), p. 88; Craig, *Politics*, p. 283; idem, *Germany*, p. 320; Ritter, *Schlieffen Plan*, pp. 103–30; Kitchen, *German Officer Corps*, p. 104; Kennedy, *War Plans*, pp. 207–10; Rich, *Holstein*, 2: 696–99.

as laid out in the memorandum dated 28 December 1905, may be defined as follows: on the west front, an opening attack lasting approximately forty days from mobilization would occur, made up of seven-eights of the available forces, or 33.5 corps, with six armies north of Diedenhofen. The heaviest armies 1, 2, and 3 would be positioned between Luxembourg and Aachen, with the lighter armies 4, 5, and 6 south of Luxembourg. Their aim would be to strike west across the Netherlands and Belgium, drive around the French left or northern flank, then decisively defeat the main French armies by attacking south down into the French rear in a giant wheeling operation intended to thrust the leading edge of the German armies close to the channel and to the far southwest of Paris. Another force of two armies, the heaviest to the south, would wait at the Meuse River hoping to entice the French armies eastward toward the Rhine. If the French attacked between Metz and Straßburg, Schlieffen felt that his forces would be able to hold at Metz long enough for the encircling German right wing to force the French to halt their invasion before they could seriously interrupt his line of communications. Depending upon what happened in the southern quadrant, two army corps could be subtracted from those between Metz and Straßburg and redirected by rail to reinforce the right wing north of Luxembourg. It is also possible that Schlieffen was thinking in terms of a complete Battle of Cannae, a double envelopment, in which case the German center would hold, and the German left wing would go forward just enough to be in position to attack north against the French right wing and rear. On the east front an opening holding action by a single army, which would await the Russian troops, split geographically by the Masurian Lakes into two forces. The German army would then move to attack each one singly, counting on slow mobilization and poor railroads to retard the Russian attack past the (forty-day) point at which the French-English force had been substantially defeated. Then east front forces could be reinforced by a number of west front corps.

As reconstructed by Gerhard Ritter, Schlieffen's memorandum of 28 December 1905 is dominated by considerations based upon a single technology, that of the railroads. Schlieffen wrote that the railroad system obliged the German army to deploy mainly on the Metz-Wesel line. Further reinforcement of this deployment by two army corps on the left blank of the Moselle would be brought up by railway as soon as the lines were cleared. This reinforcement could bring the decision. The Belgian railroad west of the Meuse River was the principle line of communication for the German right flanking force. As the German army moved forward, Schlieffen planned to reconstruct potentially destroyed Belgian and French lines and to build several entirely new railroads where none then existed, for example, from Thiaucourt to St. Mihiel and between Saales and St. Die, in this way opening up direct rail connection west of the Moselle, through Metz, and on to Paris.[83]

The plan was a daring gamble based on timing, whose vehicle was the railroad. It was a complex one with many contingencies and assumptions: (1) The inadequate Russian railroad and road systems meant that the Russian mobilization, concentration, and advance would be very slow, in fact, that it would take forty days for the Russian army to cross the German east front borders in substantial numbers. (2) The Dutch and Belgian railroad systems, the highest density systems in the world in 1905, would enable a rapid, massive, and quickly reinforced German thrust, first west, then south, to connect to the French rail system. (3) This attack would have so much momentum that it would catch the French and English by surprise. (4) It would result in a complete annihilation of these armies in thirty to forty days. (5) At that time substantial west front forces would be released and sent east by means of a second, massive railroad movement to defeat the invading Russian armies. Germany faced superior forces both east and west, but also had to confront a huge discrepancy, figured at 960 hours and caused by different transportation technologies, between the time these two superior forces would engage German troops. Schlieffen concluded on this basis that Germany's best chance was to use technology to take advantage of the narrow window of opportunity. In a plan requiring several million men, campaign areas larger than 40,000 square miles, and time pressures so great that planners feared that a delay of seventy-two hours might lose the war, only railroads offered the possibility of guaranteeing the speed, volume, and dependability needed to succeed. It was to be a modern Cannae, the complete destruction of one national opponent and the annihilation of portions of two other armies comprised of several hundred thousand, on opposite geographic frontiers.

In carrying out this plan, what kind of a war did Schlieffen

83. Ritter, *Schlieffen Plan*, pp. 138–57.

envision German forces would encounter? Four years after he retired, Schlieffen described this in a widely quoted essay which summarized his interpretation of military history after 1871 and outlined his image of future war. It is curious how closely this image parallels another war image widely discussed in Europe when it was published in 1899, Ivan S. Bloch's *The Future of War*.[84]

Schlieffen wrote that technological weapons development and a huge increase in the size of armies, both embedded in an arms race that had begun in Europe but had spread throughout the world, had created a new stage in the evolution of war. Initially Germany and France each tried to gain a decisive technological advantage, as had been the case in 1866. Neither achieved this, although at various times each held a momentary advantage, thus spurring the other on. Soon this competition spread to other states and in a few decades every power was armed with roughly equal weapons. The dual power of battle was now achieved by artillery and the size of armies. Quick-firing, lighter, and more movable artillery, accompanied by huge reserves of more powerful, smokeless shells, virtually controls the entire area from muzzle to target, Schlieffen argued. Each army corps today has 144 excellent guns, in contrast to 84 earlier, and that, plus 25,000 excellent rifles, gives the corps ten times the firepower of armies in the period of the muzzle loader. The result of these developments is a storm of shrapnel causing 68% casualties on the battlefield of Mars Le Tour in 1870 and nearly 90% casualties among the Japanese Nambu brigade in 1904. Killing with such machines is easily done; the question is how to defend against it. General conscription, once the special province of Prussia, the straitlaced military state, has spread worldwide. Today everyone who is healthy and strong is sent into the army. Peacetime service has been reduced and reserve duty increased. The results are stunning. Germany, with 62 million inhabitants, each year accepts 250,000 recruits for nineteen years of service. France, with 40 million inhabitants, accepts 220,000 recruits for twenty-five years of service. The result is that in a war Germany has 4,750,000 men and France 5,500,000! Battles will be fought with twenty times the number of forces engaged at Königgrätz in 1866!

What is the impact of all of this, Schlieffen asked? Tactically, it

84. Generalfeldmarschall Graf Alfred von Schlieffen, "Der Krieg in der Gegenwart," *Deutsche Revue*, January 1909, pp. 13–24; I.S. Bloch, *The Future of War in Its Technical, Economic, and Political Relations* (London, 1900).

meant that: (1) Artillery has to be used in close support to help infantry advance, aiming first to halt enemy artillery, then turning against the infantry, and finally destroying the enemy cover. (2) Cavalry will give up its place to infantry and artillery. Even reconnaissance, the traditional cavalry job, will be done by fleets of airplanes which can surmount the mountains, woods, and towns which hinder the horsemen's view. Heavily armed cavalry, equipped with artillery, machine guns, and carbines, will bring these weapons to bear on the enemy rear. (3) Infantry itself has to be spread out widely across a battlefield. To find cover, to secure protection, to move forward quickly, the infantry must have elbow room. In contrast to battles of the past two centuries, where fifteen men per meter or ten men to a step was used, now there will be one man to a meter with rows greatly separated. (4) This will result in a great extension of the fighting front. (5) Advancing will be done in short rushes, using the protection of trees, houses, caves, and earthen trenches and moving from position to position. (6) The final assault against the enemy, which involves crossing the last open space, will be done by digging trenches and moving from trench to trench, when possible under cover of night. (7) Forces will be dispersed, artillery going against artillery, airplane against airplane, before they unite for the final assault. Tactically, Schlieffen concluded, the battlefield of the future will look very different from those of the past, but similar to those in the Russo-Japanese War.

At the level of intermediate strategy it meant that: (1) Reserves of ammunition, ready to be brought up by truck, will be more effective than reserves of men. (2) Each corps will fight independently on its own, without being able to call up help quickly: only casualty replacements will be possible. (3) Battles will no longer be single and concentrated in one area; they will be broken up into a series of smaller but related fights, such as the Battles of Dresden and Leipzig. (4) Battles will also be spread out in time. Battles lasting several days, as in the second half of the Franco-Prussian War, for example at Orleans and Le Mans, will become common. If they do not last fourteen days, like the Battle of Mukden, they will last three to five. Each day will bring a new phase in which the commander will have to rethink his actions as conditions change. (5) Casualties will be about the same as before. Schlieffen reminded his readers that the daily battle loss in the Russo-Japanese War was only 2% to 3% of those engaged in contrast to 40% or 50%

in the wars of Frederick and Napoleon. The fourteen days of the Battle of Mukden cost the Russians and Japanese fewer losses than the few hours of Mars Le Tour cost the French and Germans in 1870.

As for grand strategy, Schlieffen asked, what was the role of the high command in all of this? No Napoleon surrounded by a splendid staff will be seen on the heights overlooking battles. For one thing, his white horse would quickly attract artillery fire. For another, even the best field glasses would not reveal very much: forces would be too large and too far away. Instead, the commander would find himself far behind the lines in a house with roomy offices where telegraph, radio, telephone, signal apparatus, motorcars, and motorcycles waited for his commands. There, seated in a comfortable chair before a large map, the modern Alexander would survey the whole battlefield. As balloons and airplanes sent in reports of enemy movements, carefully delineated as to kind and quality, he would send and receive reports from his army and corps commanders. The essential task of the commander was fulfilled long before the declaration of war.

# Chapter 5

# Moltke the Younger and Technocratic War Planning, 1906–1913

After four decades of monotonous, dreary peace, the specter of a brief, heroic, social-Darwinist war began to appear on the European horizon. In Prussian Germany, as the foreign environment darkened, the technical expert came to the fore. With nearly seven hundred officers, sixteen sections, and several buildings, the GGS was led by a man personally attractive to the Kaiser but inexperienced in GGS procedures and technology. Helmuth von Moltke the Younger lacked both a detailed understanding of the war plan and the confidence that it would work. At first he asked the chief of the RRS whether he believed the MTP would work. Later he inquired whether he really could imagine that it might work.[1] What Moltke did not lack was a belief in the inevitability of a coming war, ordained within the cosmic scheme of world history. In this mood of technological doubt and philosophical expectation there was dangerous potential for Germany and Europe.

## *Moltke: Background, Education, Interests – Steiner*

In fall 1903 Schlieffen had asked the Kaiser to begin the process of finding his replacement. In a letter to his brother-in-law he noted that he was seventy-three years old, nearly blind, half deaf, and had a bad leg. He thought the Kaiser would act soon on his request to retire. Schlieffen was ready to go. When he suffered a severe accident, kicked by one of his early morning riding companions' horses, he was unable to attend to his office for several months and did not participate in the fall 1905 Kaisermanöver. Interestingly, at these maneuvers, a contest between the Prussian Guard and the 9th Corps, the chief maneuver judge was Helmuth von Moltke the Younger, royal adjutant and recently commander of the 1st Guard

1. Staabs, *Aufmarsch*, p. 36.

Infantry Division, who only six months before had been appointed to service with the GGS.[2] The choice of Schlieffen's successor, like so many of Kaiser Wilhelm's appointments, seemed strange to everyone, including the one selected. Admittedly the problem of GGS leadership in 1905 was both formidable and sensitive. Formidable because the position had been held since 1857 by three men considered strong, if not legendary, leaders. Sensitive in that it was, in a way, the most important operative position in the Reich government. The chief of the GGS was the conductor of the war plan, the primus inter pares of the Reich bureaucracy, the technical director to whose expert opinion in war even the Kaiser deferred.

There were many choices for chief of staff in 1906. A reform-minded group was convinced that the future would be very different from the past. Their views on war were considered modern and innovative. The group included Colmar Freiherr von der Goltz, Gottlieb Graf von Haeseler, Moritz Freiherr von Bissing, and Hans Hartwig von Beseler. Goltz, author, Ottoman advisor, and chief of the Engineer and Pioneer Corps, was personally unacceptable to the Kaiser. Earlier he had apparently been Schlieffen's own choice, but later his ideas on fortress warfare turned his strategic thinking astray. Haeseler, for thirteen years commanding general of the 16th Corps in Alsace-Lorraine, had retired. Bissing, commander of the Guard Corps, failed to attract attention as a troop commander during summer maneuvers. When he disciplined officers in this most feudal corps, the Kaiser had retired him. Beseler had been GGS section chief and quartermaster, then chief of the Engineer and Pioneer Corps and inspector general of fortresses. He apparently was Schlieffen's own candidate, along with Graf Dietrich Huelsen-Haeseler and Frederick von Bernhardi. The Kaiser said he did not know Beseler. General Karl von Bülow, later war commander of the 2d Army, was also a candidate, as were Generals Georg von Alten and Karl von Endres, both of whom died prematurely. Maximilian Graf Yorck von Wartenburg, section chief under Schlieffen in the 1890s, had been a candidate but he died during the China expedition, where he was Waldersee's chief of staff.[3]

2. Kessel, *Schlieffens Briefe*, p. 304.

3. Moltke, *Erinnerungen*, pp. 306–7; Wilhelm Groener, *Feldherr wider Willen: Operative Studien über den Weltkrieg* (Berlin, 1931), p. xiv; Gaertringen, *Groener*,

The selection process was hardly consistent, uniform, or rigorous. Huelsen-Haeseler, chief of the Military Cabinet, supported his old school chum Beseler, while Plessen, Wilhelm's senior adjutant, promoted his candidate Moltke. Nobody knew who would be chosen until the last moment. It was above all Moltke's personal relationship with the Kaiser that made the difference. Moltke tried his best to refuse the office. Others – the Military Cabinet chief, the chancellor, and Wilhelm's close friend Philip Eulenburg – argued against Moltke to no avail. Ultimately the Kaiser seems to have selected a familiar face and an agreeable personality with the most famous military name in recent European history. Field Marshal von Moltke had apparently told Wilhelm that it was less important that the chief of the GGS be a genius and more important that he be a person of good character. Character was the main element tested in war. One wonders how well the Kaiser knew Moltke's character. Moltke was a close friend of Wilhelm, someone with whom he felt comfortable. Yet especially after the defeats, scandals, and disappointments of the years 1906 to 1909 – beginning with the Algeciras Conference, followed by the Moltke-Harden and Eulenburg trials, and ending with the Daily Telegraph affair and Bülow's dismissal – he was the last person in a position of responsibility whom Wilhelm could consider a trusted friend.[4]

Helmuth von Moltke the Younger was born in 1848 and was raised under the aegis of his uncle and namesake on the latter's estate at Kreisau in southwestern Silesia. Educated for the army, with a distinguished combat record while serving in the 7th Grenadier Regiment in 1870, he was then posted to the 1st Guard Regiment and to the War Academy. From 1882 to 1891, he was inseparable from "uncle Helmuth." He was assigned as an adjutant, lived in the GGS building, and traveled with him across Europe. The nephew often accompanied the uncle to dinners with Wilhelm I and as a result came to know the prince; they also served together as members of the 1st Guard Infantry Regiment. With the prince's assumption of the crown and his uncle's death, Moltke

---

p. 117; Stolberg-Wernigerode, *Unentschiedene Generation*, pp. 339–42; Görlitz, *Die Junker*, p. 298.

4. BAMA, Nachlaß Beseler, Lebenserinnerungen, p. 84; Konstantin Freiherr von Gebsattel, the Bavarian military representative in Berlin, reviewed a list of candidates in his report of 2 November 1905. BHSA, M. Kr. 41; Elze, *Tannenberg*, p. 35; Moltke, *Erinnerungen*, p. 306; Hull, *Entourage*, pp. 232–33.

in effect joined the new Kaiser's entourage. In 1893, at age fifty-four, he was promoted to lieutenant colonel and adjutant. For the next eleven years, Moltke was a close companion of Wilhelm II, meanwhile moving through a succession of prestigious commands – the Kaiser Alexander Guard Grenadier Regiment No. 1 (1896), the 1st Guard Infantry Brigade (1899), and the 1st Guard Infantry Division (1902) – guaranteed to keep him close to court and Kaiser.[5]

Contemporary as well as historical judgement of Moltke the Younger has been harsh. It is clear that he was a very different kind of person than his predecessors. They had all been serving soldiers with relatively long military careers and experience at least as staff officers. He had very little of this. It was said that he was not a hard worker and had been at court for fifteen years and was unfamiliar with tactical problems. He lacked self-confidence and leadership ability, was lethargic, and had a tendency to become bogged down in detail. He was a genial colleague, but neither a bureaucratic director nor a noble warrior whose leadership would inspire his men. He was a quiet dreamer, earnest, intelligent, and reflective. Observers praised Moltke's mental qualities. Baroness Spitzemberg described him as a highly cultivated man, surpassingly decent and of brave character. His was an intelligent, broadly oriented mind with interests in art, literature, and philosophy. He read about theology, oriental religions, and art history, appreciated Beethoven, followed history and politics in the *Preußische Jahrbücher*, visited medieval monasteries, rode in airplanes, and gave demonstrations of stereoscopic photography to Reichstag members. In many respects he appeared to be a thoroughly modern man. Yet from the days of the romantic rejection of the Enlightenment there had always been a strong antirational element in German thinking and Moltke aligned himself with the latter.[6]

5. Gaertringen, *Groener*, p. 91. Wilhelm II's nickname for Moltke, "Julius," had apparently originated when the Kaiser and Moltke both served as officers together and purchased their cigars from one Julius Denker. He sold cigars both to Moltke the Elder, called "der große Denker," and to Moltke the Younger, known as "der kleine Denker"; Moltke, *Erinnerungen*, pp. 111–246; Groener, *Feldherr wider Willen*, p. xv.

6. Hull, *Entourage*, p. 232; Stein, *Erlebnisse*, pp. 36–39; Hermann von Kuhl, *Der deutsche Generalstab in Vorbereitung und Durchführung des Weltkrieges*, 2d ed. (Berlin, 1920), pp. 140–42; Walter Gorlitz, ed., *Der Kaiser: Aufzeichnungen des Chefs des Marine-Kabinetts Admiral Georg Alexander von Mueller* (Göttingen, 1965), p. 186; Hildegard Baronin Spitzemberg, *Das Tagebuch der Baronin Spitzemberg*, ed. Rudolf

Moltke was an unexceptional man who underwent a dramatic change of personality and character in about 1904, soon after his fiftieth birthday. This change of life was based on three factors. One was his long-standing relationship with his wife, a fanatically superstitious woman who practiced spiritism and held séances. She was the dominant intellectual and psychological force in her husband's life. The second was his interest in the worldviews of Rudolf Steiner, close advisor to his wife and leader of the theosophy movement that had permeated the salons of Berlin court society. These two factors were linked together by a third, Moltke's passionate interest in knowing the future and understanding life after death.

His wife Gräfin Eliza von Moltke-Huitfeld, "Lizzy" as she was known, a distant cousin from the Danish branch of the family, was an individual with a will far stronger than her husband's. It was said she used her power over her husband in official appointments, once even making the appointment of a corps commander impossible. Above all, she brought a new philosophy into her husband's life in the form of the ideas of Rudolf Steiner. By 1897, when Steiner moved to Berlin, Eliza was well placed in Berlin society. Her friend Johanna Gräfin Keyerslingk spoke of their long membership in the Berlin branch of the theosophical society. In advancing his philosophical movement, Rudolf Steiner taught, lectured, and wrote; he also published books on Earnst Martin Haeckel and Friedrich Nietzsche. In 1900 he gave a series of talks at the home of Gräfin Brockdorff.[7]

Theosophy is a missionary philosophy, a dynamic system which presumes to move with the underlying tides and invisible forces of world history. Like religion, it is founded on belief and intuitive knowledge yet also promises a synthesis of science and religion; it combined knowledge identified to be at once scientific and spiritual. By incorporating aspects of many belief systems, it appealed to those from a variety of religious traditions. In fact, its very openness was attractive and provided a sharp contrast to the closed "thou shalt not" imperatives of conventional theologies. Fusing Eastern esotericism, Western transcendentalism, and the earliest

---

Vierhaus, 3d ed. (Göttingen, 1963), p. 450; Moltke, *Erinnerungen*, pp. 329, 343, 364–66, 377; Michael Balfour, *Withstanding Hitler in Germany*, quoted by Gordon Craig, "Facing up to the Nazis," *New York Review of Books*, January 1989, p. 11.

7. Gerhard Weber, *Rudolf Steiner: Leben, Erkenntnis, Kulturimpuls* (Munich, 1987), p. 368.

psychological speculations, it promised peace for the individual within a larger cosmic framework. The main themes in Steiner's speculative system were the raising of Lazarus, meditation, and the spiritual world in its relationship to the long-term trends of world history. Steiner's personal initiation into the Mystery of Golgotha occurred just prior to his incorporation of occultism and the beliefs of Annie Besant. The tie between Steiner and the prophetic interpretation of history is found in his inclusion of ideas from the New Testament Book of Revelation. The aim of Steiner's movement was "to prepare those who have the will to allow themselves to be prepared for the return of Christ upon earth . . . to prepare mankind . . . for the time when Christ will appear again actively among men in the sixth cultural epoch." The Book of Revelation predicted the second coming of Christ amid scenes of chaos and terror of epic proportions.[8]

Moltke began reading Rudolf Steiner in 1904, apparently to clarify his understanding of Nietzsche and Haeckel. Moltke remarked that before reading Steiner he had understood neither one, but now everything was clear. In July, aboard the royal yacht *Hohenzollern*, Moltke led a discussion of Steiner's worldviews which was listened to, according to his wife's account, as if he were "a pastor in a church." During the same tour he read Houston Stewart Chamberlain's *Foundations of the 19th Century* and Annie Besant's *Four Religions*. In certain respects, the ideas of Steiner, Chamberlain, and Besant were cut from the same cloth.

Moltke had always been interested in questions of life after death. His published letters are filled with persistent questioning in this direction. He wanted to know what happened and talked with everyone about it. Attending church services in Tulesbo, Sweden, during the North Sea trip, he fell into deep discussion with the pastor, who told him he believed in the further development of the human soul after death. The soul after death was held by a miraculous force in a congenial sphere, and higher spirits received it, enlightened it, and raised it up gradually from sphere to sphere. Moltke was impressed with the pastor's knowledge of ancient religions. On another northland cruise, Moltke and the Kaiser discussed the same topic. He reported that Wilhelm also believed in life after death and wanted to bring religion and science into accord with each other. Rudolf Steiner joined together many of

8. R.A. McDermott, *The Essential Steiner* (New York, 1984), intro., p. 282.

219

these strands in his theosophy. Eliza's spiritualism added the ingredient of communication with the dead.[9] Spiritualism was predicated on the proposition that, after death, a person's spirit could remain in close touch with the living and could relay messages back with the help of a medium, the reality of communication with identifiable deceased. Moving from disenchantment with conventional religious practices, Eliza had evolved a group, drawn from women in her social circle in Berlin, who practiced spiritualism, held séances, and talked with dead spirits. How far into occultism she went is an open question and one which need not concern us. What is important, however, is her influence over her husband.[10]

The prosaic, narrow world of old Prussian orthodoxy did not satisfy Moltke. His vision stretched far into the future, beyond the orthodox and pedantic. Rudolf Steiner's theosophy, with its mystical extension of Christian teaching, gave Moltke hope. What especially interested him was Steiner's coming to grips with the earthly and spiritual reality of Christology and with its confessional belief in mysticism and the state of Christ portrayed as a realizable power on earth.[11] Is it possible that these ideas coincided with a broad, popular religious revival? Schlieffen's traditional Pietistic fundamentalism was followed by Moltke's deep inner quest for life after death, nourished by fears, anxieties, and expectations of the imminent second coming of Christ amid an apocalyptic battle between German and Slav, the next stage in world history. Some of the roots of the conservative political revival Geoff Eley describes are probably religious. Such a revival may have undergirded the mass parties organized as pressure groups on the right at about this time. Sustained by young professionals as well as retired officers, the surging conservative movement cut a broad swath across Wilhelmian society. The faithful looked ahead hopefully and fatalistically to the next stage of world history, the second coming of Christ, and the testing of Germanic culture in a social-Darwinist

9. Moltke, *Erinnerungen*, pp. 290, 295, 300, 343, 361.

10. Janet Oppenheim, *The Other World: Spiritualism and Psychical Research in England, 1850–1914* (Cambridge, 1985), p. 165; Emily Oncken, *Panthersprung nach Agadir: Die deutsche Politik während der Zweiten Marokkokrise 1911* (Düsseldorf, 1981), p. 217; Ger van Roon, ed., *Helmuth James Graf von Moltke: Völkerrecht im Dienste der Menschen* (Berlin, 1986), pp. 10–11.

11. BAMA, Nachlaß Moltke, N78–37. "Eine Antwort an Herrn Walter Görlitz betr. das Kapitel 'Der Krieg ohne Feldherr' in seinem Buch, *Der deutsche Generalstab*," von Hauptmann a.D. Adam von Moltke, 1958, unpublished typescript, 43 pp, pp. 4–5; cf. Görlitz, *Der Kaiser*, p. 187.

contest of force. At some point after 1900, this vision of the future began to include the concept of an inevitable war. Schlieffen's legendary last words of 4 January 1913 – "It must come to a fight. Only make the right wing strong." – were mirrored in many strains of Wilhelmian thought. As early as 1905 Moltke wrote to his wife that before the spiritual era which she hoped for could come, mankind would have to endure a great deal of blood and misery. The thousand-year Reich, which mankind had awaited since Christ's time, could not be expected soon. The terrible murders in Russia were only a bloody symbol, a firebrand lighting a dark future.[12]

In retrospect, it seems that only such irrational beliefs – Bethmann-Hollweg's "leap in the dark" of 1914 – could produce a World War I and then sustain such a catastrophe for fifty-two continuous months. Many members of this generation believed that they had mystical assurance that they moved with the tides of the cosmos. As the circumstances of the foreign task environment became darker between 1906 and 1914, the Wilhelmians simultaneously tried to escape from a present with which they were increasingly uncomfortable to embrace a future which seemed more appealing. Faith in war as redeemer and deliverer became almost a creed. The religious revivalism of this period, and especially its esoteric aspects and ties to the Book of Revelation, may have been stronger than historians have suspected until now.[13]

As we move closer to 1914, the question of health must be raised in conjunction with several of the leading players, in particular Moltke. This question undoubtedly ties in with the concept of his general philosophy. Moltke was six feet three inches tall, with a large frame that tended toward rotundness. His own concern with health began in 1905: following the doctrines of one J.P. Mueller, he did morning exercises to take care of the physical body. His motto was "a sound mind in a sound body." He remarked that his health during the maneuver was excellent.[14]

12. Geoff Eley, *Reshaping the German Right* (New Haven, 1980); Moltke, *Erinnerungen*, p. 318; Hull, *Entourage*, p. 366.

13. Konrad Jarausch, *The Enigmatic Chancellor: Bethmann Hollweg and the Hubris of Imperial Germany* (New Haven, 1973), p. 159; cf. Fritz Stern, *The Politics of Cultural Despair* (New York, 1965); Roland N. Stromberg, *Redemption by War* (Lawrence, 1982).

14. Moltke, *Erinnerungen*, pp. 336, 338, 353. Eugen Bircher, "Die Krisis in der Marneschlacht," *Schweizerische Monatsschrift für Offiziere aller Waffen und Organ für Kriegswirtschaft* 30 (1926): 17–29, and Hugo Rochs, "Ärztliche Betrachtungen des schweizer Chirurgen und Oberstleutnants Bircher zum Weltkrieg," *Deutsche Medi-*

In the spring of 1911 he took a four-week leave to visit a clinic in Karlsbad. His physician told him that, as a result of the powerful action of his "deficiency," diseased material had worked its way into the body and he would probably always have to live with its consequences. Moltke's heart worked satisfactorily; there remained only a stomach indigestion and a swelling of the liver to verify. The next year 1912 he again went to Karlsbad. The doctor was satisfied with his heart, but noticed a faint irritation of the kidney. He said it would pass away in the course of the year. This diagnosis confirmed Moltke's suspicion that he had had an infection. Psychological anxieties for his own health may have begun to work on Moltke's dark vision of future events. In 1914 he went twice to Karlsbad, once in April and again in July. To take care of himself, he begged off the Kaiser's northland trip. Moltke's health became a matter of critical significance soon thereafter. As his adjutant Tieschowitz von Tieschowa wrote, during the first few days of mobilization in Berlin Moltke had two severe nervous breakdowns, crying, completely losing control of himself, and despairing, all of which were reminiscent of his actions when some aspect of a maneuver did not go according to plan. Moltke's own account of the events on the afternoon and evening of 1 August describe his breakdown when the Kaiser changed his mind twice within a few hours. Something broke within him. He was never able to get over the effects of it and went into the field under the impact of this shattering experience.[15]

---

*zinische Wochenschrift*, no. 33 (1927): 44–57, argue that Moltke suffered from arteriosclerosis and heart valve inflammation in 1906 and that these conditions worsened from then until 1914.

15. Moltke, *Erinnerungen*, pp. 358, 363, 379; Oncken, *Panthersprung*, p. 218; Görlitz, *German General Staff*, pp. 155–56; Gaertringen, *Groener*, pp. 145ff.; Ritter, *Schlieffen Plan*, p. 35; Craig, *Politics*, p. 294; Tieschowitz von Tieshowa knew Moltke well: he had worked as his adjutant for several years. The authenticity of Tieschowitz's diary is, however, open to question. In the BAMA, M Sq 1/2212, in a large file containing eight folders, most of which deal with events from 1915 on, there are only ten pages dealing directly with the events of August–September 1914. The lengthy memorandum from which Emily Oncken quotes is filled with cross-overs, cross-outs, and things added later in different handwriting. According to officials at the BAMA, additional materials from the Tieschowitz papers are anticipated from the family of German ambassador von Alten, who also wrote that they were to be deposited. On my last visit to Freiburg, however, in the summer of 1988, they had not yet been added and Ambassador Jürgen von Alten could not say exactly where these documents were or when they might be forthcoming. Letter to author of 4 February 1986.

## Moltke and the GGS Organization

Moltke was pessimistic, fatalistic, and spiritistic. And, perhaps by 1911, he was ill. The sources on him are few in number and poor in quality. He died in 1916, having been removed from office in November 1914. Bitterly attacked after the war for "watering down" the war plan or for not carrying it out energetically, he has not been well treated nor treated much at all by historians. But this may be irrelevant because there is little evidence that he had a consistent impact on war planning. Except at two points, when he altered the west front attack plan and changed the Austrian alliance, his main day-to-day influence was in his dealing with the Kaiser, chancellor, and war minister, the world outside the GGS.

The years from 1906 to 1912 were ones of almost complete cessation of army growth, during which time the ambitious "risk fleet" building program was carried out. Moltke was not a technical specialist: he was a court noble, inexperienced and lacking knowledge of GGS procedures, in particular war planning. Therefore he had to rely on others – the middle-class technical specialists brought into the GGS during the Schlieffen years – because their knowledge and experience was better than his. Moltke was Max Weber's quintessential government representative confronting an entrenched bureaucracy with a knowledge advantage. In addition, he was temperamentally unsuited to lead this bureaucracy. Moltke was uncertain, fatalistic; a hail-fellow-well-met, slap-on-the-back personality whom men especially enjoyed being around but who was simply not trained or experienced to do his job.

Not only was Moltke unprepared by education and experience to understand war planning; his disposition and life-style did not allow him the time to study or think his way into it. He was essentially not much interested in this kind of detailed work, and he never developed a taste for it. He was much more fascinated by art and philosophy, maintaining his own studio to practice his skills as an artist. In reality he did not have to become knowledgeable about war planning: he could rely on the technical experts, who were experienced and well versed in these matters. This fit in well with his daily and weekly schedule: as the Kaiser's last friend in high government circles, Moltke spent a lot of time with Wilhelm.[16] It

---

16. Hull, *Entourage*, pp. 240ff.; according to Groener, Moltke never fully grasped the main points of the Schlieffen plan. Groener Papers, roll 8, no. 35, letter of 22 June 1925.

must have been frightening for him to be in such a position, precisely because of his lack of knowledge. Thus he came to rely more and more on the technicians to provide the Reich leadership with the specialist knowledge they expected from him. As for the Kaiser, as soon as the war started he disappeared from the decision-making process. But what about the period prior to 1 August 1914? There is no reason to doubt, given the lack of regular cabinet processes and Wilhelm's established tradition of not working consistently at anything, that this same work relationship prevailed beforehand. Moltke was in charge: the Kaiser did not have to bother about it.

As an organization, the GGS of 1906–13 was a large formal bureaucracy with which Moltke had a very different relationship than Schlieffen had. Whereas Schlieffen had concentrated almost entirely on the GGS, venturing out only occasionally, Moltke operated most effectively outside, as a liaison to other Prussian bureaucratic departments. He smoothed over the differences between the GGS, the War Ministry, and the Military Cabinet that had existed during Schlieffen's time. In GGS matters the Kaiser let Moltke use his own discretion. Wilhelm II no longer led the Kaisermanöver and seldom attended war games in the GGS, as he had before. Schlieffen had put up with the vexatious imperial leadership: his tact allowed him to reconcile himself to Wilhelm's intrusions.

Moltke's viewpoint on this question was shaped by his anxiety that the Kaiser would in fact take an active leadership role. This fear revealed Moltke's level of knowledge of the war planning processes. Both in building the war plan and in practicing it in war games and in mobilization, Wilhelm was out of the decision-making loop. In war planning, the Kaiser and the GGS chief were essentially dilettantes. They lacked not only knowledge but consistency of goals, methods, and procedures. Typical of their level of effectiveness is the Langenbeck regulation incident. General von Langenbeck, in a momentary conversation at a public ceremony, proposed an entirely new infantry regulation, a single straight line attack. The Kaiser accepted it on the spot, described it to Prince Leopold of Bavaria as "our newest formation," and wanted War Minister Einem to promulgate it immediately. Since it was directly contrary to existing regulations, Einem stalled for time and asked the opinion of several older generals. A week later, when the war minister went back to the Kaiser, the latter had forgotten all about the matter.[17]

For Moltke's part, he developed no clear defense policy during the years 1906–11. He set out no new initiatives, but accepted the restrictive defence policies of War Ministers Einem and Heeringen. His influence on the preparation of the five-year defense bills was very small. Overall, the GGS was excluded from the defense decision process during these years; on the other hand, not much was expected of Moltke. Initially there were no changes in the war plan. The twice yearly winter war games were reduced in scope. The lieutenants played divisional war games and no longer pretended to lead corps or armies, as they had under Schlieffen.[18]

By 1913 the GGS was virtually up to war strength with 650 officers. At the top of the organizational chart was a technical office which directed education, publications, and land survey. Moltke, two adjutants, a chancellery head, and Freytag-Loringhoven, plus a group of twenty officers including six generals, staffed this office. It included the editor of GGS publications, the leaders of the Military Study Commission and War Academy, and the director of the Land Survey Department. A second unit was located around the corner on Moltkestraße. It included a central chancellery, ten numbered sections, a huge RRS, two military History Sections, and the very large Land Survey Department. The important functional arrangement was the section or table of organization placement, rather than the individual. The Central Section or chancellery, which was the GGS personnel office and also controlled the work flow, monitored the increasingly large paper flow by using information control techniques.

The numbered sections, each headed by a colonel, included 147 officers. The First, Third, Ninth, and Tenth were the so-called language sections whose members collected foreign intelligence. The First dealt with Russia, the Balkans, and Asia in general, including Persia and Turkey; the Third with France, including Morocco, and England, including Egypt and Afghanistan; the Ninth with Austria, Belgium, and the Mediterranean lands – Italy, Spain, Portugal – and the Netherlands, Switzerland, the Americas, and the German colonies; the Tenth with Austria and the Balkan states. The Fourth and Seventh did research on foreign military construction, especially fortresses in France and Russia. The Second Section

---

17. Einem, *Erinnerungen*, pp. 91–93.
18. Förster, *Der doppelte Militarismus*, pp. 165, 197–98; Gaertringen, *Groener*, pp. 91–93.

was for mobilization and operations, and its head was expected to become the operational advisor to the chief of the GGS in war. The Fifth and Eighth Sections handled questions of education, described as "operational studies," and were in charge of the War Academy. The Sixth Section dealt entirely with the Kaisermanöver, its preparation, execution, and evaluation. There were two Military History Sections, one for ancient and one for modern wars, and attached to them were a large library, an archive, and a map library. The Land Survey was a separate department, divided into Topographic, Trigonometric, Cartographic, and Photogrammetric Sections. The RRS was also very large.[19]

### Railroads and the Span of Control

Outside of Berlin, the GGS reached out via standardized procedures, plans, telegraph, and telephone through the umbrella-like military structures which covered the Second Reich. A greater paper flow and enhanced electric communications increased the GGS span of control and influence. This span of control operated through six bureaucratic institutions: the RRS, the corps commands, the chief of staff system, the army inspectorates, the DCs, and the chief of staff conferences.

By 1907 the RRS was the most important integrating vehicle of the GGS: it controlled the dominant technology of the war plan. When Moltke wanted to know if, in the event of war, the Italians would honor their treaty commitment, he sent the RRS chief, Hermann von Staabs, to Rome. Find out for sure if the Italians are coming or not! Moltke told Staabs as he departed. When Staabs returned, he reported that in the event of war the Italians would probably do whatever the political and military situation dictated. It was highly improbable, he said, that they would begin their MTP on the sixth mobilization day as the war plans specified.[20]

By this time German railroads were a formidable bit of social overhead capital. They operated with almost 30,000 locomotives and 65,000 passenger and 800,000 freight cars. There were 500,000 men employed on the railroad and another 200,000 in the

19. MGFA, *Handbuch*, 3: 69–72; Bergh, *Das deutsche Heer*, pp. 295–96; Jany, *Preußische Armee*, 4: 91–93; Osten-Sacken, *Preußens Heer*, 13: 489–97.
20. Staabs, *Aufmarsch*, p. 26.

telegraph system. The Prussian railroads utilized 32,847 telephones, probably the highest number per employee of any German organization of the day. The RRS and the Prussian railroads also shared certain organizational features. Prussia's railroads were headed in Berlin by a single central director, who was in addition the Prussian minister of public works. Outside Berlin were twenty-three railroad directorates. Each directorate's size depended on the amount of traffic it handled. Berlin, for example, had only 360 miles of track but heavy traffic, while Königsberg had 1,400 miles with relatively light traffic. The directories were the center of the Prussian railway system. Each had departments for traffic, operations, technical matters, and machine repair. Accordingly, a great deal of responsibility was delegated to them. Directorates controlled their own rates and fares, printed schedules, and coordinated technically and administratively with each other. Each had a construction department and a telegraph department. The German telegraph system, which had a larger network of telegraph lines than any other country in Europe, had been incorporated into the railroad administration in 1902.[21]

In addition to the decentralized directorates, system-wide central offices took care of certain tasks: an office at Madgeburg had charge of the car distribution for all of Prussia: another controlled the ordering of rolling stock; a third the purchase of roadbed materials, rails, ties, workshop supplies, and so forth. There were system-wide committees which considered technical matters such as locomotives, passenger coaches, brakes, and telegraph and block signals. One of their innovations had been the unit train rule

---

21. Ministerialrat von Voelcker, "German Transportation and Communication," *Annals of the American Academy of Political and Social Science* 92 (November 1920): 78; Bradford, "Prussian Railway Administration," pp. 310–21; Roy Morris, *Railroad Administration* (New York, 1910), pp. 156–61. In spite of a degree of unity in planning and practicing for the MTP, the German rail system in 1912 still consisted of a number of independent units. The largest were the state systems of Prussia, Bavaria, Saxony, and Baden. In addition, there were a number of private lines which remained. In 1912 an attempt began to fully unify all of these components into a Reich railroad system. For example, in April 1912 there was a Reichstag resolution which asked the Reichschancellor to introduce legislation to unify the German railroads further by laying down provisions for a Reich system. Significantly, the Reichstag resolution asked the chancellor to begin this process by creating a special commission which would include representatives from German business and from the GGS. Cf. Hermann Kirchhoff, *Vereinheitlichung des deutschen Eisenbahnwesens* (Stuttgart, 1913), pp. 1–70; L. Wehrmann, *Die Verwaltung der Eisenbahnen* (Berlin, 1913); Preußischer Minister der öffentlichen Arbeiter, *Das deutsche Eisenbahnwesen der Gegenwart*, 1: 1–25.

for mass transport of single commodities. Approximately 40% of the freight transported by rail was coal carried from the three border regions of the Ruhr, Upper Silesia, and the Saar. In each case the daily traffic was substantial: 35,000 (Ruhr), 13,000 (Silesia) and 4,000 (Saar) ten-ton cars. It is noteworthy that this replicated in various ways aspects of the MTP. Moltke had introduced the unit train into the military travel plan in 1868.[22]

The RRS was loosely organized along the lines of the Prussian railroad system. In Berlin it had eighty officers and officials, by far the largest GGS department except for Land Survey. Outside of Berlin in the twenty-three Line Commands an equal number were found. For example, Line A was Hanover, Line H was Cologne, Line L was Breslau. LCs were joined to the RRS by post, telegraph, and telephone. The electric connection permitted both speed and a large volume of communication. Each LC had substantial responsibilities: it oversaw planning and building new lines, repair and rebuilding of existing trackage, and reconciling and coordinating railroads between the different Prussian provinces and the separate railroad systems of Bavaria, Saxony, and Württemberg.[23]

Within its organization, the RRS carried out educational, representational, and analytical functions. By 1912 its continuing education program had become a formidable affair. Annually during the fall, for example, three different kinds of formal briefings were given. In October there was an all-day session for newly assigned officers. Individual lectures, limited to forty-five minutes, were prepared, with the presenters reporting to RRS chief Groener the day before to outline the talk. The briefing itself was six hours long and touched on the eight main areas of RRS activity: a general overview of the building of the German railroad network; the organization of the military railroad system in peace and war; an overview of war mobilization transportation; the specifics of the MTP; understanding and using railroad maps; the war transportation system; the supply system during war transportation; and the work of the LCs. Judging from some of the material presented, portions of this would have been classified. A second large education project, a war game briefing conducted for the LCs, took place at the beginning of November. Railroad war games had become so complex that players had to be briefed beforehand on

---

22. Dr. Weirauch, "Railway Transportation in Germany," *Annals of the American Academy of Political and Social Science* 93 (November 1920): 87.

23. Sarter, *Deutsche Eisenbahnen*, pp. 45–65.

the rules and procedures. A third in-house briefing for loading and unloading officers was held during November. The MTP could be executed only as fast as its slowest part. Loading and unloading were identified as this part, and a good deal of time was spent educating officers in how this was to be done. Finally, individual LCs spent a good part of each year, following the 1 April war plan publication date, practicing its segments.[24]

The RRS then, with the highest knowledge base of any unit within the GGS, generated a great deal of information. Specialization was such that new officers could not learn their work entirely by on-the-job experience: they were formally taught. This knowledge was practiced and transmitted not only on paper but via telegraph and telephone, which increased its volume and speed of transmission. The fact that the railroad system operated every day with a civilian traffic flow that was in quantity only less than the MTP and that numerical increases were quantifiable both in terms of the engineering principles of railroads and in terms of the size, space, and time requirements of the war plan meant that a close correlation existed between experience and theory. To some extent, the practical requirements of daily peacetime operations and the theoretical necessities of the war plan coincided. The gaps that still remained were bridged using education, training, and war games.

In contrast to other divisions of the GGS, it was only within the RRS that there was such a close correlation between theory and practice. This relationship had several ramifications. The knowledge gap between Berlin and the LCs was reduced. Routines and standard operating procedures followed a more predictable path from peace to war. Even though the changes in mobilization came in multiples rather than a few percentage points, their path and speed were predictable because technology attributes such as load, speed, and time grew in an orderly manner. Technological processes yielded a consistency or pattern, and abrupt, major deviations were uncommon.[25]

A second aspect of RRS operations was representational. As the MTP became more and more specialized, the maps and charts used

24. Groener Papers, roll 19, no. 173.
25. James R. Bright, "Technology Forecasting Literature: Emergence and Impact on Technology Innovation," in Patrick Kelly and Melvin Kranzberg, eds., *Technological Innovation: A Critical Review of the Current Literature* (San Francisco, 1978), pp. 299–334.

to describe it followed suit. By 1911 the RRS had created its own map section. In it were produced several series of maps and charts. One series at 1:100,000 showed the boundaries of each LC, along with various corps command borders. Another at 1:25,000 illustrated these by region. A third at 1:8,000 broke the LCs down into small segments and indicated their traffic capacity in terms of a flow chart. A fourth, also at 1:8,000, showed urban areas, with special reference to railroad stations, loading ramps, and storage locations within the city limits. On these maps seven different kinds of track were defined in terms of work capacity: normal gauge double track; normal gauge single track; small gauge secondary track; single track lines on which a second track was being built; double track lines under construction; single track lines being built; and full gauge small rail with good military value. On smaller-scale maps, the speeds within each block were indicated, as well as speed limitations imposed because of grade and curve. It contrast to the maps produced in the Land Survey Department, these maps plotted only absolutely precise distances. They contained the exact distance in kilometers between each marker stone. Thus the degree of time, space, and size precision was more accurate than in other kinds of GGS representation. RRS officers were trained to think in terms of very close tolerances.

The MTP was thus tied to several very precise physical and technical realities: one was track, a second the telegraph, a third the telephone. Each was worked into the MTP. For example, even in war games, movement of trains through LCs was reported by telegraph and telephone. In fact the MTP by 1912 contained precise orders telling LC officials what time to telephone, who to telephone, and what to say. A uniform speed of twenty kilometers per hour was prescribed. Exact time between trains, known as headway, was maintained. On-loading and off-loading times were precise to thirty minutes. Loading stations were listed and described in detail, including whether ramps had to be constructed and if so, the length needed, where to buy the wood, and who to charge it to. Carefully marked on the maps were loading and unloading railroad lines, travel lines with the duty to report on empty trains and through travel lines without this responsibility, supply points, and hospital stations. All of this cartographic precision worked to maintain the essential features of the MTP: (1) equal and constant speed of all trains; (2) equal and constant distance between trains on the same stretch; (3) parallelism between contiguous segments of each LC. The result was that officials had a fairly clear view of rail operations and were able to send hour-by-hour status reports to Berlin.[26]

Since railroad transportation had now become the linchpin of the war plan in both its planning and execution stages, insight into the development of that plan may be gained by examining in detail the RRS's war games. In January 1906, the RRS played through a telegraphic and telephonic war game in Magdeburg. It was the first large-scale exercise using these communication methods. By 1911 Groener had introduced the railroad war game to the LCs on a regular basis. Prior to this time the RRS had played in Berlin, but now this was extended throughout the system. Line commanders were invited to a theoretical transportation exercise in September, where they achieved a decisive victory over France on the thirtieth mobilization day, followed by the transportation of four army corps to the eastern front. The exercise simulated war conditions: track was destroyed, bridges and tunnels blocked, telegraph lines down. LCs had to create detours with the least impact on the system as a whole. Messages were sent in code. Each problem in the series had a time limit for solution, usually from three to six hours. The solution was presented and problems discussed.[27]

Later exercises were played electrically. They were sent out in code over telegraph lines and returned via rapid post. Accompanying them was a special map prepared by the Railroad Section in a scale of 1:300,000 (1 inch = 18 miles). Roughly eighteen miles was the breaking point for track stretches within LCs. In June 1912, for example, there were three problems, one for lines F, K1, K2, P, and W which began June 15; a second for lines A, B, C, D, H, J, M, Q, S, and T which began June 30; and a third for LCs G, N, R, V, and X. The exercise was secret and telegraphed in code. Between July 14 and 21 a second problem was sent out. Germany was in a war against France, whose main forces were located between Trier and Straßburg. After a decisive victory in the Eifel German forces began to follow the retreating French army. On the thirtieth mobilization day the exercise called for moving four corps quickly to the eastern front. RRS participants were asked to assess the situation and issue transportation orders.

An important goal of RRS war games was to test out and

26. Groener Papers, roll 19, no. 173.
27. Haeussler, *Groener*, p. 35; Gaertringen, *Groener*, p. 75.

improve the work capacity of each LC. The RRS continually tried to increase the number of trains and decrease the amount of time needed for their delivery through the system. The goal put forth in 1911 was to decrease the overall time by three days, from thirteen or fourteen days to ten or eleven days. There were two ways to bring this about. One was to build more tracks and bridges to thicken the system. A second was to increase the speed of travel from twenty kilometers per hour. This change required that grade, curve, and frictions were adequate to handle the increase in all of the separate stretches of the Reich railroad system. As we have suggested, locomotive power was adequate because German railroads as a whole were overpowered: there was a low ratio of locomotives to rolling stock. But to increase the speed to twenty-five kilometers per hour meant redrawing the whole MTP with its three thousand individual stretches, a task which required more than a year.[28]

In 1908 Wilhelm Groener tried to introduce greater flexibility into the war plan by suggesting the possibility of a thicker railroad network with greater work capacity. He was unable to bring this about but returned to it beginning in 1911, when he was appointed RRS chief, putting his entire program of strategic railroad building onto the table again. It consisted of three parts. Part 1 was a unitary plan for the development of transportation paths – double track railroad lines – in the border areas and across the center of the Reich which included three new Rhine River bridges at Remagen, Neuwied, and Maxau to ease the assembly of the army on the west bank of the Rhine. In the east it called for a third transportation path. Further building was envisioned to enhance the network capacity of the system. Part 2 was intended to raise the speed of the MTP using the increased work capacity of modern locomotives. In connection with the track and bridge building program, its goal was to decrease the time by which the army could be brought to operational readiness. Part 3 called for the retraining of railroad officials and corps commands in the improvised transportation of armies in war. The purpose of this training would be to move away from the fixed tabulation of travel lists to seek a more flexible procedure.[29]

28. Groener Papers, roll 19, no. 172; Gaertringen, *Groener*, pp. 132–33; Sarter, *Deutsche Eisenbahnen*, p. 4.

29. Groener Papers, roll 8, no. 35, Groener letter to Reichsarchiv, 11 November 1932.

The first obstacle to be overcome in bringing this ambitious program into reality was that of Reich-federal finances. As soon as the federal states suspected that the GGS had a special interest in a particular railroad line, the line became the focal point of an argument that it was necessary for public transportation and that the Reich, not the federal states, should pay for it. The Reich treasury, however, stalled as long as possible, trying to arrange for cost sharing or, better still, for the full cost to be paid by the states. In 1911 Groener embarked on a program of liaison with the railroad officials for all the lines. He convinced the railroads of the utility of cooperation, and through conversations with the federal ministers by the end of 1912 had persuaded them to agree to complete his plan in three to five years.

Groener's flexible approach was tested out during the return transportation movement for the Kaisermanöver. Following the disastrous experience of 1909, when troops had to be force marched to the loading stations, the MTPs for 1910 and 1911 had been completely redrawn. By 1912 the return transportation plan had been put into effect at the moment the maneuver ended. This was done on a flexible basis, with changes dependent on the configuration of the troops rather than on the MTP. An entirely new procedure was needed for this, one that was tested out theoretically in the war games and practically in the Kaisermanövers. By 1914 the RRS had not had enough experience on the basis of these exercises, and they could not replace the iron rigidity of the MTP with an improvisation put into effect at the last moment. But Groener believed that in one or two more years it would be possible. He was sometimes asked if the GGS had enough faith in the RRS to gamble everything on a last-minute change of railroad movement. He was not sure, and he was even less certain about the corps and division commands. They were so accustomed to the rigid standard procedures of the travel and march tables that it would have been a great shock to substitute new, flexible methods.

From the pure technicians' point of view, Groener believed the MTP was so certain to be carried out as written that it could be used very flexibly. Schlieffen and Groener both appear to have been prepared to allow mobilization to be completed up to the frontier, then halted while the statesmen applied political direction and control to the situation. The MTP was so trustworthy that troops were certain to be placed on the battlefield exactly at the point where a decision was to be expected. Although such a pause at the borders seems to contradict the element of surprise and the necessity for a sudden overwhelming movement, it makes sense from the standpoint of the RRS's confidence in technology. The system was so amenable to precise control and fine-tuning that the whole great mass could pause and then be hurled forward, with little diminution in potential outcome.[30]

Moltke did not draft the war plans, but delegated this to the Second or Mobilization Section, headed from 1908 to 1912 by Erich Ludendorff. At the beginning of winter, on 1 November, the RRS received a single sheet of paper on which the chief of the Second Section wrote in clear, precise outline where the different parts of the army would assemble. Based on this information, Groener's job was to prepare the railroad technical proposal. From this study further ideas, new thoughts, or entirely different plans might originate. In January and February a series of RRS war games were held. These were always in series, cumulative over a several-week period, and often included nine to twelve additions to the first problem. On the basis of these, changes in the MTP might be made. Meanwhile, Groener and his colleagues were going over the existing plans, tightening the rail schedules to achieve maximum load and minimum speed. During March the war plans were set and were published on 1 April.[31]

In addition to the RRS, there were several other integrating mechanisms in the GGS. As described above, GGS-trained officers served in key positions in each of the twenty-five corps of the Reich. Chiefs of staff, "1a" officers, were responsible, with a small staff, for handling the day-to-day business of the corps, but above all the most important questions of the corps command: mobilization, maneuvers, and the operation orders for both. His staff took care of communications, supply, and intelligence. Border corps sometimes had a second or third general staff officer to keep track of immediate cross border intelligence. They reported to the GGS special intelligence section IIIB. Peacetime corps had two divisions, and the divisional general staff officer had duties similar to those of the 1a above him. Again the most critical work in each headquarters, knowledge of how to execute the mobilization plan, was his responsibility. These officers knew and understood the

---

30. Ibid.; Gaertringen, *Groener*, p. 147.
31. Gaertringen, *Groener*, pp. 72, 77; Haeussler, *Groener*, p. 33; Sarter, *Deutsche Eisenbahnen*, p. 42.

procedures, goals, and standards established army wide for mobilization.[32]

To reinforce these goals and procedures, Moltke convened a mobilization conference of the chiefs of staffs every January. These included corps chiefs of staff and a large number of other officials concerned with mobilization. For example, the conference of 30 January 1912 included representatives from the War Ministry, Marine Ministry, Military Rail System, Reich Railroad Office, Ministry of Public Works, and various technical officers, military and civilian, from the LCs. To this group Moltke emphasized that the mobilization preparation of the winter was being carried out under the influence of the political events of the past summer, the second Moroccan crisis. He reviewed the transportation plans and experiences of the 1911 Kaisermanöver, describing the smooth functioning of the return transportation, which carried 102 battalions, 59 squadrons, and 80 batteries in 1,900 railroad cars and 188 special trains. In closing he emphasized how important it was to be fully prepared at times of political tension. During summer field exercises and maneuvers, the corps and LCs had to be ready at a moment's notice to return troops from the field. Summer exercises took place during the window of maximum war possibility from July to September. Execution of the war plan, especially the MTP, required both active army and reserves to start from fixed and prescribed positions. An army caught during a war crisis with substantial forces in the field was in an awkward position.[33]

A third integrating vehicle was the DC of the inspectors general. There were, on the eve of World War I, eight army inspectorates. It was anticipated that in war mobilization each inspector general would take command of an army, including several corps. The peacetime role of the inspectorates was instrumental in that each army inspectorate was divided into districts and each district was responsible for mobilization of the reserves, Landwehr, and Landsturm. Mobilization lists were continually being checked over and reverified. Each year the district held a "control assembly," calling in all those under its aegis in war mobilization. In addition to mobilization, the district was in charge of public assistance for retired and invalided soldiers, courts of honor for reserve officers,

---

32. Bergh, *Das deutsche Heer*, pp. 40–42; MGFA, *Handbuch*, 3: 70–72.
33. BAMA, Nachlaß Moltke, N78–25.

and annual recruitment and induction. Even though the DC was not directly under the control of the GGS, under war mobilization orders it was part of the war plan.[34]

Beginning in 1912 another integrating mechanism was the standing commission on mobilization. It included members from the Foreign Office, Treasury, Navy, GGS, Reich Statistical Office, Reichsbank, and the Prussian Interior, Economics, War, and Commerce Ministries. Wilhelm Groener, RRS chief, represented the GGS. Its purpose was to consider potential problems in forthcoming mobilization and to begin building relationships and structures to deal with them. In mobilization the main interface between the army and civilian agencies was through the MTP.[35]

### The Directional Discipline: History in Military Education

A second aspect of war planning under Moltke was educational. In the last years before 1914 the War Academy became so popular that over eight hundred officers each year took the entrance examination for the 150 places in the first-year class. In 1907 the War Academy curriculum and presumably the entire military educational system moved toward the final decisive stage in technical specialist education. Required technical courses now dominated the curriculum. Liberal arts and sciences, once considered the foundation of military education, were superceded. Emphasis was placed on the development of technical and practical matters useful to professional officers.

What is noteworthy is what happened to the study of history, called the "directional discipline" for the War Academy curriculum. No longer was history prior to 1648 studied at all; "ancient" military history, from the Greeks to the seventeenth century, had been eliminated from the curriculum. The purpose of the military history which remained was "to awaken the officer's interest in contemporary political affairs, with a concentration on the rise of Prussia and the Reich to great power status."[36] Emphasis was

---

34. Generaloberst Alexander von Kluck, *Wanderjahre–Kriege–Gestalten* (Berlin, 1929), pp. 48–50.

35. Reinhard Zilch, *Die Reichsbank und die finanzielle Kriegsvorbereitung von 1907 bis 1914* (East Berlin, 1987), p. 83 (kindness of Professor John Röhl); Haeussler, *Groener*, p. 48.

36. Bald, *Der deutsche Generalstab*, pp. 44–48, 60–63; Messerschmidt, "Militär

placed on German nationalism and the impact of old cultures on the development of modern Germany. Not only did military history exclude political and social relationships, as had been true for decades, but now its subject narrowed even more: military history was reduced to an explanatory vehicle for formal and general tactics. Military history lectures were said to provide the means to learn war in peace, to awaken enthusiasm and understanding for military history studies. They demonstrated the unchanged fundamentals of war leadership in its relationship to the changing tactical forms and showed the influence of outstanding personalities and spiritual power on the flow of circumstances.[37]

Although Moltke found no need to involve himself personally with military history, his immediate predecessor Schlieffen had set in motion a whole series of military history publications. In 1904 Schlieffen had added the *Quarterly Journal for Troop Management and Army Science* to the extensive list of GGS publications, which already included the *Military Weekly*. In addition to these journals, publication of books continued. Major series included the History of the German Regiments, Military History: Single Examples, and Studies in Military History and Tactics. These series were published under the working assumption that great examples from military history served as education for officers' minds, urging on their military imagination, spurring them toward emulation.[38] So that these examples made sense, it was necessary to impose the standard rules of contemporary relationships on the historical events of the past.[39] In other words, the GGS historical method was to superimpose the standards and expectations of contemporary war on events of the past. These war planners did not aim to recreate the past, but to take what had happened then and make it happen again under contemporary circumstances, a sort of revivification. War was approached in the same way as a revivalist communion. It was to be an emotional, spiritual re-creation. What this meant to the presentation of military history is clear. It was didactic, it always carried a message, it illustrated operational rules. When compared with factual military history it contained errors:

---

und Schule in der Wilhelminischen Zeit," p. 62; Model, *Der deutsche Generalstabsoffizier*, p. 17.

37. Kurt Koszyk, "Erhard Deutelmoser–Offizier und Pressechef," *Publizistik* 30 (10 November 1985): 513.

38. Bald, *Der deutsche Generalstab*, pp. 64–66.

39. Aschenbrandt, *Kriegsgeschichtsschreibung*, p. 13.

armies marched on roads which did not exist. Here are the fundamentals of the Schlieffen and Prussian schools of history: unchanging strategic doctrine, regardless of time period and circumstances; the influence of single great individuals; and the overwhelmingly dominant impact of spiritual power, the will to victory, over all else on the battlefield.

In addition to curriculum and history, the whole GGS approach to information processing changed after 1905. This is evident both in the control of classified information and in the dissemination of intelligence. By 1906, there were five categories of classified information: for official use only, confidential, secret, top secret, and restricted access. Information control techniques were directed by the Central Section of the GGS. There was apparently a growing feeling of insecurity, perhaps as a result of the Dreyfus affair in France and public clamor regarding revelations of war plan information. Moltke himself had a pathological fear of spies. He worried that too much information was being given away to Germany's potential enemies in GGS publications. One of the section chiefs tried to dissuade Moltke from this view, arguing that his famous uncle had himself encouraged the study and writing of military history throughout the army, that he had seen historical study as an essential aspect of general staff duty, and that he had done historical writing himself. Moltke was adamant in his objections. The outside world should not be so attentive to us, he said. Moltke retained the suspicion that the GGS's voluminious publications might be used against it by Germany's potential adversaries.[40]

Within the Prussian and Reich bureaucracies Moltke introduced the year-end intelligence review. This was a strategic assessment produced for circulation among the top leadership. Previously the GGS had done its own intelligence estimates. Now it took over the responsibility of estimating, for the government as a whole, the military situation of Europe. This report was completed in December. It included estimates of each major European army, plus the Reich's own military status quo, followed by a general conclusion. During periods of political crisis, these estimates were updated and published on demand. Sources used for the report included information from military attachés stationed abroad and from the small counterintelligence unit, section IIIB, whose work was directed

---

40. Görlitz, *German General Staff*, p. 144; Aschenbrandt, *Kriegsgeschichtsschreibung*, p. 10.

mainly against France and Russia. This section was in communication with a small group of intelligence agents stationed in the west and east border areas. Each agent controlled a group of trusted persons across the border and also sent individuals known as "tension travelers" over the border to gather specific information during periods of political tension.[41] The whole intelligence effort had a more intensive thrust, evident in the year-end summary reports. These aspects, more attention to document security, increased collection of data, and its wider dissemination, are undoubtedly related to and surely resulted in a heightened anxiety among the Reich leadership.

### Hardware Technology and War Plans

How did new weapons and communications equipment influence strategic thinking? Moltke's first years as GGS chief coincided with a turning point in hardware technology. It occurred just after the Russo-Japanese War (1904–5), to which a number of GGS officers had been sent as observers; their reports had been delivered during his first full year in office. That war emphasized the mechanical and technical aspects of war. For example, at the Battle of Yalu River, 30 April–1 May 1904, the Japanese used twelve-centimeter field howitzers which resulted in enormous Russian casualties. German artillery observers in Manchuria described the importance of concealed, indirect fire, controlled by field telephone or telegraph.[42]

Just prior to this time each Prussian division received eighteen 105-mm howitzers, and each corps got twelve 150-mm howitzers. This indicates that divisional commanders were beginning to control artillery but (1) there was not much of it, and (2) officers generally still distrusted it. The two leading questions in 1905 were: First, could the artillery with its munitions reserve keep up with the offensive movements of forward attacking troops? Second, if the number of guns in a battery increased, how large an increase did this necessitate in the number of officers, men, and horses? Heavy mortars and howitzers were added, controlled by

41. Bernd Schulte, *Vor dem Kriegsausbruch 1914* (Düsseldorf, 1980), pp. 60, 65; Bergh, *Das deutsche Heer*, pp. 171ff.
42. E. von Hoffbauer, *Schwebende Feldartillerie-Fragen* (Berlin, 1904), pp. 106–10; J.F.C. Fuller, *The Conduct of War* (New York, 1968), pp. 141–43; Bidwell and Graham, *Fire-Power*, p. 17.

divisional artillery officers to give close support to the attacking infantry. But the number of weapons remained small relative to the number of rifles. By 1908 three to five new army corps were in the planning stages, to be ready in five to six years. Every brigade was assigned a field artillery unit, two pioneer companies, and a trains squadron. In addition, the expansion of existing divisions emphasized heavy artillery, pioneer and trains, and new hand grenades and mines of simpler construction.[43]

After 1912, with the addition of many new reserve units, machine guns became more important. Although active soldiers had time to learn to shoot well with rifles, reserves did not. They fought much more effectively with machine guns, which required less training and practice to achieve combat effectiveness. To what extent this was recognized prior to the war is open to question. In the eight years following 1906, machine guns were gradually increased, concentrated in companies, and organized into small units. By 1914 machine gun companies were attached to many cavalry divisions. Still the total number of weapons was modest in contrast to rifles.[44]

Against this background advances began to be made in communications. In 1905 radio telegraph sections were added to each telegraph battalion. In 1907 a fifth signal battalion was created, more telegraph battalions were set up, and each one was given a radio telegraph capacity. In 1911 an inspectorate of military transportation brought the railroad building companies, field telegraph, air, and automobile units under one direction. Aside from the railroad building brigade, which was essentially a unit to take over, rebuild, and extend rail systems in occupied areas, very little had been completed by 1914, although a great deal was under way. For example, it was intended that the radio and telephone would eventually replace all other means of communication. In 1910 the field telegraph was virtually discarded by the German army as obsolete. Henceforth the telephone was to be the sole means of field communication, supplemented by the radio. This transition was in the process of being implemented when war broke out. By

---

43. Hoffbauer, *Feldartillerie-Fragen*, pp. 103–5; Bidwell and Graham, *Fire-Power*, p. 17; Kluck, *Wanderjahre*, p. 120. The creation of a new army corps was carried out in strict accordance with a series of regulations and formulas. Cf. BHSA, Al–165; *Organizations-Bestimmungen aus Anlaß der Bildung zweier neuer Armeekorps* (secret) (Berlin, 1889); BHSA M. Kr. 1126; Übersicht der Neuformationen bzw. Etatserhöhungen"; BAMA, Nachlaß Beseler, Lebenserinnerungen, pp. 70–71.

1912 the cavalry had begun to test out light field radios and airplanes for reconnaissance and artillery observation, but only experimentally and in very small numbers.[45]

All of this went very slowly. It met entrenched opposition from conservatives who distrusted technology. As its purchase was under the aegis of the War Ministry, the GGS could only employ what was made available. The only area where hardware technology may be said to have moved ahead consistently was in the RRS, which was tied to the Reich railroad and telegraph systems, both fully operational peacetime entities.

The representational system during these years continued to complete task cycles begun decades before. Trigonometric measuring projects were undertaken for the last of the small German states incorporated into the Reich after 1871. The duchy of Saxon-Altenburg and the principality of Birkenfeld had been completed just before 1905; in 1909 similar arrangements were made for the principality of Lippe. The year before, the patterns for a map of central Europe in the scale of 1:300,000 had been printed. In 1910 work ended on the last of the 542 sheets of the map of the German Reich at a scale of 1:100,000. In 1913, work was begun to upgrade these maps with new triangulation points, topographical survey maps, and cartography. The 3,307 survey sheets for the maps at a scale of 1:25,000, completed in the period from 1878 to 1915, indicate the long-term nature of this work.[46] Precision in estimating distances progressed via optical science. War Academy students used pocket range finders, and beginning after 1900 photogrammetric computation and evaluation were introduced to support plane table maps, partly for the ground plan and partly for the heights. These methods were used to begin a remeasurement of the land, producing maps at scales of 1:5,000. Volume printing and color lithography continued the high standards of this technically precise production.[47]

44. Ellis, *Machine Gun*, p. 116.

45. Jany, *Preußische Armee*, 4: 320–21; Paul W. Evans, "Strategic Signal Communications," pp. 34–36; Osten-Sacken, *Preußens Heer*, 3: 461.

46. Scheel, "Entwicklung," pp. 21–22; Krauss, "150 Jahre"; Stavenhagen, "Entwicklung," pp. 549–63.

47. Groener Papers, roll 18, no. 159; Krauss, "150 Jahre," p. 133.

## Moltke and War Gaming

The fourth aspect of war planning was analytical. As we move toward 1914 there are three aspects of war gaming that change. First of all, war games, which were originally unclassified, became classified information and began to be numbered and recorded. At first this was for official use only, but later documents were increasingly classified as secret and even top secret with restricted access. Like military history publications, war games closely resembled the war plan, and Moltke was anxious that their enemies not know their intentions. As his suspicions and anxieties grew, GGS information control expanded.[48] Second, war games became even more closely integrated with each other through size, space, and time progression. Their progressive nature can be identified at several levels. The most tightly organized was to be found in the RRS, where serial war gaming was carried out over a period of many months, as we saw during the first Moroccan crisis. This undoubtedly related to Schlieffen's concept of the rolling offensive, a series of loosely related but independent battles, as well as to the RRS's attempt to build greater flexibility into the MTP. Third, there was a single-minded and narrow presentation of strategy, which might be called virtually doctrinaire, emphasizing that the only way to victory was through the battle of encirclement, attacking the flanks and rear. This was a continuation of the historical concept prevalent during Schlieffen's years. During Moltke's tenure this is evident in the GGS rides, war games, and maneuvers. As Hans von Seeckt, who was in the GGS in 1906–9 wrote, success in battle as portrayed in the GGS came entirely through encirclement: surround and destroy was the rule, model, and prescription.[49]

What was Moltke's understanding of war games? Although lauded for obtaining the Kaiser's withdrawal from command in the annual fall maneuvers, a factor which had supposedly invalidated these maneuvers during Schlieffen's tenure, Moltke in fact had only a vague notion of their real value, as various evidence suggests. This applies particularly to the railroad component. The chief of the RRS wrote that Moltke tried at length and conscientiously to understand this totally alien aspect of military life, implying that he never did master it.

---

48. Gaertringen, *Groener*, p. 67; Haeussler, *Groener*, p. 19.
49. German Army, *Regulations for Maneuver*. See especially appendix 1, Chart of Maneuver Periods for the 10th Army Corps, pp. 59–60; Meier-Welcker, *Seeckt*, p. 26.

Moltke's laudatory comments on the performance of the railroads in the 1908 Kaisermanöver were made at a time when he had very little confidence that the real MTP would work. His doubts were based on a lack of knowledge.[50]

What of the Kaisermanövers? How did Moltke view them? For one thing, he expected them to go off like clockwork. When they did not, he sometimes cried and often became distraught. A simple delay or postponement could make him frantic. When they went off as planned, he was rewarded, again and again. In August 1905, for example, when Schlieffen was incapacitated with a broken leg, Moltke showed the Kaiser his outline for the coming fall maneuver. He presented his maneuver plans as a child presents something he has made to a parent. Wilhelm agreed with them and found them "charming and interesting." Moltke looked forward to a "warlike" maneuver without "outlandish" cavalry charges or other "unmilitary interferences." At this time the Kaiser was trying to get Moltke to take the job of GGS chief, but Moltke did not like the idea. After strongly remonstrating with Wilhelm, telling him that he was unsuited to be chief, Moltke finally softened and stated his conditions for accepting: the Kaiser would have to withdraw from commanding in the fall maneuvers. When the Kaiser agreed, it was seen as a great concession, an unbelievable accomplishment. Finally, after Moltke had tentatively agreed to become GGS chief, he made one more condition. He asked the Kaiser to wait until after the fall 1905 maneuvers to see if the results were satisfactory. In other words, Moltke equated his ability to plan and carry out the fall maneuvers with his ability to perform successfully as chief of the GGS, a common equation made by many generals and civilians of the time. Ferdinand Foch was appointed to the French general staff, it was said, on the basis of a single successful parade on a field bare at 3 P.M. but filled with twenty-five thousand soldiers at 3:10. The fall maneuver of 1905 went off without a hitch. The Kaiser had not interfered. In his own eyes, Moltke had been tested and validated. Before this he had been merely an untried subordinate, waiting in the wings, bound up in bureaucratic fetters. Now he was certified: the Kaiser thanked him for the "most interesting and warlike maneuvers he had ever seen." A week later Moltke received the order of the Red Adler first class and four months later he was promoted to GGS chief.

50. Staabs, *Aufmarsch*, p. 35.

After his second fall maneuver of 1906, Moltke received the Hohenzollern House order and a promotion to general of infantry. Six months later he was appointed à la suite to the Kaiser Alexander Guard Grenadier Regiment, an honor usually bestowed on elderly generals. After the third fall maneuver, in 1907, he received the grand cross of the Red Adler, with oak leaves and crown. The 1908 maneuver went off according to plan, satisfying everyone. The Kaiser was in good spirits and refrained from interference. The people in Lorraine were "enthusiastic over the royal presence." The troops were outstanding, tactical formations faultless, everything in order. Enormous marching capacity and endurance were demonstrated. The military rail transport went off without interruption, and the RRS acquitted itself brilliantly. The Kaiser gave both corps the highest commendation. Moltke's fifth maneuver in September 1909 was attended by the Archduke Franz Ferdinand who, along with foreign attachés and the press, was dazzled. Moltke received compliments from all sides and, from the Kaiser, the order of the Black Adler. He was a bit ashamed and remarked to his wife that his uncle Helmuth had won this order with a victorious campaign, whereas he got it after three days of maneuvers. The seventh maneuver also went off well, with good press reports. The Kaiser thereafter appointed him honorary chief of the Moltke Fusilier Regiment No. 38, an honor usually given to an officer in retirement. After that there were no more decorations, orders, or promotions. They had all been given out.

In military affairs the distinction between appearance and reality is defined in various ways. One is the difference between theory and practice. A second is the distinction between superficial spit and polish and fundamental combat readiness. Another is the distinction between peace and war. As with all GGS chiefs, we must ask how Moltke understood these distinctions. It often appears that Moltke was a man to whom show was very meaningful. Certainly as aide-de-camp to his uncle from 1882 to 1891, he experienced a great deal of public and royal homage paid to a military hero. It is difficult to say what his response to this was. Later evidence, however, suggests that he was impressionable. The spectacle of imperial ruffles and flourishes may have become his reality.[51]

51. Moltke, *Erinnerungen*, pp. 323–25, 342, 345–49, 350–371; for example, Moltke's description of the meeting between the Kaiser and the tsar at sea off Bjoerkoe, Finland, in July 1905 reveals that he was completely taken in. Ibid., pp. 325–30.

Were the Kaisermanöver of any military value, or were they all show? Clearly for many they were superficial, simply a waste of time, whether viewed as theoretical staff exercises or as pageantry. But a different view is also possible. Indoor war games and outdoor GGS rides were essentially paper and map exercises. In the former everything was done verbally or in writing, using maps in response to a written situation. In the latter the problem was laid out, responded to, and critiqued both verbally and on paper, with maps enhanced by the experience of riding through the terrain. Although they could be quite intense, given the antagonistic nature of two sides working against each other, both were essentially theoretical exercises. Outdoor maneuvers with large numbers of troops added several dimensions. They were still competitive, with written orders, map work, verbal and written response, and so forth, but had the added ingredient of allowing troops to live and work in the field. A Kaisermanöver, for example, could involve one hundred thousand men and eighteen thousand horses. In addition to feeding and housing these large numbers and to the practical use of terrain, maneuvers also tested certain features of the war plan, in particular, portions of the MTP, the supply system, and the communications network. If there were aspects of these maneuvers that could not substitute for the reality of war – most notably the lack of live ammunition and casualties – still in certain respects outdoor field maneuvers added realities to the war game which were not present in other varieties of military exercises.

Take for example the 1907 Kaisermanöver, conducted southeast of Hanover between the 7th and 10th Corps. The maneuver was set for the period 2 through 11 September, with parades in Hanover on 27 August for the 10th Corps and in Munster on 30 August for the 7th Corps. Aside from the royal entourage of almost a hundred, which always included a great many relatives and provincial dignitaries, the GGS, which wrote, judged, and monitored the results of the exercise, was the dominant participant. The GGS sent two contingents: the first consisted of a total of fourteen officers, including three department chiefs, two RRS officers, and a unit of telegraph and telephone experts, who together made up the headquarters group which supported the chief of the GGS and provided communications. The second group included twenty-five judges plus a staff of sixty; among the judges were the chief of Land Survey, seven section heads, and three teachers at the War Academy. The GGS contingent totaled almost a hundred men, and was top-heavy in terms of rank. The Kaisermanöver was obviously a big production, clearly equivalent to the other war exercises most favored by the Kaiser, the naval maneuvers in the North Sea usually held a week later. Files from the Naval Cabinet indicate the navy often began planning for the exercise fourteen months in advance. Obviously army leaders realized that the Kaisermanöver and the fleet exercises were in competition with each other. Who performed best in the Kaiser's eyes? Army or navy? In field maneuvers the Kaiser served as honorary chief judge, but in reality what he liked to do was to place himself at the head of four regiments of cavalry and swoop down upon an unprotected artillery position. One of Franz Adam Beyerlein's best-selling novels, *Jena oder Sedan*, described in detail how this was done. The Kaiser was so well known for this kind of frivolousness that one maneuver action, the Seydlitz attack, was named after him.

In spite of such foolishness, some real work was accomplished. In the 1907 maneuver red army had been beaten by blue army and had been pushed back against the Teutoburger Forest on 5–6 September. Blue responded by using railroad transportation to attack the flank and rear of the enemy. This maneuver was characterized by the movement of divisions by railroad line at all hours of the day and night. Troops entrained at 12:30 A.M. and detrained at 3:30 A.M., moving from rail lines into the combat formation. Cavalry forces were not used very much at all, but technical troops were heavily employed. There were airplanes, search lights, telephones, telegraph, and wireless telegraphy. Field kitchens served hot meals. Even automobiles were used. The RRS planned and carried out the transportation in the form of an MTP which, even in its cartographic designs, closely resembled the actual war plan. When it was all over, the RRS provided special trains for staff officers. They swept through the maneuver area, stopping at eleven locations, then whisked the gentlemen east to deliver them in a little more than six hours to Berlin.[52]

The 1910 maneuver again appeared to be a gigantic military show. It was held southeast of Danzig, between the Weichsel River and Allenstein, on the East Prussian highland. This general region figured prominently in the war plan and the 1910 exercise was approximately the fifteenth time that imperial maneuvers,

---

52. BAMA, *Acten des Kaiserlichen Marine-Kabinetts betreffend Herbstmanöver*, RM2–102; A. von Löbell, "Militärische Rundschau," *Der Tag*, 17 September 1907; MGFA, *Tradition in deutschen Streitkräften*, pp. 189–90.

GGS rides, or corps exercises had been held there since 1888. The maneuver began with a spectacular imperial parade in Danzig: forty battalions of infantry, foot artillery, and pioneer formed up in a seven-thousand-foot massed line, with a second line of four thousand feet comprised of cavalry, heavy artillery, and squadrons of train battalions. The imperial entourage executed a double march past, "enrapturing" the East Prussian, foreign attaché, and press viewers.[53] Placed in a land area of five hundred square miles, the maneuver pitted the 17th Corps based in Danzig against the 1st Corps based in Königsberg. Blue, led by General August von Mackenson, was given the job of attacking the fixed position of red, led by General Alexander von Kluck. Blue consisted of 42 battalions, 40 squadrons, 32 field batteries, and 8 heavy field howitzer batteries. Red had 32 battalions, 18 squadrons, 25 batteries, and 4 heavy field howitzer batteries. As a military problem, it provided eighty hours of position warfare. And as it turned out, the time frame was sufficient for the defenders but placed great pressure on the attackers, who had to carry out the prescribed land and air reconnaissance and the approach marches, fighting all the way against enemy forces in topography favorable for defense but difficult for attack. In this water-filled region of lakes, ponds, and streams, small detachments of defenders successfully interdicted larger divisional-size units. Alexander von Kluck, defending red commander, had sufficient extra time while awaiting his opponent, to spend two memorable days hunting in the company of the hospitable *Schloßherr* Graf Dönhoff. In the depths of the East Prussian forests, Kluck shot a magnificant three-year-old buck deer. After several days of action, carried on day and night by the attackers, the Kaiser brought the maneuvers to a conclusion with a splendid final summation. Again a majority of the GGS provided a

---

53. BAMA, *Acten des Kaiserlichen Marine-Kabinetts betreffend Herbstmanöver*, RM 2–105; Kluck, *Wanderjahre*, pp. 124–130. An example of "parade politics" is evident in correpondence dealing with details of the 1912 Kaisermanöver. Contested between the 3d Corps and the Guards, the Kaiser had apparently suggested a joint parade of both corps prior to the actual field maneuvers. Officials agreed that if the Kaiser ordered it, it would be done. However the War Ministry raised specific objections. For one thing the 3d Corps would notice that its uniforms were inferior to those of the Guards. In the province of Brandenburg this was to be avoided. For another, a parade of the 3d Corps by itself on Sedan Day (2 September) would bring out lots of people from Berlin and the province of Brandenburg whose sons served in the corps. Besides, a single parade would save money and the Kaiser had already seen nearly every unit of the Guards parade at various events during the summer. BAMA, Nachlaß Moltke, N78–23.

large part of the working party: seven section chiefs, the head of Land Survey, and four chief quartermasters. Moltke and his immediate staff numbered about a dozen officers. Beyond that another dozen GGS officers served as maneuver judges. In short, a majority of the ranking officers of the GGS participated. This is not surprising, for the GGS was responsible for laying out the maneuver, both in large and small detail. It was not apparent in all of the pomp and ceremony that anything of military value was accomplished. However, if one looks closely at the logistics, supply, and transportation, another story is revealed.

The 1910 Kaisermanöver placed both the attacking and defending forces squarely in the central sector of the MTP East, Part IV, Danzig Sector. The 1st Corps, headquartered at Königsberg, was located in Line Command N. The 17th Corps, headquartered at Danzig, was located in Line Command V. The 1st Corps defended fortified positions in several areas, each of which stretched along railroad lines. One stretched on an angle from Osterode and Allenstein, the southwest border towns, northwest through Mohrungen and Miswalde. The headquarters were located astride main rail lines, the corps headquarters at Liebstadt astride the line Mohrungen to Wormditt, the next echelon headquarters at Mohrungen, the juncture point of four rail lines. Major advanced outposts stretched westward along the tracks Miswalde to Marienburg and northwest on the rail line Miswalde to Elbing. In fact, both corps used virtually the same transportation and communications network each was to use four years later in August and September 1914 in the Battles of Tannenberg and the Masurian Lakes.[54] The advantages of locating along railroad lines were many. In this most difficult terrain, the Masurian region, which was filled with small lakes, swamp land, and trackless forests, the railroad lines were in many places the only way through. This was especially true in maneuvering units of divisional size, that is, forces of over twelve thousand men on a side. In addition, telegraph and telephone lines followed the railroad lines. In other words, each corps in this maneuver was operating in the difficult terrain of the central region between the area northeast and the region southwest of where the main concentrations of the Russian cross border attack were expected. Geographically East Prussia was split in this way,

---

54. Groener Papers, roll 18, no. 176, Kriegsfahrplankarte Ost, 1913/14; Dennis Showalter, "Even Generals Wet Their Pants," *War and Society*, 2, no. 1 (1984): 63–64.

and it was only the railroad, telegraph, and telephone lines through the center that allowed military forces to operate there at all. It is also interesting to note other war games in this area. Readers may recall the description of the 1888 GGS ride conducted in the same region, in which Hindenburg participated. Without including staff rides and field exercises for the East Prussian 1st, 17th, and 20th Army Corps, other such exercises were the field supply problem of May 1907, the winter tactical exercises of May and December 1912, and the LC exercise of June 1912. By 1914 many of the major players had been there before, many times.[55]

### Administrative War Gaming

After the turn of the century the War Ministry had begun to engage in war gaming. At first this took the form of joint war games with the GGS. As we have seen, intendants had been included in the GGS staff rides as early as the late 1880s. In 1906 the War Ministry began to organize war games of its own in which GGS officers participated. Known initially as "quartermaster exercise rides," implying a limited, somewhat narrow scope, they were later renamed, "administrative general staff rides." Their purpose was explicitly stated: war was like a problem in geometry which the student tried to solve only when the pressure of the teacher, standing behind him, forced him to it. Administrative rides were necessary preparation if commanders were to avoid being forced to seek solutions under pressure. What was emphasized was how much could be learned about strategy and tactics by studying logistics. Here, it was argued, was a richness of knowledge essential in preparing the army for combat readiness as well as operational freedom.[56]

As in all GGS war games, these rides aimed to incorporate the most up-to-date information on recent wars. After 1906 this included the Russo-Japanese War. To Prussian supply officers, the disastrous Russian experience demonstrated that only when the supply organization had been built and exercised during peacetime could it do the job required during wartime. Although the war was

---

55. Norman Stone, *The Eastern Front, 1914–1917* (New York, 1975), pp. 56–65; Groener Papers, roll 18, no. 173; roll 19, May and December 1912; Gaertringen, *Groener*, p. 133.

56. François, *Verwaltungs-Generalstabsreisen*, pp. 7–8.

in no way a complete surprise, Russian preparations for the supply service had been, in the Prussian view, completely inadequate. In place of army corps intendants, the Russians had used officials without peacetime experience: divisional and lower-ranking supply officers were appointed only after the war started. Plans put forward in the summer of 1903 were not seriously considered until January 1904, and they were based on erroneous assumptions of 400,000 men and 100,000 horses. The army which actually took the field was 1,500,000 men, with 200,000 horses, a difference of 400% in the former and 100% in the latter. As a result, when the war began, Russian supply was completely in the hands of local commanders.[57] At times this worked, but only up to a point. Prussian observers reported that supplies moved forward to corps and divisional magazines, but had great difficulty moving further. Food arrived late and many times did not arrive at all. Every movement of the front line threatened to destroy the supply system. Major advances broke it down completely. Fortunately the offensive of September 1905 advanced only one and one half days' march. When the armies paused, order returned to the supply system, but every movement wrenched it and battles broke it down into complete disorder. When the Russians retreated, even though the magazine was full the system failed and the troops lacked supplies. The GGS concluded from all this that the Russian army had provided itself with insufficient information to operate its system before the war or to correct deficiencies once fighting began. Supply for large armies in the field had to be carefully planned, arranged, and practiced beforehand. It depended on preparation, organization, and, above all, information.

With these examples from the Russo-Japanese War in mind, full-scale Prussian administrative GS rides began. Their general purpose was to improve regulations, formulas, rules, and procedures. They were specifically intended to familiarize the participants with the demographic and geographic statistics of the border areas and to prepare officials to respond to new situations arising suddenly. The administrative GS ride was played by officers with war mobilization assignments similar to the ones in the exercise. The conducter was generally the chief of staff of a corps. He was assisted by two or three young GGS officers and a War Ministry intendant. The GGS officers took charge of ride and administrative

57. Ibid., pp. 14, 17.

details; the composition, distribution, and collection of operation orders; reports; and communications. The intendant was in charge of the mathematical accuracy of the daily reports and statistics. Artillery staff officers were chosen from those with mobilization assignments in a rear artillery unit. The trains officer was appointed from the general command in whose region the ride took place. The medical officer's mobilization assignment was director of corps medical transportation.[58]

The ride was another example of serial war gaming. It began with simple problems and became progressively more complicated. The geographic space of the exercise was the area of operations and communications of an army. For one day's operations this was about 1,500 square miles, or a land area roughly 50 miles wide and 30 miles long. Maps used were the GGS standard map at 1:100,000, regional maps at 1:25:000, local maps at 1:8,000, and very small-scale sketch maps at 1 inch = 0.5 miles. The time was four weeks, divided into two phases. First came the preparatory phase, which took the form of an extensive indoor war game, statistically and mathematically based, and lasting four or five days. Phase two, conducted in the field, followed six weeks later.

During the preparatory phase participants were assembled and given an extensive briefing on procedures, reports, and requirements. Then they worked through a series of paper problems, and these were evaluated by the ride conductor. Officers were told that the upcoming ride was planned to include disorder and interruption in the rear lines of communication, changes in the front combat lines, retreat, and unexpectedly large expenditures of foodstuffs, munitions, and medical supplies.

The exercise was based on statistics and written work. Answers to exercise questions were expected to be brief and clearly based upon army regulations. Reports were requested to deal with transportation and communications, military geography and history, medical conditions, the supply situation, and the economics of the ride area. Every operations day ended with a report given by the director, which provided the participants with the foundation for the following day's operation. This report summarized the status quo of communication and field magazines, munitions depots, and hospitals. All these details were then put up on a large operations map. After these procedural instructions, the preparatory exercise

58. Ibid., pp. 10, 21, 27, 29.

opened with a statement by the ride conductor: "The Prussian school of strategy and tactics views the political situation only as a means to an end. We cannot bind ourselves to any particular enemy or friendly states, but change to suit the many-sided exercise object we have in mind." He went on to say that any military combination was useful even if it went against current politics. In choosing a campaign area that implied political uncertainty about Austria and the supply of an army at Dresden, no political implications were to be drawn. It was only an exercise.[59]

Preparatory phase exercises included a series of nine interconnected problems. Each was to be solved using maps, statistical tables, and mathematical formulas. The general background of the exercise was that Germany was at war with Russia, and the first mobilization day was 20 May. In East Prussia and on the Silesian-Russian border there had already been fighting. France and England stood neutral, but were ready to act as soon as the first decisive battles had been fought. Warlike actions in the Balkans necessitated Austria's reinforcing its troops in Bosnia. Germany was sending four armies against Russia, with the first attack marches beginning on 1 June. The initial problem was to devise a plan for the overall communication zone order of battle for the 1st Army. The second problem was to determine the communication order of battle in the border areas. Both were to be completed in forty-eight hours. As each solution was presented, the ride conductor gave an overall summation and the exercise participants moved on to the next problem.

Everything in these war games was measured, weighed, and timed. For example, during the opening mobilization the railroads were tied up in troop transport, therefore river transportation was used. Railroad Line Commands directed this shipping movement. The fourth problem was, how many ships were needed to move supplies and equipment to Dresden and when would they arrive? Supplies included a huge quantity of materials, for example, 300 guns with 500 shells each and equipment and trackage to build 18 miles of field railway. Travel speeds on the Elbe River were 2.5 miles per hour through the mountains and 6.5 miles per hour through the valleys. Travel was calculated at 16 hours per day, with boats tied up at anchor during darkness. Line Command T was in

59. Ibid., pp. 29, 30, 51, 70–71, 77, 80–82, 96–99, 110–15. "Für unsere strategische und taktische Schulung bleibt die politische Unterlage stets nur Mittel zum Zweck."

charge. Six days and 1,080 workers were needed for loading.

By the seventh preparatory problem, the whole exercise became computationally and statistically more complex. The intendant of 4th Corps needed to know if the duchy of Saxon-Altenburg could support a twenty-day stay by the 2d Army, with 210,000 men and 80,000 horses. GGS maps in several scales were used, as were tables prepared by the Royal Prussian Statistical Office. To deal with the problem, the ride members had to master the economy of this 820-square-mile land. Every square half mile was estimated to average 136 inhabitants, 9 horses, 50 cows, 8 sheep, 44 pigs, 11 tons of wheat, 20 tons of rye, 9 tons of barley, 18 tons of hay, and 79 tons of potatoes. A table was provided listing these averages as well as the daily needs of soldiers (0.75 pounds meat, 1.5 pounds bread, 1 pound meal bread, and 3 pounds of potatoes) and horses (13 pounds of hay). The solution was given in tabular format. The corps intendant was told that only ten days' meat rations were to be found in the duchy, and that calculation would leave only the sick, pregnant, and young animals for the inhabitants. A twenty-day supply of potatoes and bread meal was available, with enough left over for the inhabitants, but there was only a six-day supply of hay. The answer to the question posed in problem seven was negative.

With the ninth problem, the level of complexity of the exercise increased again. The size of the army was raised by almost 60,000 men and finally included a bewildering mixture of forces and arms amounting to a total of 267,735 men and 74,461 horses. To feed these required 53 magazines. In addition, the deputy intendant was authorized to purchase 1,260 oxens, 3,150 pigs, 10,710 sheep, 1,280 tons of hay, 500 tons of meal, and 100 tons of canteen goods. Delivered by rail were 10 hay trains of 2,500 tons each, 4 meal trains of 1,000 tons each, and 15 food supply trains. Ride members were asked to estimate if this was enough. At the conclusion of the ninth exercise, the preparatory phase was completed.

The administrative GS ride itself began several weeks later. Four days before, participants received complex written materials that included map requirements, printed regulations, tables, charts, and procedures. The special situation in the campaign area was that during the previous two days the German army had been fighting the Russians in the region of eastern Silesia. After making sense of a cascade of tactical data, ride participants were given the first problem, which was supply orders for the 1st Army for 7 June. The solution was to be given in terms of troop supplies, bread supplies, ecological characteristics in the region, and the supply situation in the magazines, described in twenty-category tabular columns.

The ride was laid out very precisely. It included the assembly day, seventeen exercise days, travel by railroad and horse, three general lectures, and a final summation. Frequently the exercise conductor collected his participants in the afternoons for briefings. He questioned them relentlessly. Why do supply problems stand in the foreground of all rear area activities? What are the particular difficulties of rear area supply? Historical comparisons were constantly made. For example, in 1866 in Bohemia 1.4 million rifle cartridges were expended; each weapon averaged 6 cartridges. In 1870–71 the German army fired 56 cartridges per weapon and each gun used 199 shells. The conductor emphasized that in the future such small supply requirements could not be expected. In 1870 a corps needed 736 wagons for its munitions reserve for the entire campaign. By 1910 the same corps used that number of wagons during the first six days. As illustrated in the administrative GS ride, the analytical aspects of war planning processes had developed in several ways since Schlieffen's day. There was a much greater specialization of knowledge, and this knowledge was highly structured in statistical tables, charts, and graphs. Many more support services were offered to a much larger army. Even these exercises were unable to provide adequate preparation for the supply and casualty increases of the Great War. Whereas in 1870 rifle ammunition had cost 20 million marks for the entire war, in 1914–18 the average cost per month was 200 million. In 1870 there were 43,000 killed and 100,000 wounded. After 1918 these numbers were more than two million killed and 5.7 million wounded, increases of forty-six times for the dead and fifty-seven times for the wounded.[60]

### The Bosnian and Moroccan Crises, 1908–1911

A series of war crises influenced strategic decision making in the years 1906 to 1913. It is likely that from 1906 until the World War, Moltke believed that his country confronted serious war dangers every two years, five Cuban missile-type crises over a period of

---

60. Ibid., pp. 117, 124, 231–37; MGFA, *Bedeutung der Logistik*, p. 135.

nine years: 1905–6, 1908–9, 1911, 1912, and 1914. At least in his mind he may have seen events in this way. At the end of 1906 the Bavarian military attaché reported that the military leadership in Berlin regarded war with France as inevitable. He wrote that the war would and must come. The task of German diplomacy was to delay it until Germany was fully prepared. Moltke was a man to whom the future was dark. He waited impatiently for the next stage of world history, the expected cataclysm of Revelations.[61].

The war planning and decision process of 1908 to 1909 was undergirded by several factors. First, after 1908 it seems that both the domestic and the foreign environment took decisive turns. Internally there were two crises, that of the Eulenburg scandals, whose revelations shook the Kaiser's badly inflated self-esteem, and that of the Daily Telegraph affair, an uproar in the press and Parliament which demonstrated that Wilhelm II no longer possessed the confidence of the broad mass of people in his country. After the Daily Telegraph affair he had a nervous breakdown. Some argue that he never recovered. The upshot of these crises was to reduce the Kaiser's influence and power: within the ruling circle he shrank and there was no one to replace him. At the same time nearly all of the institutional leaders who had been in place during the first seventeen years of Wilhelm II's reign, such as the chief of the Military Cabinet, the chancellor, the foreign minister, and the chief of the GGS, had been changed or were about to be. Bernhard von Bülow was in the final period of his chancellorship. The German Foreign Office had no strong leadership, except perhaps the voice of the retired Holstein. The Military Cabinet had declined to the point of insignificance after Hulsen-Haeseler's stroke while dancing for the Kaiser in the costume of a ballerina. The chief of the GGS was an inactive player in defense policy. The single institution within the Reich government which expanded its power and influence during these years was the navy.[62] At this point of semiparalysis, the foreign political situation changed from one of ominous but uncertain and vague danger before 1905 into the state of clear and present danger presented by the Anglo-French general staff talks, the Franco-Russian military talks, and the modernization and buildup of army size, weapons, and railroads

61. Lambi, *German Power*, p. 264; Moltke, *Erinnerungen*, pp. 331, 334.
62. Görlitz, *German General Staff*, p. 146; Hull, *Entourage*, p. 144; Gaertringen, *Groener*, p. 92.

by both France and Russia. Thus the foreign task environment appeared visibly more dangerous.

Moltke continued fatalistic, pessimistic, and under the Steiner influence: as Gerhard Ritter wrote, he was anything but a hearty swashbuckler. Despite occasional indignant outbursts over the seemingly weak-kneed attitude of the Foreign Ministry, he was not an activist. To his staff officers he sometimes seemed downright defeatist. Moltke reacted to those around him, to Bülow, to Ludendorff, but was not a leader within the GGS. He is not known for striking Reichstag speeches as his namesake had been or for provocative talks within the GGS or at military ceremonies as Schlieffen had been. Prior to 1912, he seems to have made little impact. With reservations about his own abilities, growing nervousness at the anti-German Entente, and anxieties about the coming test of Germanic civilization, Moltke was ready for better relations with Austria. Not only was Austria Germany's last ally but a Germanic and therefore a unique cultural partner. So Moltke looked favorably toward Austria. But he was not one to initiate.[63]

In October 1908, in the wake of the Young Turk Revolution, Austria-Hungary formally annexed the Ottoman province of Bosnia-Herzegovina. The action had been discussed between the Austrian foreign minister Alois Aehrenthal and his Russian counterpart Alexander Izvolski at a meeting in Buchlau in September. It was also agreed that Austria would not oppose the opening of the Straits to Russian warships. However no date had been set. While Izvolski set off on a leisurely tour of European capitals to obtain the consent of the powers to changes in the Straits regulations, Aehrenthal announced an immediate fait accompli. These surprise moves provoked a storm that brought Europe to the brink of war. The Serbians reacted violently to the formal incorporation of these Slavic provinces into the Habsburg empire and henceforth regarded Bosnia-Herzegovina as the Alsace-Lorraine of the Balkans. In Russia there was also strong reaction because Izvolski had not consulted his colleagues prior to concluding the Buchlau agreement. The Russian cabinet repudiated him and Izvolski was forced to ask France and Britain for support and to request either compensation or a conference from Austria. His request was refused. As the crisis dragged on Serbia and Austria prepared to mobilize against each other.

---

63. Ritter, *Sword and Scepter*, 2: 244; Hull, *Entourage*, pp. 239–45.

On 9 January 1909 Conrad von Hötzendorf, the Austrian chief of staff, wrote a lengthy formal letter to Moltke. In essence it described in detail the deployment plan for Austria's armies, set into a political and strategic context. Serbia and Montenegro, he said, were supported in their anti-Austrian activities by Russia. There was a strong possibility of an Austrian occupation of Serbia in the near future. In the event of a war between Austria and Russia, he wrote that Germany would have to join in on the side of Austria "in the spirit of the alliance of 1879." Assuming that this would also mean a war between Germany and France, that is, a general European war, he asked Moltke how he proposed to deploy his forces. Conrad's purpose in writing was to determine Germany's deployment plans precisely. In doing so, he wanted to get an unconditional guarantee that Germany would support Austria if it attacked Serbia, irrespective of other European commitments. Such a guarantee would alter radically the 1879 German-Austrian alliance, which was purely and solely defensive. The alliance provided that if either power were attacked by a third power, the other would come to its aid. It said nothing about either power attacking or what would happen in that case.[64]

The background to the German response is provided in the General Staff Strategic Assessment sent to Chancellor von Bülow, dated 29 January 1909 and covering the immediate mobilization year ahead. The French army was described as weaker than it had been the year before: war against France could be waged with confidence. Russia was also considered weaker. Its army was in the process of reorganization and there were still military burdens in East Asia. Nevertheless, new strategic railroads completed the year before had speeded up Russia's deployment by seventy-two hours. Russia would no longer be compelled to remain inactive in a war against Germany. Britain would stand by France and was ready to send an expeditionary force of 160,000 capable of appearing at Dunkirk, Calais, or Antwerp on the thirteenth mobilization day. Belgian and Dutch forces were considered inferior to German reserve troops. As for Austria-Hungary, Moltke was concerned that, if it split its forces simultaneously between Italy and Russia, it would not have enough troops to send four army corps against Serbia.[65]

---

64. Kitchen, *German Officer Corps*, p. 106; Norman Stone, "Moltke and Conrad Plan Their War," in Paul Kennedy, ed., *War Plans of the Great Powers* (Boston, 1985), pp. 226–27; Ritter, *Sword and Scepter*, 2: 239–45.
65. Lambi, *German Power*, pp. 304–6.

After consulting Bülow, Moltke replied to Conrad's ambiguous letter on 21 January. He did not reject, but instead accepted its underlying assumption. If Austria attacked Serbia and if Russia intervened, Moltke wrote, that would be for Germany a *casus foederis*. As soon as Russia began to mobilize, Germany would call up its whole fighting force. In writing, Moltke was apparently taking his lead from Bülow, who believed that as long as Germany and Austria stood together they formed a bloc which no one would attack lightly. Bülow feared Austria's losing confidence and turning away from Germany. A refusal or grudging attitude on the question of the annexation of Bosnia-Herzegovina might not be forgiven. Bülow in turn was following the advice of Friedrich von Holstein. By this response, Moltke and Bülow brought about a fundamental alteration in German foreign policy. In effect they changed the treaty of 1879 from a defensive into an offensive one and subordinated Germany to Austria in the most basic decision of foreign policy, war and peace. German leadership was giving way to a growing sense of fatalism.[66]

In early March, Serbia and Austria-Hungary began to mobilize. On 14 March Bülow issued a warning to St. Petersburg: unless Russia restrained Serbian hostility, Germany would allow matters to "take their course." An unsatisfactory Russian response led to a second warning called variously an "ultimatum," "just short of an ultimatum," and "an ultimatum in substance if not in form." Soon thereafter Russia yielded, and the crisis slowly wound down in a series of diplomatic agreements, monetary payments, and official statements. On 19 March, responding to Conrad's further plea for assurances that the German east front forces would launch a relief offensive to pin down Russian forces on the Narew River on the twenty-fourth or twenty-fifth day of mobilization, Moltke reluctantly promised an initial diversionary thrust against the Russian line to camouflage the main Habsburg assault further south. He stressed that the thirteen German east front divisions were primarily for defense east of the Vistula; however, he pledged them in support of a simultaneous Austrian offensive. He qualified this pledge by saying that in the event that enemy actions made it impossible for either Germany or Austria to carry out its intentions, it was absolutely essential that the ally be informed immediately. Conrad took Moltke's pledge very seriously. Thereafter he

66. Craig, *Politics*, p. 289; Craig, *Germany*, p. 322; Rich, *Holstein*, 2:816ff.

insisted on having it annually reconfirmed. It was referred to at the Austro-Hungarian cabinet meeting of 7 July 1914.[67]

Moltke apparently concluded during the Bosnian crisis that it offered an opportunity for war that was unlikely to reappear under such favorable conditions.[68] Exactly how he came to this conclusion is a mystery. Especially in comparison to the first Moroccan crisis of 1905–6, circumstances had changed. Russia was no longer bogged down in Asia, its western border regions denuded of troops with a revolution going on at home. As Moltke's own strategic assessment pointed out, the Russian western border provinces had returned to full strength and its railroad building program in that region had progressed. Russia was able to honor its alliance commitment to France. France too was stronger; its army had been reorganized and its east border regions were better developed, with several fortresses under construction. So the situation was very different from that of 1905. If Russia had not backed down, events might have taken quite a different course.

Up until 1911 Moltke had developed no clear defense policy of his own and his influence on preparation of the defense bills was small. War Minister Josias von Heeringen, having neither the political instincts nor the intellectual power of his predecessor, was also rather inactive. Chancellor Bethman-Hollweg and Finance Minister Wermuth were against any increases in the army budget.[69]

In 1910–11 the Mannesmann corporation, with the enthusiastic support of the Pan-German League, launched a public campaign directed at obtaining Foreign Office support for its mining interests in Morocco. In April 1911 France dispatched troops to Fez at the request of the Moroccan sultan to relieve Europeans besieged there by his insubordinate subjects. Bethmann-Hollweg advised the French to proceed with caution. On 22 April Kaiser Wilhelm welcomed French military involvement in Morocco, which would divert troops from the German border: he wanted Germany to stay in the background and to leave the protests against the French violation of the Algeciras Acts of 1906 to other powers. On 28 April Alfred Kiderlen-Wächter warned the French ambassador

67. Lambi, *German Power*, p. 307; Ritter, *Sword and Scepter*, 2: 245–46; Norman Stone, "Moltke and Conrad," pp. 228ff.
68. Herwig, "Imperial Germany," pp. 79–80; Lambi, *German Power*, pp. 305–8. Volker Berghahn, *Germany and the Approach of War in 1914* (New York, 1973), pp. 79–80; Ritter, *Sword and Scepter*, 2: 240–45; Craig, *Politics*, p. 289; Fischer, *Illusions*, pp. 60–61.
69. Förster, *Der doppelte Militarismus*, p. 94.

that if French troops stayed in Fez, Germany would regard the Algeciras Acts as dissolved and resume freedom of action. During May and June Kiderlen convinced the Kaiser to send German warships into the area to support a request for compensation. Negotiations with the French ambassador had begun when on 1 July the German gunboat *Panther* arrived in the port of Agadir. At the same time Kiderlen requested the entire French Congo as compensation from the shocked French ambassador. These two events created a full-scale crisis in the European capitals. By late July England had declared itself ready to support France in the event of war and had recalled its Atlantic fleet to Portsmouth.[70]

The military reaction to this situation began on 2 March with Moltke's strategic assessment. He did not expect the conquest of Morocco, unlike that of Algeria, to involve eighty thousand to one hundred thousand French troops annually over a period of thirty years. Nor did he think that a subdued Morocco would in the foreseeable future provide France with many native troops. Another GGS report said that if Morocco matured so that it had a population of forty million from which to draw recruits, Germany would need extensive army increases to maintain present-strength security. On 17 June War Minister Heeringen asked Under State Secretary Arthur Zimmerman if preliminary preparations for mobilization should begin. He was told that the army and navy should mobilize at the same time, but only after notification of a decision by the Kaiser. This would guarantee that a mobilization would not come into force before the political-military situation unconditionally required it and the Reich chancellor was in position to assume responsibility.

Along the way to preliminary mobilization there were certain built-in safeguards. One of these was that military attachés abroad were responsible for informing Berlin of possible war developments. During this crisis, the focus of military officials was concentrated on France. Attaché Detlev von Winterfeldt in Paris wrote in early August that he did not see any preliminary war preparations being made. By 19 August, however, he reported that the Foreign Office and war minister were preparing for a possible war against Germany, and on 24 August, he reported that large-scale French army maneuvers in the north were called off, ostensibly because of hoof and mouth disease. With the army in garrisons, he wrote, the

---

70. Craig, *From Bismarck to Adenauer*, pp. 41–42.

French had an advantage in case of mobilization. Meanwhile, English maneuvers were called off because of "wet weather." Belgium and the Netherlands took steps to "defend their neutrality."[71]

The Kaiser and Moltke were on the annual northland cruise. As soon as they heard of the French cancellation of maneuvers, they directed that, in order to avoid prejudicing a possible German mobilization, the negotiations with the French would be conducted so that no breakdown occurred during the upcoming Kaisermanöver. Kiderlen asked that one brigade be recalled to Metz from the maneuvers. The War Ministry refused to take partial measures: it was to be either a full mobilization or nothing. The navy was partially alerted for war. The fleet conducted maneuvers while in communication with Berlin. Trials of a new dreadnought, the *Helgoland*, were speeded up to allow it to enter service on 23 August, and a number of other measures were taken in August and the first part of September to increase naval preparedness. The Bavarian military plenipotentiary Gebsattel reported a warlike spirit in Berlin. He believed that the Kaiser might feel obligated to decide for war if a foreign coalition attempted to force Germany to its knees. But in that case diplomacy must ensure that Germany did not appear to be the aggressor. For only that would free the tsar of his obligation to support France.

On 7 September Moltke gave a further strategic assessment. It was impossible to say if France was now preparing for war. Neither the British army nor navy was considered ready for war. If war came, however, England would come to the aid of France, but in so far as possible shift the burden of war to its ally. If the British joined the French by means of coastal landings in Belgium or the Netherlands, a speedy German mobilization would be necessary. Franco-German negotiations went on during the summer and autumn. In late August Moltke had written to his wife that he was fed up with the wretched Moroccan affair. If Germany once again crawled out with its tail between its legs, if the Reich did not have the courage to take an energetic line and enforce it with the sword, he despaired for its future. In that case, Moltke said he would quit and would propose that the army be abolished and the Reich put under the protection of the Japanese so that the Germans could concentrate on making money. In November a new Franco-German

71. Lambi, *German Power*, p. 316; Oncken, *Panthersprung*, pp. 213, 215.

treaty was signed which recognized the French protectorate over Morocco and gave Germany 275,000 square miles in the French Congo, doubling the territory of the German Cameroons. One commentator remarked that throughout the crisis, the military was completely subordinate to the political leadership. Gebsattel concluded that the chances of war in the next few months were improbable, but the chances of war in the next few years appeared to be very great.[72]

The second Moroccan crisis was an important turning point for German public opinion. One reaction to it was the creation of the German Army League, an offshoot of several existing radical nationalist organizations, but unique because it was the first mass organization led by retired military officers. Created in December 1911, by 1913 it had become the second largest such organization in German with 78,000 single members, 190,000 corporate members, and over four hundred local units. Founded on the assumption that a European war was unavoidable and increasingly probable, the league believed the German navy would be of relatively little value in such a war. In this situation the army had to be enlarged and modernized with all possible speed. Not only was war with France and Russia inevitable, but such a war would come at a time of overall weakness in Germanic culture. Germany was at the center of a circle of evil powers threatening its existence, but there were many domestic factors also steadily weakening Germanic culture from within in subtle and insidious ways. Among these were the urbanization of the countryside, individualism, materialism, commercialism, the alienation of German women from their unique role in the family, the growing strength of socialism and pacifism, selfish German party politics, and the decline of patriotism. The result was a serious debasement of Germanic culture. Like Moltke and Steiner, the leaders of the Army League saw the coming crisis in a cosmic framework. The next war would not simply be one of victory or defeat: it would validate and decide the existence of German culture. This conservatism had a particularly nativistic tone. As General Keim, the leader of the league, said in a May 1913 speech, "You have a right to hate the enemies of your fatherland."[73]

---

72. Oncken, *Panthersprung*, pp. 216–18; Lambi, *German Power*, pp. 320–22; Fischer, *Illusions*, p. 88; Craig, *Germany*, p. 329; Jarausch, *Enigmatic Chancellor*, pp. 120ff.; Förster, *Der doppelte Militarismus*, p. 210.

73. Roger Chickering, "Der 'Deutsche Wehrverein' und die Reform der deut-

This outside agitation was soon felt within the military. As originally proposed, the five-year defense budget for the years 1911–16 provided for very small increases. But a general feeling of inferiority vis-à-vis the French and Russians was beginning to build, a kind of early "missile gap." For example, General von Gebsattel, the Bavarian military representative in Berlin, reported in April 1911 that the Reich army was quite inferior to the French army: it was not only smaller and had poorer artillery, but France could mobilize faster and had more officers and better railroad mobilization facilities. The GGS itself had long been aware of the planned expansion of the Russian railroad system in the west, a structure expected to be completed in approximately 1917 which, at that point, would greatly enhance the Russian military capabilities along the Prussian and Austrian borders. As the *Hamburger Nachrichten* put it on 31 December 1911: "We all feel with instinctive certainty that the climax of the international crisis approaches, that before long Germany's position as a rising world power must be contested with iron dice. Our enemies have long lain in wait for a suitable moment at which to attack us."[74]

In the midst of the second Moroccan crisis, in October 1911, Bethman-Hollweg asked the war minister for a new army bill. Heeringen refused: it was financially and politically impossible. But even in his own ministry, dissident voices were stirring. From the Central Department came a memorandum arguing that the political leadership should be employed to increase army size by taking advantage of the full military capacity of the population. On 29 November, Colonel Wandel wrote that army increases were unavoidable. The war minister wrote to the chancellor that he was willing to draft a new army bill. In it Belgium and the Netherlands were portrayed as potential enemies. The proposed army bill for 1912 included increases of 296 million marks annually, plus one-time additions of 144 million marks.

In 1912 the GGS internal situation dramatically changed again. General von Stein left, allowing Erich Ludendorff direct access to Moltke. Moltke was easily influenced by the energetic and knowledgeable head of the Mobilization Section. Two memorandums were sent to the war minister, one on 14 October, the second on 25 November, followed by a conference on 27 November

schen Armee, 1912–1914," *Militärgeschichtliche Mitteilungen* (1979): 15–16; cf. Roger Chickering, *We Men Who Feel Most German* (Boston, 1984).

74. Förster, *Der doppelte Militarismus*, p. 207; Fischer, *Illusions*, p. 94.

between Moltke and Heeringen and a third memorandum dated 21 December. Presenting a "worst case" scenario, the GGS memos detailed the weaknesses of the Triple Alliance and portrayed a west front with a greatly strengthened Belgian army and a numerically superior French army and an east front in which Germany's ally, Turkey, had been greatly undermined by the First Balkan War. Germany needed to enlarge its army by almost 50% to meet this threatening situation.

In October southeast Europe had begun to erupt with two wars along the frontiers of the Ottoman Empire. Against this background the famous 8 December 1912 "war council" took place, seen by some as a key event, the beginning of systematic preparation for war. The question which apparently dominated that meeting was, is Germany ready for war right now or is additional time needed? In other words, the leading military men of the Reich made the question of war and peace dependent on armaments and defense preparation. Other historians argue that this council should not be overestimated: it was not so unique compared to other meetings within the German bureaucratic system.[75]

Michael Geyer postulates that the birth of a new armaments ideology was occurring. No longer willing to work through the Kaiser and government, armament proponents went directly to the public. These proponents now extended outside of the elite and ranged far beyond the army itself. Appearing to be a "movement," it was radical in the true sense of the word, demanding the transformation of the German Reich into an armament society in order to survive in the coming international power struggle. Thus the defense package of 1913 was the largest in the forty-two years of the Kaiserreich. And it passed by acclamation!

However, a significant debate took place within the military. The GGS itself, under Ludendorff's prodding, had demanded three hundred thousand men, and showed little interest in anything technological, such as more machine guns or artillery. The War Ministry feared an abrupt increase in manpower, especially in the officer corps: it feared democratization and the decline of the old sense of honor and tradition. Neither Moltke in the GGS nor Heeringen in the War Ministry understood exactly what was

---

75. Förster, *Der doppelte Militarismus*, pp. 220–26, 266. The most recent review of this, with a bibliography which follows the historiography, is John C.G. Röhl, *Kaiser, Hof und Staat*, pp. 175ff.

happening, but younger men in both institutions did. A period of intensification of German military preparedness had begun.[76]

## Alterations in the Schlieffen Plan

As for the basic west front war plan known as the Schlieffen Plan, Moltke clearly changed it from 1906 to 1914. Groener says that because Moltke's first year in office, 1906, had been one of political crisis, he began to rethink the war plan, asking himself if it was adequate to the new dangers of heightened political tension. France and England were clearly allied and France itself had changed from advocating a defensive strategy to adopting a more aggressive posture. The Schlieffen Plan of 1905 seemed not to be in tune with these relationships; as a result Moltke altered it in several ways.

It is clear that the relationship between the right and left wings, the ratio of forces, was changed between 1906 and 1914. Groener states that it was reduced from a ratio of 7:1 to a ratio of 3:1. J.F.C. Fuller says that in percentages the Schlieffen Plan represented 100:15, the Moltke plan 100:42. From an army larger by several hundred thousand in peacetime strength and perhaps a million in wartime strength, the right wing was reduced, Len Turner says, by four divisions and the left wing strengthened by seventeen divisions, thus changing the ratios. Schlieffen's original plan called for 15% force on the left wing, 85% on the right. He planned to increase the right wing by 6% more as soon as the left wing had engaged the French in Alsace and Lorraine, thus shifting two army corps from south to north. Schlieffen's final shift gave the right wing a strength of 91%.[77]

In 1908 the German left wing, poised opposite Alsace-Lorraine, was enlarged. This was done, not by taking away forces from the right wing formations, but by maintaining the same number there and adding new forces to the left. As Gerhard Ritter wrote, this

76. Geyer, *Rüstungspolitik*, p. 89; Förster, *Der doppelte Militarismus*, pp. 190ff.
77. Wilhelm Groener, *The Testament of Count Schlieffen*, trans. W.P. Papenforth (Carlisle Barracks, Pa., 1983), p. 10 (kindness of Dr. Ed. Drea of the U.S. Army Center of Military History); L.C.F. Turner, "The Significance of the Schlieffen Plan," in Paul Kennedy, ed., *The War Plans of the Great Powers, 1880–1914* (Boston, 1985), p. 212. The "official" history of the war agrees with Groener. Reichsarchiv, ed., *Der Weltkrieg 1914 bis 1918*, 25 vols. (Berlin, 1925–35), vol.:1 *Die militärischen Operationen zu Lande*, p. 62.

technical change substantially strengthened the left wing without reducing the troop strength of the right wing in terms of absolute numbers. What it did do, however, was to alter the ratio of forces between right and left. Schlieffen had proposed to deploy fifty-nine active and reserve divisions north of Metz, nine to the south of that city. Moltke, taking advantage of additional divisions which become available after 1905, decided to deploy fifty-five divisions north and twenty-three south of Metz. The exact reasons for this change are unclear. After World War I there was a great controversy over whether Moltke had "watered down" the Schlieffen Plan and thereby lost the war at the very start. Groener said that Moltke did not have the nerve to strip Alsace-Lorraine and stake everything on a single great battle. Instead he wanted two offensives, one north and one south, and he intended to shuttle troops between them as the situation demanded. Ludendorff wrote that Moltke did not trust the war plan's timing. He feared that the MTP would not deliver sufficient forces to enable the German right wing to succeed before French forces were able to break through on the left wing and overrun the German industrial regions north of Saarbrücken.[78]

The west front was originally an incomplete triangle approximately 400 miles by 230 miles by 260 miles at its furthest extension, encompassing a land area of about 55,000 square miles. Moltke rejected the move through the Netherlands, saying that a hostile Netherlands would be disastrous, while a neutral Netherlands would protect the rear and provide a "windpipe" for imports and supplies. He admitted, however, that the west front advance would be "awkward" without the use of Dutch territory. The problem was one of compression, which forced the first and second armies to pass through a narrow twelve-mile-wide space to advance onto the Belgian plain. Von Kluck's 1st Army of 320,000 had to pass through a six-mile-wide strip between the Dutch border and Liège; von Bülow's 2d Army of 260,000 had to pass through and immediately south of Liège. Packed within a space of twelve miles were almost 600,000 men with their horses, weapons, and equipment. More important was the fact that this change necessitated another: the capture of Liège with its four railroad

---

78. Ritter, *Sword and Scepter*, 2: 219; Bucholz, *Hans Delbrück*, p. 162; Haeussler, *Groener*, p. 38; Erich Ludendorff, *Kriegführung und Politik*, 3d ed. (Berlin, 1923), pp. 71–72.

lines, as Moltke himself wrote, became the sine quo non of the whole west front advance. To do this, Germany had to keep six brigades of infantry and supporting artillery permanently on war footing in the Aachen area. It meant that almost three weeks before the main movement of the armies could begin, these six brigades had to storm Liège. The most irrevocable steps of actual war, including the violation of neutral territory, had to be taken at the first instant of mobilization. Mobilization therefore meant war. Initially this preplan attack was set for the evening of the tenth and eleventh mobilization days; later this was speeded up by 100%. This first appeared in the war plan for the mobilization year beginning 1 April 1908.[79]

From the fall of 1911 on, the RRS of the GGS was under continuous pressure to reduce the time needed to carry out the MTP. The goal was to lower it by ninety-six hours if possible, by forty-eight hours at least. Part of this ongoing process was to reexamine the capacity of every railroad stretch, trying to redraw the plan to increase capacity. Methods to do this included (1) changing the track plan to allow more trains to follow each other closer together, (2) changing the ramp plan to provide more rapid on-loading of troops and gear, (3) altering the empty wagon plan to allow faster return and reloading, and (4) speeding up the plan to prepare civilian rail cars for soldiers and horses. Each time it was tightened, the MTP became more and more fixed, rigid, and inflexible.[80]

Originally Schlieffen had not intended to put reserve forces on the front lines. Reserves were to be used as backup forces, for rear supply service, for siege and encirclement duty for fortresses, and as flank protection for combat forces. For example, north and south of the Meuse River, sixteen Landwehr brigades were to be used for siege, encirclement, and reconnaissance. Fourteen Landwehr brigades would garrison the fortresses of Namur, Maubeuge, Lille, Dunkirk, Mézières, Givet, Hirson, Longwy, and Montmédy. After the capitulation of Antwerp and Verdun, two and a half reserve corps and two Landwehr brigades would become available as reinforcement for the front and as flank protection to the front line and rear of the main army. In every division, Schlieffen had

79. Ritter, *Schlieffen Plan*, p. 166; C.R.M.F. Cruttwell, *A History of the Great War*, 2d ed. (Oxford, 1940), pp. 13–14; Groener Papers, roll 8, no. 35, von Haeften, Reichsarchiv letter of 28 January 1924 to Groener.
80. Gaertringen, *Groener*, pp. 121–133.

arranged twelve active battalions to carry the attack on the front line and in the second line, providing necessary support, eight reserve battalions. By 1912 Moltke had decided to mix reserve corps with regular troops at the forward edge of combat.[81]

Moltke closed off the year 1911 with a lengthy memorandum to Reichs Chancellor Bethmann-Hollweg in which he justified his call for a greatly enlarged army. He said all the European powers were preparing for a great war, which was expected sooner or later. Today states could not abandon their allies, for they could no longer depend on their own strength alone to confront imminent and growing dangers. The decision over a future war would be made by the different coalitions working against each other. It was the duty of states to prepare for this judgment day, when it would be decided if the Germanic state deserved, on the basis of its inner validity, to continue to exist or not. War was not only unavoidable, it was demanded by life.[82] Two aspects of this statement are worth noting. One is the idea that a great European Armageddon was an inevitable event within the coming world order. It was unavoidable, a prophetic inevitability, a cleansing action, a fulfillment which would test and validate the Germanic state at its most fundamental level, the level of culture. Moltke asked whether Germanic culture deserved to continue to exist. His answer was that it did but that it needed to be tested in war. Here the philosophical prophecies of Ecclesiasties are joined together with the scientific futurism of social Darwinism. Second, he realized that this millenial event would come about as a result of the interlinked bureaucratic technology of the war plans. When the different alliance systems became enmeshed, like cog wheels in a machine, they would pull each other forward ratchetlike into the maelstrom. Meanwhile outside the GGS, members of the Army League "rejoiced in the idea of an Armageddon for a corrupt, decadent, and materialistic world."[83]

81. Turner, "Schlieffen Plan," pp. 212–13; Sarter, *Deutsche Eisenbahnen*, pp. 42–43; Collenburg, "Schlieffen," pp. 625, 629.

82. Gerhard Granier, "Deutsche Rüstungspolitik vor dem Ersten Weltkriege: General Franz Wedels Tagebuchaufzeichnungen aus dem preußischen Kriegsministerium," *Militärgeschichtliche Mitteilungen* 2 (1985): 126.

83. Geyer, *Rüstungspolitik*, p. 530. Cf. Marilyn S. Coetzee, *The German Army League: Popular Nationalism in Wilhelmine Germany* (New York, 1990).

*Chapter 6*
# 1914
# The Great Symphony

Wilhelm Groener, head of the GGS Railroad Section in 1914, summarized the approach to war within the technical core when he wrote that the great symphony, the Schlieffen Plan, could only be attempted once, and the conductor bungled it. He went on to say that the leitmotif of the Schlieffen symphony was a strong right wing. After 1914, when poor musicians had bungled the one and only performance, many were content to place the blame for its failure on the composer.[1] Another officer carried the analogy even further. He wrote that a well-conducted war is like a great symphony. There is no lack of discords, there are players who make mistakes. No good symphonic performance is conceivable without many rehearsals and without uniform principles on which the whole orchestra is governed. He went on to describe Schlieffen's "secret of victory" not as something hidden away in a protected place, but as knowledge: knowledge of how everything had happened, how it was happening, and how it would happen again. Knowledge was the secret of victory.[2]

It is no accident that a musical score was used as a metaphor for war or that knowledge was considered the key to military success. Both defined a process. Playing a symphony combined the meticulousness and specificity of modern technical procedures with the emotions of an ancient and powerful traditional phenomenon. Modernity provided methods for large-scale integration of time, space, and size. Tradition gave ancient values and resonances and supplied the psychological force to encourage commitment, a sense of purpose, and motivation.[3] Behind all the organizational

1. Dorothea Groener-Geyer, *General Groener: Soldat und Staatsmann* (Frankfurt, 1955), p. 227; Groener, *Das Testament des Grafen Schlieffen*, pp. 47, 58, 65.
2. Friedrich von Boetticher, *The Art of War* (Bielefeld, 1951), p. 6.
3. John Child, *Organization: A Guide to Problems and Practices*, 2d ed. (London, 1984), p. 237. These sentiments describe the English department store Marks and Spencer. Surely they also fit the GGS, a different kind of organization in another cultural setting but one confronted with some of the same problems in the transition from traditional to modern operations.

procedures and technology was the esprit de corps of the most successful elite organization in an ancient military culture. In an organization whose final goal entailed some degree of death, rational bureaucracy masked the irrational clash of power.

## Four Discords

By 1914 four major aspects dominated Prussian war planning: bureaucratic routine within the technical core; unpredictable cyclicality within the ruling circle of the government; a serious knowledge gap within and between governments; and the increasingly dangerous foreign task environment. Within the technical core, the goal was consistent, uniform, predictable performance of duty which did not depend on individuals but on procedures and methods. The oft-noted anonymity of the GGS, "general staff officers have no name," is in fact the sign of the emerging organization man. The model GGS officer aimed at anonymity, professional competence, service to the state, high work capacity, and functional reliability. He was a cog in a very large machine.[4]

However such a mechanism was inevitably disaggregated. Any coherent action depended upon the synchronization of a number of routinized procedures. Each actor had a part to play, triggered by cues from other actors, almost none of whom had much discretionary power. Division and subdivision of tasks into component parts resulted in increased cycle time, greater inflexibility, more specialized manpower and longer-range planning. The result was a feeling of control, a high measure of certainty that the task would be accomplished. The application of scientific knowledge to the practical task of war planning yielded a feeling of competence. For the technical specialist the planning process was divided into manageable segments; he read and translated the flow charts, understood the timetables, and gave the "expert opinion" to which others, lacking knowledge, deferred. Bureaucratic methods tended toward uniform and consistent results. Information flows worked toward a single future. Aside from the usual Darwinian and pan-German ideas, GGS members were probably not aware of this internal dynamic because the organization masked its members.

4. quoted in MGFA, *Tradition in deutschen Streitkräften*, p. 16; Wolfgang Schall, "Führungsgrundsätze in Armee und Industrie," *Wehrkunde* 14 (1964): 10–18; cf. William H. Whyte, *The Organization Man* (New York, 1956).

Armies are future-oriented organizations maintained to compete against each other on forthcoming battlefields. Since there had been no major war in Europe in forty-three years, the GGS relied upon a particular kind of knowledge, an abstract image, derived from historical study and war games.

In this planning mechanism the feudal position of all highest warlord, which the Kaiser dreamed he held, did not exist. In its place was the modern bureaucratic functionary, the directing technical specialist. Every interference by the Kaiser with the wires and clockwork of the organized machine appeared impossible and insignificant. The specialized knowledge of the expert had became the foundation of the power position of the office holder. As Admiral von Mueller said, Germany had not had a working monarch for twenty-five years. The Kaiser reaffirmed this on 14 August 1914, when he told the Supreme Command that running the war was its responsibility, not his.[5]

Professional competence within the technical core contrasted with an unpredictable cyclicality within the ruling circle. The entourage swung between pessimism, fatalism, and irrationality on the one hand and compromise, reasonableness, and passivity on the other. Cycles came and went. The point in the cycle at which a particular issue arose or was dealt with was very important. On different occasions, the same issue might be responded to in opposite ways. With a single exception within each cycle, different players became important at different times. The exception was the Kaiser, who was also the cause of the major cyclical movements.

By 1914 a dominant philosophical tone characterized the cyclical downturns of the few persons at the top levels of Prussian leadership. Within the government it was set by the Kaiser, within the GGS by the chief. Moltke may still be poorly understood, but it is clear at least that his horizon of thought was vastly different from that of his predecessor. In trying to combat materialism, to counter feelings of insecurity, he sought answers to the large macrocosmic questions on which more orthodox contemporary philosophies were ambiguous. He turned in that direction as a refuge from the bleak material emptiness which he sensed around him in Germany. Such feelings of cultural despair were not so unusual in the Second Reich; in fact, they were held by a wide

5. Elze, *Tannenberg*, p. 36; Hull, *Entourage*, p. 268.

variety of those who sensed the massive changes taking place in their society. Rudolf Steiner after all was an avid reader of Paul de Lagarde, Thomas Mann's *praeceptor Germaniae*.[6] In his attempt to believe in something, Moltke's thinking was influenced by a man who sprinkled the jargon of natural science throughout his writing and was presumed to have mastered the limited knowledge that modern learning could provide and to have gone beyond it to offer the far profounder knowledge that Moltke sought. As Adam von Moltke confided, his father was clearly under the influence of Steiner in 1914. Far from being a negative influence, it was very strongly positive. Steiner cast contemporary life in a cosmic time frame of world cycles and rebirth. 1900 was the age of the conscious soul, part of the post-Atlantean epoch, lasting from the early fifteenth century to the mid-thirty-sixth century. Individuals were repeating former experiences and previous lives. Emphasis was placed on the uniqueness of extrasensory experience. Those who achieved this were twice-born, having achieved a spiritual rebirth, a union with the cosmic spirit. The goal was catharsis, a purification experience.[7] Curiously enough these are almost exactly the same expressions often used to describe the feelings of many Germans at the time war was declared on 1 August 1914. The "ideas of 1914" describe just such a rebirth. Contrary to some interpretations this was not just a youth movement, it was a mass movement. The older generation also sought to participate. As such it touched base with theosophy, whose goal was to prepare for the second coming of Christ in the sixth cultural epoch, a program of inevitable events within a numinous fable.[8]

Moltke's "war is coming and the sooner the better" sentiment symbolizes the power and anxiety engendered when technology and philosophy reinforce each other. It can be read as a reaction to a purely technical situation – the GGS fear that the completion of the Russian railroad building program would force it to redraw its war plan completely – or it can be understood within a larger philosophical framework – expectation of that purifying experience which would test and validate Germanic culture. There were

6. Stern, *Cultural Despair*, pp. 118–19.

7. Oppenheim, *Other World*, p. 197; McDermott, *Steiner*, pp. 144, 169–70, 249, 266.

8. Paul Fussell, *The Great War and Modern Memory* (Oxford, 1975), chap. 1; Robert Wohl, *The Generation of 1914* (Cambridge, Mass., 1979), pp. 42ff.; McDermott, *Steiner*, p. 282.

of course other purely militaristic drives evident in German war planning circles. One thinks of the happy faces, handshakes, and congratulations among officers in the Prussian War Ministry on 31 July 1914. They were pleased that Germany had finally "taken the jump." But these motivational cycles rest on more complicated mental combinations. In late July 1914 personal cycles based on chemical or psychological imbalances became intermixed with cosmic world cycles looking toward a reviving purification experience. All in all it was a heady mixture. The network of persons influenced by Rudolf Steiner's ideas and impulses was broad. Moltke's daughter apparently had a child out of wedlock by her spiritist music teacher, a shock from which, it was said, Moltke never recovered. He could not get out from under the power of his wife's influences. Steiner affected Philipp Eulenburg's son Stigwart through Axel Varnbueler's Russian wife Natascha, also under the tutelage of Lissa Moltke. Eulenburg's daughter Augusta had married her spiritist tutor Edmund Jaroljmek. The chain goes on and on.[9]

Another element in this mixture, suggested by some historians, was the fear of a domestic social uprising. This anxiety was supposedly held by various members of the Prussian ruling elite – the Kaiser, Moltke, various corps commanders, and so forth. In this view Germany sought war in 1914 partly as a way out of a deepening domestic crisis which began with the Social Democratic Reichstag victories in the 1912 elections. Clearly Wilhelm and his advisors were uneasy. How strong a contributing factor these feelings were in influencing specific actions and orders during the July crisis is still an open question. They may have enhanced the general climate of fatalism, anxiety, and doubt.[10]

A third factor was the knowledge gap. By 1914 the technical aspects of the European war systems – transportation, communication, and bureaucratization – had created an imbalance in knowl-

---

9. Bernd Schulte, "Neue Dokumente zu Kriegsausbruch und Kriegsverlauf 1914: Berichte des Generals von Wenninger," *Militärgeschichtliche Mitteilungen* 25, no. 1 (1979): 10; Röhl, *Eulenburgs Korrespondenz*, 1: 47–53.

10. Berghahn, *Germany and the Approach of War in 1914*, chap. 9; Berghahn, *Modern Germany* (Cambridge, 1982), pp. 28–37; Wolfgang J. Mommsen, "Domestic Factors in German Foreign Policy before 1914" in James J. Sheehan, ed., *Imperial Germany* (New York, 1976), pp. 223ff.; Fischer, *Germany's Aims*, chap. 1; Schulte, *Deutsche Armee*, chap. 16. But compare Michael Howard, "Europe on the Eve of the First World War," in R.J.W. Evans and Hartmut Pogge von Strandmann, eds., *The Coming of the First World War* (Oxford, 1988), pp. 4–5.

edge. Decision makers did not know vital specifics of each others' mobilization processes. This knowledge gap worsened through a change in communications methods. During the July crisis of 1914 there were three main means of communication – human, written, and electric. Human means included personal face-to-face meetings of ambassadors, ministers, and generals with each other and with their sovereigns. There were many of these traditional forms of communication. They took a long time because of the required formalities. And because of the vagaries of human relationships, they created as many ambiguities as they resolved. Participants probably considered them more meaningful than other methods; however, in fact they were probably not. A second form was written communication, which included letters, reports, official memorandums, and newspaper accounts. There were many of these written forms, mostly printed, some handwritten. These also took time: secretaries had to write them, the post office or messengers had to deliver them. Unlike personal meetings, a response time was added. Again written communications often contained ambiguities, buffering ideas in veils of rhetoric.

A third form of communication was electric. This included both telegraph and telephone. Of these the telegraph usually resulted in a printed sheet, while the telephone was virtually instantaneous and left no paper trail, except perhaps in the form of notes made by speakers. During the July crisis, the volume of human and written communication decreased, the volume and velocity of electric messages rose dramatically, and in the end, changed from telegraphic to telephonic. Analyses of telegraphic communication in 1914 list several thousand telegrams sent between the major powers between 1 July and 4 August. Many of these were encoded. Of course the Kaiser did not telephone his fellow monarchs since there was no established format for such conversations. But Moltke, when he wanted to verify that Russian mobilization notices had indeed been publicly displayed on the morning of 31 July, telephoned the corps headquarters at Allenstein and told them to go out and get one of those red notices. In two hours an officer telephoned back to Berlin. He had gotten one and proceeded to read it over the phone.[11] The speed of communications changed

---

11. Ithiel de Sola Pool and Allan Kessler, "The Kaiser, the Tsar, and the Computer," *American Behavioral Scientist* 8, no. 9 (1965): 31–38, which lists 1,400 messages, but compare this with Imanuel Geiss, *Julikrise und Kriegsausbruch 1914*, 2 vols. (Hanover, 1963) which lists over 2,569; Trumpener, "War Premeditated?"

dramatically in the transfer from human or written methods to electric. On 5 July Kaiser Franz Joseph sent his personal emissary, armed with "signature letters," to Berlin. Following the tradition that one's signature was one's bond, this act constituted an almost direct meeting between sovereigns. The whole process, including travel and formal protocol, took several days. Moltke's telephone call, which yielded knowledge of the same quality and was equally valid for war planning purposes, was turned around in two hours.

The result of these differences in the speed and nature of communication was that it enhanced the knowledge gaps that already existed. In this case it became an important flaw because knowledge was at the heart of increasingly technology-based war planning. This gap existed at many levels both within and between governments. For practical purposes it had a strong impact on the way the decision-making processes worked or did not work. More philosophically, it was an example of cultural lag, a dysfunction between humans and machines in which the speed of change was out of phase with the human ability to think, consider, and decide. The most dramatic examples are the specific details the European military and political leadership lacked about their enemies' and allies' mobilization plans. Moltke did not know exactly how long Austrian mobilization would take; the German chancellor did not have the specific details of the German mobilization plan until late in the July crisis. From the uneven knowledge base which resulted, assumptions were made by diplomats, ministers, generals, and sovereigns upon which decisions for war or peace depended.

In addition to the knowledge gap there was also a distortion in the participants' perceptions of each other. Partial mobilizations could be perceived by opponents as full mobilizations because both the complexity of the national mobilization systems and the means of communicating alert status to friends and foes were based on new technologies, bureaucratic and electric systems only completed within the decade. By 1913 few realized the high degree of counteractivity inherent in the mobilization systems. Would the great powers be pulled into the maelstrom as a result of the Balkan Wars? In spite of several partial mobilizations and countermobilizations, earlier war crises in 1905, 1909, and 1911 had not drawn them in.

---

p. 82; cf. Spitzemberg, *Tagebuch der Baronin Spitzemberg*. pp. 409, 503, for a revealing discussion of the introduction of the telephone among the ranks of the Berlin nobility.

A fourth factor in operation was the foreign task environment. Anxiety and fear complemented by a social-Darwinist urge to compete and win seemed to dominate central European politics. However at times this was offset by opposite tendencies toward rational compromise and balance of power. By 1912, after three crises in six years, the mixture was becoming unstable. With the First Balkan War in October 1912, this threatening environment took a potentially dangerous turn. By 10 November Germany's Turkish ally had been pushed back on all fronts, losing all of its European territories except for Constantinople and a narrow strip of territory along the Straits. The problem created for European armies was that of the military alliance ratchet system where mutually reinforcing alerts could ultimately involve them all. For each level of threat there was a corresponding level of military alert.[12]

From the onset of the 1912 crisis, the Russian War Ministry and general staff had shown a disposition to play with fire. In October Russia had ordered a highly provocative "trial mobilization" in Poland, which required a wide calling up of reserves. Early in November the Russians decided to retain on active duty some four hundred thousand conscripts eligible for release. On 19 November Austria put its troops in Bosnia and Dalmatia on a war footing and began to bring its Galician garrisons at Krakow, Przemysl, and Lemberg up to war strength. At that moment the Austrian heir apparent, Archduke Franz Ferdinand, and the general staff chief, Hötzendorf, arrived in Berlin for consultations, seeking confirmation of Germany's pledge of 1909. On 22 November the tsar presided over a conference attended by War Minister Sukhomlinov and the commanders of the Warsaw and Kiev Military Districts. They decided to mobilize the entire Kiev district and part of the Warsaw district and to prepare to mobilize the Odessa district. The telegrams were prepared. Meanwhile, the German court and its Austrian visitors set off on a hunting trip. A few days after their return, the chancellor reaffirmed German support for Austria if, in the course of securing its vital interests, Austria were attacked by Russia. The same day the imperial naval staff met. Tirpitz presided and asked the assembled officers what could be done preliminary to mobilization.[13]

12. Bela Kiraly and Dimitrije Djordevich, eds., *East Central European Society and the Balkan Wars* (New York, 1987); Paul Bracken, *The Command and Control of Nuclear Forces* (New Haven, 1983), pp. 220–22.

13. L.C.F. Turner, *The Origins of the First World War*, (New York, 1970), pp.

On 26 November Moltke was reported nervous, with restless, ambitious ideas but without any will of his own, lacking physical energy. His enervation may have been caused by ambiguous intelligence in a crisis setting. Some sources suggest that the first two stages of the German alert plant, "security" and "political tension," were put into effect. Baronin Spitzemberg heard from a landowner on the Oder River that the family was preparing to move west with their children and silver: Silesia would be the first area given up in a war between Germany and Russia. But tangible evidence of the imminent danger of war was not forthcoming. Military attachés and consuls in Russia reported no mobilization regulations.[14] At the last minute Russian partial mobilization was called off. The tsar had said these were intended to be purely precautionary measures directed solely against Austria: he wished to avoid war with Germany. Prime Minister Kokovtzov persuaded the tsar that no matter what he chose to call the projected measures, a mobilization remained a mobilization, which would be countered by Russia's adversaries with actual war. As the officers and ministers departed, War Minister Sukhomlinov was rebuked for thoughtlessly taking Russia to the brink of war. He replied that there would be a war anyway. It was unavoidable and it would be better for Russia to begin it as soon as possible.[15]

These sentiments were echoed in Berlin scarcely two weeks later. At the meeting of 8 December Moltke apparently wanted to launch an immediate attack. He said there had not been a more favorable opportunity since the formation of the Triple Alliance and punctuated his demand with the words, "I believe war to be unavoidable and the sooner it comes the better." The Kaiser ordered the general staff and admiralty to prepare plans for an invasion of England. In spite of this verbal bellicosity, Germany played a very minor role in the military operations of the Ottoman Empire during the First and Second Balkan Wars. In the spring of

---

44–45; Stone, "Planning Russia's Mobilization," p. 254; *New Cambridge Modern History*, 8 vols. (Cambridge, 1969–74), 18: 335; Jarausch, *Enigmatic Chancellor*, p. 133; Lambi, *German Power*, p. 376.

14. Granier, "Deutsche Rüstungspolitik vor dem Ersten Weltkriege: General Franz Wandels Tagebuch," p. 142; Spitzemberg, *Tagebuch der Baronin Spitzemberg*, p. 553; Schulte, *Kriegsausbruch 1914*, p. 154.

15. Stone, "Planning Russia's Mobilization," p. 255; Fischer, *Illusions*, p. 162; John C.G. Röhl, "Admiral von Mueller and the Approach of War, 1911–1915," *Historical Journal* 12, no. 4 (1969): 660–64; cf. Ernest R. May, ed. *Knowing One's Enemies: Intelligence Assessment before the Two World Wars* (Princeton, 1984), pp. 17–32.

1913 Major von Lossow, a military advisor in Constantinople, wrote a devastating assessment of the Ottoman army according to which it was in terrible shape physically, morally, and intellectually. Another officer advised Berlin that it was rotten from top to bottom. Berlin distanced itself from this military liability. Not only did the Balkan Wars have the potential to trigger a European war among the larger alliance systems, but they also publicly humiliated a Triple Alliance member, further isolating Germany and Austria and strengthening their enemies. As trip hammer it did not work. As isolator it had strong impact.[16]

## The GGS as Organization: Patrimonial Bureaucracy

By the spring of 1914, after an eight-year period characterized by war crises every two years, the GGS was virtually up to war strength. Although these crises failed to produce war, they did help to mold semimodern and prepared war planning organizations, not only in Germany but elsewhere as well.

The size, space, and time dimensions of the Reich war plan in the spring of 1914 were daunting. Its core technology, the MTP, entailed moving over 3,000,000 men and 600,000 horses in 11,000 trains within 312 hours. Between 2 and 18 August the Hohenzollern Bridge at Cologne was to transmit 2,150 fifty-four-car trains at ten-minute intervals. Carried on 650 trains per day, more than 560 of which crossed the Rhine River, the west army would be ready for war operations against Belgium and France on the thirteenth mobilization day, the east army for operations against Russia on the tenth mobilization day. All the while the system was threatened by the intense pressure that if it did not deliver with the speed, regularity, and dependability called for by the plans, the outcome of the whole endeavor, and with it the fate of empire, was in jeopardy. This was a modern management problem approached by technical specialists working in a bureaucratic setting.[17]

By 1914 the GGS was organized like a large business organization. There were five managements levels: (1) the chief and his control chancellery, the Central Section; (2) the deputy chiefs; (3)

16. May, *Knowing One's Enemies*, pp. 17–32; Trumpener, "German Military Involvement in the First Balkan War," in Bela Kiraly and Dimitrije Djorderich, eds., *East Central European Society and the Balkan Wars* (New York, 1987), pp. 346–62.

17. Staabs, *Aufmarsch*, p. 41.

the section chiefs; (4) the branch directors; and (5) the bureau supervisors. The Central Section was the GGS office manager. This meant that it regulated day-to-day business, supervising and directing personnel, ordering officers for attachment or temporary assignment, and taking care of financial matters. It also included Section IIIb for special intelligence operations. The first two levels worked under the direct supervision of the chief. Section, branch, and bureau heads were responsible to the Central Section for the orderly and timely completion of business.[18]

Deputy chief one included the RRS and the Second and Fourth Sections. The Second Section handled mobilization and plans. The Fourth Section had responsibility for foreign and domestic fortifications and pioneer and artillery questions. Deputy chiefs two and four comprised the language sections; their work was intelligence gathering. The Third Section dealt with France and England and their colonies, Egypt, Afghanistan, and Thailand; the Fourth Section researched Italy and its colonies, Abyssinia, Switzerland, Belgium, the Netherlands, Luxembourg, Spain, Portugal, America, and the German colonies; the First Section dealt with Russia, Persia, Turkey, Norway, Sweden and Denmark; the Tenth Section examined Austria-Hungary, Rumania, Bulgaria, Serbia, Greece, and Montenegro. Deputy chief three was in charge of GGS publications. By 1914 this was a large job and necessitated what was essentially a forms and publications office. Its responsibilities included reports such as the winter half-year activities of the army corps, the printing of appropriate regulations, the Oriental Seminar, language training, and translation and translators. There was some sharing of these tasks with the appropriate unit within the War Ministry.

18. Der Chef des Generalstabs der Armee von Moltke, *Geschäftsordnung für den Grossen Generalstab und die Landesaufnahme* (Berlin, 1913), "For Official Use Only – Restricted to GGS," p. 43; Jany, *Preußische Armee*, 4: 294–96; *MGFA Handbuch*, 3: 69–72; Bergh, *Das deutsche Heer*, pp. 167–82; Osten-Sacken, *Preußens Heer*, 3: 489–96; *Militär-Adreßbuch*. The whole question of the introduction of modern management techniques into German economic life and the problem of which sector, public or private, pioneered in this, is an area that requires research. Two aspects of these modern techniques whose importance we have seen within the RRS of the GGS, the prominence of engineering ideas and the concern for work capacity (Leistungsfähigkeit), figured prominently in German debates on these matters during the years 1902 to 1906. Cf. Homberg, "Anfänge des Taylorsystems in Deutschland," pp. 170–84; in 1980 Jürgen Kocka wrote that little research had been undertaken into the organizational structures and other procedures through which top-level managers administered large, integrated, and diversified enterprises. Kocka, "The Rise of the Modern Industrial Enterprise in Germany," p. 98.

Deputy chief five was in charge of military history. Branch one dealt with the hundred years prior to 1914, branch two with the period from the founding of the Brandenburg-Prussian army to 1815. In addition to voluminous publication of books and journals, this section acted as army censor. Works on military history written by Prussian officers on active duty were submitted to the GGS for review, "examination on behalf of his majesty the Kaiser," as it was called. One of the GGS's claims to legitimacy was based on its authority in military history. No Prussian officer could publish a work on military history without first getting GGS approval. Branch two also had charge of the war archives and the library, those materials having finally been located atop the Brauhausberg in Potsdam. Both archive and library were large, containing documents, maps, books, and journals from the previous three centuries.[19] Finally there was the very large Land Survey with its three parts, Trigonometic, Topographic, and Cartographic, its bureaus for aerial photography and photogrammetrics, and its plan room, map archive, and warehouse. This section had many hundred workers.

Communications within the GGS had become a system of formal information control. This included verbal, written, telegraphic, and telephonic communications. Reporting to the chief of the GGS was organized along the lines of reporting to the Kaiser. Mondays were reserved for deputy chief four and Section IIIB; Tuesdays for deputy chief two; Wednesdays and Thursdays were free because the chief of the GGS reported to the Kaiser; Fridays were for deputy chiefs three and five; Saturdays for deputy chief one. The mobilization Section and the RRS had no set day, but reported several times a week.[20] The Central Section communications office worked on Sundays, holidays, and the Kaiser's birthday. It operated the twenty-four-hour electric communications center; ready to alert the whole

---

19. Moltke, *Geschäftsordnung*, pp. 3, 44; Otto von Moser, *Ernsthafte Plaudereien über den Weltkrieg* (Stuttgart, 1925), p. 34; Dorothea Groener-Geyer, "Die Odyssee der Groener Papiere," *Die Welt als Geschichte* 14 (1959): 56. Bombed in early March 1945, this archive was badly damaged. Copies of GGS documents sent out to the federal states and saved in their archives, like the Bayerisches Hauptstaatsarchiv, Kriegsarchiv, and the Staatsarchiv, Stuttgart, have assumed importance as a result of this destruction. Historians who have used Prussian documents saved in the south German archives are Bernt Schulte (*Deutsche Armee* and *Kriegsausbruch 1914*) and Emily Oncken, *Panthersprung*.

20. Moltke, *Geschäftsordnung*, p. 11.

army by means of the telegraph and telephone system. Located in room 86 of the Königsplatz building on the ground floor near the stairway, it was run by the Military Telegraph Section and was open twenty-four hours a day, seven days a week, 365 days a year. It may have been the first continuous peacetime "communications room" in military history. Wired into Post Office 40 at the Lehrter Railroad Station and to the Main Telegraph Office, it also had a pneumatic system connected to Post Office 40. A telephone central board completed this system.

In 1914 a major expansion of the military communication system was underway. Prussia had begun to equip its border fortresses as radio stations for cross border transmissions. The main stations were Metz, Straßburg, and Cologne for the west front and Königsberg for the east front, each the site of an army corps headquarters and a railroad LC. They were equipped with two-kilowatt Telefunken transmitters with a range of 150 to 180 miles and were envisioned as the long-range communication link from the main headquarters to the attacking armies in the field. This system worked satisfactorily; however, the responsibility for establishing communications always lay with subordinate units placed under the command of tactical officers whose primary goal was march discipline, not communications. By 1914 there were twenty-three wire and fourteen radio companies, and the plan to use them included mobilization of eighty thousand men from the Reich Post and Telegraph Department. The genesis of a modern communication system was half completed by the summer of 1914.[21] Standards of communication efficiency, clarity, and correctness were explicit. For example, correspondence between the GGS and the Reich chancellery was to follow the form: greeting, statement of purpose, report, request, closing, salutation. To be avoided were foreign words, phrases such as "the Royal GGS hereby informs . . .," and the use of Latin script in place of German. In closing, officers on temporary assignment were to indicate their regular duty unit, not the GGS.

Each deputy chief had a chancellery which kept a registry of written materials received or dispatched by its sections. The chancellery maintained punctual and orderly transaction of the business of the unit by controlling this information flow. Like the army

---

21. Jany, *Preußische Armee*, 4: 322; Evans, "Strategic Signal Communications," pp. 34–42.

corps, each chancellery kept a meticulous catalogue of its document holdings – listings of current army regulations, a letter book indicating date, contents, and action for all correspondence, the schedule indicating the action time for each piece of work, the book of GGS regulations, the list of published documents held, the account books, a maneuver letter book, and so on. Above this level the flow of paperwork through the GGS was controlled and directed by the registrar of the Central Section. Its procedures allowed the cycle time and work capacity of each subunit to be monitored. Work was scrutinized in terms of the amount of time it was supposed to take to complete and return once assigned to the appropriate subunit. Each assigned piece of work was logged into the registry, logged out to a section, branch, or bureau, then logged back through the registry with its disposition recorded. By 1911 this process was speeded up by the use of typewriters.

The physical movement of documents within the GGS was carried out by a courier service. The master courier supervised the performance by the chancellery attendants, officials, and orderlies of their duties. He received the mail and distributed it to the appropriate office, bureau, or section and supervised the outgoing mail, whether to the regular post or within Berlin through the military post or military messenger. Maps and materials required by those officers living within the GGS buildings were delivered and picked up by the officials, with classified documents and maps released under a special sign-out system. There was a document carriage to enable couriers to distribute materials not only within the GGS but within the Berlin area. It stood ready to pick up maps and packets from the homes of officers and to forward them to the GGS building. Driver and couriers wore uniforms, were told not to stop except on official business, and reported to the chief of the GGS adjutants and to the master courier upon completion of their tasks.

Key and security control were practiced at night. After 10 P.M. officers who lived within the building or were assigned to the GGS were checked and entered their name, unit, time, and leave card number in the visitor's book. Unknown persons who wanted to visit officials living within the GGS building were escorted. A key register noted to whom keys were given and when they were taken and returned.

Very precise instructions existed for classified materials. The war plans themselves were given out only to specific officers or officials. Those who wanted access had to have a "need to know." All mobilization documents were returned, at the latest on Saturday evening at the close of business, to the register of the Central Section. The GGS had established a basic classified document policy in which the Central Section was the repository in which documents classified "top secret" or "secret" were stored and from which they were loaned and returned.[22] Two conclusions are suggested by these information controls. First, modern document classification may have originated with the German army prior to World War I. Second, if the papers from the RRS are a valid indication, this system developed only during the last two decades before 1914. The first classifications, "secret" and "for official use only," appear on RRS and War Academy documents in the early 1890s. By 1911 "top secret," "restricted access," and "confidential" also appear. Although there is no hint of personnel security checks or background investigations, the evolution of such a system indicates the development of a mentality among war planners which complements the social Darwinism and general closed-mindedness of the military prior to 1914. Document classification and access to it helped to create a particular mind set – there was a secret to victory: it was information and someone else, the "enemy," wanted it.

In summary, the GGS by 1914 resembled in many respects the prototypical bureaucracy sketched out by an early twentieth-century student of organizations, Max Weber. Although Weber did not directly study the Prussian military, he was familiar with the nature of German bureaucracy from his own experience. In addition, he described a society in transition from traditional to modern. The GGS we have been describing was partly a modern rational bureaucracy and partly a traditional royal form. In this framework, Max Weber's main categories are worthy of comment.[23]

(1) Many jurisdictional areas were bureaucratically specified, yet others depended upon who filled the office. For example, the regular activities of the RRS required personnel to be distributed in a fixed way. At the same time, Moltke's choice as chief of the

22. Moltke, *Geschäftsordnung*, pp. 51, 71–73, 76, 81, 102, 112; "Mobilmachungs-akten dürfen nur an Offiziere oder etatmäßige Bureaubeamte derjenigen Dienst-stelle verausgabt werden, zu deren Ressortarbeiten die Akten gehören," p. 57; Groener Papers, roll 19, no. 177.

23. This discussion is based on H. Gerth and Mills, *From Max Weber: Essays in Sociology*, pp. 196–204; Henderson and Parsons, *Max Weber: The Theory of Social and Economic Organization*, pp. 323–29; Michels, *Political Parties*, pp. 390–418.

GGS was a patrimonial arrangement made by the sovereign. Although within sections and in the GGS as a whole there were still some choices in which the division of labor was not fixed but depended on assignments made by the chief, this was less and less the case. By 1914 the GGS had virtually lost this feature. It had become a large impersonal organization. Except for a few key roles, such as that of chief of the railroad and mobilization sections, the chief worked through men he no longer knew.

(2) The organization of offices generally followed the principle of hierarchy yet here and there the patrimonial principle was evident. Each lower office was controlled and supervised by a higher one. At the same time the older patrimonial principle worked: authority relations were diffuse and often based on personal loyalty. Commanding generals could request chiefs of staff. Army corps were often said to reflect the character of their commanders, to the point that certain corps were known by their last names. The Kaiser continued to receive his senior generals on New Year's Day and to greet each personally.

(3) An intentionally established system of abstract rules governed many official decisions and actions, yet some of the most important were made outside these rules. Decisions were recorded in permanent files. For its major business the GGS clearly operated on this basis. Yet there were always exceptions. The process of GGS war games and rides always concluded with a final summation delivered by the chief. Often these were extemporaneous remarks, with only one officer present to write them down. Yet this was the most important part of the activity. The same applied to what could be called imperial war councils; those occasions when the Kaiser summoned his closest advisors to discuss war, such as the meeting of 8 December 1912. The only notes historians have for this meeting are those of Admiral von Mueller. A third example are the audiences between the chief of the GGS and the Kaiser. For Schlieffen, there were several hundred of these, for Moltke more than a hundred. That they took place is recorded in the *Flügeladjutant* records at Merseburg.[24] The content of some of them is known from various other sources, such as Schlieffen's letters. The format presumably followed the GGS prescription for communication – greeting, statement of purpose, report, request,

---

24. Katherine Lerman used them in her unpublished dissertation, "Bernhard von Bülow and the Governance of Germany, 1897–1909," to suggest how often the Kaiser saw various members of his entourage.

closing, and salutation – but the exact content was not laid down or recorded afterward. Again, these are official actions in which the chief of state sanctioned a fundamental instrument of state business, the war plan. That the Kaiser approved the war plan up to 1905 is clear. He participated in the GGS operational war games in the period 1899 to 1904. He clearly knew the most intimate details of the Schlieffen Plan, for example, the march through Belgium. Thereafter, as the Kaiser withdrew from leading summer maneuvers and absented himself from GGS war games and rides, his knowledge of the specifics of the war plan may have been reduced or blurred. If so, it happened at precisely the time when the war plan itself became more complicated and forms of communication between states were speeded up.[25]

(4) The tools, equipment and materials belonged to the office, not to the office holder. Personal property was clearly separated from official property and working space from living quarters. Yet the chief and other officers continued to reside in service apartments within the main GGS building. Like the sovereign, this holdover from a patrimonial system meant that there was little separation of personal from official. Schlieffen was often in the map room at 7 A.M. or at his service desk after 10 P.M. Moltke and his family resided in surroundings familiar to them from having lived there from 1881 to 1891.

(5) Officers were generally selected and promoted on the basis of technical qualification reports. However, both appointment and promotion continued in very traditional ways at three critical stages. The colonel commanding a regiment had to accept the initial officer appointment. This was then confirmed by the Military Cabinet. Personnel records included detailed personal comments on each assignment. As mentioned in chapter 5, the officer qualification report in 1902 had eliminated two very feudal provisions. However, other factors such as family background, political and social views, personality, and character counted. Who an officer was, in contrast to what he could do, remained important.

(6) Employment by the organization constituted a full-time career for an officer, yet he could always be removed at the pleasure of the ruler. A full-time employee could look forward, after a trial period of two to three years, to a lifelong career in the

25. Zoellner, "Schlieffens Vermächtnis," p. 45; Raulff, *Zwischen Machtpolitik und Imperialismus*, pp. 191–93.

army, followed by a pension and perhaps employment in a govern-ment office. However, he also served at the discretion of the king. Various actions, such as supporting Social Democratic legislation in the Reichstag or running for election as members of certain parties, could disqualify the officer and cause him to be stripped of his commission. In this sense he served at the pleasure of the ruler or his Military Cabinet, who reserved to themselves the definition of an officer's conduct.[26]

Weber's definition of organization has been criticized at those points where his formal criteria fail because of the ambiguous or dynamic nature of the Wilhelmian state. In Weber's day on-the-job experience and formal education were both discrete sources of technical competence. However the GGS, and especially its RRS, was a world of minute specialization supported by prolonged formal and continuing education. The educational and training processes were not separated from the work setting, but were a part of it.

If standardized procedures, bureaucratic esprit de corps, tra-ditional work cycles, and military history unified Prussian war planning processes by 1914, there was one additional factor which should be not be forgotten. That is personal relationships. Even in a large organization such as the peacetime active army, not to mention the war-mobilized army which was five or six times larger, personal relationships counted. How much and where is open to question. Central to the war planning processes of Prussia and the Reich was the GGS and its system. Through that system had passed most of the 1914 leadership of the Reich army. This is evident at the top levels, that is, general officer and above. How widely this personal network spread among the lower ranks is something to consider. The tooth-to-tail ratio in this army, peacetime or war-mobilized, remained very low. At each level of organization the few commanded the many. Furthermore age was an important criterion in officer selection. One source on officer ages in 1914 estimated that men averaged nineteen years in company grade and eleven in field grade assignments. Undoubtedly by that time many had retired. Generals were seldom younger than fifty, corps com-manders usually over fifty-five. Army commanders in the field were between sixty and seventy.[27] Did these men know each other?

26. Kitchen, *German Officer Corps*, p. 49; Scott, *Organizations*, pp. 68–69, 305–9.
27. Elze, *Tannenberg*, p. 2.

One kind of evidence to answer this question is found in pure numbers. For example, if the active army in July 1914 numbered 800,582 and its officers 30,741, that means that 3.8% were officers. The war-mobilized army in 1914 consisted of 3,822,450 men, and 119,754 officers: officers constituted 3.1%. In 1909 the total number of general officers for the Prussian active infantry, the largest segment of the army, was 151 with 30 full generals. Having served forty years in the same organization, these men undoubtedly knew each other.[28] A second kind of evidence, suggestive if not conclusive, comes from the war dairies of 1914. Each unit commander down to brigade level was required to keep a daily diary during war mobilization, similar to those kept during maneuvers. Although many of these have been lost, a number still exist. That these might be an important source has been mostly overlooked by historians. Karl Litzmann, *Generalleutnant*, age sixty-four in 1914, had been retired for nine years. His mobilization assignment was as commander of Rear Area Supply Region No. 3, with headquarters in Dresden. Readers may recall from chapter 3 that he knew all the main players – his own chief of staff, the commander and chief of staff of the 3d Army, and each chief of staff for its assigned corps, the 12th, 13th, and 14th Reserve Corps and the 21st Prussian. The question is of course how typical this was in the army of 1914. It is possible it was typical and customary. If so, it was certainly a strength.[29]

## Railroads and Integrative Planning

By 1914 the GGS relied upon a variety of mechanisms to vertically integrate the Reich army for war mobilization. There were two

28. Elze, *Tannenberg*, p. 15; Jany, *Preußische Armee*, 4: 329; Deist, "Zur Geschichte des preußischen Offizierkorps, 1888–1918"; Martin van Creveld, *Fighting Power* (Westport, 1982), pp. 47–51.

29. Litzmann, *Lebenserinnerungen*, 1: 184–85; war diaries were officially required from the first day of mobilization or of departure from home quarters. Information to be entered included all daily occurrences, such as marches, engagements, quarters or bivouacs, state of the weather, and so on. When the war ended the original was retained by the staff of the unit, but a certified copy was forwarded to the War Ministry, where details of supply and equipment were abstracted, with the copy itself deposited in the GGS war archive. Schellendorff, *Duties*, pp. 293–99; examples of war diaries in the BAMA include those of Gerhard Tappen, chief of the GGS Mobilization and Plans Department, Hans Hartwig von Beseler, commander of the 3d Reserve Corps, and Karl von Einem, commander of the 7th Corps.

kinds of integrating mechanisms, long-term and short-term. Let us describe the long-term methods first. These mechanisms included the RRS and LCs, the general staff system, the District Commands, the Horse Purchase Commissions, the artillery and supply depots, the Depot Administration of the Railroad Brigades, the Field Offices, and the Clothing and Food Offices. We will not deal with them all, and several have already been described. The criterion of selection is based upon the war plan. Departments and organizations responsible for executing part of the war plan were primary integrating agents. Techniques within these mechanisms included (1) standardized rules and procedures that channeled the actions of each department in a direction consistent with the actions of others; (2) plans and schedules integrating the actions of separate units; (3) meetings of groups and individuals who by mutual adjustment integrated their respective parts of the war plan.[30]

By 1914 the RRS was the major integrating mechanism for Prussian war planning. As Moltke wrote to Minister of the Interior Delbrück in May 1914, "In terms of functional reliability and work capacity, no single component of the war planning system is as important as the railroad segment." These five terms – "functional reliability, work capacity, component, system, segment" – reveal Moltke's conception of war planning. These are engineering phrases and describe an industrial process composed of segments and components and measured by means of capacity and reliability. Functional reliability suggests a high level of certainty measured numerically. Work capacity implies size and time factors: how much work could be done within a given time and space. "Component" and "segment" refer to small parts of a larger whole. "System" is that whole.[31]

The system was centered in the RRS with its eighty assigned officers. Also in Berlin was the director of the Prussian railroads, who was simultaneously Prussian minister of public works. Since this official often, prior to his civil appointment, had been head of the GGS Railroad Section, the three units – GGS Railroad, Prussian railroad, and Prussian public works – worked closely together. In addition, each one was decentralized in the same way. The RRS had twenty-six LCs outside Berlin, eighteen of them placed in locations where Prussian railroad divisions and corps commands

30. Child, *Organization*, p. 127.
31. Rahne, *Mobilmachung*, pp. 125–26.

were located. Corps commands were the primary administrative and operational level below the GGS. Railroad divisions were the primary operating unit of the Prussian railroad system. Line Commands were directly subordinate to the RRS. To each location, command, division, and corps was delegated power and influence. Outside of Prussia roughly the same configuration applied. The chief of the RRS was responsible for all the railroad lines which were to be used to execute the military travel plan, for railroad technical matters, and for leading the execution of the MTP. He worked for the GGS chief, but also with the directors of all German railroads and ministers of public works. For the GGS he was responsible that the German railroad system was ready to execute the war plan, for drawing up the MTP, and educating the railroads in its execution. He cooperated with civilian agencies in jointly maintaining and upgrading buildings, track, and facilities. As such he was one of the few GGS officers who regularly appeared before various Reichstag committees.

The power and influence of the chief of the RRS stemmed from the same source as that of the chief of the GGS: both were charged with execution of the war plan. The chief of the GGS was responsible for the plan as a whole, the chief of the RRS for its keystone, the MTP. At the declaration of war, the chief of the RRS became the director of the German railroads. LCs had military, therefore supreme, jurisdiction over the railroad systems and traffic. At mobilization officers were added to each LC: a series of station commanders, divisional supply and assembly officers, and loading commanders. The Line Command was in charge of all of these. Since its duties paralleled those of the Railroad Directorate, its organization, procedures, and ethos did as well. How important the LCs had become by May 1914 is indicated by the fact that Moltke suggested delegating to them the execution of the regional economic war plan for the country as a whole. Instead of concentrating functions in Berlin, he proposed to assign to each LC representatives of the commercial, agricultural, and trade departments of the Interior Ministry. Moltke envisioned this as an extension of normal civilian mobilization measures.[32] One reason for the

---

32. Groener Papers, roll 8, no. 35, letters to Reichsarchiv president of 11 November 1923, 3 December 1926, and 14 January 1929; Zilch, *Die Reichsbank und die finanzielle Kriegsvorbereitung*, pp. 88–89. Many obscure points are raised and discussed in the correspondence between the Reichsarchiv and various participants in German military planning and operations, 1914–1918. Copies of some of this

broad span of control of the RRS is that, unlike other GGS or War Ministry bureaus, it worked closely with the two largest civilian bureaucracies, the 774,000 officials of the railroads and the more than 300,000 in the post office, which included the telegraph and telephone systems. To these civilian officials, the authority and prestige of the army and particularly of the GGS was assumed. Many had served as NCOs or were reserve officers.[33]

The main form the war plan took was detailed at two levels, the GGS and army corps levels. At the GGS level the plan specified where the eight armies, thirty-seven corps, and ninety divisions were to go: seven armies to the west front, five distributed north of Metz and two south; one army on the east front distributed across East Prussia, with one corps to the north, one at the center, and one south. Corps war plans were distributed in blue-covered booklets describing at which of the thirty-one railroad collection points the corps was to board the trains. The link between these two levels, the army level concentrations and the corps level collection points, was the MTP: it specified times and places at which the corps units were loaded onto and off of the trains.

Within the RRS studies were continually done with the purpose of efficiently arranging the space for and decreasing the time of the MTP. As these studies were completed, they were carefully and strenuously proofed to ascertain that these two goals had in fact been achieved. Not only periods of twenty-four hours, but periods of less than twelve hours were important. An express train could travel from Berlin to the east border in a few hours and to the west border in a day. Even a war loaded corps could move from coastal Pomerania to the west front in fourteen hours. Every hour counted. The thirty minutes allocated to on-load or off-load a

---

correspondence, which must have been large judging from the numbering system used to keep track of it, are in the Groener Papers. Since the Reichsarchiv was writing and publishing its multivolume history of World War I, its members tried to investigate some of the controversies which appeared in the newspapers and journals of the times, writing to ask participants to clarify and document statements and positions. This was done in a systematic and objective manner using numbered questionnaires; the replies usually referenced the exact dated questionnaire and the numbered point in it. The process must have been very extensive because some of the typed correspondence appears on a form letter, with blank spaces left to be filled in according to whom the questionnaire was to be addressed. Often this correspondence refers to primary source documents, such as letters, war diaries, and other documents destroyed during World War II. One example is the discussion between Krafft von Delmensingen, Ernst Kabisch, and Groener over the initial combat in Alsace-Lorraine in August 1914. Groener Papers, roll 8, no. 35.

33. Rahne, *Mobilmachung*, p. 128; Gillis, *Prussian Bureaucracy*, pp. 203–4.

fifty-four-car military unit train were precisely monitored. From this process came proposals for the direction and loading of the army corps which were passed to the Mobilization Section, partly in writing and partly verbally. To these the Mobilization Section made counterproposals or stated its specific requirements. After much reworking and many conversations, the fundamentals of the war plan were laid down in a written proposal by the RRS and in a verbal presentation by the Mobilization Section to the chief of the GGS. In contrast to Schlieffen's system, where he had worked directly with the RRS chief, there were now three different levels of authority, the first two of which formulated the war plan to be presented to Moltke, who was the third level.[34]

By 1912 the RRS's maps, charts, and tables were technical in a way and to a degree hitherto unknown in German military planning. The highly detailed flow charts made to illustrate the MTP provide one example. For each LC these charts showed precisely how much traffic could be handled in both directions within a given period of time. Work capacity appeared in the form of a visual mathematical image precise in its layers of time and space. The MTP was produced in nine sheets, one each for Schleswig (I), Essen (II), Berlin (III), Danzig (IV), Mainz (V), Leipzig (VI), Breslau (VII), Straßburg (VIII), and Munich (IX). These technical segment charts illustrated the time, space, and size ratios in the exact mathematical language of engineering. It indicated supply points, hospital locations, transfer points, and the exact times for each shipment along the transportation path. These graphs were essentially industrial flow charts in which the natural and human aspects had receded into insignificance. They measured space and size in terms of time. Their scale was determined by timetable, not by the land to map ratio. Indeed, there was no map scale or legend. Instead, these maps indicated work capacity, measured mathematically – the size and space which could be covered in a given time. These maps were uniformly classified secret, to be returned to the sender.[35]

34. Groener Papers, roll 8, no. 35. Groener letter of 7 March 1924.
35. Groener Papers, roll 19, nos. 172, 176. The graphics of engineering design and construction provides the language used to communicate this engineering language to others. The language of graphics is written in the form of drawings which represent the size, shape, and specifications of physical reality. These railroad diagrams resemble logarithmic charts in which one quantity varies directly as the same power of another quantity, for example, the distance-time relationship of a moving body. Thomas E. French and Charles J. Vierck, *Engineering Drawing and Graphic Technology*, 12th ed. (New York, 1978), pp. ix, 4, 410.

A second example were the top secret echelon tables which comprised the detail sheets of the MTP. These huge forty-four- by thirty-six-inch sheets were as physically impressive as the work capacity flow charts. Called "Travel and March Tables," they were blank forms printed up by the GGS which listed in a forty-column tabular format virtually everything about the specific execution of the war plan – where and when each troop unit was to assemble and the number of officers, men, horses, guns, wagons, and supplies. Each trip was numbered. For example, a squadron and a half of the 9th Guard Ulan (10 officers, 525 men, 250 horses, and 4 guns) comprised trip number 21500, which required fifty-one cars. Its initial station was Demmin and it was to be on-loaded at 6:15 A.M. on the third mobilization day. This unit train took a two-station ride on a single track local line through Neu-Brandenburg and Straßburg Ulan to Stettin, where it made its entrance into the main line transportation path. The transportation path stretched down to the southeast, toward the off-loading point at Cammenz, south of Breslau and just north of the Polish border. The unit arrived at 5:59 A.M. on the fourth mobilization day. Mobilization day time began at 12:00 P.M. Warm food, coffee with cold food, station supplies, water for horses – all were marked on the MTP tables. Stops for food were limited to forty-five minutes, for watering the horses, to fifteen minutes. Shortening of these times due to technical problems was only possible with the permission of the transportation director. In other words, each military unit was technically under the command of the RRS line commander while in that LC's track segment. Two categories of special transportation involved movements carried out at the time of "imminent danger of war" and those for "border corps reinforcement." In both cases these trips had special designations and numbers and were transmitted in code.[36]

There were two additional and significant features of the MTP: the definition of transportation paths and the production of MTP amendment sheets. The MTP visually divided the country into huge transportation paths, literally swaths cut across Germany east to west and north to south. These paths were very clearly visible on the echelon tables; for example, to the west front were fourteen transportation paths which were scheduled to carry eleven thousand shipments. Second, the echelon tables were time

36. BHSA, Generalstabs 445/11 and 657/17-Mobilmachungs-Fahrliste 1914/15.

validated and constantly upgraded. On each sheet was stamped the phrase "good from ——" with a date. They were issued in Berlin six months before they went into effect. This lag reflected the amount of time needed to redraw the sheets, print them up, and send them out to troop units. Each phase of production required time, a process that indicates the final transition from the batch production of the 1880s to the standardized, continuous flow production of 1914. Tables were issued in four colors – grey, blue, yellow, and white, one copy for each using level. The basic MTP came out on 1 April after which changes and revisions, noted on echelon amendment sheets, followed. Revision of these tables was an industry in itself. For example, in 1911, the original MTP tables for the Württemberg War Ministry, LC K1, were dated 1 April. By October 1911, six months later, amendment numbers 417 to 502 had been issued.[37]

To master the complexities of the MTP, the RRS had become a formidable educational institution. Following Schlieffen's remark that he would take the most promising graduates of the War Academy and complete their education within the GGS, the RRS, with its huge complement of men both in Berlin and in the LCs, had become a school in itself. All newly assigned officers went through a series of all-day lectures introducing them to the main work of the section. In addition to this orientation, the RRS also offered what were in effect continuing education classes to upgrade personnel on new technical details. LC personnel worked to master the details of the MTP as it pertained to their track segment. According to Groener, this training process was continuous.

By 1911 the RRS was leading the most complex, highly technological war games of any GGS unit, which were also the most closely tied to the actual war plan. The games were complex because they entailed at least 4 LCs, each one interactive with the others, and because they were serial, extending over a period of days, weeks, or months. Serial continuation allowed each segment to be evaluated in terms of work capacity. They were technological because they involved not only the largest governmental bureaucracies in the Reich, the railroad, telegraph, and postal services, but because they used the most modern electric technology, the telegraph and telephone, and were communicated in code, with

---

37. Michael Nuwer, "From Batch to Flow: Production Technology and Work-Force Skills in the Steel Industry, 1880–1920," *Technology and Culture* 29 (October 1988): – 808–38. BHSA, M. Kr. 1581, 1582.

classified and controlled access. Afterward they were analyzed part by part, and the results were transmitted back to the LCs. As with all war games, they tested out new ideas, evaluated portions of the existing war plan, and measured players against each other.

These war games combined four qualities: operational realism, abstraction, convenience, and accessibility. In terms of operational realism, paper war games were considered the least realistic, map exercises second, and field exercises the most realistic. In this case, because the movement of troops was telephonically and telegraphically simulated through procedures identical to the war plan, there was a high degree of realism. Normal civilian rail traffic in various ways simulated military traffic, with differences between them those of degree, not kind. In executing the MTP, many of the same actions took place as in peacetime civilian traffic, only in much greater volume. The two fundamental ways to increase output within an industrial system are to increase the size of the system and to increase the velocity of the throughputs within it. Both of these occurred in the MTP. The rail system was thickened because it was devoted totally to military traffic. In this thickened system the change from peace to war meant above all increased velocity. Railroad war games retained a high degree of abstraction, yet because of the communication process and because the railroad system in war essentially increased its velocity over the same tracks, the level of abstraction did not change, but only increased in its magnitude factor. As for convenience and accessibility, since the railroad games were conducted electrically with the actual paperwork often following later, they were the easiest and most rapid to conduct. Thus, if a map exercise failed to simulate reality very closely, if the GGS rides came a bit closer and large-scale maneuvers even more, the railroad war game combined the most realistic elements of all of these with the greatest ease of execution. It was, in a sense, the highest form of game. Railroad war games also allowed for fractionalization of problems, breaking them into parts so that each could be analyzed separately. It might be asked how many trials were needed for the RRS to have some sense of the uncertainties or problems within a particular war plan. It is unclear whether the RRS used the games in this way, but if they did, they had a sound base from which to work: during Moltke's eight years there were over a hundred such trials.[38]

38. Groener Papers, roll 19, no. 172; Allen, *War Games*, pp. 4–26.

Let us consider the example of April 1914. Classified top secret, the game was conducted over a several-week period. To begin the exercise copies of the RRS train reserve orders, classified "secret-registered," were sent to each of the twenty-six LCs. To do this, the RRS made forty copies of the original document. This allows us to glimpse the volume of communication between the RRS and the LCs in the ten-day period from 13 to 26 March. If they were all three pages, as this one was, and were sent to all twenty-six LCs, the total amounted to more than one hundred pages. And this was only the start. Intended to be put into effect immediately after the main mobilization transportation (the MTP) was substantially completed, these orders indicate that the RRS planned for fluid, quick-reacting movements behind the war front. In addition to the normal task of replacing killed and wounded, the RRS expected to move seven complete corps and seven divisions, including their horses, equipment, and supplies, using over 2,700 cars. Empty trains to execute these orders were to be arranged in grouped units. Locomotives and personnel were to be ready to move quickly to on-loading stations.[39] The purpose of the April 1914 exercise was to war game four possible scenarios for these trains.

The first problem involved a Russian attack in Galicia which pushed German forces in Upper Silesia back behind the Oder River along the line Ratibor to Oppeln. East of the Oder there were only Landwehr troops at Namelau and Groß Wartenberg. Heavy Russian forces were located at Pless, Gleiwitz, and Lublinitz. A decisive battle appeared about to begin. Meanwhile on the west front, French forces in Alsace-Lorraine had been decisively defeated on the twenty-first mobilization day. On the morning of the twenty-second mobilization day the high command directed the chief of the field railroad to transport the 11th Corps, which stood south of St. Avold, to Silesia. Whether it was to go to the right or left bank of the Oder River was not yet determined, thus off-loading sites remained open. Transportation was to begin on the evening of the twenty-third mobilization day. Game participants were told to set up the whole movement in large and small detail, with echelon tables, encoded communications, and appropriate liaisons with corps commands. The solution entailed the main west to east transportation path from LC P, Saarbrücken,

---

39. Groener Papers, roll 19, no. 177.

through LC C, Frankfurt, to LC Y, Erfurt, thence via Halle to LC E, Dresden, then on to LC L, Breslau. From there the corps was divided into three parts and moved southeast along a complicated network of secondary lines which crisscrossed the rugged mountain terrain in southeastern Silesia.

In the second problem, French forces had invaded Alsace-Lorraine, and German forces had retreated to the east bank of the Rhine. On the twenty-fifth mobilization day the 14th Corps in Freiburg, plus four brigades, a division, and two detachments, conducted a defensive-offensive movement against this invasion using railroads.

In the third problem after a successful west front decision on the twenty-third mobilization day, the transportation of one army plus three corps was directed from the west front to the area east of the Weichsel River. LC H, Cologne, was given major responsibility, with LC B, Münster, D, Cassel, and Q, Elberfeld, all standing ready to execute orders.

The fourth and last problem described weak German forces confronting an overwhelmingly strong French attack through Upper Alsace and west Switzerland. German forces retired east of the Black Forest on a line Freudenstadt to Sökasch. On the twenty-eighth mobilization day railroads were used to organize a defensive offense against this invasion, which concluded with formation of a new army in southwestern Bavaria and its transportation into combat along the Rhine.

In each case game solutions were presented in a series of forty-column echelon tables describing LC orders. The level of complexity of the serial game was substantial. Three modes of telegraphic communication were used: the military telegraph, the railroad telegraph, and the Reich telegraph. Many telegrams were encoded and, judging from these transmissions, the sending and receiving of messages was time-consuming; each telegram with thirty series of five-code groups had to be encoded and then decoded. Telegrams raised the level of complexity and specificity by recording the day, hour, minute, and station of transmission. By 1914 the RRS was ready for a variety of possible situations and had prepared for them using simulations which combined a high degree of operational realism with a level of abstraction that replicated in substantial detail the velocities of August 1914.

## Mechanisms of Coordination

In addition to the RRS, four additional long-range integrating mechanisms were the chief of staff system, the corps commands, the DCs, and the Horse Purchase Commissions. Each of these has been described previously and therefore needs only brief mention here. The general staff system integrated the twenty-five active corps of the German Reich. Each of the chiefs of staff was the mobilization officer for the corps, and the war plan drew these men into a single network. But the network itself was loosely constructed. Direct communication lines – telegraph and telephone – linked the GGS to each corps.

At mobilization, corps commands were responsible for seeing that subordinate war structures were created. The rule was that each active army staff and unit prepared mobilization schedules not only for itself but for all lower-level units formed under its command. Supplies of equipment, weapons, and clothing were stored at the point where the complete unit came together during mobilization. Heavy weapons and munitions for active troops, as well as the newly mobilized units, were stored in the central artillery depots of the army corps. The exceptions to this were the rapid mobilization units and cavalry and field artillery regiments, whose weapons were in their own possession. Detailed, timed railroad transport supported this arrangement. Corps depots were included in the mobilization schedules and had to guarantee the quick evacuation of their weapons, supplies, and equipment.[40]

By 1914 there were 314 DCs. With over ten million men to be called up for some kind of service, young reserve officers were rotated through the post of DC adjutant so they could obtain a close view of the mobilization process. Between 1900 and 1914 more than four thousand officers got a close look at the mobilization preparation of the DC through these assignments. At the spring 1914 chiefs of staff meeting in Frankfurt an der Oder officers remonstated that DCs should be headed by capable and energetic officers, urging that the larger DCs be commanded by regular officers. However, it was noted that regular officers were rotated through new commands too often for such posts, which

40. This following discussion is based on Rahne, *Mobilmachung*, pp. 120–24. Cf. Elaine G. Spencer, "Police-Military Relations in Prussia, 1848–1914," *Journal of Social History* 19 (Winter 1985): 305–17.

required long-term assignment in order to master all of their complexities.

A fourth long-range integrating mechanism was the system of Horse Purchase Commissions. For the mobilization year beginning 1 April 1914, this system of automatic mobilization based on previously issued orders was extended to motor cars and trucks. In addition, by working with civilian authorities, each corps command prepared to mobilize personal cars, wagons, buses, and hospital ambulances. Also included were power riverboats, sea steamers, and harbor boats. Mixed civil-military commissions were established to oversee this process.

The preparation of these measures called for the closest coordination between military and civil authorities. Accordingly, the Interior Ministry for each federal state put out a list of mobilization responsibilities for each police region. These included publicizing mobilization orders throughout the region, especially in outlying villages and estate areas, and protective measures to be taken for railroad lines, border areas, seacoasts, and riverbanks, as well as press censorship. Under Reich law civil authorities also had the responsibility for mustering the Landsturm, to insure that no one liable for service avoided his duty and that troops called up but unable to be fed and housed within the garrison itself, were housed and fed in private quarters or public facilities.

In addition to long-range integration, by the spring of 1914 the GGS employed a variety of mechanisms to integrate the war plan on a short-term or immediate level. These included reinforcement call-up, test mobilizations, officer apportionment, advanced readiness for border units, and mobilization planning conferences.[41]

The army law of 1913 authorized the army to increase the peacetime strength of all units significantly. A portion of the reservists were assigned to reinforcement call-up, a system for gradually increasing the size of certain active army units without public notification. This advanced call-up included five stages: winter troop increase, political tension, imminent danger of war, immediate danger of war, and rapid deployment. Each one put into effect certain specific measures. For example, at the stage of imminent danger of war, the 12th Corps, located in eastern Saxony with headquarters at Dresden, inconspicuously added 360 to 480 reservists to infantry regiments, 75 to 80 reservists to cavalry

41. Rahne, *Mobilmachung*, pp. 125–32.

regiments, 60 to 120 reservists to field artillery regiments, and 120 men to pioneer batallions. For the entire army this meant that 104,000 reservists were called up, that is, approximately 4,000 men or 10% per army corps, before official or public notification. During the winter months calling up reservists during political tension was done only in the west and east border regions. Between 1901 and 1910 more than three million reservists and Landwehr participated in reinforcement call-up exercises.

In fear that the always more complicated mechanism of mobilization would fail at the declaration of war, various levels of the army carried out test mobilizations. The results were carefully monitored. Thus, in a communication from the command of the 19th Corps (Leipzig) of 7 January 1914, for example, it was reiterated how important it was for the DCs to prepare for a rapid and certain mobilization, to put everything in order beforehand, and to test out all possibilities. As test exercises went on in the DCs, the corps commands drew two conclusions. First, at the outset of mobilization, the administrative personnel in the DC had to be rapidly and substantially increased. Second, both reserves and new troop units should be exercised in test mobilizations. Some corps commands carried out practice mobilizations of their horse purchase plans. Others practiced plans for loading provision and munition trains from corps storage depots. The RRS of the GGS routinely ordered loading exercises of troop units at railroad stations. For financial reasons only active personnel participated in most of these exercises. In the final months prior to August 1914, practice alerts continued, going deeper into the tactical formations of the army to test the "functional reliability" of the system. For example, on 13 July 1914 the commander of the 24th Division alerted the second company of Field Artillery Regiment 78 in Wurzen. Even as late as 29 July 1914, the 19th Corps carried out a test mobilization in fourteen units.

In mobilization, care was taken to assign active officers to those positions where they were most needed. For this allocation the war-mobilized army was divided into five categories: (1) field troops were required to have two active officers per company, three in all border companies; (2) reserve troops required company, battery, and squadron commanders to be active officers, with a minimum of three per battalion; (3) Landwehr troops were given active officers only from the overflow from categories 1 and 2; (4) substitute troops received one active officer per company; (5) substitute troops of reserve units had no active officers. For the mobilization year 1914–15 the Military Cabinet planned to leave unchanged all twenty-five corps commanders and twenty-two of the chiefs of staff. At divisional level, of the forty-five active Prussian, Saxon, and Württemberg divisions, thirty-seven commanders would lead their troops into war, with eight new commanders appointed.

The final war plan time schedule directed twenty-one border region brigades to move out within hours after war was declared. Others, reinforced with artillery and cavalry, moved at the twentieth hour of the first mobilization day. Cavalry divisions moved on the second mobilization day, and most active units went during the first six days. Reserve army corps moved on the seventh mobilization day, reserve Landwehr brigades on the eighth, substitute divisions assigned to field units during the first twelve days, units of the trained Landsturm, assigned to remain in position where they were, between the eighth- and fifteenth days.[42]

## Mobilization Planning, Spring 1914

Some of the problems of integrating this massive war system are clear in the GGS mobilization planning meeting of 21 January 1914. Called the Chiefs' Conference on Mobilization Planning, it was held in Frankfurt an der Oder, according to one report to avoid the publicity which such a meeting would have attracted had it been held in Berlin. Chaired by Colonel Gerhard Tappen, chief of the Mobilization Section, aided by Major Walter Nicolai of GGS Section IIIb (counterintelligence), along with Generalmajor Wild von Hohenborn, head of the Central Department (mobilization) of the War Ministry, and his aid, Colonel Ernst von Wrisberg. The meeting was attended by the chiefs of staff of all twenty-five active corps.[43] The conveners made a number of general points before the conference was opened up to a question and answer format. The main topic was mobilization, the rapid and smooth conversion of forces to war strength and war structure. Between 1911 and 1913 the Reich had made three increases in army size, changing the peacetime army structure and necessitating alterations in the

---

42. Ibid., pp. 123–40.
43. The following is based on Werner Knoll and Hermann Rahne, "Bedeutung und Aufgaben der Konferenz der Generalstabschefs der Armeekorps in Frankfurt a.M. am 21.Januar 1914," *Militärgeschichte* 25, no. 1 (1986): 55–63.

mobilization plan. It was recognized that this raised many problems for chiefs of staff. Although the GGS was in the midst of revising the war plan which would go into effect on 1 April certain advance information was provided. For each corps the forthcoming plan would list the exact kind and number of officers prescribed by staff, formation, and troop and would detail the personnel arrangements for reserve and Landwehr formations adjusted between areas of heavy and light population.

Recently issued special orders were carefully reviewed. The officers were reminded that at noon on the first day of mobilization, every fifth one of the 106 infantry brigades of the active army would begin immediate movement to the border at peacetime strength. These twenty-one brigades were to form the war shield. The staffs of cavalry corps and divisions to be created at mobilization would be formed up when the government declared a state of political tension, alert stage two. At alert stage three, imminent threat of war, the state of siege would go into effect in all corps commands. It was emphasized that an essential precondition for the successful completion of mobilization was that everything remain secret as long as possible. The bulk of the session was carried out in question and answer format. The discussion revealed that many officers were confused by the complexity of the plans. For example, chiefs of staff asked what was legally required at each alert stage.

There were seven stages in the mobilization for war. Stage one was a precautionary warning period called "state of security," which alerted the army to unexpected and ominous new intelligence. Like the release of a safety catch on a weapon, the alert served to warn officers to be sure units were fully prepared to mobilize. Stage two was a second preliminary warning period called "political tension," in which commanders took certain preliminary steps toward beginning to build up their forces to war strength. Leaves were cancelled, maneuver plans were halted, staffs of reserve cavalry corps and divisions were called up. Stage three was "imminent threat of war." Whereas the first two stages were classified secret, stage three was made public. Here commanders put the other half of the measures begun in stage two into effect. This was very significant for eleven of the twenty-five corps: the six east front and five west front corps called up the Landsturm. This meant that large numbers of troops, regular and reserve, were freed to join the war-mobilized army as their places were taken by the Landsturm. Reserves assigned to maneuver duty but not then on maneuvers could also be called up in stage three. Finally, state of siege law went into effect. This was significant to quell anxieties over civilian unrest, a specter on the minds of conservatives that turned out to be a pure chimera. The army leadership emphasized that corps should not take any action in stage three that tied their hands, for example, purchasing horses.

Stage four was "war mobilization"; active, reserve, and Landwehr troops reported to their military units, horse and automobile purchase plans went into effect, and twenty-one brigades moved to the borders. The 8th Corps, LC S, headquarters Saarbrücken, was loaded in peacetime strength and sent to Luxembourg to capture the Alzette. Six brigades of infantry with supporting artillery moved across the border from Aachen against Liège. In East Prussia, evacuation moved civilians in border areas out of the way of the expected incoming Russian cavalry.

Stage five was the MTP, which began 4 August and ran through 20 August. It positioned seven armies along the line Aachen-Metz, Saarburg-Millhausen. In the east the 8th Army was placed in a ready position between Hohensalza and Insterburg. One Landwehr corps was sent to Upper Silesia. The essentials of the MTP were the equal and constant speed and interval of all trains on the same stretch. Parallelism in touching systems allowed officials hour by hour status reports.

Stage six was the "concentration": troops were off-loaded from transportation and formed up for the border crossing. Stage seven was the "attack march." Chiefs of staff were familiar with what followed. Stage eight was the attack. If combat was not expected, field and service trains were placed directly behind their divisions; if combat was anticipated, trains moved to the rear of the corps. It took twenty-four hours to reform a war-mobilized corps of 41,000 men, 14,000 horses, and 2,400 wagons because in march formation its road space was roughly thirty miles.[44]

Chiefs of staff were worried that the MTP was too complicated and under the direction of too many different commands. For

---

44. Turner, "Schlieffen Plan," p. 213; Groener Papers, roll 12, "Der Deutsche Eisenbahn in Weltkriege"; Stabbs, *Aufmarsch*, pp. 41–51; Sarter *Die deutschen Eisenbahnen*, pp. 40–64. Hermann von Kuhl and General von Bergmann, *Movement and Supply of the German First Army during August and September 1914* (Fort Leavenworth, 1929), p. 214 indicate that this is almost thirty-seven miles; Elze, *Tannenberg*, p. 365, says it is thirty miles; in either case it was some distance.

example, they argued that troops immediately dispatched to secure borders in the first hours of war should remain under the control of their corps instead of LC authority. During the MTP, line commanders, majors, or captains were technically superior to unit commanders, including general officers. Discussion followed. It was agreed that this was a problem to be worked on.

Chiefs of staff were also concerned that the increased speed in forming up accelerated mobilization units, especially up to the fourth mobilization day, was dangerous because the horse complement for these forces could not be organized so quickly. The units referred to were those brigades made up of mixed forces – two infantry regiments, including a machine gun company, a cavalry squadron, and a foot artillery battery – whose job it was to secure the concentration area on the French and Belgian borders and to seize Luxembourg and Liège. Chiefs of staff argued that this acceleration would make the mobilization of the army corps very difficult, putting into question possible action against domestic unrest, making it difficult for reserve forces, and leading to a situation in which the brigade itself would only be fully up to strength much later than expected. The general staff representatives replied that they were aware of the difficulties of accelerated mobilization and would try to avoid further speed but that the early concentration of these brigades could not be avoided. The corps command might, in certain cases, delay the inclusion of cavalry squadrons to the brigades before their departure, in other words, add them at a later location. If so, it was nevertheless the responsibility of the corps to inform the GGS by 15 November of each specific case and request a waiver. In all cases, however, the late added forces had to arrive in the brigade by the time it reached the border.[45]

Could the RRS inform the corps commands when it gave orders to the LCs, so that the corps and line commanders could work more closely together? Very difficult, replied the GGS, because too many technical factors come into play. Line commanders, however, were responsible for establishing and maintaining relationships with the corps command and especially for reporting personally to the chief of staff of the corps. The dual chain of command worried chiefs of staff.

---

45. Rahne, *Mobilmachung*, p. 107; *Groener Papers*, roll 8, no. 34; Groener letter to General von Haeften, 28 January 1924, Knoll and Rahne, "Bedeutung," p. 59.

How could railroad protection be coordinated between the army corps on the west bank of the Rhine? The GGS replied that from the first mobilization day to the end of the MTP railroad security would be taken care of by Landsturm or Landwehr forces located in the vicinity of the railroads to be secured. Weapons, munitions, and accoutrements for this operation were stockpiled in local railroad stations. Every year there were exercises in which the designated forces were informed of their obligations and looked over their weapons and equipment under the direction of the railroad administration. In other words, the RRS organized its own security outside the corps command channels and even practiced this operation. The GGS said that orders for the distribution of weapons at railroad offices were under the command of the Railroad Directorate. At a declaration of political tension, stage two, at the specific request of the government railroad officials could protect the railroad. At the same time the corps command could take steps to protect important buildings.

It was desirable that anyone whose mobilization assignment was as acting district commander spend a few days in peacetime practicing these duties. The GGS approved this suggestion. The annual test mobilizations of the DCs were discussed. Three days would be sufficient to call up the reserves, examine them, give them supplies, and ready their transportation. The chiefs of staff urged test mobilizations for munitions and supply trains and for the horse purchase program.[46]

## The Military Travel Plan (MTP)

As finally conceived, the MTP itself was divided into six phases. The first was a forty-eight hour preparatory period after war mobilization was announced. This phase included transportation for those troops in "rapid mobilization" and for the coaling of the fleet. LCs and local railroad offices opened their classified war time schedule and went over its contents – track and ramp plans; preparation of materials needed for loading; orders for the disposition of freight and passenger cars when public transportation was suspended; measures necessary for transition to the MTP; and preparation of the 244,000 railroad cars needed for troops, horses,

---

46. Knoll and Rahne, "Bedeutung," pp. 59–60.

and equipment. The second was a seventy-two hour period for the completion of the mobilization transport, that is, when men reported to their units. For the first three to six days, the period during which reserves moved from civilian life to their units and those units were transported to their rail collection points, transportation moved in irregular sequences. For example, the characteristics of some corps was such that their units were brought up to war strength with troops and horses from outside their region. During the first six days, two border corps in the east were completed by adding 148,000 men mainly from the Rhineland and Berlin, whereas the corps and forts in Alsace-Lorraine were filled up with 112,000 men and 23,000 horses from those same areas. For the navy, approximately 74,000 men from all over Germany had to be transported to their mobilization posts in the harbors of the North and East Sea. Phase two also called for Germans visiting abroad to return and moved East Prussian border families westward. Phase three allowed twelve days for the deployment transportation of the west army. Phase four assigned five days for the deployment transportation of the much smaller east army. Phase five consisted of three days' mobilization transport for the fortress and reserve troops, and finally, phase six allowed twenty days for all additionally required mobilization transport.[47]

Phases three and four involved a tightly scheduled, continuous run of train sequences through specific transportation paths. As soon as the troops began to move along these paths in fifty-four car unit trains, ten minutes apart, telegraphs and telephones monitored their movement through the LCs. For example in LC S, Saarbrücken, it was estimated that sufficient cars were on hand to move the 11th Corps, running forty troop trains or 2,160 cars daily. Disposition of empty cars was arranged by telephone with adjoining LC H, Cologne, and LC C, Fankfurt am Main, so that the empty trains moved back through the rail system on different tracks from the advancing troop trains. Delays were reported by telegraph, which also monitored at what hour food supplies were given to the troops and animals. LCs controlled each corps for a set number of hours and prescribed the steps of its progress. Thus 1st Corps was in LC J for 29 hours, 4th Corps in LC A for 30.5 hours, 11th Corps in LC J for 25 hours. Station directions prescribed

47. Gaertringen, *Groener*, p. 72; Rahne, *Mobilmachung*, pp. 126–27; Sarter, *Die deutschen Eisenbahnen*, p. 43.

location; number of unit trains to be loaded per hour, usually two; and loading ramps. A military train was between 200 and 400 meters long and generally required four loading stations.[48]

By 1914, within the RRS several forms of technology influenced war planning. One was the mechanical technology of the railroads. A second was the informational technology of bureaucracy, the war plan, and the telegraph and telephone. A third was automation technology, which combined mechanical and informational aspects to monitor and adjust the machines and the mobilization by means of electric feedback.[49] The MTP was the only phase of the war plan amenable to these three forms of technological manipulation. As such, the RRS was under continuous pressure to reduce the execution time of the MTP. As pointed out above, amendment sheets were added to the MTP at the rate of several hundred per year. Each change was an attempt to gain time and to increase the work capacity of the three thousand segments of the MTP. The pressures to do this came mainly from technological changes outside Germany. To officers within the RRS, it appeared that French and Russian railroad construction was developing swiftly in these matters. The nature of these fears is revealed in Wilhelm Groener's classified testimony to the Reichstag finance committee.[50]

France, he began, had a spatial advantage over Germany in war mobilization: its military travel distances were half those of Germany. This created a dangerous time differential because the less space there was, the more rapid the mobilization could be. Since 1870, both France and Russia had built more railroads than Germany. In terms of railroad track per inhabitant, he said Germany's had increased by 44%, whereas France had enlarged its system by 77%. Similarly, overall railroad construction had increased by 312% in Germany, and by 531% in Russia. Differentials were especially evident in the thickness of the rail systems. France had spent over one hundred million francs on small connecting lines. Germany had also enhanced the density of its system, yet still lagged behind. Lack of density was a major source of congestion.

48. Groener Papers, roll 19, "Prüfung der Eisenbahn Kriegsspiel," RR Sektion Berlin, 31.7.1912, nos. 173, 174, 175. H. Bauer, *Deutsche Eisenbahner im Weltkriege, 1914–1918* (Stuttgart, 1927), p. 9; Elze, *Tannenberg*, pp. 112–14. Kuhl and Bergmann, *Movement and Supply*, p. 81.

49. Child, *Organization*, p. 245.

50. "Auszug aus dem Bericht des Württembergischen Militärbevollmächtigten von Graevenitz, 25 April 1913, quoted in Schulte, *Kriegsausbruch*, pp. 165–72.

Wherever main lines met, a potential source of congestion existed; several of these might create dangerous situations during mobilization. To illustrate this, Groener used a series of charts and maps which demonstrated that: (1) the overall travel time for the French army was less than that for the German army; (2) German horse transportation was mainly from east to west, whereas French horses were more evenly distributed; (3) food and fodder movements were mainly from east to west; (4) coal for the navy was transported mainly from the Ruhr: some also came from Silesia, but the route near the Polish border was considered dangerous; (5) rail transportation of war material had increased during the last ten years from 19,000 to 522,000 tons; (6) France had increased its number of through railroad lines more than had Germany. In 1870 Germany had nine, France four. By 1914 Germany had thirteen, France sixteen. Groener's conclusion was that Germany needed to add to the density of its system. He also suggested building additional Rhine River bridges, especially one at Rüdesheim, where construction should begin immediately.

Over Easter week Groener and two other lieutenant colonels, one Austrian, one Italian, went over the transportation lists. By that time the *Terminkalendar*, the classified timetables to be opened at mobilization, had been distributed to the twenty-six LCs. They contained specific details of the loading sites, ramp plans, orders for the disposition of freight trains at suspension of civilian traffic, preparation of cars for men and horses, and the complete program for going over to the MTP. The chiefs of the Austrian and Italian general staffs had attended German field maneuvers. Representatives from trade, industry, and agriculture had met to plan the distribution of coal at mobilization. Enough coal was to be stockpiled to supply Germany for three to four weeks. Public utility needs were assessed. Secondary railroad lines and canals were instructed to be prepared to keep food, coal, and milk supplies moving to the large cities and to industry during the time that the main rail lines were being utilized for mobilization. The four military railroad companies prepared to extend their work into a war zone of occupied territory, creating seventeen new companies, each of which was to take responsibility for thirty miles of track.[51]

---

51. Sarter, *Die deutschen Eisenbahnen*, pp. 43–46; Gaertringen, *Groener*, pp. 137ff.

## *The July Crisis: Traditional Terror and Modern Mechanisms*

Although the July crisis is beyond the scope of this book precisely because it was a countervailing mechanism and is not fully understandable without considering the actions of all five opening round belligerents, some approaches to it can nevertheless be suggested by considering certain factors already touched upon. By July 1914 the GGS technical war plan was loaded and the organizational control system was cocked. The field of fire was well known: it included only full mobilization, a seven-stage process that was enhanced by various preplan attacks. Within this framework, there was continual change. The railroad building program stretched several years into the future. Modifications in the MTP were continuous. In terms of conceptualizing war, although war games, GGS rides, and maneuvers were not a description of the actual course of a war any more than GGS history precisely approximated what had actually happened, nonetheless, all these images played a powerful role in shaping German officers' ideas of the future. Their very simplicity offered one means of coping with the enormous complexity of German military planning. Officers were trained to think in terms of the future conditional. The defense establishment was prepared to fight a seventy- to ninety-day war aimed, at least in the west, at integral operations and continuous movement. The objective was not any specific battlefield or concentration but the dynamics of military action unfolding against a whole nation. In place of individual battles, there was integrated and continuous movement, war as uninterrupted forward motion. The war was envisioned as a series of battles of annihilation beginning in Luxembourg and Belgium and ending southwest of Paris, where the west front war would be concluded. [52]

The July crisis was the fifth in a series which had begun in 1905. All dealt with great power politics as they revolved around third world countries: in 1905 Morocco, in 1908 Bosnia-Herzegovina, in 1911 Morocco, in 1912 the Balkans, and in 1914 Serbia. It is tempting to speculate that, up until 1914, many of the same factors had been present but in a different configuration. They had not coalesced, and the outcome in each case was peace, not war. In 1905 Schlieffen and Holstein seem to have counseled war, but the Kaiser, the war minister, and others had been against it. In

52. Geyer, "German Strategy," p. 532; Haeussler, *Groener*, pp. 48–49.

1909 Germany and Austria threatened war, but Russia backed down. In 1911 neither the Kaiser nor the French government wanted war, even though Moltke was probably in favor of it and England certainly appeared ready to support France. In the early Balkan Wars the partial Russian and Austrian mobilizations augered in the direction of war, but these were called off. Only in 1914 was there a falling together, a coalescence. It is surprising how suddenly this typhoon wave overwhelmed the European great powers. In Germany it was as if the technical focus within the GGS was so narrowly defined that no one really expected to implement the plans, not next month nor next year. Within a general framework of expectation supported by deep-future-oriented planning, the war seems to have caught them unawares. The major turning point in modern history after 1815 was up on them before they realized it.

The July crisis began as an act of traditional nineteenth-century terrorism, the grotesque, almost comic opera-like assassination of visiting royalty. It ended in the launching of the first modern mechanical war, a major industrial catastrophe which had world wide repercussions. The crossing point from traditional to modern crisis came with the forty-eight-hour Austrian ultimatum to Serbia of 6 P.M., Thursday, 23 July. With it the time clock of the war planning processes began ticking. By then the industrial planning mechanisms imbedded in the structures of the European armies were so fully prepared that in Austria-Hungary and Germany the main war planners took a several-week vacation immediately before the ultimatum was issued. However, outside the general staffs, it was an entirely different matter.

In Germany there were no governmental processes that corrected for the concentration of the assessment function in a single person, the Kaiser.[53] Almost fifty people had direct access to him but there were no routines to discuss or coordinate among or between them or to share the important and discrete information that each possessed. No established or regular councils existed for that purpose. Even information about the war plan was top secret and restricted to those who had a need to know: it was not shared between the GGS, the War Ministry, the Military Cabinet, the Admiralty, the Naval General Staff, and the Foreign Office. The same was true of intelligence. As the crisis developed, therefore, there was no management, no consideration of options, no weighing

---

53. Herwig, "Imperial Germany," pp. 89–94.

of alternatives. As Paul Bracken has written, a nation's actions in crisis are profoundly influenced by the security institutions it builds years before the crisis occurs. In the case of Imperial Germany, these institutions included no provision for anything resembling crisis management. On the contrary, all that was left was the Kaiser's ad hoc, spur-of-the-moment approach. In this final crisis of the nineteenth century, such methods were archaic and in-sufficient. The means for making war, weapons, transportation, and communications, had progressed into the twentieth century, while the German entourage operated in a nineteenth-century cabinet atmosphere in which the whim of the monarch called the tune. These two mechanisms, like many other institutions of the indus-trial feudal state, were mismatched and out of sychronization. As a result, clear understanding of a rapidly changing situation, that became more complicated as it developed was clouded and ir-rational. A twentieth-century crisis – communicated by means of electricity – was conducted using nineteenth-century cultural forms – royal protocol, ethnic honor, and mystical cosmology.

Compounding the absence of consulting processes was a lack of knowledge. European diplomats and monarchs lacked clear under-standing of the various kinds of mobilization. Within a broad frame-work, each country had its own unique methods. Germany, we have argued, had seven distinct stages. Russia allowed for only full mobilization but the tsar believed there were other options. Aus-tria had war cases R and B. France had Plan 17. Each one was measured in stages, hours, and days: all were technical devices dependent on railroads. Beyond trains, complex notificaton pro-cedures meant that communication processes were lengthy. Be-cause of the public, visible, and complicated mechanics needed to get their war-mobilized armies into the field, each state was anxious about the others' actions. Preliminary military steps by one were considered ominous or dangerous by others. Information about such preparatory moves was poor at best, but guaranteed, under the circumstances, to be examined, misunderstood, and reacted to by opposing powers. Every action was measured in terms of time and space. They were quantifiable: officers thought of them in terms of numbers. As General Joffre said on 31 July every twenty-four-hour delay in calling up reservists resulted in abandonment of twelve to fifteen miles of territory.[54]

54. Kern, *Culture of Time and Space*, pp. 270–73.

As opponents began to mobilize against each other, all European general staffs felt the urgency of time. There was a point – different for each state – at which countervailing mobilizations were triggered technologically, that is, by the knowledge or by the suggestion of opponents' bureaucratic and operational moves. Because of the interlinked designs of the European war plans, there were various points along the trajectories of the planning mechanisms that, once reached, forced additional engagements. There were other points at which, once the mechanisms crossed, actions could not be reversed but had to proceed along a predetermined course.

Four examples of this countervailing mechanism may be suggested. As early as 2 July, the Rumanian government announced that in any future Austro-Serbian war it would remain neutral. For Conrad von Hötzendorf, chief of the Austrian general staff, this statement was immediately interpreted as a double negative: the loss of four hundred thousand soldiers fighting against Russia and the release of three additional tsarist corps for use against Austria.[55] At the Austrian ministerial council of 7 July it was made clear that during the first five days of the military transportation plan, Austria could mobilize against Serbia and then, if necessary, turn about and mobilize against Russia. After the fifth rail transportation day, however, it was impossible to redirect the mobilization from south to east without massive disruptions in the overall war plan.[56] On 28 July, one hundred twenty hours after the Austrian ultimatum, Moltke sent a secret situation report to Chancellor Bethmann-Hollweg. In it, Moltke stated that Germany's options were gone: the direction and movement of events were out of control. Only the speed could still be determined. He concluded that the next seventy-two hours were crucial and that Germany could not allow these to slip away without acting because it would otherwise suffer the most grievous consequences.[57] Finally, on the afternoon of 1 August, after the mobilization order had been signed and the implementing orders were being prepared, the Kaiser changed his mind. Having heard from his ambassador in London that there was apparently some possibility of English neutrality, he ordered a halt to the west front deployment and a redeployment of all forces

---

55. Luigi Albertini, *The Origins of the War of 1914*, 3 vols. (London, 1952–57), 3: 132.
56. Stone, "Moltke and Conrad," pp. 233–37.
57. Groener Papers, roll 8, no. 34; cf. Fischer, *Germany's Aims*, pp. 74–75.

against Russia. Moltke, after many remonstrances, finally convinced the Kaiser that this was impossible. The result would be an impotent formless mass, a swarm of disorganized troops on the east front with a fully war-mobilized French army on the west front, at Germany's back. The final war plan, the result of a full year's work, Moltke said, could not be altered if Germany was to avoid the most disastrous confusion. Moltke would take no responsibility for this chaos.[58] The German government telegraphed London, declaring that the deployment could not be stopped for technical reasons.

58. Imanuel Geiss, *July 1914: The Outbreak of the First World War* (New York, 1974), pp. 337ff.; Gaertringen, *Groener*, pp. 145–46; Görlitz, *German General Staff*, p. 155; Fischer, *Germany's Aims*, pp. 86–87.

# Conclusion
# The Invention of
# Twentieth-Century War

We began this book with a defeated army reacting to its losses at the hands of a more modern army. The participants were officers serving a fallen great power, a kingdom which had been created and sustained by an army once so powerful that it was described in the eighteenth century as the only one in Europe with its own state. In response to defeat, Prussia created the nucleus of a new approach crafted, above all, by the application of organized knowledge to the practical skills of war.

This approach had its source in the idea of preparing for the future. During peacetime officers were to plan for future contingencies by studying possible opponents, by regular exercises simulating combat in specific terrain, and by combining theoretical staff work with practical troop duty. This required a new kind of organization. During the succeeding century each of these procedures became institutionalized in the GGS: war plans in the Mobilization Section, mapping in the Land Survey Section, education in the War Academy, and war games in the GGS ride and Kaisermanöver. Organizational and procedural patterns instituted at the top of the Prussian army were replicated in corps, divisions, and regiments. Thus was born the first deep-future-oriented war planning system in world history. From the start there were disagreements over how this system should be defined. Theoretical goals conflicted with practical ones, humanistic education warred against technical professional learning, artistic terrain images contrasted with mathematical likenesses. After more than a half century of gradual development, three rapid, unexpected military victories simultaneously overturned the European balance of power, created a new nation-state, and validated the instrument of these achievements, the Prussian war planning process.

During the next forty-three years there were no wars in Europe. For the first two decades the new Germany, under Bismarck's aegis, worked to maintain a balance of power between Russia to the east and France and England to the west, while the Prussian war system expanded slowly throughout the Reich. With stable foreign policy and reduced military threats, the evolution of war planning slowed in every aspect but one. The historical image of war upon which war planners depended for their clues to the future changed dramatically. GGS historians projected Prussia's strategic methods of 1866 and 1871 over the entire military past. In this image Prussian strategy – total war by battles of annihilation – had been followed by all previous field commanders in western history from Napoleon to Frederick the Great and back to the Romans and Greeks. Any other conception of war was illegitimate.

After 1890, when this radical image of the past was firmly established, a sea change in foreign and defense policy occurred. Germany gave up attempts to keep the balance of power and instead sought a place in the sun of European politics. In response an iron ring of military alliances formed around it. A climate of social Darwinism and a new defense philosophy accompanied the development of these competing alliance systems. Defense bills aimed at long-term goals: personnel-intensive armament gave way to the materially intensive military industrial complex. Reserve forces mushroomed and weapons technology changed. By 1905 the largest armies in world history confronted each other in central Europe, armed with the greatest number of lethal weapons. Armies twenty times larger than those that fought in 1870 were readied by the four great continental powers. Each minute a brigade of three thousand men with its artillery could discharge a volume of fire equal to that of the whole of Wellington's army of sixty thousand firing volley and salvo at Waterloo.[1] As Schlieffen said, the problem was not how to kill with these instruments but how to defend against them.

Accompanying the changed foreign and defense policy was a greatly enlarged, more professional, more intellectual GGS, an organization poised between patrimonial and modern forms. Its chief set himself apart from the Prussian and Reich leadership. Unlike the Kaiser, who was often considered a kind of ill-fated child, Schlieffen maintained an aura of intellectualism and mystery enhanced by the distance he imposed between himself and others. Schlieffen appeared the quintessential man of honor and service;

1. John Keegan, *Mask of Command*, p. 248.

correct and incorruptible. This leadership style allowed him to meld task-oriented work methods with traditional goals of power in the increasingly dangerous international climate. As dangers increased, the influence of Schlieffen, the sphinx who knew the secret of victory, grew. Confronted by the lethal environment of a new strategic era, the second founder of Prussian war planning groped for a way out. He found it in railroads and in history. Railroads promised the essentials of speed, volume, regularity, and dependability by which a smaller army could defeat two larger ones on opposite geographic frontiers. History provided an example of the means to this end tailored to the brutal firepower conditions of early twentieth-century Europe, the battle of annihilation accomplished by attacking flank and rear. Schlieffen accepted the interpretation of war current in the GGS and turned it in a new strategic direction: the rolling offensive, a series of loosely related battles, which avoided frontal attack and culminated in the defeat of France in forty days. Although he tried many war plans for both the east and west, in the war crisis of 1905 he settled on using the highest-density railroad network in Europe to effect a revivification of the great Cannae victory of the Carthaginians over the Romans.

When Schlieffen retired on the final day of 1905 his war plan, which was intended to meet the immediate circumstances and necessities of that moment in time, that is, the first Moroccan crisis, was handed over to his successor Helmuth von Moltke the Younger. Because of Schlieffen's dominance and Moltke's ineffectiveness in the GGS and in spite of the fact that the war planning process went on as before, testing and evaluating dozens of possibilities, the Schlieffen Plan was treated as an inviolable legacy. From then until 1914 it was modified in only two aspects. Schlieffen's successor lacked interest in the mechanics and details of the war plan and he lacked knowledge of the process that created it. Moltke the Younger was inexperienced in GGS procedures, a dilettante confronting technical experts. But what Moltke did not lack was a vision of the future. It was dark, dominated by the belief in the inevitability of a coming war which would test and validate Germanic civilization. Cosmic cycles of a millenarian nature would bring the Parousia. In 1909, when Conrad von Hötzendorf initiated the transformation of the German-Austrian alliance so that Germany would be subordinate to Austria in the event of war, Moltke accepted the suggestion of his Germanic ally.

On the eve of the great war, the GGS had become a technically specialized bureaucracy that commanded a complex network of interacting procedures and had a generally recognized knowledge advantage over the political leadership. The bottom line for this system, the actual instrument to which everything else related, was the war plan. The fulcrum of the war plan was stage five, the MTP. Only stage five allowed the military bureaucrats the greatest degree of control, prepractice, and ability to foreshorten. Consequently the RRS built up a technological array of procedures, language, symbols, intricate charts, and complex plans. The spatial location of the Schlieffen Plan was dictated mainly by the railroads: through using them the GGS expected to gain and maintain the only advantage Germany would have in a future two-front war, the advantage of time. In the chaos of war, it was railroads, that dominant vehicle of the nineteenth-century industrial revolution, that guaranteed the essential, modern goals of speed, volume, regularity, and dependability. It was the only variable by which officers could set their watches. Even the Kaisermanöver, often considered a spectacular but frivolous public show, in reality practiced a segment of the MTP. Corps commanders hunted in the depths of the East Prussian forests, reliving heroic tradition, while underlying their practice was the *moteur* of the German war machine, railroad technology. The Battles of Tannenberg and Masurian Lakes illustrate deep-future-oriented planning. Whether or not these battles represented a model of what decision making for war should look like, many participating officers had been there before, working through simulations more than a dozen times during the previous quarter century. They had considered the strategic and tactical possibilities; they were familiar with the terrain; they knew the relationships of size, space, and time. They had also traveled along the railroads, the skeleton for strategic decision making.

By 1914 rising conservative clamor matched Moltke's belief that his country was subject to hidden powerful forces beneath the world of appearances that foretold an apocalypse. A total transformation of a degenerate civilization would occur, bringing a new Germanic nation, cleansed and strong. These views were mirrored in the general society, and more specifically in Pan Germanism and the Army League, which also sought a redemptive Armageddon. This belief came together with a timed military crisis to precipitate the great war. On the philosophical level, it fulfilled a long awaited expectation. At the technical level it created real conditions simulated by the system in games for a decade. Between the philosophy and the technique, little space remained for decision making. We might ask how philosophy and technology conjoined in these circumstances.

One definition of this situation is provided by reactionary modernism: where technology was incorporated into the cultural system of German nationalism without retaining the latter's romantic and antirational aspects. The reactionary modernists were nationalists who turned the romantic anticapitalism of German radical conservatism away from backward-looking pastoralism, pointing it ahead toward the outlines of a new order. That order would replace the formless chaos of capitalism with a united, technologically advanced nation. Moltke may have subscribed to some of this attitude. Germany's clumsy, dangerous attempts to find its place in the sun of European power politics made him uneasy and impatient. In the midst of the 1911 crisis he remarked that if Germany crept away with its tail between its legs, he would abolish the army and hire the Japanese to protect his nation. His countrymen could forget about national security and devote themselves to making money. Clearly his thoughts fit the format of reactive nationalism. However they do not necessarily reflect modernist views. Modernism includes not only a positive view of hardware technology and an affirmative stance toward progress but also idealist dreams of the past, "a highly technological romanticism" as Thomas Mann once called it.[2] Instead of Moltke's vision, it was the GGS image of war that fit this pattern, one highly technological in its dependence on knowledge and railroad delivery systems and strongly idealist in its attempt to resuscitate an historical strategy and make it reoccurr. In this, German planners shared the war images of the French, Russians, Austrians, and English: all believed that the only legitimate form of war consisted of the *offensive à outrance*.

By 1914, a transformation had taken place within the GGS which supported this war image. Intellect above character, professional education over general education, technical above general knowledge, mathematical accuracy above artistic representation – in all of these aspects the GGS had turned decisively toward the technical, professional, and modern. The state could not be simul-

2. Jeffrey Herf, *Reactionary Modernism: Technology, Culture, and Politics in Weimar and the Third Reich* (Cambridge, 1984), p. 2.

taneously strong and technologically backward. Within the RRS culture and technology had been reconciled; however, this reconciliation did not fit the definition of reactionary modernism. Rather it grew out of traditional Prussia's confrontation with modernity, where ambiguities about identity and security found their resolution in technology. Within the GGS technology guaranteed speed, volume, regularity, and dependability. Officers looked ahead to the great symphonic performance in which the technical and the cultural were to merge. The meticulousness and specificity of bureaucratic planning – goal oriented and rationalized – combined with the appeal to the senses, the emotional and psychological force of the ancient and traditional drive for power. Because its ultimate goal entailed some degree of death, the GGS was one of those industrial institutions that not only possessed the attributes of organization, power, and technical perfection but also generated spiritual impulses, social models, and cultural ideals.[3]

As Michael Geyer has written, the Prussian army described here was an industrial organization which was able, even before the outbreak of World War I, to dissolve the long-standing boundaries between civil and military society. It did so by employing methods of war preparation which amounted to a comprehensive managerial effort at national organization. In the process, the relationship between mass participation, institutional domination, and elite formation was readjusted. As a result of this, as well as for its historic contribution to nation building, the GGS became a part of the national mythology. In a rapidly changing society suffering from both an identity and a security crisis, the GGS was a symbol of both patrimonial and rational values.[4]

Generally speaking, railroads influenced Prussian-German war planning in four ways.[5] One was through increased performance, which produced intensification. It marked the beginning of an era

---

3. This is how the Allgemeine Elektricitäts-Gesellschaft (AEG) under Emil and Walter Rathenau was described. Cf. Tilmann Buddensieg, *Industriekultur: Peter Behrens and the AEG*, trans. I.B. Whyte (Cambridge, 1984), p. 2. For provocative commentary on the relationship between humans and technology, see J. David Bolter, *Turning's Man: Western Culture in the Computer Age* (Chapel Hill, 1984), chaps. 1 and 2.
4. Michael Geyer, "The Militarization of Europe, 1914–1945," pp. 70–80.
5. Wolfgang Schivelbusch, *The Railway Journey: The Industrialization of Time and Space in the 19th Century* (Berkeley, 1986), pp. 16–26; Michael Geyer has argued that a "machine culture" and the dominance of the technocrats in the German High Command came in late 1916, with the arrival of Hindenburg and Ludendorff.

in which military expectations were such that, at some point in time, all cogwheels would operate without play. The disappearance of "play," or a narrowing of tolerances, has been used as a paradigm for the machine in general. Up to a point, railroads generally had this impact on war, both forcing and allowing for a more precise interaction between the individual parts of armies. In contrast, in the Napoleonic armies there was always a great deal of play between the individual parts. Even Moltke the Elder's corps could arrive late. By Schlieffen's day, however, a great deal of play had been squeezed out and by 1914 it was further reduced, both in the war plans and, more importantly, in the minds of the planners. Close tolerances of time, space, and size had begun to be assumed.

A second influence of railroads was felt when mechanical regularity began to triumph over natural irregularity. The replacement of animal and human power by steam power in one stage of the war plan assumed the guise of a guarantee. The natural irregularities of the terrain were replaced in the planner's mind by the sharp linearity of the railroad. A machine ensemble had interjected itself between the railroad and the land. War planners now began to think about the land as it was filtered through the machinery. The character of this new vision was one of great technical discipline.

A third general influence of railroads on Prussian war planning dictated the reorganization of traffic according to the hardware technology of the railroad. If Schlieffen chose his initial attack point based upon considerations of European rail density, his successor hinged his entire plan upon the capture of a single traffic point, a rail junction. Huge transportation paths defined war plan cartography. On these maps there was no distance scale, but instead there was time and size. These industrial flow charts measured work capacity and measured it mathematically. Not only was the traffic reorganized, it was also gauged and timed according to rail technology.

Finally, the very ethos of the GGS was shaped by its confrontation with technology. Armies have often been considered the first modern organizations in traditional societies. In the case of Prussian war planning, the metamorphosis from patrimonial to rational management resulted in a shift of power from rulers to

---

Keeping in mind that Ludendorff was head of the Mobilization Section of the GGS from 1908 to 1913, perhaps this "conversion to a technical paradigm of war" began earlier. Michael Geyer, "German Strategy," pp. 527–54 and the discussion of it in Tim Travers, *The Killing Ground*, pp. 261–62.

subordinates, from generalists and dilettantes to technical specialists. The systematic application of organized knowledge applied to practical problems of war planning resulted in the division of labor. Tasks became conterminous with established areas of engineering knowledge. The more thoroughgoing the application, the longer the task cycle, the more complex the procedures, the more specialized the personnel, the larger the organization, the greater the division of labor and the more information was needed. Finally, power passed to those who had the knowledge for important decisions. The GGS was a new kind of organization shaped by knowledge. As the Prussian army became dependent upon railroads, the task of size, space, and time coordination created a new kind of officer. The general staff officer became one who gave consistent, dependable, technical performance: he was interchangeable. His goals were functional reliability and high work capacity. The GGS ethos derived from its technical core, the railroads.

As Schlieffen wrote in 1909, future battles would be directed by a commander far behind the lines in a house with spacious offices, where he would be surrounded by telegraph, radio, telephone, and signal apparatus and motorcars and motorcycles would be at his disposal. Seated before a large map, he would receive intelligence reports from balloons and airplanes and send and receive orders from his army and corps commanders. The commander's essential task had meanwhile been fulfilled long before the war began.

Five years later, Schlieffen's successor saw the fruition of this vision. On 29 August, twenty-seven days after mobilization, Moltke sat in an empty schoolhouse in Luxembourg, the temporary quarters of the GGS. There was neither gas nor electricity, only a few dim oil lamps. In spite of the darkness he was bathed in brilliant light waves which poured over him as he read the reports of his armies and absorbed the images of what appeared to him to be great victories.[6]

6. Moltke, *Erinnerungen*, p. 382.

# Glossary

| | |
|---|---|
| *Abitur* | secondary school graduation certificate |
| *Dienstzeugnis* | testimonial of character, on an officer's personnel records (before 1902) |
| *Einjährig-Freiwilliger* | secondary school graduate who serves one year as a soldier, paying for his uniform and food, prior to commissioning. |
| *Fachliteratur* | specialized research materials |
| *Freiherr* | duke |
| *Frontdienst* | military service with an active duty troop unit |
| *Graf* | count |
| *Grafenstand* | all the counts in Germany, as a social group |
| *Gründerjahre* | founding years of German Second Reich, 1864–71 |
| *Immediatstellen* | positions with direct, personal access to the Kaiser |
| *Immediatvorträge* | reports presented directly to the Kaiser |
| *Kaisermanöver* | annual maneuvers attended by the Kaiser |
| *Kriegsakademie* | War Academy |
| *Kriegskunst* | art of war |
| *Kriegsspiel* | war game |
| *Kriegswissenschaft* | science of war |
| *Landwehr* | reserve military force |
| *Leutnantzeit* | an officer's years as a lieutenant |
| *Militär-Wochenblatt* | *Military Weekly* |
| *Nachlaß* | assembled personal papers of a person, usually in a library or archive |
| Railroad Directorate | one of twenty-six regional civilian railroad headquarters (1914) |
| *Septennat* | custom of voting for military appropriations every seven years in the German Reichstag |

| | |
|---|---|
| *Stalldienst* | taking care of regimental horses |
| transportation path | double track railroad line used in the war plan |
| *Würdigkeitsurteil* | judgment of worth, on an officer's personnel record (before 1902) |

# Bibliography

## Unpublished Sources

### Bundesarchiv-Militärarchiv, Freiburg (BAMA)

| | |
|---|---|
| RM 2 | Kaiserliches Marinekabinett |
| RM 94–108 | Herbstmanöver von Armee und Marine (1894–1914) |
| N30 | Nachlaß Hans Hartwig von Beseler |
| N30–46 | Lebenserinnerungen |
| N36 | Nachlaß Wilhelm von Hahnke |
| N37 | Nachlaß Max Hoffmann |
| N43 | Nachlaß Alfred Graf Schlieffen |
| N56 | Nachlaß Gerhard Tappen |
| N324 | Nachlaß Karl von Einem |
| N78 | Nachlaß Helmuth von Moltke the Younger |
| | 20 5. Garde-Infanterie Brigade-Manöver und -Besichtigung, Bericht, 27.7.1898 |
| | 37 "Eine Antwort an Herrn Walter Görlitz betr. das Kapitel 'Der Krieg ohne Feldherr' in seinem Buch, *Der deutsche Generalstab*," von Hauptmann a.D. Adam von Moltke, 1958 |
| | 22 "Bemerkungen zu den Herbstübungen 1905," General von Bülow, III Armeekorps, General-Kommando, Sekt. 1a, Nr. 5289, 9. März 1906 |
| | 22 "Bemerkungen zu den Brigade- und Divisions-Manöver, 1906," General von Bülow, III Armee, General-Kommando, Sekt. 1a, Nr. 1439 |
| | 17 Berichte des Hauptmanns Friedrich Erckert vom Militärbezirk Hasuur an das Kaiserliche Kommando Süd, 25. März 1907–26. April 1907 |
| | 19 Taktische Aufgaben für die Offiziere beim Generalstab, 1883 |
| | 23 Kaisermanöver, 1912 |
| | 25 Konferenzen des Generalstabs der Armee mit Vertretern der Heeresverwaltung, der Marine sowie der Militär-Eisenbahnen, Protokolle, 30. Januar 1912 |
| M Sq 1/2212 | Nachlaß Tieschowitz von Tieschowa |

*Bibliography*

## Bayerisches Hauptstaatsarchiv-Kriegsarchiv, Munich (BHSA)

### Königlich-Bayerisches Kriegsministerium (M. Kr.)

M. Kr. M 27 Bezirke des IV, XI und XVIII Armeekorps vom 1. April 1899

M. Kr. 43 Abtransport nach Schluß des Kaisermanövers, 1907

M. Kr. 41–44 reports of K.B. Militär-Bevollmächtigter in Berlin, Karl Ritter von Wenninger and Konstantin von Gebsattel, 1911–14

M. Kr. N 33 Übersicht über die auf Grund des Gesetzes über die Friedenspräsenzstärke des Deutschen Heeres vom 27. März 1911 und des Ergänzungsgesetzes vom 14. Juni 1912 getroffenen und noch zu treffenden Maßnahmen

M. Kr. 1125 Übersicht der vorhandenen Truppen-Einheiten der größeren Staaten Europas," geheim, 1893

M. Kr. 1126 "Übersicht der Neuformationen bezw. Etatserhöhungen."

M. Kr. 1128 III Armeekorps, Nürnberg, 1911–20

M. Kr. 1129 K.B. Inspektion der Fuss-Artillerie 16. März 1900, geheim

M. Kr. 1130 K.B. Inspektion der Kavalerie, 1904–5

M. Kr. 1133 Beiordnungs-Blatt, 30. Juli 1913

M. Kr. 1576 Deckblätter Nr. 40–142, Mobilmachungs-Bestimmungen, 1901–2, Sächsische Armee, geheim

M. Kr. 1581 Deckblätter, 1909–12

M. Kr. 1582 Deckblätter for 1913, change sheets numbers 405–547, dated November 1912, good from 1 April 1913

M. Kr. 1583 Mobilmachungs-Plan für die K. Bayerische Armee, 8. September 1913, geheim


### Königlich-Bayerischer Generalstab

Holdings under "Generalstab" are very large; there is a 235-page catalogue describing them. They trace the evolution of the independent Bavarian general staff up to 1866 and its relationship with the Prussian general staff in Berlin thereafter.

Generalstab 358 Eisenbahnwesen-Zugstaffel, 1908–14

Generalstab 357 Linienkommandantur, 1886–95

Generalstab 657 Mobilmachungs-Fahrliste 1914/15, Linienkommandantur: Stuttgart, Straßburg Els L.K. II, M. QI, P,T, V,W,Y (the MTP for the Bavarian army corps)

Generalstab 444 mobilization year 1913–14, LC loading stations for I, II and III Armeekorps

Generalstab 445 General-Kommando XX A.K., 39 Infant. Division, 9 Fahr- und Marsch- Tafel, series for the years 1896 to 1904

*Papers of Wilhelm Groener, U.S. National Archives, Washington, D.C., (microfilm)*

These extensive materials are contained on twenty-seven rolls of microfilm. They deal with Groener's entire life, but most of the documents date from the years 1895 to 1935. Many letters both to and from Groener are included.

**roll 3**  Groener War Diaries
**roll 8**
no. 34  Groener letters to Hermann von Kuhl, Ernst Kabisch
no. 35  Groener answers to Reichsarchiv question letters
**roll 12**  Groener, "Die Eisenbahn im Weltkrieg"
**roll 13**
no. 125  wartime RRS operations, 1914 bridges destroyed
no. 126  Groener's review of Reichsarchiv history of World War I
no. 127  Groener on strategy
**roll 18**
no. 157  Groener War Academy notes, 1894
no. 158  Groener War Academy terrain studies
no. 159  Groener War Academy tactical studies
no. 160  Groener War Academy tactical sketches and maps
no. 161  Groener War Academy notes
no. 162  Groener War Academy notes: siege studies, 1895–96
no. 163  Groener War Academy sketches
no. 164  War Academy final ride, 1896
no. 165  War Academy examination papers
no. 168  GGS RRS problems and papers, 1905–6
**roll 19**
no. 170  war game problems, GGS, RRS, 1911–14
no. 172  1912 RRS war games
Introduction to the RRS for Newly Assigned Officers
assorted maps
no. 173  RRS LC war games, 1912
War Plan Reporting Requirements
Transportstraßenkarte for I, IV, XI, and XVIII Armeekorps
no. 174  RRS LC war games, 1913
no. 176  RRS war games, 1913; War Travel Plan East, 1913/14
no. 177  RRS war games, 1914
no. 178  RRS war games, 1914
no. 180  Groener's tactical notes, 1892
War College tactical exam, 1893
War College tactical examination, 1903
**roll 20**  1907 GGS ride: final critique

*Bibliography*

**Papers of Alfred Graf Schlieffen (U.S. National Archives microfilm).**

These materials are contained on five microfilms. In spite of Eberhard Kessel's skepticism regarding anything approaching full documentation for Schlieffen, there is a good deal of material from which to draw.

**roll 1**
  nos. 1–13  family photographs, documents, and memorandums
**roll 2**
       family photographs, letters, and memorandums
**roll 3**
  no. 29    Erinnerungen Alfred Graf Schlieffen
  no. 30    Schlieffen's letters to his mother
  no. 32    Schlußbesprechung, Kriegsspiel, 23 December 1905, 25 maps
**roll 4**
       family photographs and letters
**roll 5**
       Schlieffen's letters to his mother and father, 1859–90
       letters of Anna Schlieffen to Alfred, 1866–70
       documents and maps from the Kaisermanöver, 1901
       Denkschrift dated December 1905, "Krieg gegen Frankreich," with maps
       Denkschrift dated 28 December 1912, with maps

**Books, Articles, Theses**

Addington, Larry. *The Patterns of War since the Eighteenth Century.* Bloomington: Indiana University Press, 1984.

Aitken, Hugh. *Scientific Management in Action: Taylorism at Watertown Arsenal, 1908–1915.* Princeton: Princeton University Press, 1985.

Albertini, Luigi. *The Origins of the War of 1914.* 3 vols. London: Oxford University Press, 1952–57.

Allen, Thomas B. *War Games.* London: Heinemann, 1987.

Allison, Graham. *Essence of Decision: Explaining the Cuban Missile Crisis.* Boston: Little Brown, 1971.

Andreski, Stanislav. *Military Organization and Society.* Berkeley: University of California Press, 1971.

Aschenbrandt, Heinrich. *Kriegsgeschichtsschreibung und Kriegsgeschichtsstudium im deutschen Heere.* Königsten: U.S. Army Historical Division, 1953.

Bald, Detlev. *Der deutsche Generalstab, 1859–1939.* Hamburg: Sozialwissenschaftliches Institut der Bundeswehr, 1972.

——. *Vom Kaiserheer zur Bundeswehr, Sozialstruktur des Militärs: Politik der*

*Rekrutierung von Offizieren und Unteroffizieren.* Frankfurt: Peter Lang, 1981.

———. "Zum Kriegsbild der militärischen Führung im Kaiserreich." In Jost Dülffer and Karl Holl, eds., *Bereit zum Krieg: Kriegsmentalität im Wilhelminischen Deutschland, 1890–1914.* Göttingen: Vandenhoeck & Ruprecht, 1986.

Barnard, Henry. *Military Schools and Courses of Instruction in the Science and Art of War.* 2 vols. Philadelphia: J.B. Lippincott, 1862.

Bauer, H. *Deutsche Eisenbahner im Weltkriege, 1914–1918.* Stuttgart: Chr. Belser, 1927.

Beniger, James. *The Control Revolution: Technological and Economic Origins of the Information Society.* Cambridge, Mass.: Harvard University Press, 1986.

Berdahl, Robert M. *The Politics of the Prussian Nobility: The Development of a Conservative Ideology, 1770–1848.* Princeton: Princeton University Press, 1988.

Bergh, M. von dem. *Das deutsche Heer vor dem Weltkrieg.* Berlin: Sanssouci Verlag, 1934.

Berghahn, Volker. *Germany and the Approach of War in 1914.* New York: St. Martin's Press, 1973.

———. *Modern Germany.* Cambridge: Cambridge University Press, 1982.

Bidwell, Shelford, and Graham, Dominick. *Fire Power: British Army Weapons and Theories of War, 1904–1945.* Boston: Allen & Unwin, 1985.

Bigler, Robert M. *The Politics of German Protestantism: The Rise of the Protestant Church Elite in Prussia, 1815–1848.* Berkeley: University of California Press, 1972.

Bircher, Eugen. "Die Krisis in der Marneschlacht." *Schweizerische Monatsschrift für Offiziere aller Waffen und Organ für Kriegswirtschaft* 30 (1926): 17–29.

Bircher, Eugen, and Bode, Walter. *Schlieffen: Mann und Idee.* Zurich: Albert Nauck, 1937.

Bloch, I.S. *The Future of War in Its Technical, Economic, and Political Relations.* London, 1900.

Boehn, Hubert von. *Generalstabsgeschäfte.* Potsdam, 1875.

Boetticher, Friedrich von. *Alfred Graf Schlieffen.* Göttingen: Musterschmidt, 1957.

———. *The Art of War.* Bielefeld: U.S. Army Historical Division, 1951.

———. *The Schlieffen Problems.* Fort Leavenworth, Kansas: U.S. Army Command and General Staff School, 1925.

Bolter, J. David. *Turning's Man: Western Culture in the Computer Age.* Chapel Hill: University of North Carolina Press, 1984.

Bradford, Ernest S. "Prussian Railway Administration." *Annals of the American Academy of Political and Social Science* 29 (March 1907): 66–77.

Bracken, Paul. *The Command and Control of Nuclear Forces.* New Haven: Yale University Press, 1983.

Bramsted, Ernest K. *Aristocracy and the Middle Classes in Germany: Social Types in German Literature, 1830–1900*. Chicago: University of Chicago Press, 1964.

Brandt, Heinrich von. *Aus dem Leben des Generals der Infanterie z.D. Dr. Heinrich von Brandt*. Berlin: E.S. Mittler, 1868.

Brecht, Martin. "Der Spätpietismus: Ein vergessenes oder vernachlässigtes Kapitel der protestantischen Kirchengeschichte." *Pietismus und Neuzeit* 10 (1984): 124–51.

Bright, James R. "Technology Forecasting Literature: Emergence and Impact on Technology Innovation." In Patrick Kelly and Melvin Kranzberg, eds., *Technological Innovation: A Critical Review of the Current Literature*. San Francisco: San Francisco Press, 1978, pp. 299–334.

Bucholz, Arden. *Hans Delbrück and the German Military Establishment: War Images in Conflict*. Iowa City: University of Iowa Press, 1985.

Budde, Hermann. *Die französischen Eisenbahnen im deutschen Kriegsbetriebe, 1870–71*. Berlin: E.S. Mittler, 1904.

Buddensieg, Tilmann. *Industriekultur: Peter Behrens und die AEG*. Translated by I.B. Whyte. Cambridge, Mass.: MIT Press, 1984.

Bunsen, Marie von. *Zeitgenossen die Ich Erlebte, 1900–1930*. Leipzig: Koehler & Ameland, 1932.

Burchardt, Lothar. *Friedenswirtschaft und Kriegsvorsorge: Deutschlands wirtschaftliche Rüstungsbestrebungen vor 1914*. Boppart am Rhein: Harald Boldt, 1968.

———. "Technischer Forschritt und sozialer Wandel: Das Beispiel der Taylorismus-Rezeption." In Wilhelm Treue, ed., *Deutsche Technikgeschichte*. Göttingen: Vandenhoeck & Ruprecht, 1977, pp. 52–98.

Burtt, Philip. *Control on the Railways*. London: George Allen & Unwin, 1929.

———. *Principal Factors in Freight Train Operation*. London: George Allen & Unwin, 1923.

Büsch, Otto. *Militärsystem und Sozialleben im alten Preußen, 1713–1807*. Berlin: Walter de Gruyter, 1962.

Caemmerer, General August von. *Die Entwicklung der Strategischen Wissenschaft im 19.Jahrhundert*. Berlin: Wilhelm Baensch, 1904.

Campbell, Joan. *Joy in Work, German Work: The National Debate, 1800–1945*. Princeton: Princeton University Press, 1989.

Canis, Konrad. *Bismarck und Waldersee: Die außenpolitischen Krisenerscheinungen und das Verhalten des Generalstabes, 1882–1890*. East Berlin: Akademie Verlag, 1980.

———. "Bismarck, Waldersee und die Kriegsgefahr Ende 1887." In Horst Bartel and Ernst Engelberg, eds., *Die großpreußisch-militaristische Reichsgründung 1871*. East Berlin: Akademie Verlag, 1971.

Carlson, Brigitta. "Good Teachers: Honoring a Tradition." *University of Chicago Magazine* 78, no. 2 (Winter 1986): 14–18.

Cecil, Lamar. *Wilhelm II: Prince and Emperor, 1859–1900*. Chapel Hill: University of North Carolina Press, 1989.

Chandler, Alfred D, Jr. *The Visible Hand: The Managerial Revolution in American Business*. Cambridge, Mass.: Harvard University Press, 1977.

Chandler, David, ed. *A Guide to the Battlefields of Europe*. 2 vols. Philadelphia: Chilton Books, 1965.

Chickering, Roger. "Der 'Deutsche Wehrverein' und die Reform der deutschen Armee, 1912–1914." *Militärgeschichtliche Mitteilungen* 1 (1979): 1–35.

——. *We Men Who Feel Most German*. Boston: Allen & Unwin, 1984.

Child, John. *Organization: A Guide to Problems and Practices*. 2d ed. London: Harper & Row, 1984.

Clapham, J.H. *The Economic Development of France and Germany*. 4th ed. Cambridge: Cambridge University Press, 1963.

Coetzee, Marilyn S. *The German Army League: Popular Nationalism in Wilhelmine Germany*. New York: Oxford University Press, 1990.

Colin, Jean. *The Transformations of War*. Translated by L.H.R. Pope-Hennessy. London: Hugh Rees, 1912.

Collenburg, Freiherr Ludwig Rüdt von. "Graf Schlieffen und die Kriegsformation der deutschen Armee." *Wissen und Wehr* 8 (1927): 605–34.

Craig, Gordon. *The Battle of Königgrätz*. Philadelphia: J./B. Lippincott, 1964.

——. "Facing Up to the Nazis." *New York Review of Books*, January 1989, pp. 10–15.

——. *From Bismarck to Adenauer: Aspects of German Statecraft*. Rev. ed. New York: Harper Torchbook, 1965.

——. *Germany, 1866–1945*. New York: Oxford University Press, 1978.

——. *The Politics of the Prussian Army*. New York: Oxford University Press, 1955.

Creveld, Martin van. *Command in War*. Cambridge, Mass.: Harvard University Press, 1985.

——. *Fighting Power*. Westport, Conn.: Greenwood Press, 1982.

——. *Supplying War: Logistics from Wallenstein to Patton*. Cambridge: Cambridge University Press, 1977.

Cruttwell, C.R.M.F. *A History of the Great War*. 2d ed. Oxford: Clarendon Press, 1940.

Dalton, Herman. *Johannes Goßner: Ein Lebensbild aus der Kirche des neunzehnten Jahrhunderts*. 3d ed. Berlin-Friedenau: Buchhandlung der Goßnerschen Mission, 1898.

Dannhauer, General von. "Das Reisswitz-Kriegsspiel von seinem Beginn bis zum Tod des Gründers, 1827," *Militär-Wochenblatt*, no. 56 (11 July 1874): pp. 524–32.

Deist, Wilhelm. "Zur Geschichte des preußischen Offizierkorps, 1888–1918." In H.H. Hoffmann, ed., *Das deutsche Offizierkorps,*

*1860–1960*. Boppard am Rhein: Harald Boldt, 1979, pp. 39–57.

Delbrück, Hans. *Geschichte der Kriegskunst im Rahmen der politischen Geschichte*. 4 vols. Berlin: George Stilke, 1900–1920.

——. *Historische und politische Aufsätze*. Berlin: Georg Reimer, 1886.

——. *Das Leben des Feldmarschalls Grafen Neidhardt von Gneisenau*. 2 vols. Berlin: George Stilke, 1880.

——. "Moltke." In *Erinnerungen, Aufsätze und Reden*. Berlin: Georg Stilke, 1902, pp. 546–75.

——. *Die Strategie des Perikles erläutert durch die Strategie Friedrichs des Großen*. Berlin: Walther & Apoland, 1890.

Demeter, Karl. *The German Officer Corps in Society and State*. London: Weidenfeld & Nicolson, 1965.

Dissow, Joachim von. *Adel im Übergang: Ein kritischer Standesgenosse berichtet aus Residenzen und Gutshäusern*. Stuttgart: W. Kohlhammer Verlag, 1961.

*Documents Relating to the Fixing of a Standard Time*. Ottawa: Brown Chamberlain, 1891.

Douglas, Mary. *How Institutions Think*. London: Routledge and Kegan Paul, 1987.

Drucker, Peter F. *The New Realities*. New York: Harper & Row, 1989.

Eckardstein, Herman Freiherr von. *Lebenserinnerungen und politische Denkwürdigkeiten*. Leipzig: Verlag Paul List, 1920.

Einem, General von. *Erinnerungen eines Soldaten, 1853–1933*. 6th ed. Leipzig: R.F. Koehler, 1933.

Eley, Geoff. *Reshaping the German Right*. New Haven: Yale University Press, 1980.

Ellis, John. *The Social History of the Machine Gun*. Baltimore: Johns Hopkins University Press, 1975.

Elze, Walter. *Tannenberg: Das Deutsche Heer vor 1914: Seine Grundzüge und deren Auswirkung im Sieg an der Ostfront*. Breslau: Ferdinand Hirt, 1928.

Evans, Paul. W. "Strategic Signal Communications: A Study of Signal Communications as Applied to Large Field Forces, Based upon the Operations of the German Signal Corps during the March on Paris in 1914." *Signal Corps Bulletin* 82 (1935): 24–58.

Evera, Stephen van. "The Cult of the Offensive and the Origins of the First World War." In Steven Miller, ed., *Military Strategy and the Origins of the First World War*. Princeton: Princeton University Press, 1985, pp. 58–107.

*Festschrift des königlich-preußischen statistischen Bureaus*. Berlin: Verlag des königlichen statistischen Bureaus, 1905.

Fischer, Fritz. *Germany's Aims in the First World War*. New York: W.W. Norton, 1967.

——. *War of Illusions: German Policies from 1911 to 1914*. New York: W.W. Norton, 1975.

Fontane, Theodor. "The Eighteenth of March." In Peter Demetz, ed., *Theodor Fontane: Short Novels and Other Works*. New York: Continuum, 1982. pp. 224–34.

"Foreign War Games." Translated by H.O.S. Heistand. In *Selected Professional Papers*. Washington, D.C.: U.S. Government Printing Office, 1898.

Förster, Stig. *Der doppelte Militarismus: Die deutsche Heeresrüstungspolitik zwischen Status-Quo-Sicherung und Aggression, 1890–1913*. Stuttgart: Franz Steiner, 1985.

——. "Optionen der Kriegführung im Zeitalter des 'Volkskrieges' – Zu Helmuth von Moltkes militärisch-politischen Überlegungen nach den Erfahrungen der Einigungskriege." In Detlef Bald, ed., *Militärische Verantwortung in Staat und Gesellschaft: 175 Jahre Generalstabsausbildung in Deutschland*. Koblenz: Bernard & Graefe, 1986.

François, Hermann von. *Verwaltungs-Generalstabsreisen*. Berlin: Reichsdruckerei, 1910.

Fremdling, Rainer. "Germany." In Patrick O'Brien, ed., *Railways and the Economic Development of Western Europe, 1830–1914*. New York: St. Martin's Press, 1983.

French, Thomas E., and Vierck, Charles J. *Engineering Drawing and Graphic Technology*. 12th ed. New York: McGraw-Hill, 1978.

Freytag-Loringhoven, Hugo Freiherr von. "Introduction." In Alfred Graf Schlieffen, *Cannae*. Fort Leavenworth: U.S. Army Command and General Staff School, 1931.

——. "Introduction." In Großer Generalstab, ed., *Alfred von Schlieffen: Gesammelte Schriften*. 2 vols. Berlin: E.S. Mittler, 1913, pp. 7–36.

Fulbrook, Mary. *Piety and Politics: Religion and the Rise of Absolutism in England, Württemberg, and Prussia*. Cambridge: Cambridge University Press, 1983.

Fuller, J.F.C. *The Conduct of War*. New York: Funk & Wagnalls, 1968.

——. *A Military History of the Western World*. 3 vols. New York: Funk & Wagnalls, 1954.

Fussell, Paul. *The Great War and Modern Memory*. Oxford: Oxford University Press, 1975.

Gaertringen, Freiherr Hiller von, ed. *Wilhelm Groener: Lebenserinnerungen*. Göttingen: Vandenhoeck & Ruprecht, 1957.

Galbraith, John K. *The New Industrial State*. 2d ed. London: Penguin Books, 1972.

Gall, Lothar. *Bismarck: The White Revolutionary*. Vol. 1, 1815–1871. London: Allen & Unwin, 1986.

Gawthrop, Richard L. "Lutheran Pietism and the Weber Thesis." *German Studies Review* 12, no. 2 (May 1989): 237–48.

Gebsattel, Ludwig Freiherr von. *Generalfeldmarschall Karl von Bülow*. Munich: J.F. Lehmanns, 1929.

Geiss, Imanuel. *Julikrise und Kriegsausbruch 1914*. 2 vols. Hanover: Verlag für Literatur und Zeitgeschehen, 1963.

——. *July 1914: The Outbreak of the First World War*. New York: Harpers, 1974.

Generalstab des Heeres. *Geschäftsordnung für den Großen Generalstab und die Landesaufnahme*. Berlin: Reichsdruckerei, 1913.

Generalstab des Heeres, Kriegswissenschaftliche Abteilung, ed. *Bestimmungen über Generalstabsreisen*. Berlin: E.S. Mittler, 1908.

——. *Dienstschriften des Chefs des Generalstabs der Armee Generalfeldmarschall Graf Alfred von Schlieffen*. 2 vols. Berlin: E.S. Mittler, 1937.

——. *Die französische Armee*. Berlin: E.S. Mittler, 1909.

——. *Der Schlachterfolge, mit welchen Mitteln wurden Sie erstrebt?* Berlin: E.S. Mittler, 1903.

German Army. *Regulations for Maneuver*. Translated by the War Office General Staff. London: Harrison and Sons, 1908.

*German Army Handbook*. Translated by the War Office. Reprint of *The Handbook of the German Army in War*. London: War Office, 1918; London: Arms and Armour Press, 1977.

Gerth, Hans H., and Mills, C. Wright, eds. *From Max Weber: Essays in Sociology*. New York: Oxford University Press, 1946.

Geyer, Michael. *Deutsche Rüstungspolitik, 1860–1980*. Frankfurt: Suhrkamp, 1984.

——. "German Strategy in the Age of Machine Warfare, 1914–1945." In Peter Paret, ed., *Makers of Modern Strategy from Machiavelli to the Nuclear Age*. Princeton: Princeton University Press, 1986, pp. 527–97.

——. "The Militarization of Europe, 1914–1945." In John Gillis, ed., *The Militarization of the Western World*. New Brunswick: Rutgers University Press, 1989, pp. 65–103.

Geyl, Egon Freiherr von. *General von Schlichting und sein Lebenswerk*. Berlin: E.S. Mittler, 1913.

Gilbert, Felix, ed. *The Historical Essays of Otto Hintze*. Princeton: Princeton University Press, 1975.

Gillis, John R., ed. *The Militarization of the Western World*. New Brunswick: Rutgers University Press, 1989.

——. *The Prussian Bureaucracy in Crisis, 1840–1860: Origins of an Administrative Ethos*. Stanford: Stanford University Press, 1971.

Gispen, Kees. *New Profession, Old Order: Engineers and German Society, 1815–1914*. Cambridge: Cambridge University Press, 1989.

Gleich, Generalmajor a.D. von. *Die alte Armee und ihre Verirrungen*. Leipzig: R.F. Koehler, 1919.

Goldschmidt, Hans. *Das Reich und Preußen im Kampf um die Führung*. Berlin: Carl Heymanns Verlag, 1931.

Gollwitzer, Heinz. *Die Standesherren: Die politische und gesellschaftliche Stellung der Mediatisierten, 1815–1918*. 2d ed. Göttingen: Vandenhoeck & Ruprecht, 1964.

Görlitz, Walter. *History of the German General Staff*. New York: Praeger, 1957.

——. *Die Junker: Adel und Bauern im deutschen Osten*. 4th ed. Limburg: C.U. Starke Verlage, 1981.

——, ed. *Der Kaiser: Aufzeichnungen des Chefs des Marine-Kabinetts Admiral Georg Alexander von Mueller*. Göttingen: Vandenhoeck & Ruprecht, 1965.

"Graf Alfred von Waldersee." *Deutsche Illustrierte Zeitung*. 60 (October 1888): 1003–4.

Granier, Gerhard. "Deutsche Rüstungspolitik vor dem Ersten Weltkriege: General Franz Wandels Tagebuchaufzeichnungen aus dem preußischen Kriegsministerium." *Militärgeschichtliche Mitteilungen* 2 (1985): 123–62.

Greenhood, David. *Mapping*. Chicago: University of Chicago Press, 1964.

Groener, Wilhelm. *Feldherr wider Willen: Operative Studien über den Weltkrieg*. Berlin: E.S. Mittler, 1931.

——. *Das Testament Graf Schlieffen*. Berlin: E.S. Mittler, 1930.

——. *The Testament of Count Schlieffen*. Translated by W.P. Papenforth. Carlisle Barracks, Pa.: U.S. Army War College, 1983.

Groener-Geyer, Dorothea. "Die Odyssee der Groener Papiere." *Die Welt als Geschichte* 14 (1959): 52–64.

——. *General Groener: Soldat und Staatsmann*. Frankfurt: Societas Verlag, 1955.

Hacker, Barton C., and Hacker, Sally L. "Military Institutions and the Labor Process: Noneconomic Sources of Technological Change, Women's Subordination, and the Organization of Work." *Technology and Culture* 28, no. 4 (October 1987): 743–75.

Hagerman, Edward. *The American Civil War and the Origins of Modern Warfare*. Bloomington, Ind.: Indiana University Press, 1988.

Haines, Henry S. *Efficient Railway Operation*. New York: Macmillan, 1919.

Hammer, Karl. "Die preußischen Könige und Königinnen im 19. Jahrhundert und ihr Hof." In Karl F. Werner, ed., *Hof, Kultur und Politik im 19. Jahrhundert*. Bonn: Ludwig Röhrscheid Verlag, 1985, pp. 90–110.

Hartmann, Julius von. *Lebenserinnerungen, Briefe und Aufsätze*. Berlin: Verlag von Gebrüder Paetel, 1882.

Haeussler, Helmut. *General William Groener and the Imperial German Army*. Madison: State Historical Society of Wisconsin, 1962.

Hausrath, Alfred H. *Venture Simulation in War, Business, and Politics*. New York: McGraw-Hill, 1971.

Henderson, A.H., and Parsons, Talcott, eds. *Max Weber. The Theory of Social and Economic Organization*. Glencoe, Ill.: Free Press, 1947.

Hensmen, Howard. "French and German Manoeuvres: Some Comparisons." *United Service Magazine*, November 1909, pp. 195–210.

Herf, Jeffrey. *Reactionary Modernism: Technology, Culture and Politics in Weimar and the Third Reich*. Cambridge: Cambridge University Press, 1984.

Herwig, Holger. "Imperial Germany." In Ernest May, ed., *Knowing One's Enemies*. Princeton: Princeton University Press, 1984, pp. 62–97.

*History of Railroads*. 2 vols. London: Times-Mirror, 1972.

Höbett, Lothar. "Schlieffen, Beck, Potiorek und das Ende der gemeinsamen deutsch-österreichisch-ungarischen Aufmarschpläne im Osten." *Militärgeschichtliche Mitteilungen* 12 (1984): 7–30.

Hoffbauer, E. von. *Schwebende Feldartillerie-Fragen*. Berlin: E.S. Mittler, 1904.

Homberg, Heidrun. "Anfänge des Taylorsystems in Deutschland vor dem Ersten Weltkriege." *Geschichte und Gesellschaft* 4 (1978): 170–84.

Hull, Elizabeth. *The Entourage of Kaiser Wilhelm II, 1888–1918*. Cambridge: Cambridge University Press, 1982.

Hutten-Czapski, Bogdan Graf. *Sechzig Jahre Politik und Gesellschaft*. 2 vols. Berlin, 1935.

Henderson, W.O. *The State and the Industrial Revolution in Prussia, 1740–1870*. Manchester: University of Manchester, 1958.

Hillard, Gustav. "Epilog auf den preußisch-deutschen Generalstabsoffizier." *Neue Deutsche Hefte* 100 (July–August 1964): 90–99.

Hoffmann, Joachim. "Der Militärschriftsteller Fritz Hönig." *Militärgeschichtliche Mitteilungen* 1 (1970): 12–33.

Hoffmann, Max. *War Diaries*. London: Martin Seecker, 1921.

Holborn, Hajo. *A History of Modern Germany*. 3 vols. New York: Alfred Knopf, 1969–71.

Hoppenstadt, Julius. *Wie studiert man Kriegsgeschichte?* Berlin: E.S. Mittler, 1904.

Hostetler, John. *Hutterite Society*. Baltimore: Johns Hopkins University Press, 1974.

Howard, Michael. "Europe on the Eve of the First World War." In R.J.W. Evans and Hartmut Pogge von Strandmann, eds., *The Coming of the First World War*. Oxford: Clarendon Press, 1988, pp. 1–17.

——. *The German-French War*. New York: Collier Books, 1969.

——. "Men against Fire: Expectations of War in 1914." In Steven Miller, ed., *Military Strategy and the Origins of the First World War*. Princeton: Princeton University Press, 1985, pp. 41–57.

Huntington, Samuel P. *The Soldier and the State*. Cambridge, Mass.: Harvard University Press, 1957.

Irvine, Dallas D. "The French and Prussian Staff Systems before 1870." *Journal of the American Military History Foundation* 2 (1938): 192–203.

——. "The Origins of Capital Staffs." *Journal of Modern History* 10, no. 2 (June 1938): 161–79.

Jacob, Herbert. *German Administration since Bismarck: Central Authority versus Local Autonomy*. New Haven: Yale University Press, 1963.

Jähns, Max. *Feldmarschall Moltke*. 2d ed. Berlin: Ernst Hoffmann, 1906.

——. "Das Militair-Wochenblatt von 1816 bis 1876." In *Max Jähns:*

*Militärgeschichtliche Aufsätze*. Edited by Ursula von Gersdorff. Osnabrück: Biblio Verlag, 1970, pp. 287–304.

James, Harold. *A German Identity, 1770–1990*. London: Weidenfeld and Nicolson, 1989.

Janowitz, Morris. *The Military in the Political Development of the New Nations*. Chicago: University of Chicago Press, 1964.

Jany, Kurt. *Geschichte der preußischen Armee vom 15. Jahrhundert bis 1914*. 2d ed. 4 vols. Osnabrück: Biblio Verlag, 1967.

Jarausch, Konrad. *The Enigmatic Chancellor: Bethmann Hollweg and the Hubris of Imperial Germany*. New Haven: Yale University Press, 1973.

Johns, Emory J. *Railroad Administration*. New York: Appleton, 1910.

Jones, P.B. "Teaching Surveying in a School of Civil Engineering." In D. Campbell-Allan and E.H. Davis, eds., *The Profession of Civil Engineering*. Sidney, Australia: Sidney University Press, 1979, pp. 71–81.

Keegan, John. *The Face of Battle*. New York: Viking Press, 1976.

——. *The Mask of Command*. New York: Penguin Books, 1987.

Kehr, Eckart. *Economic Interest, Militarism, and Foreign Policy: Essays on German History*. Translated by Grete Heinz. Edited by Gordon Craig. Berkeley: University of California Press, 1977.

Keiger, John F.V. *France and the Origins of the First World War*. New York: St. Martin's Press, 1983.

Kennan, George. *The Fateful Alliance: France, Russia, and the Coming of the First World War*. New York: Pantheon Books, 1984.

Kennedy, Paul, ed. *The War Plans of the Great Powers, 1880–1914*. Boston: Allen & Unwin, 1985.

Kern, Stephen. *The Culture of Time and Space*. Cambridge, Mass.: Harvard University Press, 1983.

Kessel, Eberhard. *Generalfeldmarschall Graf Alfred Schlieffens Briefe*. Göttingen: Vandenhoeck & Ruprecht, 1958.

——. *Moltke*. Stuttgart: K.F. Koehler, 1957.

——. "Moltke und die Kriegsgeschichte." *Militärwissenschaftliche Rundschau* 2 (1941): 99–105.

——. "Die Tätigkeit des Grafen Waldersee als Generalquartiermeister und Chef des Generalstabs der Armee." *Welt als Geschichte* 14 (1954): 192–221.

Kiraly, Bela, and Djordevich, Dimitrije, eds. *East Central European Society and the Balkans Wars*. New York: Columbia University Press, 1987.

Kirchhoff, Hermann. *Vereinheitlichung des deutschen Eisenbahnwesens*. Stuttgart: J.G. Cotta, 1913.

Kitchen, Martin. *The German Officer Corps, 1890–1914*. Oxford: Clarendon Press, 1968.

Kittel, Helmuth. *Alfred Graf Schlieffen: Jugend und Glaube*. Berlin: Verlag des Evangelischen Bundes, 1939.

Kluck, Generaloberst Alexander von. *Wanderjahre – Kriege – Gestalten*.

Berlin: R. Eisenschmidt, 1929.

Knoll, Werner, and Rahne, Hermann. "Bedeutung und Aufgaben der Konferenz der Generalstabschefs der Armeekorps in Frankfurt a.M. am 21. Januar 1914." *Militärgeschichte* 25, no. 1 (1986): 55–63.

Kocka, Jürgen. "The Rise of the Modern Industrial Enterprise in Germany." In Alfred D. Chandler, Jr., and Hermann Daems, eds., *Managerial Hierarchies: Comparative Perspectives on the Rise of the Modern Industrial Enterprise*. Cambridge, Mass.: Harvard University Press, 1980, pp. 77–99.

——. *Unternehmensverwaltung und Angestelltenschaft am Beispiel Siemens, 1847–1914*. Stuttgart: Ernst Klett, 1969.

Konvitz, Josef. *Cartography in France, 1660–1848*. Chicago: University of Chicago Press, 1987.

Koszyk, Kurt. "Erhard Deutelmoser – Offizier und Pressechef." *Publizistik* 30 (10 November 1985): 511–34.

Kranzberg, Melvin, and Kelly, Patrick, eds. *Technological Innovation: A Critical Review of the Literature*. San Francisco: San Francisco Press, 1972.

Krauß, Georg. "150 Jahre preußische Meßtischblätter." *Zeitschrift für Vermessungswesen* 94, no. 4 (April 1969): 125–35.

Kriegsgeschichtliche Abteilung des Großen Generalstabs. *Der deutsch-französische Krieg, 1870–71*. 8 vols. Berlin: E.S. Mittler, 1874–81.

——. *Der Feldzug von 1866 in Deutschland*. Berlin: E.S. Mittler, 1867.

Kuhl, Hermann von. *Der deutsche Generalstab in Vorbereitung und Durchführung des Weltkrieges*. 2d ed. Berlin: E.S. Mittler, 1920.

Kuhl, Hermann von, and Bergmann, General von. *Movement and Supply of the German First Army during August and September 1914*. Fort Leavenworth: U.S. Army Command and General Staff School Press, 1929.

Ladebur, Freiherr Ferdinand von, ed. *Die Geschichte des deutschen Unteroffiziers*. Berlin: Junker & Dünnhaupt Verlag, 1939.

Lambi, Ivo. *The Navy and German Power Politics*. Boston: Allen & Unwin, 1984.

Lancken-Wakenitz, Oscar Freiherr von der. *Meine dreißig Dienstjahre, 1888–1918*. Berlin: Verlag für Kulturpolitik, 1931.

Lebow, Richard Ned. "Windows of Opportunity: Do States Jump through Them?" In Steven E. Miller, ed., *Military Strategy and the Origins of the First World War*. Princeton: Princeton University Press, 1985, pp. 147–86.

Lenoir, Timothy. "A Magic Bullet: Research for Profit and the Growth of Knowledge in Germany Around 1900." *Minerva* 26 (Spring 1988): 66–88.

Lerman, Katherine. "The Decisive Relationship: Kaiser Wilhelm II and Chancellor Bernhard von Bülow, 1900–1905." In John Röhl, ed., *Kaiser Wilhelm II: New Interpretations*. Cambridge: Cambridge University Press, 1982, pp. 221–47.

——. "Bernhard von Bülow and the Governance of Germany, 1897–1909." Ph.D. dissertation, University of Sussex, 1984.

Lexis, W. *Die Hochschulen für besondere Fachgebiete im Deutschen Reich.* Berlin: A. Ascher, 1904.

Lieven, D.C.B. *Russia and the Origins of the First World War.* New York: St. Martin's Press, 1983.

Liss, Ulrich. "Graf Schlieffens letztes Kriegsspiel." *Wehrwissenschaftliche Rundschau* 15 (1965): 161–67.

Litzmann, Karl. *Lebenserinnerungen.* 2 vols. Berlin: E. Eisenschmidt, 1927.

Livonius, Otto. "Erinnerungen eines alten Blücher-Husaren." In Gerd Stolz and Eberhard Grieser, eds., *Geschichte des Kavalerie-Regiments 5.* Munich: Schild Verlag, 1975, pp. 197–269.

Löe, Freiherr von. *Erinnerungen aus meinem Berufsleben.* Stuttgart: Deutsche Verlags-Anstalt, 1906.

Löbell, A. von. "Militärische Rundschau." *Der Tag,* 17 September 1907.

Lossow, Walter von. "Mission Type Tactics versus Order Type Tactics." *Military Review* 57 (June 1977): 87–91.

Ludendorff, Erich. *Kriegführung und Politik.* 3d ed. Berlin: E.S. Mittler, 1923.

Luvaas, Jay. *The Military Legacy of the Civil War: The European Heritage.* Chicago: University of Chicago Press, 1959.

Mann, Thomas. *Königliche Hoheit.* Berlin: S. Fischer Verlag, 1919.

Manstein, Erich von. *Aus einem Soldatenleben.* Bonn: Athenaeum Verlag, 1958.

Marx, Generalleutnant a.D. *Die Marne – Deutschlands Schicksal?* Berlin: E.S. Mittler, 1932.

——. "Über Schlieffen Geist und Haeseler Geist." *Militär-Wochenblatt,* no. 12 (1934): 444–48.

Massenbach, Christian von. "Über die Nothwendigkeit der engern Verbindung der Kriegs- und Staatskunde." In *Memoiren zur Geschichte des preußischen Staats unter den Regierungen Friedrich Wilhelm II und Friedrich Wilhelm III.* 3 vols. Amsterdam: Verlag des Kunst- und Industrie, Comptiors, 1809, vol. 2.

May, Ernst, ed. *Knowing One's Enemies: Intelligence Assessment before the Two World Wars.* Princeton: Princeton University Press, 1984.

Mayer, Arno. *The Persistence of the Old Regime.* New York: Pantheon, 1981.

McDermott, R.A. *The Essential Steiner.* New York: Harper & Row, 1984.

McNeill, William H. *The Pursuit of Power: Technology, Armed Force, and Society since A.D. 1000.* Chicago: University of Chicago Press, 1982.

Meier-Welcher, Hans. *Seeckt.* Frankfurt: Bernard & Graefe, 1967.

Messerschmidt, Manfred. "Militär und Schule in der Wilhelminischen Zeit." *Militärgeschichtliche Mitteilungen* 1 (1978): 51–75.

——. Das preußisch-deutsche Offizierkorps." In H.H. Hoffmann, ed., *Das deutsche Offizierkorps, 1860–1960.* Boppart am Rhein: Harald Boldt, 1978, pp. 21–38.

——. "Schulpolitik des Militärs." In Peter Baumgart, ed., *Bildungspolitik in Preußen zur Zeit des Kaiserreichs*. Stuttgart: Klett-Cotta, 1980, pp. 242–55.

Michels, Robert. *Political Parties*. Translated by Eden and Cedar Paul. Glencoe, Ill.: Free Press, 1949.

*Militär-Adreßbuch (Taschen-Rankliste) aller Offiziere und oberen Militärbeamten der Standorte Groß-Berlin, Charlottenburg, Potsdam und Spandau sowie des Gardekorps*. Charlottenburg: Verlag Litz, 1913.

Militärgeschichtliches Forschungsamt, ed. *Die Bedeutung der Logistik für die militärische Führung von der Antike bis in die Neuzeit*. Bonn: E.S. Mittler, 1986.

——. *Handbuch zur deutschen Militärgeschichte, 1648–1945*. 5 vols. Pt. 5, *Von der Entlassung Bismarcks bis zum Ende des Ersten Weltkrieges*, edited by Wiegand Schmidt-Richberg, Edgar Graf von Matuschka, and Karl Koehler. Munich: Bernard & Graefe, 1979.

——. *Tradition in deutschen Streitkräften bis 1945*. Bonn: E.S. Mittler, 1986.

Model, Hansgeorg. *Der deutsche Generalstabsoffizier*. Frankfurt: Bernard & Graefe, 1968.

Mohs, Hans. *Generalfeldmarschall Alfred Graf von Waldersee in seinem militärischen Wirken*. 2 vols. Berlin: E.S. Mittler, 1929.

Moltke, Chef des Generalstabs der Armee. *Geschäftsordnung für den Großen Generalstab und die Landesaufnahme*. Berlin: Reichsdruckerei, 1913.

Moltke, Helmuth von. *Erinnerungen, Briefe, Dokumente*. Stuttgart: Der Kommende Tag, 1922.

Mommsen, Wolfgang J. *The Age of Bureaucracy: Perspectives on the Political Sociology of Max Weber*. New York: Harper & Row, 1974.

——. "Domestic Factors in German Foreign Policy before 1914." In James J. Sheehan, ed., *Imperial Germany*. New York: Franklin Watts, 1976, pp. 223–68.

——. *Max Weber and German Politics, 1890–1920*. Translated by Michael S. Steinberg. Chicago: University of Chicago Press, 1984.

Monkhouse, F.J., and Wilkinson, H.R. *Maps and Diagrams*. 3d ed. London: Metheun, 1971.

Morozowicz, General von. "Die Königlich-preußische Landes-Aufnahme." *Militär-Wochenblatt*, Beiheft (1879): 1–35.

Morris, Roy. *Railroad Administration*. New York: D. Appleton, 1910.

Moser, Otto von. *Ernsthafte Plaudereien über den Weltkrieg*. Stuttgart: Chr. Belser, 1925.

Müller, Theo. "Die topographischen und kartographischen Vorschriften für die preußischen Meßtischblätter." *Kartographische Nachrichten* 34 (1984): 174–79.

Nelson, Richard. "Notes on the Constitution and System of Education of the Prussian Army." *United Service Magazine* (1839), pt. 3, 497–522.

*New Cambridge Modern History*. 8 vols. Cambridge: Cambridge University Press, 1969–74.

Nichols, J. Alden. *Germany after Bismarck: The Caprivi Era, 1890–1894.* New York: W.W. Norton, 1968.

——. *The Year of the Three Kaisers.* Urbana: University of Illinois Press, 1987.

Nicholson, Michael. "Games and Simulations." In Amos Perlmutter and John Gooch, eds., *Strategy and the Social Sciences.* London: Frank Cass, 1981, pp. 68–85.

Nottebohm, W. *Hundert Jahre des militärischen Prüfungsverfahrens.* Berlin: E.S. Mittler, 1908.

Nuwer, Michael. "From Batch to Flow: Production Technology and Work-Force Skills in the Steel Industry, 1880–1920." *Technology and Culture* 29 (October 1988): 808–38.

O'Etzel, F.H.O. *Terrainlehre.* 2d ed. Berlin: Verlag von Friedrich August Herbig, 1834.

Oncken, Emily. *Panthersprung nach Agadir: Die deutsche Politik während der Zweiten Marokkokrise 1911.* Düsseldorf: Droste, 1981.

Oppenheim, Janet. *The Other World: Spiritualism and Psychical Research in England, 1850–1914.* Cambridge: Cambridge University Press, 1985.

Osten-Sacken, Ottmar Freiherr von. *Preußens Heer.* 3 vols. Berlin: E.S. Mittler, 1914.

Otto, Helmuth. "Alfred Graf von Schlieffen: Generalstabschef und Militärtheoretiker des imperialistischen deutschen Kaiserreiches zwischen Weltmachtstreben und Revolutionsfurcht." *Revue internationale d'histoire militaire* 39, no. 3 (1979): 74–88.

——. "Die Herausbildung des Kraftfahrwesens im deutschen Heer bis 1914." *Militärgeschichte* 28, no. 3 (1989): 227–36.

Palmer, R.R. "Frederick the Great, Guibert, Bülow: From Dynastic to National War." In Peter Paret, ed., *Makers of Modern Strategy from Machiavelli to the Nuclear Age.* Princeton: Princeton University Press, 1986, pp. 91–119.

Paret, Peter. *Clausewitz and the State.* New York: Oxford University Press, 1976.

——. *Yorck and the Era of Prussian Reform.* Princeton: Princeton University Press, 1966.

Perlmutter, Amos. "The Military and Politics in Modern Times: A Decade Later." *Journal of Strategic Studies* 9, no. 1 (March 1986): 5–15.

Petter, Wolfgang. "Die Logistik des deutschen Heeres im deutsch-französischen Krieg von 1870–71." In Militärgeschichtliches Forschungsamt, ed., *Die Bedeutung der Logistik für die militärische Führung von der Antike bis in die Neuzeit.* Bonn: E.S. Mittler, 1986 pp. 109–33.

Pollard, Sidney. *The Genesis of Modern Management.* Cambridge, Mass.: Harvard University Press, 1965.

Pool, Ithiel de Sola, and Kessler, Allan. "The Kaiser, the Tsar, and the Computer." *American Behavioral Scientist* 8, no. 9 (1965): 31–38.

Poten, Bernhard. *Geschichte des Militär-Erziehungs- und Bildungswesens in den Landen deutscher Zunge.* 4 vols. Berlin: A. Hoffmann, 1889.

Powis, Jonathan. *Aristocracy.* London: Basic Blackwell, 1984.

Preußischer Minister der öffentlichen Arbeiten, Bayerischer Staatsminister für Verkehrsangelegenheiten, Eisenbahn-Zentralbehörden anderer deutscher Bundesstaaten. *Das deutsche Eisenbahnwesen der Gegenwart.* 2 vols. Berlin: Reimar Hobbing, 1911.

Pye, Lucian W. "Armies in the Process of Political Modernization." In John J. Johnson, ed., *The Role of the Military in Underdeveloped Countries.* Princeton: Princeton University Press, 1962, pp. 69–90.

Radziwill, Dr. Carl Prinz. *Entwicklung des fürstlich-Stolbergischen Grundbesitzes.* Jena: Verlag von Gustav Fischer, 1899.

Rahne, Hermann, *Mobilmachung.* East Berlin: Militärverlag der Deutschen Demokratischen Republik, 1983.

Rassow, Peter. "Schlieffen und Holstein." *Historische Zeitschrift* 173 (1952): 297–313.

Raulff, Heiner. *Zwischen Machtpolitik und Imperialismus: Die deutsche Frankreichpolitik, 1904–1906.* Düsseldorf: Droste Verlag, 1976.

Reichsarchiv, ed. *Der Weltkrieg 1914 bis 1918.* 25 vols. Berlin: E.S. Mittler, 1925–35.

Reisswitz, G.H.R. "Anzeige." *Militär-Wochenblatt,* no. 42 (6 March 1824): 2973–74.

Rich, Norman. *Friedrich von Holstein: Politics and Diplomacy in the Era of Bismarck and Wilhelm II.* 2 vols. Cambridge: Cambridge University Press, 1965.

Ritter, Gerhard. *The Schlieffen Plan: Critique of a Myth.* London: Oswald Wolff, 1958.

———. *The Sword and the Scepter.* Translated by Heinz Norden. 4 vols. Miami: University of Miami Press, 1969–73.

Robinson, Arthur H.; Sale, Randall D.; Morrison, Joel L.; and Muehrcke, Phillip C. *Elements of Cartography.* 5th ed. New York: John Wiley, 1984.

Rochs, Hugo. "Ärztliche Betrachtungen des schweizer Chirurgen und Oberstleutnants Bircher zum Weltkrieg." *Deutsche Medizinische Wochenschrift,* no. 33 (1927).

———. *Schlieffen: Ein Lebens- und Charakterbild für das deutsche Volk.* 2d ed. Berlin: Vossische Buchhandlung, 1921.

Röhl, John C.G. "Admiral von Müller and the Approach of War, 1911–1915." *Historical Journal* 12, no. 4 (1969): 651–73.

———. *Germany without Bismarck: The Crisis of Government in the Second Reich, 1890–1900.* Berkeley: University of California Press, 1967.

———. "Higher Civil Servants in Germany, 1890–1900." In James J. Sheehan, ed., *Imperial Germany.* New York: Franklin Watts, 1976, pp. 129–52.

———. "Hof und Hofgesellschaft unter Kaiser Wilhelm II." In Karl F.

Werner, ed., *Hof, Kultur und Politik im 19. Jahrhundert*. Bonn: Ludwig Röhrscheid, 1985, pp. 230–69.

——. *Kaiser, Hof und Staat: Wilhelm II und die deutsche Politik*. Munich: C.H. Beck, 1987.

——. *Philipp Eulenburgs politische Korrespondenz*. 4 vols. Boppart am Rhein: Harald Boldt Verlag, 1976–86.

——. ed. *Kaiser Wilhelm II: New Interpretations*. Cambridge: Cambridge University Press, 1982.

Roon, Albrecht Graf. *Denkwürdigkeiten aus dem Leben des Generalfeldmarschalls Kriegsministers Graf von Roon*. 5th ed. 5 vols. Berlin: Eduard Trewendt, 1905.

Roon, Ger van, ed. *Helmuth James Graf von Moltke: Völkerrecht im Dienst der Menschen*. Berlin: Droste Verlag, 1986.

Ropp, Theodore. *War in the Modern World*. New York: Collier Books, 1961.

Rosenberg, Hans. *Bureaucracy, Aristocracy, and Autocracy: The Prussian Experience, 1660–1815*. Boston: Beacon Press, 1966.

Rosinski, Hubert. *The German Army*. Washington, D.C.: The Infantry Journal, 1943.

Rothenburg, Gunther. "Moltke and Schlieffen." In Peter Paret, ed., *Makers of Modern Strategy from Machiavelli to the Nuclear Age*. Princeton: Princeton University Press, 1986, pp. 149–75.

Sagebiel, Martin D. "Alltag bei Hofe zur Zeit Fürst Leopold II zur Lippe." *Lippische Mitteilungen aus Geschichte und Landeskunde* 53 (1984): 207–27.

Samuel, H. *Railway Operating Principles*. London: Adhams Press, 1961.

Sarter, Adolf. *Die deutschen Eisenbahnen im Kriege*. Stuttgart: Deutsche Verlags-Anstalt, 1930.

Schaible, Camill. *Standes- und Berufspflichten des deutschen Offiziers: Für angehende und jüngere Offiziere des Stehenden Heeres und des Beurlaubtenstandes*. 3d ed. Berlin: R. Eisenschmidt, 1896.

Schall, Wolfgang. "Führungsgrundsätze in Armee und Industrie." *Wehrkunde* 14 (1964): 10–18.

Scharfe, Wilhelm. "Preußische Monarchie, preußische Kartographie." In I. Kretschmer, J. Doerflinger, and F. Wawrik, eds., *Lexikon zur Geschichte der Kartographie: Von den Anfängen bis zum Ersten Weltkrieg*. Vienna: Verlag Franz Deuticke, 1986, pp. 636–42.

Scharfenort, Louis. *Die königlich-preußische Kriegsakademie, 1810–1910*. Berlin: E.S. Mittler, 1910.

Scheel, Günter. *Die Entwicklung der deutschen Landesvermessung mit den wichtigsten Daten aus den geodätischen Nachbarbereichen und Fachinstitutionen*. Wiesbaden: Hessische Landesvermessung, 1978.

Schellendorff, Bronsart von. *The Duties of the General Staff*. 4th ed. London: His Majesty's Stationery Office, 1905.

Schichfuß und Neudorff, Erich von. "Der Sieger." In Generalleutnant a.D. von Cochenhausen, ed., *Von Scharnhorst zu Schlieffen, 1806–1906: Hundert Jahre preußisch-deutscher Generalstab.* Berlin: E.S. Mittler, 1933, pp. 145–65.

Schieder, Theodor. *Das Deutsche Kaiserreich von 1871 als Nationalstaat.* Cologne: Westdeutscher Verlag, 1961.

Schivelbusch, Wolfgang. *The Railway Journal: The Industrialization of Time and Space in the 19th Century.* Berkeley: University of California Press, 1986.

Schlieffen, Alfred Graf. *Cannae.* Fort Leavenworth: U.S. Army Command and General Staff School Press, 1931.

———. *Gesammelte Schriften.* 2 vols. Berlin: E.S. Mittler, 1913.

———. "Der Krieg in der Gegenwart." *Deutsche Revue,* January 1909, pp. 13–24.

Schmerfeld, Ferdinand von. *Die deutschen Aufmarschpläne, 1871–1890.* Berlin: E.S. Mittler, 1929.

Showalter, Dennis. "Even Generals Wet Their Pants." *War and Society* 2, no. 1 (1984): 61–86.

———. *Railroads and Rifles: Technology and the Unification of Germany.* Hamden, Conn., 1975.

———. "Prussia, Technology, and War: Artillery from 1815 to 1914." In Ronald Haycock and Keith Neilson, eds., *Men, Machines, and War.* Montreal: Wilfred Laurier University Press, 1987.

Schröder, E., ed. *Zwanzig Jahre Regierungszeit: Ein Tagebuch Kaiser Wilhelms II von Antritt der Regierung 15. Juni 1888 bis zum 15. Juni 1908.* Berlin: Verlag Deutscher Zeitschriften, 1909.

Schröder-Hohenwarth, Joachim, "Die preußische Landesaufnahme von 1816–1875." *Nachrichten aus dem Karten- und Vermessungswesen,* Reihe 1: Deutsche Beiträge und Informationen 5 (1958): 5–60.

Schulte, Bernd. *Die deutsche Armee, 1900–1914.* Düsseldorf: Droste Verlag, 1977.

———. "Neue Dokumente zu Kriegsausbruch und Kriegsverlauf 1914: Berichte des Generals von Wenninger." *Militärgeshichtliche Mitteilungen* 25, no. 1 (1979): 87–114.

———. *Vor dem Kriegsausbruch 1914.* Düsseldorf: Droste, 1980.

Scott, W. Richard. *Organizations: Rational, Natural, and Open Systems.* Englewood Cliffs, N.J.: Prentice Hall, 1981.

Seeckt, General von. *Thoughts of a Soldier.* London: Ernest Benn, 1930.

Sell, Frederick C. *Die Tragödie des deutschen Liberalismus.* Stuttgart: Deutsche Verlags-Anstalt, 1953.

Shils, Edward. "The Military in the Political Development of the New States." In David E. Novack and Robert Lakachman, eds., *Development and Society: The Dynamics of Economic Change.* New York: St. Martin's Press, 1964, pp. 393–405.

Spencer, Elaine G. "Police-Military Relations in Prussia, 1848–1914." *Journal of Social History* 19 (Winter 1985): 305–17.

Spitzemberg, Hildegard Baronin. *Das Tagebuch der Baronin Spitzemberg: Aufzeichnungen aus der Hofgesellschaft des Hohenzollernreiches.* Edited by Rudolf Vierhaus. 3d ed. Göttingen: Vandenhoeck & Ruprecht, 1963.

Staabs, Hermann von. *Aufmarsch nach zwei Fronten auf Grund der Operationspläne von 1871–1914.* Berlin: E.S. Mittler, 1925.

Stavenhagen, W. "Die geschichtliche Entwicklung des preußischen Militär-Kartenwesens." *Geographische Zeitschrift* 6 (1900): 435–49, 504–12, 549–65.

Stein, General von. *Erlebnisse und Betrachtungen.* Leipzig: Koehler, 1919.

Steiner, Zara. *Britain and the Origins of the First World War.* New York: St. Martin's Press, 1977.

Stern, Fritz. *Dreams and Delusions.* New York: Alfred Knopf, 1987.

———. *The Politics of Cultural Despair.* New York: Doubleday, 1965.

Stolberg-Wernigerode, Otto Graf zu. *Die unentschiedene Generation: Deutschlands konservative Führungsschichten am Vorabend des Ersten Weltkrieges.* Munich: R. Oldenbourg, 1968.

———. "Prussia." In David Spring, ed., *European Landed Elites in the Nineteenth Century.* Baltimore: Johns Hopkins University Press, 1977, pp. 45–67.

Stone, Norman. *The Eastern Front, 1914–1917.* New York: Scribners, 1975.

———. "Moltke and Conrad Plan Their War." In Paul Kennedy, ed., *The War Plans of the Great Powers.* Boston: Allen & Unwin, 1985, pp. 222–51.

Stradonitz, Stephan von. "Über die Zuständigkeit des preußischen Heraldsamts." *Archiv für öffentliches Recht* 18 (1903): 191–211.

Stromberg, Roland N. *Redemption by War.* Lawrence, Kans.: Regents Press of Kansas, 1982.

Synder, Jack. *The Ideology of the Offensive: Military Decision Making and the Disasters of 1914.* Ithaca: Cornell University Press, 1984.

Teske, Hermann. *Colmar von der Goltz.* Göttingen: Musterschmidt, 1957.

Thadden, Rudolf von. *Prussia: The History of a Lost State.* Cambridge: Cambridge University Press, 1987.

Thaer, Albrecht von. *Generalstabsdienst an der Front und in der O.H.L.* Edited by S.A. Kaehler. Göttingen: Vandenhoeck & Reprecht, 1958.

Thiede, Dr. "Das Zentraldirektorium der Vermessungen im preußischen Staat und sein Einfluß auf das preußische Vermessungswesen." *Zeitschrift für Vermessungswesen* 64 (1935): 148–59.

Tönnies, Ferdinand. "Deutscher Adel im neunzehnten Jahrhundert." *Neue Rundschau* 2 (1912): 1041–63.

Totten, Charles A.L. *Strategos.* New York: D. Appleton, 1880.

Travers, Tim. *The Killing Ground: The British Army, the Western Front, and the Emergence of Modern Warfare, 1900–1918.* London: Allen & Unwin, 1987.

Treue, Wilhelm, ed. *Deutsche Technikgeschichte*. Göttingen: Vandenhoeck & Ruprecht, 1977.

Trumpener, Ulrich. "German Military Involvement in the First Balkan War." In Bela Kiraly and Dimitrije Djorderich, eds., *East Central European Society and the Balkan Wars*. New York: Columbia University Press, 1987, pp. 346–62.

——. "Junkers and Others: The Rise of Commoners in the Prussian Army, 1871–1914." *Canadian Journal of History* 4, no. 1 (April 1979): 29–47.

——. "War Premeditated? German Intelligence Operations in July 1914." *Central European History* 9 (March 1976): 58–85.

Turner, L.C.F. *The Origins of the First World War*. New York: St. Martin's Press, 1970.

——. "The Significance of the Schlieffen Plan." In Paul Kennedy, ed., *The War Plans of the Great Powers, 1880–1914*. Boston: Allen & Unwin, 1985, pp. 199–221.

Über militärisches Schrifttum im preußisch-deutschen Heere von Scharnhorst bis zum Weltkriege." *Militärwissenschaftliche Rundschau* 4 (1938): 463–482.

Vagts, Alfred. *A History of Militarism*. Greenwich: Meridian Books, 1959.

——. *The Military Attaché*. Princeton: Princeton University Press, 1967.

Vernois, Julius Verdy du. *Beitrag zum Kriegsspiel*. 2d ed. Berlin: E.S. Mittler, 1881.

——. *Studien über den Krieg*. 3 vols. Berlin: E.S. Mittler, 1902.

Viktoria Luise, Herzogin. *Im Glanz der Krone: Erinnerungen*. Munich: Wilhelm Heyne Verlag, 1967.

Voelcker, Ministerialrat von. "German Transportation and Communication." *Annals of the American Academy of Political and Social Science*, 92 (November 1920): 76–86.

Walker, R.T., Jr. "Prusso-Württembergian Military Relations in the German Empire, 1870–1918." Ph.D. dissertation, Ohio State University, 1974.

Wartenburg, Yorck von. *Napoleon als Feldherr*. 2 vols. Berlin: E.S. Mittler, 1901.

Weber, Gerhard. *Rudolf Steiner: Leben, Erkenntnis, Kulturimpuls*. Munich: Koesel Verlag, 1987.

Wehler, Hans-Ulrich. *The German Empire, 1871–1918*. Leamington Spa: Berg Publishers, 1985.

Wehrmann, L. *Die Verwaltung der Eisenbahnen*. Berlin: Julius Springer, 1913.

Weirauch, Dr. "Railway Transportation in Germany." *Annals of the American Academy of Political and Social Science*. 93 (November 1920): 87–90.

Wellner, Arnold, ed. *Anne Countess zu Stolberg-Wernigerode*. London: Strahen & Co, 1873.

Werdermann, Johannes. "Der Heeresreform unter Caprivi." Ph.D. dissertation, University of Greifswald, 1927.

Wheeler, Everett L. "The Modern Legality of Frontinus' Strategems." *Militärgeschichtliche Mitteilungen* 43 (January 1988): 7–29.

Whyte, William H. *The Organization Man*. New York: Anchor Books, 1956.

Wilkinson, Spencer. *Essays on the War Game*. Manchester: Manchester Tactical Society, 1887.

Winsen, Peter. "Der Krieg in Bülows Kalkül." In Jost Dülffer and Karl Holl, eds., *Bereit zum Krieg: Kriegsmentalität im Wilhelminischen Deutschland, 1890–1914*. Göttingen: Vandenhoeck & Ruprecht, 1986, pp. 161–93.

Winton, Harold. *To Change an Army: General Sir John Barnett-Stuart and British Armored Doctrine, 1927–1938*. Kansas City: University Press of Kansas, 1988.

Wischermann, Clemons. "Zur Industrialisierung des deutschen Braugewerbes im 19. Jahrhundert: Das Beispiel der Reichgräflich zu Stolbergischen Brauerei Westheim im Westfalen, 1860–1913." *Zeitschrift für Unternehmensgeschichte* 30 (1985): 143–80.

Witt, Peter-Christian, "The Prussian Landrat as Tax Official, 1891–1918." In Georg Iggers, ed., *The Social History of Politics: Critical Perspectives in West German Historical Writing since 1945*. Leamington Spa: Berg Publishers, 1985.

Wohl, Robert. *The Generation of 1914*. Cambridge, Mass.: Harvard University Press, 1979.

Zeitz, Hugo. "Der Schirmer des geeinten Reiches." In Generalleutnant a.D. von Cochenhausen, ed., *Von Scharnhorst zu Schlieffen, 1806–1906: Hundert Jahre preußisch-deutscher Generalstab*. Berlin: E.S. Mittler, 1933.

Ziekursch, Johannes. *Hundert Jahre schlesischer Agrargeschichte*. 2d ed. Aalen: Scientia Verlag, 1978, pp. 215–48.

Zilch, Reinhard. *Die Reichsbank und die finanzielle Kriegsvorbereitung von 1907 bis 1914*. East Berlin: Akademie Verlag, 1987.

Ziolkowski, Theodore. *German Romanticism and Its Institutions*. Princeton: Princeton University Press, 1990.

Zobeltitz, Fedor von. *Chronik der Gesellschaft unter dem letzten Kaiserreich*. 2d ed. 2 vols. Hamburg: Alster-Verlag, 1922.

Zoellner, Generalleutnant a.D. von. "Schlieffens Vermächtnis." *Militärwissenschaftliche Rundschau*, Sonderheft (4 January 1938).

Zorn, Wolfgang. "Unternehmer und Aristokratie in Deutschland." *Zeitschrift für Firmengeschichte und Unternehmerbiographie*. 8, no. 6 (1963): 241–54.

# Index

# Index